Uniting Africa

The Politics of Regional Integration and Development Cooperation in the Continent

Malusi Mncube

UNIVERSITY OF JOHANNESBURG

UJ Press

Uniting Africa: The Politics of Regional Integration and Development Cooperation in the Continent

Published by UJ Press
University of Johannesburg
Library
Auckland Park Kingsway Campus
PO Box 524
Auckland Park
2006
https://ujpress.uj.ac.za/

First published 2025

https://doi.org/10.36615/9780906785676
978-0-906785-66-9 (Paperback)
978-0-906785-67-6 (PDF)
978-0-906785-68-3 (EPUB)
978-0-906785-69-0 (XML)

This publication had been submitted to a rigorous double-blind peer-review process prior to publication and all recommendations by the reviewers were considered and implemented before publication.

Proofreading: Paul Giess
Cover design: Hester Roets, UJ Graphic Design Studio
Typeset in 9/13pt Merriweather Light

Contents

Dedication

This book is dedicated to Africa's people's continentally and globally, to forever assert our minds, values, and the undying teachings of Africa's global ancestors the philosophy of Ubuntu (Humanity),umuntu ngumutu ngabantu!!!

Dr Malusi Mncube
Department of Politics and International Relations
University of Johannesburg

Acknowledgements

I express my gratitude to Professor Bhaso Ndzendze, Head of the Department of Politics; Professor Suzy Graham, the Deputy Executive Dean; and Professor Kamilla Naidoo the Executive Dean for affording me an enabling environment and space to pursue, as much as is feasible, truth and academic objectivity. My thanks go to all lecturers, students, staff, and visitors who have impacted me both directly and indirectly, as well as all humanity at the University of Life. I also express my sincere gratitude to the Faculty of Humanities, University of Johannesburg for providing me with affiliate status during the completion and production of this book, and for allowing me the opportunity to contribute to global African knowledge. Furthermore, thanks go to the global gallant African philosophers, who have fearlessly lived and fought for the ONENESS OF ALL HUMANITY (UMUNTU NGUMUNTU NGABANTU).

Thokoza
Camagu
Ndawu

Dr Malusi Mncube
Department of Politics and International Relations
University of Johannesburg

Abbreviations

AACB	Association of African Central Banks
AAPC	All-Africa Peoples' Conference
ACB	African Central Bank
ACBF	African Capacity Building Foundation
ACDEG	African Charter on Democracy, Elections and Governance
ACERWC	African committee of experts on the rights and welfare of the child
ACHPR	African Commission onHuman and Peoples' Rights
ACIRC	African Capacity for Immediate Response to Crises
ACP	African, Caribbean, and Pacific Group of States
ACRWC	African Charter on the Rights and Welfare of the Child
AEC	African Economic Community
AFCFTA	African Continental Free Trade Area
AfCHPR	African Court on Human and People's Rights
AfDB	African Development Bank
AFISMA	African Led International Support Mission to Mali
AFREXIM	AfCFTA Secretariat and African Export and Import Bank
AFRICOM	United States Africa Command
AGA	Africa Governance Architecture
AGOA	African Growth and Opportunity Act
AHSG	Assembly of Heads of State and Government
AHSTN	Africa High Speed Train Network
AIDA	Accelerated Industrial Development for Africa
AIMS	Africa Integrated Maritime Strategy
AISA	Africa Institute of South Africa
AMF	African Monetary Fund
AMDC	African Minerals Development Centre

AMIB	African Union Mission in Burundi
AMIS	African Union Mission in Sudan
AMISON	African Union Mission in Somalia
AMU	Arab Maghreb Union
AMV	Africa Mining Vision
APF	Africa Peace Facility
APRM	African Peer Review Mechanism
APSA	African Peace and Security Architecture
AQIM	Islamic Maghreb
ARIPO	African Regional Intellectual Property Organisation
ARV	Anti-Retroviral
ASF	African Standby Force
ASEAN	Association of Southeast Asian Nations
ATAF	African Tax Administration Forum
A3	The Three African Members of the UNSC
ATMIS	African Transition Mission in Somalia
AU	African Union
AUABC	African Union Advisory Board on Corruption
AUC	African Union Commission
AUCIL	African Union Commission on International Law
AUCPCC	African Union Convention on Preventing and Combating Corruption
AUHDG	African Union Heads of State and Government
AUMS	African Union Member States
BIAT	Boosting Intra-African Trade
BIT	Bilateral Investment Treaty
BRICS	Brazil, Russia, India, China, and South Africa
BRI	Belt and Road Initiative
BWIs	Bretton Woods Institutions
B2B	Business-to-Business
B2C	Business-to-Consumer

Abbreviations

CAADP	Comprehensive Africa Agricultural Development Programme
CAR	Central African Republic
CAECU	Central African Economic and Customs Union
CBTP	Cross-Border Programme
CCSA	Competition Commission of South Africa
CCU	Continental Customs Union
CCUCA	Customs Union of Central African States
CEAO	Communauté Economique de l'Afrique de l'Ouest / West African Economic Community
CEMAC	Central African Economic and Monetary Community
CEN-SAD	Community of Sahel-Saharan States
CET	Common External Tariff
CEWS	Continental Early Warning System
CFA	Communauté Financiè re d'Afrique
CFTA	Continental Free Trade Area
CHS	Commission on Human Security
CIDO	Citizens and Diaspora Organisation Directorate
COMESA	Common Market for Eastern and Southern Africa Facilitation Programme
CONOPS	Concept of Operations
CT	Counter-terrorism
CSO	Civil Society Organisations
CSSDCA	Conference on Security, Stability, Development, and Cooperation in Africa
CTTFP	Comprehensive Trade and Transport
DDR	Disarmament, Demobilisation, and Reintegration
DFID	UK Department for International Development
DFTA	Digital Free Trade Area
DIRCO	Department of International Relations and Cooperation
DoUF	Directives on the Use of Force
DRC	Democratic Republic of the Congo

DTRP	Dependency Theory Research Programme
DTSA	Digital Transformation Strategy for Africa
EAC	East African Community
EASF	Eastern Africa Standby Force
ECCAS	Economic Community of East African States
ECGLC	Economic Community of the Great Lakes Countries
ECOWAS	Economic Community of West African States
ECOSOCC	Economic Social and Cultural Commission
ECU	Equatorial Customs Union
EEC–ACP	European Economic Community–African Caribbean Pacific Countries
EITI	Extractive Industries Transparency Initiative
EPA	External Partnership Agreement
EPF	European Peace Facility
EU	European Union
FAL	Final Act of Lagos
FDI	Foreign Direct Investment
FDSM	Defence and Security Forces of Mali
FemWise	Network of African Women in Conflict Prevention and Mediation
FOCAC	Forum on China Africa Cooperation
4IR	Fourth Industrial Revolution
FMP	Free Movement of Persons
FTA	Free Trade Area/Agreement
FTAA	Free Trade Area of the Americas
GATT	General Agreement on Tariffs and Trade
GDP	Gross Domestic Product
GGC	Gulf of Guinea Commission
GAO	Government Accountability Office
GSP	Generalised System of Preferences
GTAP	Global Trade Analysis Project
GVC	Global Value Chain

G5	Group of Five for the Sahel
G20	Group of 20
G77	Group of 77
HAND	Human Rights and Advocacy Network for Democracy
HANDS	Humanitarian Action and Natural Disaster Support
HIPC	Heavily Indebted Poor Countries
HIPPO	High-level Independent Panel on Peace Operations
HSGIC	Heads of State and Government Interim Committee
HRW	Human Rights Watch
ICGLR	International Conference on the Great Lakes Region
ICSID	International Centre for Settlement of Investment Disputes
ICRC	International Committee of the Red Cross
ICT	Information Communication Technology
ICU	Islamic Courts Union
IDP	Internally Displaced Person
IEG	Independent Evaluation Group
IFIs	International Financial Institutions
IGAD	Intergovernmental Authority on Development
IISD	International Institute for Sustainable Development
IHL	International Humanitarian Law
IHRL	International Human Rights Law
ILO	International Labour Organisation
ILO	International Law Office
IMF	International Monetary Fund
IOC	Indian Ocean Commission
IPA	Investment Promotion Agency
IoT	Internet of Things
IPE	International Political Economy
IPEP	Independent Panel of Eminent Persons
IPR	Intellectual Property Rights
IR	International Relations

IRG	International Crisis Group
ISI	Import Substitution Industrialisation
ISS	Institute for Security Studies
ITU	International Telecommunication Union
JAES	Joint Africa-EU Strategy
JICA	Japan International Cooperation Agency
JF-G5S	Joint Force of the G5
LCB	Lake Chad Basin
LCBC	Lake Chad Basin Commission
LDCs	Least Developed Countries
LGA	Liptako-Gourma Authority
LPA	Lagos Plan of Action
LRA	Lord's Resistance Army
MAES	African Union Electoral and Security Assistance Mission
MAP	Millennium African Recovery Plan
MDC	Movement for Democratic Change
MDG	Millennium Development Goal
MDRP	Multi-Country Demobilisation and Reintegration
MERCOSUR	Mercado Común del Sur
MFN	Most Favoured Nation
MINUSMA	United Nations Multidimensional Integrated Stabilization Mission in Mali
MIP	Minimum Integration Programme
MNC	Multinational Corporation
MNJTF	Multinational Joint Task Force
MONUC	United Nations Mission in the DRC
MOU	Memorandum of Understanding
MRTA	Mega-Regional Trade Agreement
MRU	Mano River Union
MSMEs	Micro, Small, and Medium Enterprises
MUJAO	Movement for Oneness and Jihad in West Africa

MULPOCS	Multinational Programming and Operational Centres
NAI	New Africa Initiative
NAM	Non-Aligned Movement
NARC	North African Regional Capability
NATO	North Atlantic Treaty Organisation
NDB	New Development Bank
NDC	National Democratic Congress
NIEO	New International Economic Order
NEPAD	New Partnership for Africa's Development
NFTA	North American Free Trade Agreement
NGO	Non-Governmental Organisation
NPoA	National Programmes of Action
NPP	New Patriotic Party
NTB	Non-Tariff Barriers
OAPI	Organisation Africaine de la Propriete Intellectuelle
OAU	Organisation of African Unity
ODA	Overseas Development Assistance
ODeL	Open Distance and e-Learning
ODM	Orange Democratic Movement
OECD	Organisation for Economic Cooperation and Development
OPEC	Organisation of Petroleum Exporting Countries
PAIC	Pan-African Investment Code
PAIPO	Pan-African Intellectual Property Organisation
PanWise	Pan-African Network of the Wise
PAP	Pan-African Parliament
PAPSS	Pan African Payments and Settlement System
PCRD	Post-Conflict Reconstruction and Development
PIDA	Programme for Infrastructural Development in Africa
PKO	Peacekeeping Operation
PNU	Party of National Unity

PoC	Protection of Civilians
PoW	Panel of the Wise
PPIAF	Public Private Infrastructure Advisory Facility
PPP	Public–Private Partnership
PRC	Permanent Representatives Committee
PRIDA	Policy and Regulation Initiative for Digital Africa
PRSP	Poverty Reduction Strategy Paper
PSC	Peace and Security Council
PSO	Peace Support Operation
PSOD	Peace and Security Department
PSSG	Police Strategic Support Group
RDC	Rapid Deployment Capability
R2P	Responsibility to Protect
RCI–LRA	Regional Cooperation Initiative for the Elimination of the Lord's Resistance Army
RCM	Regional Consultation Mechanism
REC	Regional EconomicCommunity
REG	Regional Economic Grouping
RISDP	Regional Indicative Strategic Development Plan
RM	Regional Mechanism
ROE	Rules of Engagement
ROO	Rules of Origin
RVC	Regional Value Chain
SAATM	Single African Air Transport Market
SACU	Southern African Customs Union
SADC	Southern African Development Community
SADCC	Southern African Development Coordination Conference
SAPP	Southern African Power Pool
SAP	Structural Adjustment Programme
SAPRI	Structural Adjustment Participatory Review Initiative

SAPRIN	Structural Adjustment Participatory Review International Network
SDG	Sustainable Development Goal
SFM	Self-Financing Mechanism
SPMU	Support Management Planning Unit
SPS	Sanitary and Phytosanitary
SRC	Southern Rhodesia Customs Union
SRO	Sub-regional Organisations
SSR	Security Sector Reform
STC	Specialised Technical Committee
TBT	Technical Barriers to Trade
TCC	Troop-Contributing Countries
TCE	Training Centre of Excellence
10YCBP	Ten-Year Capacity-Building Programme
TFG	Transitional Federal Government
TFTA	Tripartite Free Trade Area/Agreement
TPLF	Tigray People's Liberation Front
TNC	Transnational Corporation
ToT	Terms of Trade
TPP	Trans-Pacific Partnership
TRALAC	Trade Law Centre
TRIPS	Trade-Related Aspects of Intellectual Property Rights
TTIP	Transatlantic Trade and Investment Partnership
UEMOA	Union Economique et Monetaire Quest Africaine (West African Economic and Monetary Union)
UK	United Kingdom
UN	United Nations
UNAMID	UN-AU Mission in Darfur
UNCTAD	United Nations Conference on Trade and Development
UNECA	United Nations Economic Commission for Africa
UNGA	United Nations General Assembly

UNIDO	United Nations Industrial Development Organisation
UNMIS	United Nations Mission in Sudan
UNOB	United Nations Operations in Burundi
UNSC	United Nations Security Council
UNSOA	United Nations Support Office for ANISOM
UNITA	National Union for the Total Independence of Angola
UNWTO	World Tourism Organisation
USA	United States of America
USSR	Union of Soviet Socialist Republics
USTR	Office of the US Trade Representative
WAAC	West African Airways Corporation
WACB	West African Currency Board
WACM	West African Common Market
WACRI	West African Cocoa Research Institute
WAEC	West African Examinations Council
WAEMU	West African Economic and Monetary Union
WAGP	West African Gas Pipeline
WAMZ	West African Monetary Zone
WAPP	West African Power Pool
WB	World Bank
WCO	World Customs Organisation
WEF	World Economic Forum
WTO	World Trade Organisation
WWI	World War I
WWII	World War II

Editorial Foreword

Jo-Ansie Van Wyk

University Of South Africa
Co-Series Editor: African Political Science
and International Relations in Focus

In *Uniting Africa: The Politics of Regional Integration and Development Cooperation in the Continent*, Malusi Mncube integrates a key component of Pan-Africanism and the Organisation of African Unity's (OAU) emphasis on unity, as well as the that of the successor of the OAU, the African Union (AU), established in 2002.

In Chapter 1, Mncube states the primary aim of his book, namely to 'reach a better understanding of Africa's efforts to incrementally advance Pan-Africanism, and its consolidating efforts to attain socio-economic inclusive growth, political stability, and continental security'. To achieve this objective, he offers 'neo-functional arguments to support the actualisation of the aims and objectives of the AU as an intergovernmental organisation constituted under the Constitutive Act' of the African Union, the AU's founding charter.

Mncube proceeds to outline the dominant intellectual perspectives on regional integration before addressing the transition from the OAU to the AU by emphasising competing discourses. He anchors his research in Samir Amin's Dependency Theory Research Programme (DTRP)/centre-periphery framework to conduct a neo-functionalist examination of the continent's regionalism efforts through three main mechanisms and principles, namely the positive spillover effect, the transfer of domestic allegiance, and technocratic automaticity.

Hereafter, the focus shifts to the AU's notion of self-reliance and the African Governance Architecture (AGA) and the African Peace and Security Architecture (APSA). In terms of the AGA, Mncube outlines the continent's various commitments, agencies, mechanisms and institutions to achieve the AU's objectives such as self-reliance and good governance, whereas,

1

in the context of the APSA, a set of institutions, legislation, and procedures intended to address conflict prevention and promote peace and security in Africa, is analysed by referring to, among other aspects, the pillars of the APSA as well as the AU's peace-making efforts through AU peace missions and hybrid missions with the United Nations (UN).

Mncube continues to address the AU pursuit of socio-economic self-reliance with an emphasis on the African Continental Free Trade Area (AfCFTA) and the continent's role and position in global multilateralism. The author also analyses the role and contribution of the AfCFTA to the security-development nexus to foster achieve peace and development on the continent through intra-African cooperation on security. Mncube also emphasises that the AfCFTA will enable a more cooperative security regime to accelerate human security and development on the continent in the context of Agenda 2063. Mncube proceeds to address regional cooperation and integration in the context of the AU's development blueprint, Agenda 20263: The Africa we Want (Agenda 2063), adopted in 2015.

The author also addresses the AU 2007 Audit Report and the Report on the Proposed Recommendations for the Institutional Reform of the African Union (The Kagame Report) compiled by an AU designated panel under the leadership of President Paul Kagame of Rwanda released in 2017. The 2007 Audit Report commissioned a high-level Panel to conduct an audit review of the AU. Former UN Under-Secretary-General and Executive Secretary of the United Nations Economic Commission for Africa (UNECA) Adebayo Adedeji served as the chairperson of the 12-member high-level twelve-member panel. Mncube concludes that the AU has been unable to implement and manage its programmes towards continental self-reliance as outlined in the Constitutive Act and its agenda without external support.

Mncube concludes that Africa's aspirations for political and economic self-reliance have produced partial results due to a variety of complex factors endogenous and exogenous to the continent. He cites, for example, the embeddedness of corruption and neo-patrimonialism, and global financial and economic power structures obstructing the continent achieving self-determination and sustainable development.

Finally, Mncube contends that there is a need to evolve African integration further and anchored in the neo-neo-integrationism of post-neo-functionalism or postmodern integrationism of post-neo-nationalism that emphasises the initial integration of security matters through post-nationalism.

Mncube's book is a valuable contribution to the series African Political Science and International Relations in Focus. He convincingly and skilfully manoeuvres the complexity of the realisation of the historical ideals of Pan-Africanism in contemporary Africa and the plethora of challenges to its practical implementation. Mncube's emphasises the link between these ideals, the continent's contemporary normative commitments via the AU, and its Agenda 2063. He is also mindful of the complex challenges to African integration at continental and regional level, unity and solidarity but lauds the incremental, albeit relatively slow, progress by offering a critique of existing scholarship on African integration and a succinct and innovative theoretical analysis based on neo-functionalism in the context of Samir Amin's DTRP)/centre-periphery framework. Moreover, Mncube offers practical solutions to achieve Pan-Africanism and continental integration by, for example, linking security and development as a panacea for the continent's future political and economic self-reliance. Finally, he calls an end to embedded corruption in African governance and calls for an agile continent who can respond to a complex geo-political context and deeper and wider self-reliance in the context of regional integration.

Prologue

The Evolution of Global Finance from Africa's Black Slavery to Continuing Neocolonial Exploitation

The history of global finance is deeply intertwined with Africa's exploitation, a legacy that stretches from the brutal era of black slavery to contemporary forms of neocolonial domination by multinational corporations (MNCs). This prologue contextualises this historical exploitation, illustrating how slavery, colonialism, and genocide laid the economic foundations for Africa's ongoing subjugation. It further examines how neocolonial practices, which continue to this day, perpetuate the economic marginalisation of the continent.

The transatlantic slave trade remains one of the most brutal and economically exploitative systems in history. European powers, driven by an insatiable quest for wealth, turned to Africa as a source of cheap labour. The profits generated from the trade in human beings fuelled the industrial growth of European economies and contributed to infrastructure development in Europe and the Americas (Curtin, 1990). In the process, African societies were destabilised, families were torn apart, and economies were left in ruins, all in service of the European demand for cheap labour.

Colonialism further entrenched economic exploitation in Africa. European powers carved up the continent into colonies, extracting vast quantities of raw materials while exploiting the labour of indigenous populations to fuel industries in their homelands (Amin, 1972). Colonial administrations imposed extractive economic systems that ensured the flow of resources and wealth to Europe, leaving African nations impoverished and underdeveloped. As the colonialists built railways, ports, and plantations, the financial gains overwhelmingly enriched the colonising powers, while African societies remained trapped in cycles of poverty and dependency, perpetuating a legacy of economic disparity and underdevelopment (Rodney, 1973).

The end of formal colonial rule did not mark the end of Africa's economic subjugation. In the post-independence era, MNCs continued the legacy of economic domination through unfair trade practices, resource extraction, and political manipulation. These corporations, often backed by their home governments, maintained control over Africa's resources, effectively continuing the patterns of economic exploitation established during colonialism (Petras and Veltmeyer, 2001). In many instances, the wealth generated from Africa's minerals, oil, and agricultural products was funnelled out of the continent, with little benefit to the local communities. Moreover, lax regulatory frameworks, corruption, and weak governance structures allowed corporations to maximise their profits while further impoverishing African nations (Sachs, 2005).

In contemporary Africa, neo-colonialism remains a potent force, shaping the continent's economic landscape. Although formal colonisation has ended, the structural and power dynamics established during the colonial era continue to exert influence. Foreign MNCs, in collaboration with Western governments and international financial institutions (IFIs), wield considerable power over African economies, often dictating policies that prioritise foreign interests over the welfare of African citizens (Nkrumah, 1965). One of the central features of neo-colonialism is the phenomenon of debt dependency. African nations, burdened with unsustainable levels of debt, often find themselves forced into accepting unfavourable terms from institutions such as the International Monetary Fund (IMF) and the World Bank (WB). These loans are typically used to finance projects that disproportionately benefit foreign interests, further entrenching cycles of poverty and dependency (Gyekye, 2010).

Furthermore, the monopolistic dominance of MNCs in key sectors, such as agriculture, telecommunications, and finance, has crowded out local entrepreneurship and innovation. Small businesses in Africa struggle to compete with the immense resources and global reach of these corporate giants, resulting in continued economic marginalisation for local populations (Moyo, 2009). The combination of multinational dominance, external debt, and continued resource extraction constitutes a modern form of economic neo-colonialism, where Africa remains subjugated to the financial interests of global powers.

The African Union (AU), formed in 2001 as the successor to the Organisation of African Unity (OAU), stands as a symbol of hope for the continent. Its mission to promote unity, development, peace, and security has been central to its objectives. Despite this, the AU has struggled to overcome the deep structural challenges it inherited, including political instability, authoritarian leadership, and economic dependence on global capital. As a pan-African Organisation, the AU aims to address the legacy of slavery, colonialism, and exploitation that continues to shape Africa's political and economic landscape (Shivji, 2008). The AU's founding principles, enshrined in the Constitutive Act of the African Union of 2000 (hereafter, the Constitutive Act), emphasise sovereignty, territorial integrity, and non-interference in the internal affairs of member states. However, Article 4(h) of the Constitutive Act also grants the AU the power to intervene in the case of war crimes and genocide, a mandate that underscores the Organisation's commitment to continental peace and security (AU, 2000).

Despite some notable achievements, such as the African Standby Force (ASF) and the African Continental Free Trade Area (AfCFTA), the AU has faced significant setbacks. One of the key challenges is the persistence of authoritarian regimes and undemocratic governance in many member states. Leaders often cling to power through electoral manipulation and repression, undermining the AU's principles of democracy and human rights (Mkandawire, 2012). Additionally, the AU's reliance on external financial donors has hindered its ability to act independently and effectively, often leaving it vulnerable to the geopolitical and economic interests of global powers (Gillespie, 2013).

At the heart of the AU's struggles is the phenomenon of elite patronage, where political leaders prioritise their own interests and those of the wealthy elite over the needs of ordinary citizens. This system of cronyism, corruption, and nepotism has led to widespread inequality and exclusion, with millions of Africans living in poverty despite the continent's vast natural resources. The concentration of power in the hands of a few elites exacerbates social tensions and undermines efforts to combat poverty and promote sustainable development (Baldwin, 2015).

In conclusion, the evolution of global finance from Africa's black slavery to modern-day neocolonial exploitation serves as a sobering reminder of the enduring legacy of exploitation, genocide, and economic domination. While the AU holds the potential to lead Africa toward greater unity and prosperity, it must confront the dual challenges of external exploitation and internal elite corruption. True progress will require a concerted effort from Africa's civil society to dismantle patronage networks, strengthen democratic institutions, and prioritise the needs of the continent's most vulnerable populations. The global public must also overcome their apathy to demand greater transparency and accountability in the decision-making processes that affect Africa's future. Only through genuine collaboration and solidarity can Africa hope to break free from the shackles of exploitation and build a more just and equitable future for all its people.

Chapter 1

Introduction

The primary aim of this book is to reach a better understanding of Africa's efforts to incrementally advance Pan-Africanism[1], and its consolidating efforts to attain socio-economic inclusive growth, political stability, and continental security. The book makes neo-functional arguments to support the actualisation of the aims and objectives of the AU as an intergovernmental organisation constituted under the Constitutive Act. The limited neo-functionalist achievements of the AU's policies and programmes are critiqued using dependency theory as a research method and as a framework of analysis focused on a centre-periphery analysis (Kvangraven, 2018 and Amin, 2021). These theories are premised on existing theories deployed in earlier studies and critical analyses of Africa's political economy, international relations (IR), and security issues in the period 2000 to date. The book also provides a historical-critical analysis of the regional experiments in Africa, and it therefore expands on the transition from the OAU to AU. It considers the eight officially recognised regional economic communities (RECs), i.e., the East African Community (EAC); Southern African Development Community (SADC); Arab Maghreb Union (UMA); Common Market for Eastern and Southern Africa (COMESA); Economic Community of West African States (ECOWAS); Economic Community of Central African States (ECCAS); and Community of Sahel-Saharan States (CEN-SAD),the Intergovernmental Authority on Development (IGAD) as the building blocks of the AU. The book further assesses African security mechanisms, the key actors involved, and the factors that contribute to Africa's continental security. The book additionally emphasizes Pan-African economic integration and argues that global economic inequality warrants a reinstatement of the New International Economic Order (NIEO) adopted by the United

---

[1] Mamdani (1996). 'Citizen and Subject: Contemporary Africa. For Critical perspectives on Pan Africanism.' Princeton University Press. 18(3). 521–42.

Nations (UN)[2]. Furthermore, the book advocates for regional communities in the global south to adopt stronger partnerships and trade relationships that will level the global playing field to engender equitable opportunities in all socio-economic facets for the benefit of all stakeholders.

Africa's journey and efforts towards true self-reliance can be said to have begun in the 1980s with the institution of the 1980 Lagos Plan of Action (LPA)[3]. The LPA was conceived as a 'formal inward regionalism' made up of state actors in response to the impact of the adverse global economy. This was followed a decade later by the 1991 Abuja Treaty, which was created to respond to Africa's debt and the Global North's neoliberal onslaught. These policies, characterized by deregulation and privatization, reflected the neoliberal principles advocated by the Washington Consensus. The revitalised 1991 Abuja Treaty articulated a vision to promote self-reliance and sustainability through the African Economic Community (AEC), which is now an integral part of Agenda 2063.

To date, Africa's journey towards complete self-reliance has, unfortunately, been met with several unpredictable variables in the global political economy, which are in constant flux, and continue to have a negative impact on its overarching goal of self-reliance and sustainability. Multiple global challenges have

---

2   Origins and Principles of the NIEO. See Shepherd, G.W. Jr. (1990). 'The Politics of International Economic Relations.' Oxford University Press. See: Barakat 2004; Igwe (2011a); Hoogvelt (2001). See Lee (2002:284) and Strange (2011:71). 'Declaration for the Establishment of a New International Economic Order': 2229th plenary meeting of the United Nations General Assembly Document A/RES/S-6/3201.

3   Lagos Plan of Action see: Adedeji, A. 'Africa within the World: Beyond Dispossession and Dependence.' (Zed books, 1989). The Declaration of Tripoli on the World Bank Report 'Accelerated Development in Sub-Saharan Africa: An Agenda for Action by the ECA Conference of Ministers' at the 17th Session of the Commission held in Tripoli from 27 to 30 April 1982. Browne, R.R., Cummings, R. (1984). 'The Lagos Plan vs. The Berg Report. Contemporary Issues in African Economic Development.' Brumswick Publishing Company. Virginia. The 'Lagos Plan of Action: ECA Revised Framework.' See: World Bank 1981. 'Accelerated Development in Sub-Saharan Africa: An Agenda for Action' (Washington D.C.: World Bak) Brown and Cummings, 'The Lagos Plan of Action.' 83–84.

militated against Africa's development, all of which have been entirely out of the continent's control but for which it has suffered bitterly. During the 1980s, for example, there was a downturn in Africa's political economy – commonly referred to as Africa's 'lost decade' – which was, in part, sparked by the 1973 oil crisis[4] (Oen, 2005). As a result of the decision taken by the member states of the Organisation of Petroleum Exporting Countries (OPEC) to increase the price of oil four-fold, Africa's terms of trade (ToT) worsened, and the price of its primary commodities declined. Ultimately, by the time the Berlin Wall fell, signalling the end of the Cold War in 1989, Africa found itself in trade and fiscal deficits and heavily indebted as it sought to integrate itself into the liberalised global economy. Africa's economic growth and competitiveness stagnated due to its increased debt, further militating against its independent development policy space. This is supported by figures showing an increase of US$16.4 billion in the continent's current account deficit between 1980 and 1988 as well as an annual 10% loss in its export earnings (Ajiki, Adedeji, 2002)

Additionally, between 1978 and 1988, its foreign debt increased by US$181.1 billion. This undoubtedly harmed the continent's economic growth rate, which fell to zero percent between 1980 and 1985.

Against the backdrop of exogenous factors that impede Africa's integration efforts, internal challenges, such as corruption perpetrated by Africa's elite leadership, sustain neo-patrimonial[5] networks. These practices prioritise personal gains

---

4   See 'The 1973 Oil Crisis: A Retrospective.' Eugene G. (ed.) (2011). Stanford University Press. See: Merrill, Karen. 'The Oil Crisis of 1973-1974: A Brief History with Documents'. Bedford/St. Martin's. Boston. 2007. See Palyi, M (1972), 'The Twilight of Gold.' Henry Regnery. Chicago. See Triffin (1960), ' and the Dollar Crisis.' Yale University Press. New Haven. Hart, A.G., Kaldor, N., Tinbergen, J. 'The Case for an International Commodity Reserve Currency.' In Kaldor, N. Essays on Economic Policy, vol. 2 (Norton, 1964). See Hart, A. G. (1976). 'The Case as of 1976 for International Commodity-Reserve Currency,' *Weltwirtschaftliches Archive*. 12(1). 1-32.
5   Erdman, G., Engel, U (2007). 'Neo-patrimonialism Reconsidered: Critical Review and Elaboration of an Elusive Concept.' *Commonwealth & Comparative Politics*. 45(1). 95-119. [13]. See

for family and associates to the detriment of Africa's population. Africa's leadership often lead ostentatious first-world lifestyles amidst the desperate abject poverty of the majority of Africa's population. The book critiques their empty rhetoric, hypocrisy, duplicity, and sloganeering, as their empty words do not translate into policy implementation.

Africa's corrupt elite leadership has been complicit in hindering the continent's progress in terms of economic development before and during the 1990s. Its average annual gross domestic product (GDP) decreased by 0.2% (from 2.5 to 2.3%) between the 1980s and 1990s. Many credit Africa's persistent economic development woes to the onslaught of structural adjustment programmes (SAPs) imposed on African countries at the insistence of the IMF and as a condition for loans. Structural adjustment programmes, with their stringent accompanying austerity measures, have resulted in many African people falling further into poverty without any relief from their governments.

Africa's extreme global economic vulnerability extended into the 2000s. Despite its arguably relatively weak links to the global economy, the continent was not spared from the negative impact of the 2008 global economic crisis. Its average annual GDP more than halved from 5.5% between 2005 and 2008 to 2.5% in 2009 as a result of low remittances and commodity prices. This, undoubtedly, had an impact on Africa's most poor and vulnerable who lost their sources of income (OECD 2010). Recently, the outbreak of the 2019 coronavirus (COVID-19) global pandemic as well as the heightening of the Russo-Ukrainian War (previously referred to as the Ukrainian crisis) in 2021 have both taken their toll on Africa's economies.

The COVID-19 pandemic saw a significant downturn in economic activity as the health crisis brought all economic sectors to a near halt, costing the continent an estimated loss in outputs of US\$115 billion for the year 2020. Consequently, Africa's real GDP plummeted from 2.9% in 2019 to -1.8% in 2020 (AfDB, 2021).

Franciso, A.H. (2010). 'Neopatrimonialism in Contemporary African Politics.' E-International Relations.

Compounding Africa's dire economic situation and robbing it of its promised and much-anticipated post-pandemic recovery has been the escalation of the Russo-Ukrainian war, which reached greater heights following Russia's invasion of parts of Ukraine in February 2022. The war has resulted in increased food and fuel prices (which fuelled a high inflation rate of 7.5% in 2023), disrupted trade, restricted the fiscal space, and limited the amount of development finance previously available to the continent. As a result, Africa's economic growth rate fell from 4.1% in 2021 to 3.6% in 2022 and was projected to fall further to 3.1% in 2023 (AfDB, 2024). Africa's sluggish rate of economic growth has done little to uplift the many Africans who live in poverty. It has also hindered the continent's ability to achieve sustainable economic self-sufficiency.

Africa has also faced many challenges in its pursuit of self-reliance and self-sustainability in the domains of peacebuilding and peacekeeping. The call for this was first advocated by the late Kenyan political scientist, Ali Mazrui through his concept of Pax Africana. For Mazrui, it is crucial for Africa to achieve and maintain continental jurisdiction over its own peace and security matters. He further argues that the continent should not rely on the intervention of external actors in what are essentially internal matters.

At the start of the new millennium, Pax Africana found its institutional expression in the AU's African Peace and Security Architecture (APSA)[6]. The APSA consists of the following five pillars: the AU Peace and Security Council (PSC), the Panel of the Wise (PoW), the ASF, the Continental Early Warning System (CEWS), and the AU Peace Fund. However, the APSA has

---

[6]   Tiyanjana. (2003). 'The Constitutive Act of the African Union and Institution Building in Post-Colonial Africa', *Leiden Journal of International Law*. 16. 157-70. Article 5 2UJDQVRIWKH8QLRQ1. The organs of the AU shall be: 1, (a) The Assembly of the AU; (b) The Executive Council; (c) The Pan-African Parliament; (d) The Court of Justice; (e) The Commission; (f) The Permanent Representatives Committee; (g) The Specialized Technical Committees; (h) The Economic, Social and Cultural Council; (i) The Financial Institutions. 2, Other organs that the Assembly may decide to establish.

experienced several obstacles to its peacekeeping operations (PKOs) and, consequently, the achievement of Pax Africana.

These obstacles include a lack of political will, an overreliance on external funding (which signifies a lack of financial ownership on the part of African states), funding constraints, lack of capacity, and poor coordination between the five institutional pillars listed above.

The achievement of good and inclusive governance remains indispensable to Africa's pursuit of self-reliance and self-sustainability, without which, it will be impossible for the continent to meet its economic, peace and security, and social goals.

As noted by the former UN Secretary, General Kofi Annan, "Good governance is perhaps the single most important factor in eradicating poverty and promoting development." The achievement of good governance has been listed as one of the seven key aspirations in Agenda 2063: "an Africa of good governance, democracy, respect for human rights, justice and rule of law."

Since the concept of 'good governance' arose in popularity in the 1990s, many African countries undertook institutional reforms to rectify their governance structures. Ghana, for example, set out to radically transform its governance structures to include, "the design and adoption of a new democratic constitution, which places emphasis on the separation of powers with checks and balances to transform its political system."

Its governance reforms were put to the test in its 2016 elections and proved sufficient in the peaceful transfer of political power following the defeat of the incumbent National Democratic Congress (NDC), led by President John Mahama, by the main opposition party, the New Patriotic Party (NPP), led by Nana Akuffo Addo.

Between 2008 and 2017, a handful of African states made substantial strides towards good governance, as noted in the Ibrahim Index of African Governance. These states included Kenya, Morocco, and Côte d'Ivoire. However, several African countries are riddled with weak governance structures, which have allowed the persistence of dictatorships, corruption and poor economic performance. These countries include the Central African Republic (CAR), Eritrea, Somalia, and South Sudan. The challenges faced by Africans in achieving good governance include a lack of political will, poor leadership, and persistent sectarian violence.

In all of this, the LPA, the New Partnership for Africa's Development (NEPAD),[7] and now Agenda 2063, stand out as development policies and programmes dedicated to extricating Africa from marginalisation and global vulnerability. However, since the establishment of the 1980 LPA, it can be argued that Africa has struggled to truly attain the self-reliance that it envisages for itself. After the limited successes of both the LPA and 1991 Abuja Treaty in achieving regional economic integration on the African continent, the NEPAD was adopted in 2002 under the aegis of the AU, and is now a programme under Agenda 2063. In this regard, the AU, as an intergovernmental continental institution, seeks to become a self-sufficient global powerhouse, in which its states are integrated and united and its people live in peace and prosperity.

This has been more rhetorical than tangible, with little evidence of key results having been attained. The AU, in its efforts to achieve an integrated, cooperative, peaceful, and prosperous Africa, strives to pursue the following ideals:

- Establishing a codified and binding supranational entity, which overrides nation-states' sovereignties and their neo-patrimonial-based RECs or an intergovernmental AU with incrementally shared values and policies;
- Timeously receiving mandatory budgetary contributions from all nation-states to the AUC to give effective and further traction towards an AfCFTA (finally ratified on 30 May 2019);
- Addressing the issue of multiple and overlapping memberships within RECS, which have contributed to inter and intra-state conflicts;

---

7   See: Adepoju, A, (2016). 'Challenges and Prospects of NEPAD in Africa's development.'

- Establishing the AU's Agenda 2063, which echoes the objectives of the 1991 Abuja Treaty.
- Overcoming the widely-held perception that Agenda 2063 is an elitist government-driven agenda with few or imperceptible contributions from the public and civil society fraternity. Here, many are aggrieved that the formulation of Agenda 2063 had bypassed institutions such as the NEPAD, Economic Social and Cultural Commission (ECOSOCC), and the Pan-African Parliament (PAP), which are intended to serve as a platform for both vertical and horizontal participation and activism (Akokpari, 2008; Bah, 2012; Weltz, 2014).

For this reason, a critical approach towards policies and programmes, such as the 1980 LPA, 1991 Abuja Treaty, Constitutive Act, NEPAD, AfCFTA, and Agenda 2063, is imperative to establish why the AU has failed to realise its intended aims and objectives.

The adoption of the LPA was Africa's assertion of independence, an attempt to define itself against global hegemonic forces. It has had limited success. The lack of human and monetary capital has been a contributory factor to the limited achievements of Africa's developmental policies.

Subsequently, the 1991 Abuja Treaty[8] emerged in response to the limited and poor implementation of the LPA. It differed from its predecessor in that it was informed by the neoliberal orthodoxy, which dominated the international development discourse at the end of the Cold War with the fall of communism. However, the treaty asserted that the deficit of human and monetary capital and the increase in Africa's financial debt to IFIs constrained its fiscal and monetary capacity to pursue its development policies.

Therefore the adoption and ratification of the AU-NEPAD in 2002 and later Agenda 2063 in 2015, were informed by Africa's pragmatic and eclectic approach to its development frameworks. The aforementioned developments took place

---

8   Abuja Treaty. See: Ndulo, M. (1994). 'The Abuja Treaty Establishing the African Economic Community.'

against an asymmetrical, indifferent and dismissive global economy dominated by neoliberal capital. However, both the NEPAD and AfCFTA, to date, have experienced limited success, which has contributed to the difficulties in comprehensively realising Agenda 2063. Furthermore, the continued deficit in both continental and foreign direct investment (FDI) has restricted the effective actualisation of the AU's development policies (Nagar, 2020:1–310; Martin, 1982:221–238; Adebajo, 2004:449). Linked to this, as the NEPAD, AfCFTA, and Agenda 2063 enter their implementation phases, their key stakeholders seem disengaged, displaying indifference and a lack of political will. This attitude underestimates the implicit risks involved in the successful implementation of its intended aims and objectives. Against the backdrop of these shortcomings, the 2007 AU Review Report and the 2017 Kagame Report offer reform recommendations to make the AU fit for purpose.

This book therefore focuses on Africa's efforts, through the AU's policies and institutions, to attain true and comprehensive self-reliance and sustainability in the areas of socio-economic development, peace and security, and governance. This introduction has offered a prelude to the study by briefly discussing Africa's initial pursuits towards self-reliance and sustainability.

This chapter has, therefore, made the call for Africa to assume full ownership and responsibility in all areas to prevent it from being subjected to the throes of the global political economy and being further marginalised within the global arena. Only through African agency can the continent reach its full potential in assuming its role as a global actor and powerhouse.

Chapter 2 considers the contrasting viewpoints on regional integration towards uniting Africa. What are the divergent and converging politics of regional integration and development cooperation in Africa?

Chapter 3 explores the competing intellectual arguments and considers the successes and failures of both the LPA and NEPAD. The LPA is considered to be only a rhetorical policy blueprint under the aegis of the OAU, which was replaced by AU–NEPAD in 2002. However, different observers have asserted differences of opinion in the economic orientation and underlying paradigms that define AU–NEPAD. Some reports have argued that NEPAD development policies are inward-looking and self-reliant.

Other critics have challenged this view, and believe that the NEPAD is a market-driven, outward-looking framework that is directed at emasculating Africa's development states in line with the Washington Consensus neoliberal orthodoxy.

Chapter 4 identifies and problematises the gaps within the work in progress of the AU thus far. It evaluates the organisation's governance, particularly focusing on the African Governance Architecture (AGA).

Chapter 5 focuses on the APSA. This includes the peace and security institutions and initiatives (e.g., APSA/AGA/AUC/ECOSOCC/PAP and their PKOs) in Burundi; Sudan; Somalia; Comoros, Mali and the Sahel, and Uganda, and considers the actions of the Lord's Resistance Army (LRA).

Chapter 6 explains the AU's socio-economic institutional performance regarding the AU. In a global marginalising economy dominated by the Bretton Woods Institutions (BWI), including the IMF, WB, and World Trade Organisation (WTO), the AU aligns with a progressive reformist antithetical multilateralism. This multilateralism is supported by the ratification and adoption of the AfCFTA, membership of the group of 20 (G20), WTO, Brazil, Russia, India, China, and South Africa (BRICS), and the New Development Bank (NDB). It is also supported by being a participant in the Belt and Road Initiative (BRI) and the Forum on China–Africa Cooperation (FOCAC). It is against this backdrop that the institutional standards and agreed criteria will hopefully enable the materialisation of the African Union Agenda 2063 as the continent's economic blueprint.

Chapter 7 explores the regional cooperation and integration towards realising Africa's Agenda 2063.

Chapter 8 presents the findings and recommendations of the 2007 AU and 2017 Paul Kagame report in terms of:

Africa's mining vision; human peace and security (also in public health); financial integration and convergence; free movement of persons (FMP) and right of residence and establishment; movement of capital goods and services in Africa; comparison of trade policies and multiple REC membership; and rules of origin (ROO).

Chapter 9 presents the conclusion, findings, and recommendations. It synthesizes the research findings, emphasising the significance of the book's core message. Furthermore, this chapter reasserts the importance of agency in the continental integration project and the ongoing work in progress of Agenda 2063.

Chapter 10: Epilogue.

Chapter 2

The Dominant Intellectual Perspectives on Regional Integration

2.1 Introduction

The classical proponents of dependency theory[9] are Hans Singer and Raul Prebisch. This chapter's arguments are essentially predicated on their dependency theory paradigm using centre-

9   See: Kvangraven, I. (2021) 'Beyond the stereotype: Restating the relevance of the dependency research programme.' *Development and Change.* 52(1). 76–112. Löwy, Mi. (2010). 'The Politics of Combined and Uneven Development: The Theory of Permanent Revolution.' Haymarket Books. Chicago. Arrighi, G. (2002) 'Global Inequalities and the Legacy of Dependency Theory.' Radical *Philosophy Review* 5(1/2). 75–85. Arrighi, G., Silver B.J., Brewer, B.D. (2003). 'Industrial Convergence, Globalization and the Persistence of the North–South Divide.' *Studies in Comparative International Development.* 38: 3–31.
See: Bonizzi, B., Kaltenbrunner, A., Powell J. (2019). 'Subordinate Financialization in Emerging Capitalist Economies.' In Mader, P., Mertens D., van der Zwan N. (eds.) 'The International Handbook of Financialization.' 177–87. Routledge. London.
See: Durand, C., Milberg., W. (2019) 'Intellectual Monopoly in Global Value Chains', Review of International Political Economy. DOI: https://doi.org/10.1080/09692290.2019.1660703 See: Fischer, A.M. (2015) 'The End of Peripheries? On the Enduring Relevance of Structuralism for Understanding Contemporary Global Development.' *Development and Change.* 46(4). 700–32. Fischer, A.M. (2018). 'Debt and Development in Historical Perspective: The External Constraints of Late Industrialisation Revisited through South Korea and Brazil.' *World Economy.* 41.(33). 59–78. Fischer, A.M. (2019) 'On the Origins and Legacies of Really Existing Capitalism: In Conversation with Kari Polanyi Levitt.' *Development and Change.* 50(2). 542–72.
See: Giraudo, M.E. (2020. 'Dependent Development in South America: China and the Soybean Nexus.' *Journal of Agrarian Change.* 20(1). 60–78. See: Goda, T., García, A.T. (2017). 'The Rising Tide of Absolute Global Income Inequality during 1850–2010: Is it Driven by Inequality Within or Between Countries?' *Social Indicators Research.* 130(3). 1051–72.

periphery theory as a research framework (Amin, 1977:107; Amin, 2019a). The theory possesses adequate explanatory values and analytical utility to critically explain the defects of neo-functionalist regionalism in Africa throughout the preceding decades. Neo-functionalism is a theory of regional integration/supranationalism predicated on the roles of regional organisations such as the AU and European Union (EU). The Dependency Theory Research Programme (DTRP)/centre-periphery framework (Amin, 1977:107) was applied to examine the fostering of

See: Hauge, J. (2019). 'Should the African Lion Learn from the Asian Tigers? A Comparative Historical Study of FDI-oriented Industrial Policy in Ethiopia, South Korea and Taiwan.' *Third World Quarterly.* 40(11). 2071–91. See: Kufakurinani, U. et al. (eds.) (2017). 'Dialogues on Development – Dependency Theory.' Institute for New Economic Thinking. New York.

See: Kvangraven, I.H. (2017). 'A Dependency Pioneer – Samir Amin.' In Kufakurinani, U. et al. (eds) 'Dialogues on Development – Dependency Theory.' 12–17. Institute for New Economic Thinking. New York. Kvangraven, I.H. (2018). 'Unpacking and Repackaging Dependency Theory.' In Kvangraven I.H. 'Essays on Global Development, Trade and Finance,' 1–55. ProQuest LLC. Ann Arbor, MI. Kvangraven, I.H. (2019) 'Samir Amin: A Third World Activist and Pioneering Marxist.' *Development and Change.* 51(3). 631–49.

See: Milanovic, B. (2015) 'Global Inequality of Opportunity: How Much of Our Income is Determined by Where We Live?' *Review of Economics and Statistics.* 97(2). 452–60. See: Palma, G. (1978). 'Dependency: A Formal Theory of Underdevelopment or a Methodology for the Analysis of Concrete Situations of Underdevelopment?' *World Development.* 6. 881–924. Palma, G. (1995) 'Underdevelopments and Marxism: From Marx to the Theories of Imperialism and Dependency.' In R. Ayers (ed.) 'Development Studies: An Introduction through Selected Readings,' 161–210. Greenwich University Press. Dartford.

See: Palma, G. (2016). 'The "Dependency School" and its Aftermath: Why Latin America's Critical Thinking Switched from One Type of Absolute Certainties to Another.' In Reinert, E., Ghosh. J., Kattel, R., (eds) 'Handbook of Alternative Theories of Economic Development,' 386–415. Edward Elgar Publishing. Cheltenham.

See: Powell, J. (2013). 'Subordinate Financialisation: A Study of Mexico and its Non-Financial Corporations.' PhD dissertation, SOAS, University of London. See: Ram, R. (2004). 'Trends in Developing Countries Commodity Terms-of-trade since 1970.' *Review of Radical Political Economics.* 36(2). 241–53.

See: Ricci, A. (2018). 'Unequal Exchange in the Age of Globalization.' *Review of Radical Political Economics.* 51(2). 225–45. See: Smith, J. (2016). 'Imperialism in the 21st Century – Globalization, Super-exploitation, and Capitalism's Final Crisis.' Monthly Review Press. New York.

regionalism through three main mechanisms and principles: the positive spillover effect, transfer of domestic allegiance, and technocratic automaticity.

This will help to assess the progress, problems, and prospects of the AU in its self-reliance and sustainability. This chapter argues that the DTRP/centre-periphery framework fittingly describes the postcolonial dispensation as a form of neo-colonialism. In this context, the core economies of the Global North (which now include China and industrialised countries) develop and dominate the global economy at the expense of the peripheral developing economies of the Global South, such as Africa.

The ramifications of this dependent versus dominant configuration are also evident in these peripheral countries, in addition to their hierarchical internal structures of production and social and political structures.

The DTRP/centre-periphery framework remains relevant and useful, and continues to be used to analyse the widening inequalities between rich and poor countries, or in analysing the structural divisions within a developed or developing country context (Ferraro, 2008: 58–64; Heidus et al., 2011: 55–64; Amin, 2010; Amin, 2019a).

Moreover, De Coning and Cloete (2000:29) assert that "the development of various theories in disciplines such as political science, sociology, and public administration and others is highly relevant to policy application." Agenda 2063 continues to demand supra-nationalistic development frameworks of policy implementation, thus testing and validating the object of inquiry within a scientific paradigm.

It is for these reasons that this chapter maintains that the DTRP/centre-periphery framework is most suited to the analysis of the AU's policies and institutions towards its goal of self-reliance and sustainability. The chapter will define the DTRP and the concept of centre-periphery (Kvangraven, 2018; Amin, 2019a), and outline the chosen theories that comprise the meta-theoretical framework. It does so by providing perspectives on theoretical policy implementation frameworks, which are interlinked with DTRP and other approaches that inform their pragmatism and relation to the object of study. Moreover, this chapter will provide some perspectives on the above-mentioned policy implementation theoretical frameworks, which together explain how the dominant liberal politico-economic world system has worked to marginalise the African continent and how the AU's development policies and supporting institutions have emerged within this context. Finally, the chapter will conclude by discussing the analytical and explanatory strengths of the DTRP/centre-periphery framework as it relates to the study.

2.2 Dependency Theory Research Programme and Metatheories

The DTRP was applied with accompanied interrelated, analytical frameworks in this work. According to Kvangraven (2018:1–55), the DTRP is a combination of interdisciplinary and systematic approaches, anchored in an analysis of a global historical approach to development: the analysis of structures and ownership of production; technological dependence and its polarising tendencies; the uneven effects of domestic and foreign investments; consumption patterns; and financial constraints. These approaches denote "a situation in which the economy of certain countries is conditioned by the development and expansion of another."

In assessing the AU's policies and institutions, this book leverages DTRP/centre-periphery framework to explain how the global economy and world system has, in part, through its liberal economic (capitalism) and political (democracy) systems marginalised the African continent. This dynamic has led Africa further away from its goals of self-reliance and self-sustainability.

Considering the diverse and asymmetrical perspectives in global development and within development theories, the collective body of research in this field can be termed a program. This designation accommodates the disagreements while establishing a shared foundation for approaching the study of development. The core hypothesis associated with the DTRP is the polarising impact of capitalist development, related to the structures of production and the constraints related to peripheral development. The theoretical policy implementation models that form part of this study's DTRP include the following:

· Centre-periphery theory
· Neo-functionalism;

2.2.1 The Dependency Theory Research Programme-Centre-Periphery Framework

The core-periphery theory in the context of Samir Amin's analysis is organised around three major themes: first the necessity of what Amin describes as an analysis at the world level; second his characterisation of peripheral economies; and third his characterisation of economic relationships between centre and periphery. The analysis of world capitalism is conducted in terms of two categories, centre and periphery (Amin,1977:107; Amin, 2019a). The basic difference between the centre and periphery is that capitalist relationships in the centre developed based on the expansion of the home market, whereas capitalist relationships in the periphery were introduced from the outside.

Thus, in the centre, Amin asserts that "the tendency of the capitalist mode of production to become exclusive, when based on expansion and deepening of the home market is accompanied by a tendency for the social structure at the centre to come close to the pure model of *Capital,* characterised by the polarisation of social classes into two basic classes: bourgeoisie and proletariat, with new strata all situated within the framework of the essential division between bourgeoisie and proletariat" (Amin, 1976:2 9; Amin 2010). Conversely, at the periphery, because the capitalist mode of production is introduced from outside, it does not tend to become exclusive, only dominant.

The social structure of the periphery is a truncated structure that can only be understood when it is situated as an element in a world social structure (Amin, 1976:294). The structure is truncated because it is dominated by the 'absentee' metropolitan bourgeoisie. Moreover, "since the peripheral economy exists only as an appendage of the central economy, peripheral society is incomplete; what is missing from it is the metropolitan bourgeoisie, whose capital operates as the essential dominating force" (Amin, 1976: 345). Unequal exchange means that the problem of the class struggle must necessarily be considered at the world scale (Amin,1974:599-600; Amin, 2019a). Having asserted that underdevelopment can be understood only at a world level, Amin provides various accounts of the forces that propel the world system, although these accounts contradict each other. Basically, the theory of underdevelopment and development is a theory of the accumulation of capital on a world scale, i.e., between the world bourgeoisie and the world proletariat (Amin, 1977:277).

Having indicated, albeit briefly, Amin's justification for the necessity of a world-level analysis, we can now determine his characterisation of the nature of peripheral economies, in this case, Africa. The peripheral capitalist mode of production has the dual feature of modern technology (hence high productivity) and low wages within the framework of the capitalist social organisation. The integration of Africa into the world capitalist system implies that the balance between the development level of the productive forces and the value of labour-power is not to be found at the level of the peripheral formation but only at the level of the world system, into which the labour-power is integrated.

This lack of internal correspondence between the two elements in question results in a vicious circle of peripheral development; hence, the failure of Africa's integration over the decades to date (1977:218). The approach adopted in Amin's characterisation of peripheral capitalism is to compare peripheral capitalism with central capitalism.

Africa's peripheral capitalism is manifested as two kinds of distortion: first, the distortion towards export activities (extraversion), and second the abnormal enlargement (hypertrophy) of the tertiary sector. This reflects (a) the difficulties of realising surplus value at the centre and (b) the limitations of peripheral development that result in inadequate industrialisation and rising unemployment.

The transition of Africa to peripheral capitalism was a result of slavery, colonialism, and ongoing neo-colonialism. This is fundamentally different from the transition to central capitalism of the Global North because it effected an external onslaught upon the Global South (Africa) causing peripheral capitalism that was determined from the centre (Amin, 1977:222). This has been expressed as extreme unevenness in the distribution of productivity and in the system of prices transmitted from the centre; disarticulation because of the adjustment of the economy to the needs of the centre; and economic domination by the centre. As economic growth proceeds in Africa, the situation becomes unsustainable as the features of underdevelopment are accentuated; autocentric growth is impossible, whatever output per capita is achieved (Amin, 1976:213).

Moreover, Africa's countries perennially suffer from vulnerability in the balance of payments. None of them have achieved self-sustained growth in their own currencies and their foreign exchange reserves are dependent on the reserve currencies of the Global North that have global convertibility. Therefore, growth in Africa's peripheral economies is 'blocked' because the periphery is 'complementary and dominated' (Amin, 1976:288). The periphery is prevented from accumulating capital indigenously because capital generated at the periphery is transmitted to the centre.

Because of the domination by the centre, the development of underdevelopment is neither regular nor cumulative, unlike the development of capitalism at the centre. In contrast, it is characterized by intermittent phases of rapid growth, interspersed with abrupt halts or blockages (Amin, 1976:289; Amin, 2019a).

Finally, building on the aforementioned core-periphery theory, this work scrutinises the AU's impractical neo-functional frameworks for regional integration, emphasising their inadequacy in achieving self-reliance and sustainability. Africa's underdeveloped countries have no freedom of manoeuvre in relation to world capitalism: "So long as the underdeveloped country continues to be integrated in the world market, it remains helpless, the possibilities of local accumulation are nil" (Amin, 1974:131). Thus economic policy at the national level in a peripheral capitalist economy is largely ineffective.

The establishment of a national currency does not grant local authorities significant control as long as a country remains integrated into the global financialised market. Even with control over exchange and transfer rates, the transmission of fluctuations in the value of the dominant currencies of the centre cannot be prevented. Money or the globally dominated financialisation system by the Global North (centre) constitutes the outward form of an essential relationship of dominance that makes the AU's neo-functional approaches to integration, self-reliance, and sustainability unworkable (Amin, 1974:483; Amin, 2019a).

2.2.2 Neo-Functionalism

Neo-functionalism[10] is a political theory of regional integration and supranationalism, predicated on pluralistic assumptions of asymmetrical global interdependence. It involves bargaining processes aimed at achieving convergence and identifying common interests (Keohane and Nye, 1977; Mattli, 1999:28; Schmitter, 2005:25; Nagar, 2016).

Therefore, neo-functionalism also shares a common basis with new regionalism and human security. The neo-functional framework supports the evolving workings of the AU, particularly in the establishment of a continental supra-authority to action the Agenda 2063 goals. Therefore new regionalism is contingent on the participation of both state and non-state actors. Thus, pushing robust regional cooperation and allowing the free flow of production factors, such as transboundary water governance, green development, and climate change, which all inform human security theory.

To the neo-functionalists, "interests, rather than common ideals or identity, are the driving force behind the integration process, but actors may learn and develop common ideals and identities" (Schmitter and Ernst, 2005: 258). Drawing on the

---

10   See: Schmitter, P.C. (1969). 'Three Neo-Functional Hypotheses about international integration .'

above assertion, neo-functionalism is pragmatic in its process of regional integration. It argues that states and non-state actors are important participants in the integration process (Niemann and Schmitter, 2009).

Thus, neo-functionalism asserts supranationalism as the "only method available to the state to secure maximum welfare, underpinning the idea that there are inseparable linkages between the social, economic and political domains in integration" (Biswaro, 2012:31 and Jiboku, 2015).

This has resulted in African member states transforming the OAU to the AU to consolidate economic, political, and security matters in the continent. It is therefore apparent, that the adoption of a neo-functionalist framework is required to appraise the metamorphosis of the OAU to AU in Africa, notwithstanding its failure as critiqued by the DTRP/centre-periphery framework (Kvangraven, 2018; Amin, 2010, 2019a).

The framework is able to highlight the weaknesses of the AU as a continental organisation and its inability to adapt to the new postcolonial era. One example of this is the reluctance of AU member states (AUMS) to cede aspects of their sovereignty to a continental supra-authority to effectively action Agenda 2063 goals. According to Nagy (2013:1–41), human security has evolved. It is no longer only about regime or state security but has broadened and deepened as a field of inquiry.

It now includes non-state activism in the areas of non-military threats, such as environmental degradation, overpopulation, mass refugee migrations, and asymmetric transnational terrorism. Therefore, neo-functionalism, new regionalism, and the human security development nexus are underpinned by the DTRP. These frameworks all address the dynamics of integration, and their underlying assumptions are coordinated with the AU's Agenda 2063.

According to Haas (1970:627) and Newman (2001:239–251), interdependent national and supranational elites have become the architects of the macro-convergence of continental regional policies. This is in recognition of the limitations of anachronistic sovereignties and their narrow national policy solutions (Adedeji,

2002). Thus, the transitioning of the OAU to the AU and its Constitutive Act serve as a definitive commitment to work towards realising the normative centripetal integration policies of the AEC and Agenda 2063.

For example, notable achievements have been made by the AU institutions in peace and human security outcomes, with actors having learnt from their cooperative decision-making (Haas, 1958:291; Okhonmina, 2009:86–95)

Once established, regional institutions acquire a degree of policy-making autonomy. Africa's regional integration is predicated on the principle of (regional) subsidiarity to its RECs, as they are the building blocks through which the policies of Agenda 2063 are to be realised. Thus, the foundational achievements of the Tripartite Free Trade Agreement (TFTA) of COMESA and ECOWAS have become the benchmarks by which other RECs measure their progress. This has had a catalytic effect, resulting in greater convergence towards Africa's integration and Agenda 2063.

State and non-state actor activism in this enterprise of regional subsidiarity, is evident, as was the case in the materialising of the Southern African Power Pool (SAPP) and the West African Power Pool (WAPP) in energy supply cross-border cooperation (Karaki, 2017; Vanheukelom, 2016). Policy decisions by regional institutions tend to be gradual and incremental, based on successive compromises and marginal adjustments (Haas, 1970:627).

This is the case in Africa's integration project. Its nation-states and RECs, in some respects, reflect incremental gradualism and in others reflect unevenness and stagnation. The drive for integration possibly implies impending supranational authority; however, it threatens and compromises states' sovereign policy spaces in their fiscal and monetary actions to raise taxes for the benefit of the elite.

The unpredictability of fiscal compensation for revenue loss by AU institutions results in hesitant, gradual, and incremental support to completely abdicate sovereignty to a supranational authority. Contrary to the realist axiom of zero-sum national self-interest, neo-functionalism is characterised by positive-sum outcomes (Haas, 1964:66). This shift towards positive-sum outcomes has contributed to Africa's improved peace and human security under the auspices of the AU. National, sub-national and supranational actors have become more interdependent and embedded in the global political economy nexus. This asymmetrical and often predatory marginalising interdependence is inescapable. The problems and challenges should be engaged eclectically and pragmatically.

The assumptions of the neo-functionalism analytical approach benefit integration theory due to its comprehensive nature. The concept of spill-over tasks plays a critical role in this framework, whereby integration deepens in various sectors and is regionally enabled by sustainable human security and peace. This in turn creates push and pull dynamics enhancing further integration in regional, harmonised, standardised, and streamlined value chains along with the interpenetration of regional institutions (Haas, 1968; Tranholm-Mikkelsen,1991; Selwyn, 2013). The spill-over effect, which converges towards supranational institutions, resonates with Lindberg as follows:

"Spill-over refers to a situation in which a given action, related to a specific goal, creates a situation in which the original goal can be assured only by taking further actions, which in turn create a further condition and a need for more action, and so forth" (Lindberg, 1963:10).

However, the automaticity of the functional spill-over effect as a linear and singular process loses its relevance in Africa's integration project. This has occurred against a myriad of geo-strategic factors and asymmetrical interests that continue to impact Africa unevenly, such as global terrorism and climate change.

According to Nye (1971:202), these competing asymmetrical interests result in group coalitions of interest groups that compete for favourable positions vying for advantageous positions to advance either further integration or disintegration. This has been evident in the adoption of the AfCFTA, where there is ongoing lobbying by state and non-state actors to retain and promote their interests in these formations.

In this rivalry and contestation of class interests, both centripetal and centrifugal factors have an impact on the integration project, asymmetrically and in diverse ways (Selwyn, 2015:253–274; UNCTAD, 2016). Neo-functionalism, is a dependent variable constrained by its inherent limitations. Its applicability or inapplicability to asymmetrical conditions, globally – and more specifically – in Africa, have rendered its theoretical predictions occasionally invalid and unreliable.

This challenge of unpredictability has been expressed as: "They do not now provide an explanation of a recurring series of events made up of dimensions of activity causally linked to one another" (Haas, 1971:19). In addition to global asymmetrical interests, which have an impact on Africa's integration and Agenda 2063, the spontaneous assumptions of spill-over in neo-functionalism also play a significant role. However, the comprehensive body of metatheories is a useful prism through which some aspects of its assumptions and hypotheses that are relevant to Africa's integration and Agenda 2063 can be evaluated.

Neo-functionalism explains the process of regional integration with reference to the way three causal factors interact:

- Growing economic interdependence between nations, such as the formation of the SAPP to effectively and efficiently harness regional energy capability.
- Organisational capacity to resolve disputes and build international legal regimes, such as the AU's PSC, which assists in peacekeeping across Africa.
- Supranational market rules, which replace national regulatory regimes, such as the AfCFTA.

The mechanism of transfer of certain aspects of sovereignty and domestic allegiances within the neo-functionalist approach is catalysed by the non-viability of the nation-state to operate on its own. The nation-state is encouraged to be part of a (larger) whole, as is shown in the structural relationship between the AU and its organs. The consequence of this is greater regulatory complexity to enable the functionality of the whole with its constituent parts, such as the AU and its RECs.

In this regard, integration is transferred to higher levels of the decision-making processes. For example, in the case of the AU, the heads of states and governments are not only the highest decision-making bodies but also play a role in considering the horizontal policy contributions of non-state actors. Technocratic automaticity describes the way in which integration proceeds. Supranational institutions are set up to oversee the integration process and take the lead in sponsoring further integration as they become more powerful and more autonomous of the member states.

In the Haas-Schmitter model (1958;1961;2004), the size of the unit, rate of transactions, pluralism, and elite complementarity are the building blocks on which the process of integration depends. As asserted by Rosamond (2000:37), political integration will then become an 'inevitable' side effect of integration in economic sectors.

2.3. Assessing the Analytical and Explanatory Strengths of The DTRP/Centre-Periphery Framework

The combination of these elements forms a holistic and comprehensive approach to uneven development, which characterises the research programme (Kay,1989; Grosfoguel, 2011; Kvangraven, 2017)The DTRP/Centre-periphery framework has been ble to show that the slave trade, colonialism, and postcolonial African governments are factors within a politically, culturally, and economically marginalising and exploitative global environment (Amin, 2001; Adi, 2012; Grosfoguel, 2020: Maldonado-Torres, 2011; Ndlovu-Gatsheni, 2013a).

Given the successful political decolonisation of Africa under the aegis of the OAU, the continent (as forewarned by the late president of Ghana, Kwame Nkrumah) has been forcibly Balkanised to remain an extractive, primary resource appendage to the Global North – and lately China (Benyera, 2020a; Ndlovu-Gatsheni, 2013a; Shivji, 2009).

There are multiple global challenges, as briefly explained by the centre-periphery framework, that have worked against Africa's neo-functionalist development approaches. However, the LPA and NEPAD have been two notable programmes that have sought to extricate Africa from global vulnerability and marginalisation. The policy formulation and design of the LPA was not matched by any policy implementation. The Abuja Treaty (1991) was created to revitalise the aims and objectives of the LPA within a supranational and authoritative framework to implement its policies (Adedeji; 2002). From the 1970s to the late 1990s, Africa's global socio-economic position worsened, despite the quixotic rhetoric of both the OAU and LPA. This resulted in the transitioning of the OAU to the AU and the adoption and ratification of the AU-NEPAD in 2002 (Adejumobi, 2009:405).

The DTRP/centre-periphery framework, with its interlinked theoretical frameworks, provided the motivation for the norm-based LPA, Abuja Treaty, NEPAD, and Agenda 2063. These norms are: self-reliance, good governance, corporate governance, human rights, the rule of law, peace and security, and transparency and accountability. It has been argued that "Theoretical frameworks tell us what sort of world we have, what sort of explanations to provide, of which particular problem" (Preston, 1996:10). After World War II (WW II) and the rise of the decolonisation process in the third-world, regional economic integration became the blueprint for newly independent states. It helped them to effectively leverage their comparative advantages within the global economy (Baran, 1968; Nkrumah, 1974; Ruthman, 1985:9–36; Kvangraven, 2017:12–17).

The DTRP/centre-periphery framework explains the nature of the least developed countries (LDCs). Specifically, Africa is itself a historical product of the international division of labour, which was structurally entrenched largely during colonialism. This bequeathed a dominant, hegemonic 'centre' position to the industrially advanced North and relegated Africa and the third-world countries to a peripheral status in the 'zone of the nonbeing.'[11] Characteristically, the 'peripheral' countries were small and fragmented, devoid of any industrial productive capacity. They became locked into competitively supplying raw materials to the Global North without complimenting their own 'supply-side' factor endowments to harness economies of scale (Satgar, 2009:35; Thompson, 2009:299).

This deficit finds resonance in the DTRP/centre-periphery framework and is not addressed in traditional theories of regional integration. Axline (1994) points out that:

> "A number of essential conditions relating to the process of integration differed in the new setting. Principle among these were the conditions of economic underdevelopment, the absence of pluralistic democratic political systems, and the vulnerability of the region to external factors" (Axline, 1994:49).

This uneven relationship has kept the third world as an extractive exporter of primary commodities to the buyers of finished commodities from the Global North.

This configuration resulted in the continued economic development of the industrialised Global North but was also responsible for the underdevelopment of the Global South. Haas and Schmitter (1964), writing within the neo-functionalist tradition, stated:

> "Our argument then is that the shared fear of the industrialised world, and special regional mechanisms for converting this fear into mutual accommodation, may act as a functional equivalent for the shared positive expectations among elites in other settings, and thus regional integration in the North" (Haas and Schmitter, 1964:250).

After the failure of the NIEO in 1979, the strength of the DTRP/centre-periphery framework influenced the adoption of the LPA

---

11   See Nkrumah, K. (1965). 'Neo-Colonialism: The Last Stage of Imperialism.' International Publisher. New York.

in 1991. This prevented Africa from becoming debt-distressed and enabled it to become self-reliant. The dynamic nature of the DTRP/centre-periphery framework remains relevant in evaluating and understanding contemporary development challenges (Kvangraven, 2017:12–27; Amin, 2010, 2019a).

Furthermore, the DTRP is a research programme rather than a singular theory predicated on a historical global approach. It focuses on analyzing the polarizing factors of global capitalism, examining the components of production structures, and addressing the specific challenges faced by peripheral economies, especially in Africa (particularly due to the chaos, which the BWI's SAPs caused in Africa) (Kvangraven, 2018:1–55; Patalano, 2016; Amin, 2019a). Although these elements are evident in contemporary theories, what makes the DTRP unique, and a particularly strong research programme, is the combination of these varied elements.

The DTRP/centre-periphery framework requires a deep and broad understanding to appreciate the persistence of Africa's uneven development and how it is relevant in understanding the difficulties in attaining Agenda 2063. The four approaches constitute a multi-disciplinary combination to form a holistic and comprehensive approach, which characterises the research programme (Kay, 1989:194). The DTRP/centre-periphery framework makes it possible to address both the strengths and weaknesses of individual theories because it permits ongoing research *and* the discovery of new outcomes. Therefore, it helps to assess the overall rising global inequalities and the way in which structural inequality is produced and reproduced, as well as the uneven development of the global economy. This benefits the highly industrialised countries at the expense of the peripherals, such as Africa (Lakatos, 1978; Fischer, 2015; Evans, 1994:449).

Contrary to the DTRP/centre-periphery framework, traditional regional economic integration theories have been criticised for having little relevance when applied to the development of Africa (Langan, 2014;101–121; Zack-Williams, 2005:501–503; Heidus, 2011:55–64). Models and theories developed from the experience of advanced industrialised societies have proven to be unsuitable to the conditions of extractive – and predominantly – dependent agrarian countries, which tend to be small, fragmented, and clouded by a multiplicity of rival ideologies. With this in mind, the LDCs and Africa designed the LPA based on the DTRP/centre-periphery framework, realising they were an extractive appendage economy supplying raw materials to the Global North. This self-reliant strategy was deemed post-positivist. It was empowering and emancipatory as it sought to structurally delink itself from the exploitative traditional development theories. Therefore, after the failure of the NIEO in 1979, the strength of the DTRP/centre-periphery framework influenced the 1980 adoption of the LPA (Amadi, 2012:191–203; Jalata, 2013:1–43; Tarhan, 2013:411–418).

For example, market forces that rely on highly developed institutions of the West are a crucial factor that has been absent in the LDCs. Leys and Tostensen (2007:52) have observed that:

> "In contrast to Western Europe where commodity trade and capital movements across national boundaries have increasingly integrated, strengthened, and corporatized the political economies of the area, the hidden hand of the market has not had the same effect on African economies."

Thus, certain variables, such as dependency and under-development, the influence of foreign governments, and their transnational corporations (TNCs)), which are ignored in the traditional theories, were factored into the architecture of the LPA.

The impact of external actors on Africa's integration schemes is reflected in superpower ideological confrontation. Former colonial powers sought to entrench their neocolonial ties and extend the interests of MNCs in securing access to sources of raw materials, cheap labour, investment areas, and markets.

The DTRP/centre-periphery framework explains the problems of dependency and underdevelopment in Africa and its poor performance in regional economic integration projects.

This also explains Africa's lack of an industrial base and why its unprocessed commodity economies have been structured as appendages to supply the Global North metropoles. These commodities are linked to the vagaries of global price volatility, determined not by Africa but by countries of the Global North (Ferraro, 2008:58; Jalata, 2013:1-43; Kay, 2005:1177; Kay, 2011:523-538). One key insight of the DTRP/centre-periphery framework is the critique of the internal dynamics of the rentier class in the peripheral states concerning the dynamics of the core centre countries. This is how the elite, collaborative relationship of the centre and the periphery is disaggregated to gender and race in support of neo-patrimonial policies. The chasm of inequality between developed and developing countries is therefore further widened (Cardoso, 1977; Dos Santos, 1970; Kay, 1989; Vasconi, 1971; Fischer, 2015: 727).

In the new millennium, where asymmetry and unpredictability with no singular and linear theoretical approach exist, the NEPAD and Agenda 2063 are the organising templates for the political and socio-economic development of Africa. They share similarities and differences with the previous LPA. In this comparative undertaking, this chapter has provided some perspectives on the theoretical frameworks of various policies, which display a converging similarity between the LPA, NEPAD, Agenda 2063, and their diverging factors.

For example, Marxist theory explains that the process of integration is predicated on class struggle, which is equally attributable to DTRP (Evans, 1994:484–504; Fischer, 2019:542–72; Amin, 1974; Grosfoguel, 2000: 347–74; Kvangraven, 2018; Marx, 1967; Mkandawire, 2001:289–313; Ndlovu-Gatsheni, 2013). It is therefore fundamental to not only analyse the instruments and policies used in the traditional theories but also to question who is being integrated and for whose benefit.

It is also necessary to understand the specific conditions within which integration is sought, including the reasons for and forces behind the integration. This sentiment was supported by the late president of Tanzania, Mwalimu Julius Nyerere (Nyerere, 2012:36):

"Our experience also forces us to question what result we will obtain from greatly expanding our output of exportable agricultural commodities. If all the African producers succeed in increasing their cotton production for example, the first result is likely to be a price collapse and perhaps a reduction in their individual cotton earnings. The market for primary commodities is inelastic: the total demand depends more upon the economic state of the Developed Countries than any other single question."

In support of Amin's centre-periphery theory (Amin, 1974, 2019a), Paul Baran, A.G. Frank assert that the activities of MNC's and FDI in Africa are there to establish exploitative relations and structurally repress Africa's growth. Profits are repatriated back to the Global North rather than being re-invested in the periphery. Therefore, structural economic dependence is seen to have contributed to the underdevelopment of Africa and acts as a hindrance to further development (Rodney, 1973; Singer 1970:208–33; Amin, 2019a).

2.4   Conclusion

The study investigated the AU's self-reliance and sustainability by examining its problems and prospects, as well as its progress towards materialising Agenda 2063. Against an asymmetrical and unpredictable global landscape in constant flux, it would be disingenuous to allocate a one-size-fits-all theoretical framework. Instead, the objectives of Agenda 2063 were investigated with a pragmatic approach focused on achieving tangible results.

On balance, the DTRP/centre–periphery framework adopted in this chapter is a suitable approach to problematise the progress, problems, and prospects of the AU in materialising Agenda 2063.

The framework adopted in this chapter further provides a causal theoretical grounding with which to analyse the AU's initiatives, development policies, and processes, as well as the way each contributes towards theoretical understandings.

The relevant integrative and intersubjective theoretical frameworks are inextricably interwoven with the concept and objectives of the study. Using these theoretical frameworks, a comparative analysis of the AUC/LPA/AGA/AfCFTA/APSA/NEPAD, and Agenda 2063 was conducted.

Using the DTRP/centre-periphery framework, this chapter explained that the concept of regional integration along with its norms and theories, were spread and replicated in post-colonial 1960s Africa by its former colonisers. This occurred under the banner of modernising theories that would enable Africa to catch up with the civilised First World. The DTRP/centre-periphery approach has subsequently challenged and debunked these theories. The deployment of the DTRP/centre-periphery framework was relevant to an analysis of materialising Agenda 2063. For example, trade liberalisation and expansion, without addressing the problem of Africa's structural dependency, have resulted in stunted economic development. Therefore, from the formation of the OAU-LPA to their transitions to the AU and NEPAD and then to Agenda 2063, the historically conditioned structural imbalances in Africa – on which regional economic integration is based – are likely to still prove unviable for Africa.

This is compounded by the fact that Africa's political, economic, and military weakness is in stark contrast to the strength of the West and all the permanent members of the United Nations Security Council (UNSC). While the literature on integration has focused on evaluations of the means and instruments used, such as the traditional free trade areas (FTAs), customs unions, and common markets, few studies have examined the questions relating to the specific conditions within which the LPA, NEPAD, and Agenda 2063 were established. Fewer still have concluded that it is due to dependency on a multipolar superpower rivalry. In addition to the other integrative aspects of established metatheories, the DTRP/centre-periphery framework (Kvangraven, 2017:12–27; 2018:1–55; Amin, 2010, 2019a) contributes important elements highlighting Africa's historical and contemporary constraints. This framework challenges the dominance of past and present hegemons, such as the United

Kingdom (UK), France, Russia, United States of America (USA), and now China.

Chapter 3

The Transition from the Organisation of African Unity to the African Union: Competing Intellectual Discourses

3.1   Introduction

This chapter examines the core issues influencing the progress, problems, and prospects of the AU from 2000 onwards in materialising Agenda 2063. To meet this objective, this book problematises both the external and internal shocks that limit and somewhat stagnate Africa's socio-economic development. In terms of the former, the historically marginalising global economy with its deep-rooted institutions renders Africa an extractive appendage supplying raw materials to the Global North. In terms of the latter, it is Africa's coopted leadership, a buffer class that serves the interests of the globalists, paying lip service to the desperate abject poverty of the majority of Africa's people. Both the Global North and Africa's leadership are an enduring partnership in global crime and corruption. Africa's leadership must be held to the same level of scrutiny, accountability, and condemnation as the colonisers are.

The book will argue (and prove in the oncoming chapters) that, to date, Africa has applied the neo-functionalist approach to express and institutionalise its normative ideas and concepts of wholistic self-reliance and sustainability (within the areas of socio-economic development, governance, and peace and security), within an impressive and vast array of policies, flagship programmes, regional groupings, and organs. This chapter asserts that poor policy implementation can be better understood using the DTRP/centre-periphery framework that will show the limitations of the AU's neo-functionalist policy approaches.

This is evident in the lack of institutional and human capacity. Africa's poor standing in the global economy is a key hurdle that may prevent the continent from becoming a fully-fledged global powerhouse.

In summary, Africa's aspirations for self-reliance have been only partially achieved, primarily due to the lack of consistent and comprehensive political will to give effect to genuine AU development policies and support institutional architecture, thereby failing to effectively realise Agenda 2063.

This lack of political will could be more appropriately considered a total disinterest by Africa's corrupt leadership, who are only invested in the AU as a ruse and a fashionable façade for profit accumulation for themselves, family, and associates. They display total disrespect and disdain for Africa's people, not in sloganeering and sophistry but by watching their actions and following the scent of money. They are in it for themselves and to hell with the masses.

Against this backdrop, the book provides a historical analysis aimed at enhancing our understanding of the incremental institutional intergenerational global power of the Global North, i.e., the colonisers. Starting with the 1870-1914 international monetary system, the first section examines the historical evolution of Pan-Africanism and integration prior to the formation of the OAU/AU. Furthermore, it considers the causes and factors that witnessed the formation of the OAU, LPA, and the transition to the AU. Moreover, an examination of the factors that led to the conclusion of the LPA reveals that the failure of two development decades played a significant role (the 1960s and 1970s). This resulted from Africa's internal structural weaknesses, including military coups, and the LPA was established in 1980 to kick-start Africa's development. The historical analysis highlights and discusses important global events, such as the world regional development initiatives, the Cold War (1946–1991), the 1970s Oil Crisis, the emergence of the NIEO, the failure of the NIEO Campaign in the late 1980s, and the need for 'home-grown' African development programmes. Given the asymmetrical and complex global factors that continue to impact the AU's implementation programmes, the multiple metatheoretical foundations offer a methodological eclecticism, which is non-dogmatic but will be of benefit.

This is a demonstration of the DTRP/centre-periphery framework, whereby advanced developed countries' policies continue to structurally exploit the developing peripheral countries. The explanatory focus which provides the basis for these theories necessitates an openness to quantitative and qualitative data and study designs (Lor, 2011; Sousa, 2010; Bhaskar, 1998; Barron, 2013:117–130). In Africa's pursuit of integration and self-reliance, metatheories give precedence to reality over disciplinary positions, which sometimes distort, impoverish, and narrow accounts of reality.

This enables a post-disciplinary approach, as Africa is inextricably embedded in a geo-strategic milieu with asymmetrical competing global interests (Sayer, 2000; Clark et al., 2008; Cruickshank, 2012:71–82). These competing global interests spawn, reinforce, and promote, racism, prejudice, bigotry, coups, wars, genocide, and ethnic cleansing, compartmentalising certain pedigrees of humans as sub-humans, sheep that must be mass sedated or exterminated. This is a real-time global phenomenon; simply observe your surroundings, and you will witness and hear for yourself.

3.1 International Experiences in Regional Development

i.   **The 1870-1914 International Monetary System and the Historical Evolution of Pan-Africanism Prior to the Organisation of African Unity to the African Union**

The pre-1914 gold system was predicated on an international financial system structure where the key currency standard was underpinned by Great Britain's pound sterling. In this regard, Britain was the world's hegemonic regime of the international monetary order (Eichengreen and Flandereau, 2010; McKinnon, 1993:1–44).

This gave London power in global financial policy formulation and control. In this section, this book will consider the historical processes of the international monetary system from 1870 to 1914. The role played by the USA, especially after WW II, will be examined (Triffin, 1964; Ali et al., 2011). Using integrative metatheories this book will historically examine why and how the countries of the Global North created international monetary institutions and structures reflective of their white racist dominance and influence.

This deliberate racist structural imbalance disadvantaged the countries of the Global South and catalysed Africa's development policy initiatives. In the period from 1870 to 1914 the international monetary regime was predicated on the gold standard and dominated by Great Britain. Among the developed industrial countries, the gold exchange contributed to the balance of payment adjustments, thereby facilitating the ease of international trade and investments (Bloomfield 1959; Scammell 1965; Dayer 1988; Silverman 1982:58).

For example, a balance of payments surplus in one country would trigger an increase in import supplies with a multiplier effect of decelerating exports and reducing the surplus. When Britain (or any other country), experienced a balance of payments deficit, the Bank of England (or the central bank in the other countries) would raise the bank rate. This would increase domestic interest rates, which in turn would reduce the money supply. The Bank of England would act as a lender of last resort to stabilise the global economy within the gold standard regime.

This arrangement helped capital-exporting countries to mitigate the consequences of their balance of payments deficit and domestic inflation, which would erode the value of currencies and dampen margins, thereby threatening their ability to convert gold into the local currency. This would cause the global economy to stagnate by producing deflationary downward pressure on currencies. The same balance of payment adjustment by Great Britain had a disadvantageous effect on countries on the periphery, or Britain's colonies, including several African countries (Triffin 1964; Schwartz and Bordo 1984; Conan 1966;

Schenk 2010). This was a deliberate racist policy measure by Great Britain, that institutionally enabled capital surplus accumulation from Africa to fund their perceived comfortable lifestyles and notion of civilisation. This epitomizes corruption; indeed, corruption by any other name remains corruption.

The gold standard dominated by Britain was vertically and hierarchically arranged with Africa at the bottom as an extractive colonial appendage of finished European goods. This arrangement allowed Britain to continuously draw surplus capital from the peripheral colonies, which had underdeveloped financial markets and no manufacturing base.

As argued by Walter Rodney (1973), the arrangement of the Western systems, including the gold exchange regime and their classical theory of economics espoused by Adam Smith in 1776 in *The Wealth of the Nations,* were exploitative, racist, and impartial towards Africa. These competitive global tensions reached a critical mass and when World War I (WWI) broke out in 1914, the gold standard collapsed. With the demise of Great Britain as the sole global financial and economic hegemonic centre, different countries sought their own policy positions. In the post-WWI period, between 1920 and 1930, repeated efforts were made to reinstate the pre-war gold standard, with limited success.

The USA, which remained an unscathed global power after the war, became the net creditor nation to the devastated nations of Europe and demanded that its debts be repaid. The lack of structures, rules, and institutions to coordinate, sequence, and regulate the global financial system in the aftermath of WWI, resulted in the Great Depression during the 1930s as countries applied competitive counter-currency devaluations and protectionist policies to safeguard their economies. The burden of debt repayment fuelled nationalistic discontent and contributed to the rise of Nazism in Germany, resulting in WWII. In its aftermath, a new monetary reconstruction programme arose, which was considered at the 1944 Bretton Woods Conference (Eichengreen 1985; Devereux 2002; Bernake 2009). The Bretton Woods conference of July 1944 resulted in the formation of the WB and IMF under the hegemonic dominance of the USA. It is against this backdrop that the US dollar, which had performed well prior to the 1914 gold standard, became the medium of international exchange. It is from this point that the global rules and instructions of a neoliberal world economy were dictated.

Using DTRP/centre-periphery framework as a prism, Africa's unequal and asymmetrical position from a colonial to a postcolonial continent within the global political economy was clearly articulated. Amidst the dominance of the Western international monetary system, the evolution of Pan-Africanism represented a significant undercurrent in resisting slavery, colonialism, and the contemporary challenge of present-day neo-colonialism.

Ake (2003) noted that the idea of regional integration as a means of collective self-reliance for promoting economic integration and cooperation has been around in Africa for a long time. Historically, integration in Africa preceded European colonialism and predated European integration. Africa has a long tradition of regional cooperation, with its trade and monetary integration schemes being the oldest in the developing world.

Chronologically, integration in Africa has undergone three important phases: the first phase (Islamisation and Arab colonialism), the second phase (diaspora pan-Africanism and European colonialism), and the third phase (modern pan-Africanism and post-colonialism) (Okafor and Aniche, 2017). Islamisation and Arab colonialism in Africa started in the 10th century, or even earlier with the gradual but steady Islamisation of the continent under Arab colonialism. From the coasts of the Mediterranean and the Red Sea to the coasts of the Atlantic and Indian Oceans, or from Saharan Africa (covering the whole of North Africa) to sub-Saharan Africa, the rampaging Arabs continued the conquest and Islamisation of Africa. Thus, this first phase was essentially, although not exclusively, centred on religious aspects. This was subsequently curtailed by European incursions into Africa between the 18th and 19th centuries. During the scramble for Africa, the various European powers defeated the Arabs, and both the Islamised and yet-to-be-Islamised African kingdoms, culminating in the Berlin Conference (1884–5), and subsequent European colonialism (Coleman, 1958; Okafor and Aniche, 2017).

Diaspora Pan-Africanism and European colonialism during this period of integration in Africa began with diasporic Pan-Africanism during the European colonial era. This was pioneered by the African diaspora in the Americas and Europe, spearheaded by the likes of Henry Sylvester-Williams, Edward Wilmot Blyden, Marcus Garvey, W.E.B. du Bois, and Malcolm X (Coleman, 1958; Walters, 1997). A good example of the leading role played by the African diaspora in Pan-Africanism was the role played by Henry Sylvester-Williams in the formation of the African Association in 1897 (later renamed the Pan-African Association) and the organisation of the First Pan-African Conference in London in 1900 (Hooker ,1975; Sherwood, 2010).

The aims were to unite all people of African descent, both those in Africa and those in the diaspora in the Americas and Europe; and to tackle racial discrimination and segregation, racism, colonialism, imperialism, alien religions, and slavery against blacks; as well as pursuing freedom, self-determination, self-government, independence, and decolonization for Africa (Gassama, 2013). This phase of integration in Africa primarily encompassed socio-cultural and political dimensions (Okafor and Aniche, 2017).

This was the beginning of black nationalism. This also coincided with the era of European colonialism, in which European powers sought to integrate their various colonial territories in Africa. Thus, the first experiment with integration in Africa began in 1910 with the formation of the Southern African Customs Union (SACU) (Attuquayefio, 2009; UNECA, 2004). The pervasive influence of Europe on existing integration projects in Africa can also be traced to the colonial period when Britain and France made spirited efforts to amalgamate their respective colonial territories to enhance cost-effectiveness in their administration and exploitation.

In what is generally regarded as the first economic integration scheme in the region, Britain created the West African

Currency Board (WACB) in 1912 as the sole institution responsible for the issue and management of currency. It was also charged with issuing the legal tender for its four colonies – Gambia, Ghana, Nigeria, and Sierra Leone – to ease trade transactions. This was followed by the West African Airways Corporation (WAAC) to facilitate air transportation and the West African Examinations Council (WAEC) to standardise examinations for university admission in the four colonies.

The West African Cocoa Research Institute (WACRI) was also established (Agbonkhese and Adekola, 2014; Attuquayefio, 2009; Sesay and Omotosho, 2011). There were similar institutions and arrangements in the French colonies. France embarked on the same integration trajectory, albeit in a more inclusive manner, by creating a monetary union using the Communauté Financiè re d'Afrique (CFA) in 1945, in its colonial territories. It also served as legal tender following the establishment of a central bank in Dakar, Senegal, which acted as a clearing house. Unlike their Anglophone counterparts, the French colonies retained the CFA as legal tender after independence making it relatively easy, in theory, to promote trade among them (Agbonkhese and Adekola, 2014; Sesay and Omotosho, 2011). Subsequently, the Southern Rhodesia Customs Union (SRCU) emerged in 1949 between Apartheid South Africa and colonial Rhodesia (present-day Zimbabwe) (Mistry, 2000; Qobo, 2007).

It was this attempt by European colonial powers to integrate their various colonial territories in Africa for large-scale economic exploitation that Pan-Africanists in the diaspora and the emerging African Pan-Africanists resisted. Thus, traditional Pan-Africanism was sustained by African-educated elites in the later stages of European colonialism.

This was the period when the Manchester (Pan-Africanist) Conference of 1945 spelt out the need for African unity in detail. The struggle of decolonisation saw the Pan-Africanists' demands being strongly echoed (Anyang, 1990; Antwi-Danso, 2009; Saasa, 1991; Sherwood, 1995). However, there was tension between the African Pan-Africanists who saw Pan-Africanism as the true path to sustainable African liberation and development and emerging

African nationalists who favoured nationalism as the realistic approach to decolonisation, self-determination, self-governance, and independence.

Despite this tension, Pan-Africanism remained the leitmotif of Africa's developmental framework. As a result, regional integration became the pillar of Africa's developmental strategy soon after the independence of most African states. This period marked the genesis of Afrocentrism within the realms of modern Pan-Africanism and post-colonialism.

It was towards this period that the first All-Africa Peoples' Conference (AAAP) took place in Accra, Ghana, in December 1958. It was attended by more than 300 delegates representing over 200 million Africans from 28 African countries and colonies. Thus, unlike the Pan-African Conference, which was spearheaded by Africans in the diaspora, the AAAP was dominated by Africans. However, the objectives of the latter did not depart significantly from those of the former. For example, the objectives, resolutions, and recommendations of the conference were anti-colonial struggles or national wars of liberation, decolonisation of Africa, abolition of all forms of racial segregation and discrimination, and rejection of economic dependence, neo-colonialism, and imperialism (Legum, 1962; Wallerstein, 1967).

The AAAP thus succeeded and replaced the Pan-African Conference. Subsequently, the second and third AAAPs were held in Tunis, Tunisia, in January 1960 and in Cairo, Egypt, in March 1961, respectively. Unfortunately, the fourth AAAP that was scheduled to take place in Bamako, Mali, in February 1962 never happened for various reasons, leading to its eventual demise (Legum, 1962; Wallerstein, 1967). Subsequently, contemporary regionalism in Africa during this period was spearheaded in large measures by the OAU and UNECA, partly as a response to the last vestiges of colonialism, but also in an attempt to spur political and economic progress on the continent; and partly as a political instrument to deal with the power imbalances in the international system (Mistry, 2000; Qobo, 2007; UNECA, 1995).

Thus, since independence, African states have been using regional integration as a strategy for solving their developmental challenges. For example, following the inspiration of Kwame Nkrumah, Ghana and Guinea announced in 1959 that they had formed a Union of African States. In May 1959, Côte d'Ivoire (then Ivory Coast), Burkina Faso (then Upper Volta), Niger, and Benin (then Dahomey) reacted immediately by forming the Conseil du l'Entente (all Francophone countries). In an address delivered to a meeting of the committee of African organisations held in London in August 1961, Nnamdi Azikiwe proposed a West African Common Market (WACM) as a strategy for achieving unity in the sub-region (Adedeji, 1970; Adetula, 2009).

Nevertheless, the Ghana–Upper Volta Trade Agreement between Ghana and Upper Volta (now Burkina Faso) started in 1962, as did the African Common Market linking Algeria, United Arab Republic (Egypt), Ghana, Guinea, Mali, and Morocco. In the same year, Cameroon, CAR, Chad, Congo, and Gabon formed the Equatorial Customs Union (ECU), the predecessor to the Customs Union of Central African States (CCUCA) (Aworawo, 2016; UNECA, 2004).

This was followed by the unification of various blocs (e.g., the Brazzaville, Casablanca, and Monrovia blocs), culminating in the establishment of the OAU/AU, 1980 Lagos Plan, and Abuja Treaty of 1991 that gave birth to the AEC.

This unification was led by African leaders such as Haile Selassie, Julius Nyerere, Ahmed Sékou Touré, Kwame Nkrumah, Nnamdi Azikiwe, Léopold Sédar Senghor, and Kenneth Kaunda. The aims were to achieve the unification of Africa and the integration of the fragmented African economies through the fight against neo-colonialism, Apartheid, and white minority rule (especially in South Africa, Lesotho, and Zimbabwe). This included the movement for African renaissance, African revivalism, revival of African culture, philosophy, religion, arts, science, technology, ideology, common heritage, African socialism, African democracy, and African welfarism; and the struggle for decolonisation and independence of the remaining African territories under colonial rule, such as Namibia, Angola, and Mozambique. It also condemned dependency and stressed the need for collective self-reliance (Sherwood, 2012).

As expected, there was a flurry of diplomatic initiatives and activities among the new states aimed at promoting collective self-reliance and regional integration. For example, in January 1964, President William Tubman of Liberia conveyed a meeting of four West African countries – Côte d'Ivoire, Guinea, Liberia, and Sierra Leone – to explore the feasibility of setting up an FTA. Almost a year later, in February 1965, diplomats from the four states met again in Freetown, Sierra Leone, to draw up a document that would have led to the formation of what they called an organisation for West African cooperation. However, these early initiatives did not materialise due to a lack of sincerity on the part of the West African leaders and their strong adherence to their newly won political sovereignty (Sesay and Omotosho, 2011).

In the east of Africa, the EAC – comprising Kenya, Tanzania, and Uganda – began in 1967 as perhaps the most far-reaching of the early modern integration attempts in Africa. However, most of these early experiments in Africa have been dissolved or transformed. New groups have formed, reflecting African countries' continued desire for economic cooperation and integration (UNECA, 2004).

The second decade of independence witnessed an upsurge in the establishment of regional integration schemes. Consequently, in West Africa alone, three economic communities emerged in four years.

This began with the Mano River Union (MRU) in 1971 between Liberia and Sierra Leone, which was established to promote economic and political cooperation between their contiguous countries, and was joined by Guinea under Sékou Touré a decade later in 1983. Another was the formation of the French Speaking West African Economic Community or Communauté Economique de l'Afrique de l'Ouest (CEAO) in 1972. This was followed in 1975 by the ECOWAS (Attuquayefio, 2009).

The next group to be established was the Community of West African States (which became the West African Economic and Monetary Union, WAEMU) in 1973. Elsewhere, the Central African Economic and Customs Union (CAECU) was transformed in 1974, followed by the establishment of the Economic

Community of the Great Lakes Countries (ECGLC) in 1976 (Sesay and Omotosho, 2011; Tolentino, 2011; UNECA, 2004). The 1974 declaration by the UN of the NIEO recognized regional economic cooperation among developing countries as the cornerstone for their future development.

Subsequently, the United Nations Economic Commission for Africa (UNECA) took up the challenge and convened a series of meetings in various parts of Africa to promote regional cooperation and integration (Agbonkhese and Adekola, 2014). Prior to the 1980s, African leaders pursued regional integration schemes as part of a strategy to meet the continent's daunting development challenges, especially during the Cold War era. After the 1980s, African regional integration received renewed attention through various summits and meetings, culminating in the Monrovia Declaration, LPA, and Abuja Treaty (Ofei-Nkansah, 2009). The impetus for the Abuja Treaty was largely attributed to the new wave of democratisation on the continent.

The era of modern Pan-Africanism and post-colonialism differed from the two previous phases of integration in Africa in many ways.

First, it emanated from Africa and represented the first attempt by Africans to integrate their territories. The first phase was imposed from outside (specifically the Arabs) while the second phase was spearheaded by Africans in the diaspora.

Second, as a corollary to the above, the third phase is referred to as African integration in this book, unlike the first and second phases, which are more aptly described as 'integration in Africa.' In other words, while integration in Africa is an institutive integration because it was imposed by non-Africans, African integration is constitutive integration because it was driven by Africans, even as it is currently driven by African leaders.

Third, the third phase of African integration occurred largely in the economic sphere, with the target of ultimately embracing other spheres, such as the political, security, and social spheres; whereas the first and second phases were more focused on religious and socio-cultural cum political spheres, respectively.

Fourth, from an African historical perspective, the third phase of African integration was modelled on European civilisation, integration, and neo-functionalism as a form of modern integration or neo-integrationism. In contrast, the first phase of integration in Africa was based on the classical integrationism of Arabian Islamic tradition or civilisation, while the second phase of integration in Africa epitomized neo-classical integrationism, revolving around African cultural revival and civilisation (Okafor and Aniche, 2017).

Consequently, African integration is currently targeted at continentalism through regional integration and democratic reforms, as well as the struggle against military rule and authoritarian regimes or agitations for multiparty democracy modelled after neo-functionalism. However, neo-functionalism and its revised version, neo-neo-functionalism, are essentially theories of European integration (Gehring, 1996; Haas, 2001; Laursen, 2008; Mattli, 1999; McGowan, 2007; Niemann and Schmitter, 2009; Schmitter, 1970; Warleigh, 2006).

Therefore, these theories are not able to explain the defects, failures, and drawbacks of African integration. Most of the European countries that adopted a neo-functional approach to regional integration, resulting in the formation of the EU have transcended problems of national unity, de-industrialisation, and national insecurity (Aniche, 2015). The explanatory value of neo-functionalism suffered a serious setback as a result of the unpredictable trajectory of the upsurge of nationalism in the EU, such that many of its proponents and exponents began to question it (Haas, 1975; Hoffmann, 1966; Schmitter, 2003; Tranholm-Mikkelsen, 1991). Thus, there is a need to deconstruct them in the quest for a paradigm shift in African integration.

One of the major defects of neo-functionalism is that it assumes that regional integration is a gradual and linear process, making an explanation of its shortcomings impossible (Haas, 1976; Schmitter, 1969). Another of its defects is that neo-functionalism assumes that state integration is an integration of interdependence, and therefore cannot adequately explain the incidence of dependence of African economies on Western economies and the integration of the dependence of the African states to another state (Aniche, 2018).

This book therefore contends that there is a need to evolve the fourth phase of African integration anchored on the neo-neo-integrationism of post-neo-functionalism or postmodern integrationism of post-neo-nationalism that emphasises the initial integration of security matters through post-nationalism. This is an appropriate theoretical approach given the enormous security challenges confronting the continent. This will be followed by a phase of subsequent and gradual integration of the economic and political spheres after many years of nation-building, national integration, and national development, through neo-nationalism or a combination of political and economic nationalism. This should also be driven by the people or private sector rather than the government or the public sector, as embedded in humanism. Post-neo-functionalism is effectively a hybrid of neonationalism, post-nationalism, and humanism (Okafor and Aniche, 2017).

ii.   The Organisation Of African Unity's initial Paradigm of Africa's Integration

The formation of the OAU was preceded by the rise of diasporic Pan-Africanism during the European colonial era. This was spearheaded by the likes of Henry Sylvester-Williams, Edward Wilmot Blyden, Marcus Garvey, W.E.B du Bois, and Malcolm X (Coleman, 1958; Walters, 1997). This culminated in the first AAAP held in Accra, Ghana, in December 1958 (Legum, 1962; Wallerstein, 1967). This was followed by the 1959 Union of African States between Ghana and Guinea as the Casablanca Group that was pushing for an immediate United States of Africa. In contrast, the Brazzaville and Monrovia blocs led by Dr Nnamdi Azikiwi and the late President of Tanzania Kambarage Nyerere respectively preferred a gradual, incremental step-by-step institutional building of Africa's nation-states.

This ideological divide was followed by a compromise and unification of all the blocs resulting in the formation of the OAU on 25 May 1963 (Sherwood, 2012:106-26). The OAU initiated the varied strands of Africa's integration.

The deployment of the DTRP/centre-periphery/neo-functionalist integration theories provides a supporting framework to assess the gaps and interventions towards Africa's integration. These theories are transboundary and non-territorial and both factor in state and non-state actor activism (Owens, 2010:165; Schmitter, 2005:25). Therefore, the DTRP/core-periphery/neo-functionalist nexus will show and explain the global historical approach; the economic theorising that addresses the polarising tendencies of capitalist development; and the dominant Global North structures of production vis a vis the peripheral Global South. It is these colonial exploitative structures and systems that resulted in the formation of the OAU and its later transition to the AU. The post-WWII period was dominated by Cold War rivalry between the former Union of Soviet Socialist Republics (USSR) and the USA. The former materially, diplomatically, and politically, supported the anti-colonial struggles of the third world against the Global North's foreign and alien rule (Wolfers, 1988:14). The support by the USSR and other Eastern Bloc countries for the Global South was provided to enhance its geopolitical influence against the Global North countries led by America (Wolfers, 1988:14). It was during this time that the OAU was established in Addis Ababa on 25 May 1963. It aimed to continue the struggle for continental decolonisation (Hargreaves, 1996:219).

Article III of the Charter of the OAU proclaimed its principles as the sovereign equality of all states; non-interference in other states' internal affairs; respect for the sovereignty and territorial integrity of each state, and acceptance of their inalienable rights to independent existence and self-determination. An African Group in the UN General Assembly pursued the principle of decolonisation and self-determination (Hargreaves, 1996:219). Ochieng (1999) reinforced Africa's pursuit of anti-colonialism and unity by proposing that the idea of the unification of Africa originated during the anti-colonial struggles. This idea was mainly associated with the late president of Ghana, Kwame Nkrumah, who stated "we are looking forward to solving our problems but this can only be achieved through the unification of African States" (Ochieng, 1999:91).

Africa's anti-colonial struggles were supported by the USSR and other Eastern Bloc countries, meanwhile, the USA and other Western countries pursued overt and covert destabilisation tactics. This interplay of soft and hard power dynamics contested the third world arena for hegemonic control over its populace's hearts and minds (Hart, 1985:148).

The increasing tension of the Cold War rivalry enabled the developing countries to extract value from both the USSR and USA protagonists with minimal conditionality. Mengisteab (1996:153) attests to the aforementioned assertion that the Group of 77 (G77), the Non-Aligned Movement (NAM)[12], the United Nations General Assembly (UNGA), the United Nations Conference on Trade and Development (UNCTAD), and the United Nations Industrial Development Organisation (UNIDO) were among the international forums where the developing countries leveraged their influence on the global agenda and participated in global processes concerning the space presented by the superpower Cold War rivalry. Regional initiatives in Africa became extensions of superpower proxy wars, by vying for spheres of influence in Africa. The regional initiatives were therefore bereft of homogeneity and orientation in their goals and purpose. They all subscribed to Africa's cooperation and unity within the OAU but with divergent superpower allegiance and loyalty. These dynamics led to constraints, even in the OAU and the UN, regarding the principle of non-interference in the affairs of a sovereign and autonomous state.

There was no commitment to long-term regional goals and the equitable distribution of benefits. Other global forums and agreements, such as the European Economic Community (EEC), African, Caribbean, and Pacific Group of States (ATP) (1966–1975) and the Generalised System of Preferences (GSP) (1971) of the General Agreement on Tariffs and Trade (GATT) (1986-1994), were some of the Cold War era concessions that enabled value to

---

12   See Adams, D. 'Overview of the Non Aligned Movement' Council on Foreign Relations,' www.cfr.org.

be extracted from African countries. The coalescing of the third world around the NAM in support of OPEC and the success of third world anti-colonial liberation struggles catalysed and reinforced confidence in Africa to support the NIEO and later the LPA strategies. This interplay of global processes made a substantial contribution to Africa's continent-wide LPA.

iii.　The Emergence of the New International Economic Order

The OPEC global oil crisis and the collapse of the USA gold standard worsened the USA balance of payments deficit. This threatened the loss of dominance of its currency in the global economy. These developments had an impact on the structure and workings of the BWIs, making the hegemonic dominance of the USA through the gold standard untenable.

The USA delinked from the BWIs gold standard regime in August 1971, under the Nixon presidency. It was during this period that the USA applied its hard power military engagement, enforcing its policies through the IMF by destabilising third world countries, including those in Africa.

These contrivances by the USA had already been predicted in Kwame Nkrumah's book: *Neo-Colonialism*, which envisaged forced policy subjection, indirect imperialism, dependency, and a debt trap for the third world.

In the aftermath of the collapse of the BWIs gold standard system in 1971, the IMF conditionality vested its power to dictate the domestic policy of borrower nations, specifically the third world. As a response to this, the countries of the Global South began calling for a NIEO. This would become the set of proposals demanded by Third World countries through the UNCTAD, with their combined voices becoming the G77. The adoption of the UN General Assembly (UNGA) resolution on the 'Declaration of the Establishment of a NIEO', states:

> "[We] solemnly proclaim our united determination to work urgently for the establishment of a New International Economic Order based on equity, sovereign equality, interdependence, common interest, and cooperation

among all States, irrespective of their economic and social systems which shall correct inequalities and redress existing injustices, make it possible to eliminate the widening gap between the developed and developing countries and ensure steadily accelerating economic and social development, and peace and justice for present and future generations (1 May 1974, A/RES/S-6/3201)."

Against the aforementioned exploitative structural relations benefiting the Global North at the expense of the Global South, the declaration of the NIEO by the G77 demonstrated their agency in demanding an equitable economic global order benefiting all nation-states. The economic structural dominance of the Global North over the Global South was unacceptable to the latter.

iv. The Emergence of the 1979 Monrovia Strategy and the 1980 Lagos Plan of Action

The 1979 Monrovia Strategy and 1980 LPA were pivotal. There were, however, three main regional plans which triggered the need to fast-track African regionalism in the third phase of African integration (or the era of modern Pan-Africanism and post-colonialism) as a strategy of African development and transformation. Thus, the narratives about modern African regionalism and Pan-Africanism cannot be complete without mentioning the 1979 Monrovia Strategy, 1980 LPA, and 1991 Abuja Treaty (Tandon 2016). The 1979 Monrovia Strategy for the Economic Development of Africa and the Monrovia Declaration of Commitment on the Guidelines and Measures for National and Collective Self-reliance in Economic and Social Development for the Establishment of a New International Order were the outcomes of the African Heads of State and the Council of Ministers of the OAU meetings in their 16th Ordinary Session and 23rd Ordinary Session, respectively. This was concluded in Monrovia, Liberia, in July 1979 (OAU 1979; Asuk 2011; Tandon 2016).

The document, described as Africa's economic Magna Carta, committed Africa to establish an AEC by 2000, to foster the economic, social, and cultural integration of the Continent. The LPA emphasised self-reliance and African ownership of and control over its own resources. It proposed a bold programme of action based on regional building blocks that would eventually lead to the economic unity of the African continent (Ravenhill, 1984; Tandon, 2016). The Plan was Africa's regional approach to the economic decolonisation of the continent providing long-term socio-economic restructuring and development (Aniche, 2020b; Benachenhon, 1983).

However, one major similarity in the policy thrusts of the Monrovia Strategy and the LPA was to accelerate the process of regional economic integration through cooperation (Adedeji, 1991; Aniche, 2020b). Both documents emerged on the African development agenda as a critique of development approaches derived from the modernisation thesis, particularly the WB's Berg Report (Asante, 1991; Browne and Cummings, 1984; Eyoh, 1998; OAU, 1979; Sekgoma, 1987; Shaw, 1983). The major defect in the two documents was that they simply consisted of a political declaration, a development strategy, a set of priorities, sectoral programmes of action, and a blueprint for regional and sub-regional integration, and therefore did not consider the elaborate theoretical issues of development economics, political economy, and public policy (Adedeji, 1991; Aniche, 2020b).

The NIEO demanded a recalibration of the balance of forces arising from the post-WWII international order, upheld by the IMF, WB, GATT and later the WTO (formed in 1995), which were unjust and biased against the Global South (Adedeji, 1984; Adejumobi, 2009:405; Adogamhe, 2008:1–34;Kingston, 2011:110-130).

The proposals and demands put forward by the Global South to restructure and create an equitable global new order were in direct opposition to the Global North's hegemonic dominance and interests. The Global North was only agreeable to selective reforms in international trade, and financial and investment relations, which still left their global hegemony unscathed.

It was evident that by 1979, no fundamental or comprehensive policy overhaul enjoyed any support from the Global North and that the NIEO campaign had been a failure, as described by Adebayo Adedeji:

"In spite of the 6th and 7th special sessions of the UN General Assembly, in spite of the UNCTAD IV and V, we are no nearer to establishing a NIEO now than we were in 1974. One is not being alarmist if one says that between 1974 and 1979, the international situation has gone from bad to worse."Walters and Blake (1992:221) explain that the failure of NIEO further reinforced a coalescing of third world forces in their economic and political agencies to capitalise on its agenda setting. This gave legitimacy to the global principles as demanded by the NIEO UN resolution. It was against this backdrop that the formulation of Africa's self-reliant development strategy, contained in the LPA, resonated with the 1957 demands of Kwame Nkrumah for a United States of Africa. The global multiple crises, as predicted by President Kwame Nkrumah, predisposed Africa to the violent mechanisation of the West's neo-colonialism.

The practical failure of the NIEO campaign and the aftermath of coerced political and economic policies forced on Africa's governments by the Global North's institutions, left no doubt that Africa's leadership had to chart their own domestic development path. The LPA emerged as a response to the failure of the NIEOs and was compounded by the multiple global crises. This highlighted the marginalisation and vulnerability of Africa's economy within the global economic framework.

This book presents the Pan-African agency within the framework of the LPA. The aims of Africa's integration were validated using a metatheoretical methodology to show the differences between early post-independence regionalism, as espoused by the Monrovia and Brazzaville gradualist and incrementalist school, and the way it differed from the continent-wide LPA as envisaged by Nkrumah as early as 1957.

The LPA and NEPAD are significant for comparing their effectiveness relative to the goals of Agenda 2063. The LPA was inward-looking: its development strategy was based on Import Substitution Industrialisation (ISI), while NEPAD focused on export-led growth and development. After the failure of NIEO to meet the Global South expectations, the countries of the Global North, and their institutions, increased their efforts to maintain their global hegemony (Adedeji, 1982:2). This led to the OAU working together with the UNECA to review the development policies that Africa had pursued since independence.

This was in response to UNGA resolution 3508 (xxx), which called upon the UNECA and the other four regional economic commissions to prepare studies of the long-term trends in and forecasts of the economic development of their respective regions. The UNECA undertook (and published in 1977) a preliminary assessment of long-term development trends and prospects in Africa (UNECA, 2002; 2005).

The assessment confirmed that the global oil crisis of the 1970s had an adverse impact on Africa's balance of payments and continuing debt, as well as its downward economic trajectory since 1971 (UNECA, 2002).

This resulted in a global negative ToT and a current account deficit, which created a debt crisis for Africa, as shown in (Table 3.1).

Figure 3.1: Africa's Share in world merchandise
Source: WTO (2003).

Negative ToT, which was Africa's position, resulted in meagre export earnings, an unsustainable balance of payments, and unsustainable debt servicing with no foreign currency earnings. This forced African countries to borrow from IFIs with conditions that kept their economies afloat at the expense of public services and the development of their citizens (Kingston, 2011:110; Kvangraven and Amin, 2019:631–649).

Between 1948 and 2002, Africa had the lowest share of world merchandise among the world's continents. Its economy was mainly based on extracting primary resources destined for processing in the Global North and China (UNCA, 2005).

The UNECA study predicted poor prospects for Africa within the prevailing international economic order if its peripheral position continued. It was imperative to establish home-grown development policies and strategies as alternatives to the colonial and neocolonial policies, which were being practised by independent African countries (Adedeji, 1983:1)

This resulted in the 1979 Monrovia Strategy for the Economic Development of Africa for National and Collective Self-Reliance in Social and Economic Development. The Assembly of the Heads of State and Government (AHSG) adopted this in July 1979 and in 1980 the LPA was adopted to implement the strategy.

The inward-looking development strategy of the LPA prioritises the development of the domestic market rather than a dependence on the foreign Global North markets, which are at the heart of Africa's development efforts. It emphasises the fundamental importance of indigenous factor inputs in the development process. In contrast to the Western neoliberal export-oriented development, as espoused by the NEPAD, the LPA argued that the central concern of development should be the African individual and communities without the destruction of their culture (Adedeji, 1980:4). Three factors underpinned the self-reliant, self-sustaining process of development: the rediscovery of self-confidence; mastering sovereignty over natural resources and strengthening the leadership role of government in socio-economic engineering.

The last factor was in contrast to the Washington Consensus neoliberal stricture of delinking the state and government from the free market (Adedeji, 1984). This book argues, however, that the LPA and NEPAD have been unable to delink from the global economy and that this has been widely demonstrated. In comparison, NEPAD has exhibited global export-led initiatives, while the LPA's lofty rhetorical claims remain unattainable.

Nevertheless, the recovery of self-confidence, as articulated by the LPA, was not only a technical treatise but also a political document. It articulated the assertion of self-confidence as an indispensable factor for Africa's recovery and development (Adedeji, 1980:48). The WB report entitled 'Accelerated Development in Sub-Saharan Africa: An Agenda for Action' was diametrically opposed to the LPA, which had described Africa's governments and nation-states "as intrusive in the domain and operations of a free and deregulated market system."

The LPA, contrary to the WB report, demanded establishing effective control over Africa's natural resources, which had become the property of MNCs. This aspect of the LPA further contrasts with the NEPAD's export-oriented trajectory for Africa, with the LPA rejecting foreign trade as the engine for growth and development. In contradistinction, the development of the domestic continental African market highlighted the LPA's self-reliant and self-sustaining processes of development strategy, with the government at the epicentre:

"If substantial meaning is to be given to self-reliant, dynamic growth and diversification, governments are expected to play a larger role in the process of socio-economic transformation than they have explicitly and formally agreed to play so far. In view of the multiple objectives of socio-economic policy, governments will inevitably find themselves performing several roles. They will act as planners, instituting state-wide planning networks and linkages, plan monitoring facilities, control mechanisms, information systems and feedback effects; and act as entrepreneurs running state enterprises and as allocators of national resources through fiscal and monetary policies, incentives, and disincentives."

Undoubtedly, this emphasises that the AUMS and non-state actors should drive the implementation of policies to materialise Agenda 2063. This was anathema to the WB's programme for

Africa, which sought to weaken the African state and give ease of operation to the invisible hand of the privatised market economy. In the Berg Report, Browne and Cummings (1984:24–33) asserted the WB's vision of the way the global economy should be ordered, and that the LPA was inimical to Western interests.

By emphasising the interdependence of the global economy, the 1981 Berg Report ensured that Africa remained "the storehouse of natural resources necessary for the maintenance of the West's hegemonic global industrial dominance."

The LPA's self-reliant development strategy was perceived as antithetical and a threat to the capitalist system of the West. The projections of the LPA contended that maintaining unchanged neocolonial structures and systems would result in a bleak future for Africa. The LPA study correctly projected that by 2008, Africa would become more economically dependent and marginalised within the global political economy. Africa's position as an exploited, extractive source of primary resources for the Global North was robustly and pedantically maintained because it supported their business model. More importantly, this strategy was contingent not only on the Global North's coordination of soft power, but also of its hard power (e.g., its military might, which was unleashed on Iraq in 2003 and Libya in 2011). Since the inception of the LPA to the present-day NEPAD, nowhere has AU agency countered the Global North's military hard power. This is in comparison to China, which has a nuclear deterrent capability and North Korea, which engages in nuclear sabre-rattling as a countervailing strategy.

This fundamental weakness of Africa not to aspire to equal or neutralise the Permanent Five (P5) of the UNSC will always be a lingering failure of the AU. This book further argues that soft and hard power strategies are inextricably intertwined, and the latter engenders a balance of power among (the P5) equals, of which Africa is not a part. It is, however, a step in a positive direction for the continent-wide LPA regional programme, which was an attestation to Pan-African agency and epistemic restoration. This approach stands in stark contrast to the pre-LPA regional initiatives in Africa.

The LPA was a comprehensive economic blueprint under the aegis of the UNECA and was ratified by the OAU, thus it became comprehensively institutionalised. Nevertheless, a mismatch has existed in Africa from the 1970s to date, between its rapid growth in population and urbanisation, and a deterioration in food production and supply to its population. Within the DTRP/centre-periphery theoretical framework calculus, this has increased dependence on food imports resulting in negative ToT.

This has meant that foreign exchange resources have secured expensive food supplies at the expense of financing self-sustaining development programmes. As Africa lacks hard power capability in both its LPA and NEPAD policy documents, it is not clear in which ways Africa could become industrialised and globally competitive without the kind of hard power leverage that China has and exercises in its geo-political space. Trade and tariff wars with either the West or the USA would not be sufficient. The DTRP, as an intersubjective metatheoretical framework constituting causal models, will help to analyse and problematise these unpredictable, non-benchmarked asymmetrical challenges. The implementation of Agenda 2063 programmes offers the solution to these development challenges (Adler, 2001: 95-118; Carlsnaes,1992:245–270; Ricci, 2018:225; Shivji, 2016:240).

As argued by McMichael (2011), the mono-cash crop export economy dominated by Western MNCs has encouraged rent-seeking agri-policies benefitting the few among the ruling elite. This is at the expense of a self-sustainable comprehensive holistic food and agricultural policy framework, which would sufficiently promote and sustain both urban and rural livelihoods. In support of sufficient food production and supply, the LPA programme recommended a 50% reduction in post-harvest food losses.

In this regard, a regionally integrated and interdependent African economy would be the initial building block towards establishing an African common external tariff (CET), African central bank (ACB), and single common currency and market, thus establishing a singular diversified and dynamic AEC. The LPA's policy insisted that Africa's almost total reliance on the export of raw materials should change. The OAU, however, believed that Africa's development and growth should be based on a combination of Africa's considerable resources, its entrepreneurial, managerial, and technological resources, and its markets (restructured and expanded), to serve its people.

With the onset of the Global North's financial globalisation under the aegis of the BWIs, the LPA document called for increased south-south cooperation in all facets of the global political economy, creating preferential trade areas within the framework of the UNECA-Multinational Programming and Operational Centres (MULPOCS). This new global redesign and rebalancing by the LPA within the south-south NIEO, was aimed at extricating Africa from its role as an extractive colonial appendage supplier of unprocessed primary commodities for the West. Thus, the gradual elimination of the exploitative and dependent north-south trade patterns and relations would give way to a fairer NIEO. The LPA promoted an interventionist developmental state, in contrast to the WB's Berg Report neoliberal free market without involvement. The LPA aimed to enforce capital account controls and a tax regimen, which would constrain multinational monopolistic dominance.

Within the context of the NIEO, the LPA demanded that developed countries eliminate their protectionist measures, especially their farm subsidies, which rendered Africa's exports inaccessible to the Global North markets. However, the LPA's self-reliant economic programme did not preclude global financial assistance, as long as it was not exploitative in intent. Furthermore, the LPA, through the NIEO initiative, called for the reform of the global monetary and economic system as well as the cancellation of restrictive conditions and debt. Increased Overseas Development Assistance (ODA) from the Global North was requested through the LPA in support of an equitable NIEO.

Both the LPA and NEPAD demanded increased ODA. This opened a plethora of criticism of an externally dependent, self-reliant sponsored programme. Ravenhill (1986) commented that "for the most part, the plan appears to be little more than a plea for externally generated resources; international donors are expected to foot the bills".

In principle, both the LPA and NEPAD involve sourcing external funding support for Africa's self-reliant economic programme. This reinforces the assumption and stereotype that Africa is ever dependent on handouts for its socio-economic programmes. In 1984, Africa experienced multiple crises of drought and desertification, which spread to 36 of its 50 (now 55) member states.

This was a form of stress test for the LPA. The global economic recession and its attendant collapse of commodity prices affected Africa's balance of payments negatively. This resulted in external mounting debt levels and confirmed Africa's deteriorating economic crisis.

Unlike the NEPAD, which has taken responsibility for also contributing to Africa's economic failure, the LPA apportioned the blame to the persistence of the colonial and neo-colonial mix of economic policies. The 1984 food crisis was induced by drought on top of the colonial economic policy (Adedeji, 1984:14). The colonial economic policy had concentrated all resources on the production and marketing of mono-cash crops for export, neglecting the production and marketing of food crops, which were left largely to the subsistence sector.

During this period, Africa's population grew rapidly at 3% per annum and the urbanisation rate was approximately 5% per annum. This rural-urban migration was unsustainable, due to low productivity in the food production sector and negative current account balances. The structure of the LPA included short, medium, and long-term interventions. The short-term interventions were for emergencies (for example, the food crisis), but were supported by medium and long-term interventions to structurally reposition the African economy to be self-reliant. In support of food security, the LPA called for immediate reforestation programmes for soil stabilisation, and the exploitation of underground water for irrigation to mitigate the effects of droughts. It also called for the establishment of meteorological and hydrological monitoring stations to enforce strict sustainable land management.

The implications of the 1984 global recession had a deleterious impact on the implementation of the LPA. As the WB confirmed:

"The crisis management of recent years has resulted in widespread neglect of programmes dealing with the long-term constraints on development; schools are unable to teach effectively because of shortages of books and other materials; clinics are without medicines; deforestation, overgrazing and other environmental hazards are not being checked."

The persistent and declining trend in net capital flows to Africa, particularly to bolster productive investment and industrialisation policies, has been apparent from the era of the LPA to NEPAD. This affirmed Bogdanowicz-Bindert's (1982:286) prediction for Africa, which foresees "a continuation of economic stagnation and human misery, recurrent crises, and stop-gap measures." The transitioning of the LPA to the NEPAD in the new millennium has demonstrated Africa's resolve to fight against Afro-pessimism, which is a product of colonialism and neo-colonialism directed at sapping Africa's optimism and confidence. Support for an optimistic outlook for Africa began to emerge from various quarters. The WB's 1984 report 'Towards Sustained Development in Sub-Saharan Africa', stated the following:

"Against this disquieting background, is it possible to look with hope toward the future? The World Bank has answered with an emphatic 'yes.' This optimism can be justified by recent experience in both Africa and elsewhere. For instance, the despair that is now focused on Africa was matched by a comparable feeling about India in the early 1960's. In recent years, India, despite its terrible poverty, has emerged from despair to hope in the eyes of the world. This change has been achieved largely through sustained improvement in the government's policies and programmes, with support from donors wherever their finance, technical assistance, or advice could be useful. There are many other cases around the world of mutually reinforcing roles of good domestic programmes and appropriate external assistance. The same combination of domestic reform and donor support can be successful in Sub-Saharan Africa."

Optimism about Africa's future was also prevalent at the 'Special Memorandum by the UNECA Conference of Ministers on Africa's Economic and Social Crisis', which was presented at the 1984 Second Regular Session of the Economic and Social Council of the UN. It stated that "Africa is capable, in the not-too-distant future of establishing at national, subregional and regional levels truly dynamic, self-reliant and interdependent economies, capable of functioning as effective partners in the international economic system." This statement heralded the transition of the LPA to the NEPAD.

v.   Challenges for the 1980 Lagos Plan of Action, the 1991 Abuja Treaty, and African Regionalism Architecture

From the 1980s onwards, the LPA supported Pan-African agency in IR in pursuit of equitable economic development and cooperation. The creation of new regional economic groupings (REGs) was encouraged to improve and support the existing groups, as pillars and building blocks towards a continent-wide economic community.

However, Africa continued to display only rhetorical success with no practical policy application or implementation. This was despite a plethora of multi-membership RECs and the signing of the Abuja Treaty in 1991 to revitalise the implementation of the stagnated aims and objectives of the LPA in establishing the AEC[13]. This stagnation and lack of policy implementation was recognised by Ravenhill:

> "Regional self-reliance has been given the same symbolic status in the 1980s as was accorded Pan-Africanism in the 1960s: a concept to which lip service is paid but one which is largely ignored when it comes to policy implementation (Ravenhill: 1986)."

---

13   See: Smith, J. (2015). 'The African Economic Community: A comprehensive overview.'

Taking into consideration this commentary, this section will expand on the factors and actors that led to the LPA being followed by the Abuja Treaty (1991), within an interplay of metatheoretical frameworks. This section will also demonstrate their application in cost-benefit calculus criteria, which informed the Abuja Treaty and the AEC. These evaluative processes help to identify comparative advantages and economies of scale that will benefit the integration project.

The section will further explain the rationalising of more than 19 RECs in addition to the eight officially recognised by the AU. The principle of norm subsidiarity and variable geometry represents an anti-one-size-fits-all strategy, which has modelled and guided the AU's eight REC programmes in sequence, given their asymmetrical levels of development. This section argues for an intersubjective framework of a cost-benefit analysis, which for Africa's leadership means choosing between the long-term benefits of the LPA and the perceived short-term costs for African governments. Opting for the implicit short-term costs would have been perceived as a threat, requiring sacrifices from populations for the long-term welfare gains promised by the LPA.

Not only would this be a recipe for domestic destabilisation, but it would also invite the Global North's soft and hard power zero-game tactics to maintain its hegemony. Without the Global North's financial input and skills, Pan-African agency will be stagnated and compromised to some degree.

However, the LPA programme suffered from a litany of problems, ranging from the overlapping memberships of its RECs, through to unfulfilled commitments (Dinka and Kennes 2007; Draper et al., 2007; UNECA, 2006; 2008). The policy rhetoric of the LPA was not matched by the reality of implementation in key result areas. This was after the 1884 Berlin Conference, which arbitrarily divided Africa into small, weak domestic economies, which were largely underdeveloped and rural based.

These subsistence-based states had weak productive capacities concentrated in dependent export industries, as appendages of the metropoles. Hitherto, they had been part of an immense continental infrastructure for supply-side and demand-side deficits, which militated against rationalised competitive integration into the global value chains of the global economy (Collier, 2007:7).

The absence of effective and adequate institutional incentives, such as the payment of a country's revenue loss, accentuated collective action problems, and disinterest added to a deficit of trade facilitation measures. Trade facilitation measures are predicated on sophisticated and effective measures, which engender trade liberalisation to unlock and attract both foreign and intra-regional investments.

Under these circumstances, the rationalisation and harmonisation of sectoral industries would have benefited other regions and countries more than others. This would have resulted in the loss of tariff revenues as a source of revenue for most African governments. This arrangement would have constricted the patronage networks and therefore created disinterest in the LPA. At the time, the only highly industrialised country in Africa was Apartheid South Africa and its racist policies were antithetical to the LPA.

The comparative balance between trade creation and trade diversion encouraged the smaller economies of Africa to support the LPA programme through shared market institutions and they jointly formulated regulatory policies. This was perceived as threatening individual African governments in terms of their sovereignty and discretionary authority over economic policy formulation. Trade creation, therefore, consisted of shifting the production of goods and services from a less to a more efficient member of the AU. For example, within the SACU and Southern Africa Development Conference (SADC), South Africa benefited more from trade creation than the other members.

Conversely, trade diversion involved the shifting of production and services from an efficient non-union member to a less efficient union member. The UK, for example, which is neither a member of the AU nor of any of its RECs, enters into trade agreements with Africa's less developed RECs and enjoys superior economies of scale. It could be said that these trade agreements threaten the implementation of the LPA and NEPAD, thereby jeopardising the establishment of the AEC.

The disinterest of some African governments towards the LPA is underscored by the cost-benefit analysis between trade creation and trade diversion. Trade creation, whereby production would shift from small and less efficient regional producers to more efficient RECs, threatened the immediate and short-term economies of weaker member countries despite the welfare benefits of the LPA.

In the north-south divide, the LPA's proposals emphasised by the failed NIEO campaign, required a trade diversion configuration. This would shift production from the more efficient Global North (i.e., the developed world) to the less developed regional producers of the Global South, with welfare-enhancing benefits. This kind of trade diversion, initially demanded by the G77 NIEO campaign and then by the 1980 LPA, was perceived to be a challenge and inimical to the Global North's hegemony.

For example, the LPA would have demanded the reviewing and re-configuration of EEC-ACP preferential trade agreements within the Lomé convention protocols, and the common currency arrangements and CETs between Francophone Africa and France.

Their removal from Africa was demanded by the LPA. The process of disentanglement was a continent-wide initiative to disentangle Africa from the perpetuation of the exploitative pattern of the Global North.

At the onset of the LPA, Browne and Cummings (1984:24) countered the LPA supported by two WB reports: (1) the Berg Report, and (2) the 'Accelerated Development in Sub-Saharan Africa: An Agenda for Action.' Both WB Reports were antithetical to the LPA. The former emphasised colonial export-oriented economies in contrast to the LPAs inward-looking self-reliance and industrialisation.

The WB advocated for a minimised role of government with greater neoliberal privatisation and unfettered movement of global capital. The LPA was considered inimical to Western interests, and as a consequence, had to be marginalised (Browne and Cummings, 1984:33).

The WB's Berg Report claimed that Africa's economic demise was due to gross resource mismanagement by its political elite leadership, overvalued national currencies, faulty exchange rate policies, excessive state intervention, public subsidies, and pervasive corruption (Obare, 2011:57).

The WB's Berg Report became the neoliberal Washington Consensus policy doctrine, which further marginalised Africa's aims and objectives towards integration and self-reliance. Consequently, African public services were compromised to maintain external debt servicing and more funds were borrowed from the IMF and WB to feed its populations. According to S.K.B. Asante:

> "Unless governments can be convinced that economic cooperation and eventually integration will strengthen their capacity to cope with urgent domestic problems better than they could on their own, they will continue to be preoccupied with managing policy issues with a national orientation and lose sight of the significant benefits that regional cooperation can bring."

This was demanded and enforced by the WB, IMF, and its global military-industrial complex represented by the North Atlantic Treaty Organisation (NATO). The credit rating agencies as gatekeepers of monopoly global capital (for example, Standard and Poor and Moody's and Fitch) enforced the Washington Consensus IMF/WB neoliberal regime of a free market economy with minimal government intervention, thereby rendering African states' development and the LPA defunct. Most African governments were in no position to challenge the Global North, diplomatically, militarily, or otherwise and followed the SAP scripts of the North (Akokpari, 2001:147–169; SAPRIN, 2002:21; Amin, 2010; Kingston, 2011:110–130).

Table 3.2: Sub-Saharan Africa's arrears and debts, 1980-93 (%)

	1980	1986	1987	1988	1989	1990	1991	1992	1993[p]
				DSR and ISR on Cash Base*					
WDT 1993									
ISR	6.2	11.4	9.4	10.3	9.7	9.0	9.2	8.6	7.3
DSR	9.7	24.9	19.6	21.0	18.0	18.0	17.1	16.9	13.5
*WDT 1992**									
ISR	5.7	11.6	9.2	11.5	10.2	8.9	10.0	8.8	—
DSR	10.9	28.2	22.1	24.7	21.8	20.0	19.8	18.5	—
				Contractual DSR and ISR					
WDT 1993									
ISR_d	6.4	15.8	16.3	19.7	20.5	20.9	23.4	25.7	26.8
DSR_d	11.2	39.4	39.1	50.5	48.0	50.2	56.7	64.9	68.0
*WDT 1992**									
ISR_d	6.1	18.7	20.3	26.9	27.7	27.2	32.6	34.5	—
DSR_d	11.2	49.4	49.4	67.9	64.6	64.0	76.6	—	—

Notes:
* DSR = debt service ratio: (actual) total debt service/exports of goods and services (TDS/XGS);
ISR = interest service ratio: (actual) interest payments (INT/XGS).
** Data for 1992 provisional estimates.
$_d$ indicates that actual payments plus arrears are used in the numerator.
[p] indicates projected.

Source: WDT (1992,1993)

The IMF concentrated on providing loans to stabilise countries with balance of payments deficits that were unable to service their external debt obligations (Kingston, 2011:116).

Kingston (2011:116) argues that the late 1970s multiple crises of rising oil prices, rising interest rates, and falling prices of primary commodities left African countries unable to repay mounting foreign debts. In the early 1980s, Africa's debt crisis worsened, as the ratio of its foreign debt to export income grew to 500% (SAPRIN, 2002:21). Against this background western IFIs enforced conditions on African governments for them to qualify for loans. The two policy frameworks (SAPs and LPA) were diametrically opposed.

The former SAPs conditionalities tended to reinforce neoliberal policy norms by forcefully integrating African extractive primary commodity exports to the Global North against LPAs self-reliant production and integration programmes.

The combination of regional integrated production and the intra-African cooperation of the LPA was an approach that effectively integrated individual African countries as appendages of the foreign trade and monetary exchange regime. In the spirit of GATT, the BWIs demanded the elimination of tariff barriers and capital account controls to facilitate financial globalisation. Global capital converged with open trading regimes to allow free market enterprise and diverged with closed protectionist economies underpinned by ISI. The policy divergences between SAPs and the LPA were expressed and reflected by the architects of the LPA:

> "The goals, objectives, and characteristics of the strategy contained in the World Bank's Berg Report are in many ways inconsistent with those of the LPA. The implication of the recommended approach is to make Africa more dependent on external markets for its agricultural and mineral products and for its essential factor inputs. This is contrary to the principles of self-reliant and self-sustaining development of the LPA."[14]

The goal was to delink the role of the state in business and economics, while refraining from capital account controls, thus allowing the unhindered movement of global capital with no import tariffs to raise taxes. Allowing repatriation of foreign profits by TNCs was a precondition for structural adjustment loans (Obare, 2011: 57–64). This section argues that the authors of the LPA displayed naivety by not factoring in the failure of the NIEO campaign, of which they were a part. It was assumed that the policies of the LPA, although shown to be welfare enhancing, would not be reciprocated forcefully by the Global North.

Furthermore, Africa did not have the means to assert or use power effectively in the realm of hard and soft power dynamics essential for the institutionalization of the LPA. The IMF and WB represent a combined membership of 186 countries. The UK's voting weight exceeds that of 43 African countries together:

> "This structure is compounded by the structure and functioning of the IMF and WB board's where rich countries hold 62% of the votes, despite only possessing 21% of the

---

14   Personal Interview with Dr Odilile Ayodele senior researcher at the Institute of Pan African Thought and Conversation. 2022.

world's population and providing 23% of the Bank and Fund's income. Developing countries, who provide 77% of the institution's income and hold 79% of the world's population, have just 39% of the votes on the boards of IFIs."

The Global North member states are economically more powerful, and this translates to them holding a majority of votes, thereby selecting leaders of their choice for the daily management of the IFIs. Drawing on the functional policy theory highlighted in Chapter 2, the agenda-setting dominant discourse and interest is in line with their objectives and aims. This aligns with the findings of the Structural Adjustment Participatory Review Initiative (SAPRI) report, echoing the sentiments of critics within the developing countries, especially Africa and Latin America:

"To them structural adjustment programmes (SAP) and other expressions of the neoliberal agenda are seen as reforms that, despite the free market rhetoric, 'regulate' capital accumulation at a world level to the benefit of the interests of dominant economic and political elites."

In John Perkins book, 'Confessions of an Economic Hit Man: How the US uses Globalisation to Cheat Poor Countries Out of Trillions', it is asserted that IFIs dominated by the US, UK, and France, imposed loan conditions (such as the SAPs) as a means of control over indebted countries and their natural resources, labour, and land on a global scale.

For debtor countries to qualify for development loans, the senior members of the country's Central Bank should be independent of government influence and intrusion in matters pertaining to austere fiscal and monetary discipline.

In this regard, public subsidies that support education, health, and food security are cut to service external debt obligations. Interest rates are increased to limit the money supply to the general population, but simultaneously to earn large profits for global speculative capital, which does not contribute to a country's productive industrialisation. The former vice president of the WB and Nobel-prize winner in economics made the following statement about the IMF and WB:

> "They were interested in one thing. They looked at the country and thought, "they need to repay the loans they owe to Western banks. How do we get that to happen?" So they would never ask, "should we give this developing country a bankruptcy procedure so they can have a fresh start?" They thought that bankruptcy was a violation of the sanctity of contracts, even though every democracy has a bankruptcy law for people who have persistently failed. They were interested in milking money out of the country quickly, not rebuilding it for the long-term."

This section asserts that this is why the IMF and WB demanded an independent central bank and the elimination of capital account controls to facilitate their global speculative financial flows. The multiple crises of the 1970s forced many developing countries into debt and they therefore needed to turn to the IMF and WB for development finance. This entailed cutting public subsidies in health, education, housing, and food security.

The IMF and WB dictated the terms of repayment. In particular, they demanded that Africa's export earnings should pay for the servicing of its debt and that priority should be given to service the external global debt owed. These conditions show that not only is the idea of a free market economy false but there is also a systematically entrenched and exploitative system that benefits the global elite with their neo-patrimonial cronies.

This marked the de-industrialisation of most African countries and the rise in poverty levels. Hitherto, Africa had largely remained an extractive economy whose commodities peaked and dipped unpredictably due to the vagaries and dictates of the elite globally controlled economy. A critical mass of global challenges led to the creation of the 1991 Abuja Treaty against further marginalisation of Africa's political economy.

This marked the ascendancy of global neoliberalism, exemplified by its legitimacy and hegemony over communism as underscored by the demise of the USSR in 1991. With the implosion of one-party state governments in Africa, which had been supported by the now-defunct USSR, the 1990s ushered in a new period of democratic ethos. The Washington Consensus, the BWI's victorious ideological package, demanded that African governments follow the principles of democracy to qualify for loans and balance of payments to support their governments.

These conditions were proffered as democratic principles, including multi-party general elections leading to a multi-party constituted government, the separation of powers in the executive government, legislature, an independent judiciary, and the fourth estate – a free media (Mkandawire, 2004:289; Kingston, 2011:110-130).

These principles constitutionalised horizontal public participation and scrutiny of all processes of government, a practice that was anathema to the one-party state governments that had created the LPA. Furthermore, the BWI's demanded minimal intervention from the government in the economy, emphasising the importance of upholding the rule of law and protecting private property rights. The changed neoliberally dominated space required an alternative to the LPA that could be more aligned with the dominant neoliberal hegemon of the Global North.

For African governments to qualify for the BWI's much-needed loans, the Abuja Treaty adopted the neoliberal precepts of private free market enterprise and economic openness – a fundamental departure from its precursor LPA programme, which had sought to partially disengage from the West's exploitative dominant global economy in pursuit of an inward-looking regionalism. Percy Mistry has observed how the SAPs of the BWIs were haphazardly embraced by African states and recorded how the autonomy of the state was diminished through the neoliberal markets. As in the LPA, the Abuja Treaty maintained its aims and objectives towards an integrated AEC. However, this now had to be pursued within a supranational authority with harmonised and rationalised RECs as its pillars and building blocks. The AEC revised treaties of the LPA inspired the various RECs to amend and adopt the Abuja Treaty to align with the new compliances in procedural and systematic demands towards continental economic integration.

The 1991 Abuja Treaty and African regionalism architecture were significant milestones in the continent's integration journey. The 1991 OAU Summit or meeting of African leaders in Abuja, Nigeria, which metamorphosed into the 1991 Abuja Treaty was primarily and initially meant to assess the 1979 LPA that succeeded the Monrovia Strategy (Tandon, 2016).

The fallout of this Treaty, adopted by the OAU at the meeting of the Heads of State Government in Abuja, Nigeria in June 1991, was the establishment of the AEC. The Treaty of AEC, also known as the Abuja Treaty, came into force after the requisite ratification of members in May 1994. It provided for the AEC to be set up through a gradual process (a neo-functional approach,) which would be achieved by the coordination, harmonisation, and progressive integration of the activities of existing and future RECs in Africa (Aniche, 2020a).

The stated goals of the AEC include the creation of FTAs, a customs union, a single market, a central bank, and a common currency; thus, establishing an economic and monetary union (Aniche, 2020b).

There are multiple regional blocs in Africa, many of which have overlapping memberships. The RECs consist primarily of trade blocs and, in some cases, political and military cooperation. Most of these RECs form the 'pillars' of the AEC. Several of these pillars also contain subgroups with tighter customs and/or monetary unions. It is often hoped that, due to the high proportion of overlap in memberships of these pillars of the AEC, some states with several memberships will eventually drop out of one or more of the RECs (Aniche, 2015).

The RECs include the CEN-SAD (established in February 1998); COMESA (formed in December 1994, replacing a Preferential Trade Area, which had existed since 1981); the new EAC (established in November 1999 and entered into force in July 2000 following its ratification by the three original partner states); ECCAS (established in 1985); ECOWAS (founded in May 1975 with the signing of the Treaty of Lagos); Intergovernmental

Authority on Development (IGAD, founded in 1986); SADC formed in Lusaka, Zambia in April, 1980 as the Southern African Development Coordination Conference (SADCC), and following the adoption of the Lusaka Declaration transformed into SADC in August 1992 in Windhoek, Namibia; and AMU formed in 1989 (Aniche 2014; Aniche and Ukaegbu 2016).

Some of the RECs, including the ECCAS, ECOWAS, and SADC contain sub-groupings. For example, the Central African Economic and Monetary Community (CEMAC) is a sub-bloc of ECCAS; the West African Economic and Monetary Union (UEMOA) and West African Monetary Zone (WAMZ) are sub-groups of ECOWAS; and the SACU is a sub-group of SADC. Consequently, some countries belong to a customs union, yet continue to negotiate towards establishing other customs unions (Aniche and Ukaegbu, 2016).

By the end of April 2019, the Agreement was ratified by the required 22 countries (specifically 24 AUMS). It came into force on 30 May 2019, exactly 30 days after ratification. The operational phase was launched on 7 July 2019 at an AU Summit in Niger (TRALAC, 2019). Unlike the LPA, which lacked the force of legal institutional sanctions, the provisions of the Abuja Treaty have binding provisions to enable the realisation of AEC. The Abuja Treaty, unlike the LPA, is predicated on market integration. It focuses on all processes within the production value chain, operating at the sector level and within the region, to unleash the full potential of economies of scale.

This uniformity in planning and execution, synchronisation of paces and sequences, and leveraging complementarities of factor endowments aims to achieve optimal returns on investments. The Abuja Treaty was signed in 1991 to revitalise the shortcomings of the LPA. Just as with the LPA programme, the AEC only became operational four years later in 1994 because the member states were reluctant to cede aspects of their sovereignty to affect a supranational authority. Similarly to the LPA, the Abuja Treaty remained a declaration of intent with no implementation of its aims and objectives and could be seen as another failure in the annals of Africa's economic development history. Africa's vulnerability and marginalisation had incrementally worsened from the 1970s. This chapter argues that a rhetorical shift to strengthen the Abuja Treaty, without domestically mobilised resources, skills, and a military capability to leverage Africa's integration aims and objectives, would be utopian.

This book argues that from the outset, the LPA programme lacked an overarching, continental supra-institutional authority to incrementally sequence, coordinate, and enforce its legally binding provisions towards the fulfilment of its objectives.

Within the naivety and the assumption of political voluntarism on which the LPA's design was predicated, the authors of the LPA and the AHSG did not attempt to institutionalise any soft or hard power tenets in anticipation of internal or external resistance to the programme.

From the outset, the lack of institutional incentives and enforcement of a binding mechanism to 'lock in' African governments, which were prone to reneging on LPA commitments and processes, was a miscalculated oversight. The failure to sanction non-compliance encouraged free-riding and indifference. Hence, the LPA became a rhetorical mouthpiece with neither monitoring nor evaluative mechanisms to measure progress. With the increased vulnerability and marginalisation endured by Africa from the multiple crises of the 1970s, to their escalation in the 1980s, the 1991 Abuja Treaty sought to institutionally remedy this indifference.

The RECs were endowed with normative supranational authority to enforce and sanction non-compliance towards the LPA but this mandate was never ratified and adopted. The lack of coordinated continental planning resulted in multiple memberships and heterogeneity in aims and objectives. This militated against the convergence of policy formulation and their implementation because there was no enforceable legal framework with which to sanction non-compliance.

This was against the background of the UN's and OAU's provision of 'non-interference in the internal affairs of a sovereign state.' The top-down intergovernmental vertical structure of the LPA lacked horizontal public participation. It was this lack of transparency and accountability that resulted in its stagnation. The late or non-payment of budgetary contributions by member states reflected on the fragmented vision of the LPA.

This chapter argues that the LPA was rendered little more than a talk-shop, due to two interrelated conditions. The first was the disinterest of Africa's leadership and the second was the result of being trapped between the two superpowers, whose rivalry entrenched divisions created polarity and mistrust among African leaders.

The demise of the USSR in 1991 and its embrace of *glasnost* and *perestroika* were coordinated with the West's open and private market enterprise, the neoliberal doctrine, which promoted a free market economy. As both were championed by Prime Minister Margret Thatcher of the UK and President Ronald Reagan of the US, they earned unchallenged legitimacy and hegemony.

vi.   Transitioning from the Organisation of African Unity 1980 Lagos Plan of Action Towards the African Union[15]

The transition from the OAU to AU was examined from the perspective of the DTRP/centre-periphery framework. The OAU was formed on 25 May 1963 in Addis Ababa, Ethiopia. This was the first ever intergovernmental organisation in Africa operated by Africans. Its raison d'etre was the decolonisation of Africa from foreign and racist occupation and domination (Padmore, 1972; Mark, 1979; Young, 2016). Prominent Pan-Africanists, notably, Henry Sylvester-William, Kwame Nkrumah, Dedan Kimathi, Kenneth Kaunda; Julius Nyerere, Herbert Macaulay, Gamal Abdel Nasser, Jomo Kenyatta, and Abubakar Tafawa Balewa mobilised the anti-colonial struggle (Chirisa et al., 2014:1–8; Johnson, 1962:426–429).

While the OAU successfully achieved some of its aims and objectives, particularly in eliminating colonial and Apartheid rule in the African continent (Young, 2016), the OAU failed to achieve several other goals for the continent (Williams, 2007; Saho, 2012; Obayiuwana, 2013:4; Mathews, 2011). This stagnation and failure

---

15   Interview with Professor Siphamandla Zondi Director at the Institute of Pan African Thought and Conversation. 2022.

on the part of the OAU engendered its metamorphosis into the AU. Several meetings and conferences by African leaders preceded the transformation of the OAU to AU, which included the Conference on Security, Stability, Development, and Cooperation in Africa (CSSDCA), a product of the Kampala Movement of 1991; the Algeria Summit of 1999; the 35th Summit of AHSG held in September 1999 in Sirte, Libya (Sirte Declaration); and the 36th Summit of OAU, held in Lomé in July 2000. It was at the 36th Summit of the OAU that the draft of the Constitutive Act was formally ratified by the member states (Packer and Rukare, 2002:365–379).

Following the ratification of the Act, the AU was officially launched on 9 July 2002, with the convergence of 53 African leaders in Durban, South Africa (Tieku, 2004). Researchers of neo-functionalism identified with the functionalists' propositions on the common pursuit of welfare needs through interstate cooperation of both state and non-state actors (Biswaro, 2012). In 'The Uniting of Europe – Political, Social and Economic Forces, 1950–1957', Hass argued that in contrast to the predictions of functionalism, the process of integration is not only restricted to the intensification of policy collaboration in a specific functional area, economic or technical but also encompasses its political approach (Dosenrode, 2008). This is relevant to the AU.

To the neo-functionalists, "interests, rather than common ideals or identity, are the driving force behind the integration process, but actors may learn and develop common ideals and identities" (Schmitter and Ernst, 2005: 258). Drawing on the above assertion, the Neo-functionalist approach was adopted by the AU in its process of regional integration. It argues that states and non-state actors are important participants in the integration process and demonstrates how neo-functionalism has been limited in realising Africa's integration towards Agenda 2063 (Niemann and Schmitter, 2009).

Neo-functionalism posits supranationalism as the "only method available to the state to secure maximum welfare, underpinning the idea that there are inseparable linkages between the social, economic, and political domains in integration". However, as revealed by the DTRP/centre-periphery framework the neo-functional pursuit of Africa's integration has proven unworkable within the intergovermentalism of the AU and self-reliance and sustainability has not been realised (Biswaro, 2012:31; Jiboku, 2015).

The works of Naldit and Magliuerast (1999), Obeng-Odoom (2013), and Makinda et al. (2016), describe the inability of the OAU to promote and attain the 1980 LPA and the 1991 Abuja Treaty socio-economic goals and objectives embedded in Article II of the organisation's charter (Opiko, 2013; Adar et al., 2010; Adar and Bamidele, 2016).

The realisation of economic integration to actualise the AEC was conceptualised and codified in the LPA and subsequently, the Abuja Treaty, led by Nigeria and other committed African countries. At this point, the RECs began to be considered as the building blocks for the AEC (Murithi, 2014).

The concept of Africa's integration towards the AEC also resonated with Adejumobi and Olukoshi (2008:82), who affirmed that "only if the regional integration efforts can be fully developed through a developing macro-states approach that would better strategies for integration be facilitated in a globalized world". This particular approach was employed during the transition of the OAU to AU, while highlighting the limitations faced by the OAU.

The failure of the OAU as a continental organisation was not restricted to achieving its goals and objectives to promote economic prosperity and growth in the African continent. It also failed as an institutional structure, which could not handle the functional tasks set in the AEC (Parker and Rukare, 2002:367). The African leaders of Nigeria and South Africa, Olusegun Obasanjo and Thabo Mbeki respectively, embarked on reform packages, which led to the formation of the NEPAD African Peer Review Mechanism (APRM) (Tieku, 2004).

Moreover, the non-interference policy of the OAU caused great stagnation and instability, threatening the safety and human rights of its own citizenry. This failure was due to the anachronistic principles of respecting sovereignty and non-interference in the internal affairs of other states, which were contained in Article III of the organisation (OAU Charter, 1963).

This paralysed decision-making in the OAU and prevented it from responding to pressing issues on the continent, exacerbating atrocities and the violation of human rights (Murithi, 2008; Zoubir, 2015; Hanspeter, 2016).

The ratification of the Constitutive Act at the Summit called for the public pronouncement of the AU as the successor to the OAU (Francis, 2006; John-Mark, 2016). The official inauguration of the AU was made during the convergence of 53 African leaders in Durban, South Africa, on 9 July 2002, at the summit of the OAU AHSG (Jaoko, 2016). In the meantime, South Sudan became the 54th member of the AU on 9 July 2011 (Bamidel, 2016) and Morocco rejoined the continental institution on 30 January 2017 (Abubeker, 2017; Gaffey, 2017).

However, Adejo (2001:125) and Onuoha (2004:370), have critiqued the transition of the OAU to the AU, still referring to the AU, as a "talking club", "toothless bulldog", and as a continuation of the same institution. Adejo (2001:119) described the AU as nothing but "an old wine in a new bottle". In support of Adejo and Onuoha's views, Kimenyi (2011), Kura (2013), and Ubaku (2014) observed that despite the transformation from the OAU to the AU in 2002, the AU was still confronted with a myriad of challenges in achieving regional cooperation in the continent and remains heavily donor dependent. As argued by Hentz (1997), Adesope and Asaju (2004), and Wapmuk (2014:72–73), economic stagnation in Africa could be attributed to Afro-pessimism and the policies of the IFIs. From 1960 to 1980, Africa's investment declined from 30.7% to 2.5% (Wapmuk, 2014:72).

The Constitutive Act and the transformation of the OAU to the AU are major developments in the evolution of African integration. For the continent to experience meaningful development, there is need to promote human security, which holistically encapsulates preventive diplomacy, peace, security, and ongoing post-conflict reconstruction, and stability (Lamidi, 2010). These needs informed the shift from non-interference to a policy of non-indifference in the Constitutive Act (Packer and Rukare, 2002; Kioko, 2003; Hunt, 2016; Karen, 2016).

The policy empowers the AU with the right to intervene in the internal affairs of member states, where there is a crime against humanity. Article 4(h) upholds the right of the AU to intervene on the recommendation of the PSC (Lamidi, 2010; Solomon, 2010). In particular, Article 4(p) sanctions governments that usurp power through unconstitutional means, such as coups d'états, manipulating constitutions (to extend a leader's stay in power), or refusing to hand over power after an election loss. Governments, therefore, that have gained control over a country under these conditions will not be recognised by the AU (McGowan, 2003; Ngoma, 2004). As asserted by Usov and Kongwa, the normative pillar on which the Constitutive Act is constructed, provides opportunities to enhance centripetal factors towards greater convergence and integration towards the realisation of Agenda 2063 (Usov, 2003:29; Kongwa, 2002:13–14).

The Constitutive Act, as a result, reverses the understanding and scope of the application of the principles of state sovereignty and non-interference previously embraced by the OAU (John-Mark, 2016; Murithi, 2012; Omorogbe, 2012; Murithi, 2012;9; Nitin, James and Shakur, 2001:1–2: Nkusi, 2016:1; Sipalla, 2016:32). The following subsections explain the AU's policy of non-indifference and where it has been applied.

i. The African Union Doctrine of Non-Indifference

The existence of the AU is an expression of Pan-Africanism. Historically, Pan-Africanism has manifested itself as the desire for greater solidarity and collaboration to address the domestic and global challenges that confront the continent. One of the ways in which this solidarity is now being put to the test concerns how the AU is addressing human security challenges. Realising the ideal of Pan-Africanism means that African countries can no longer remain indifferent to the suffering and plight of their neighbours. In what would be a paradigm shift from common AU practice the implementation of a policy of non-indifference will require the generation and sustaining of a political will to address crisis situations.

As already mentioned, the AU has the primary responsibility for establishing and operationalizing the continent's peace and security architecture. The AU's Doctrine of Non-Indifference involves a collective pooling of sovereignty to enable the AU to act as the ultimate guarantor and protector of the rights and well-being of African people.

This principle was articulated and promoted by the first Chair of the AUC and former President of Mali, Alpha Oumar Konare. Konare believed that it was no longer tenable for African countries to remain silent in the face of atrocities being committed in neighbouring countries. This is in keeping with the philosophy of Pan-Africanism and continental solidarity. The principle of non-indifference, continental solidarity, and collective security is now indispensable.

ii. Implementing Non-Indifference: From Rhetoric to Reality

Following the AU's Doctrine of Non-Indifference, the SADC was tasked by the AU to address the Zimbabwean crisis. The AU retained a role as part of the Reference Group, together with the UN and other international partners. In January 2008, at the Annual Summit of the AHSG, held in Sharm-el-Sheik, Egypt, the parties in the Zimbabwe crisis were called to meet and agree on steps to establish peace and national reconciliation.

The AU Summit also asked the parties to establish an inclusive government. The AU endorsed and supported the SADC mediation initiative, led by President Thabo Mbeki. On September 15, 2008, in Harare, the key parties to the crisis, ZANU-PF led by President Robert Mugabe, and the two Movement for Democratic Change (MDC) formations led by Morgan Tsvangirai, as the Prime Minister, and Arthur Mutambara, as the Deputy Prime Minister, signed an agreement that outlined a government of national unity. The AU's engagement in the Zimbabwe issue, in a supporting role, demonstrated a commitment to non-indifference.

The diplomatic non-indifference agency by the AU was also in evidence during the presidential elections held in Kenya on December 27, 2007. The results of the poll were heavily contested by the two main political parties, the Party of National Unity (PNU) and the Orange Democratic Movement (ODM), which resulted in civil unrest.

The situation subsequently required a process of political dialogue that was conducted under the auspices of the AU Independent Panel of Eminent Persons (IPEP), led by Kofi Annan, the former UN Secretary-General. These talks included representatives from the key actors in the crisis, the PNU and the ODM. A power-sharing agreement signed by the parties on 28 February 2008 outlined the basis of a government of national unity under the auspices of the AU. This underscored the AU's commitment to implementing its Doctrine of Non-Indifference and fulfilling its responsibility to protect (R2P).

iii. Military Non-Indifference

Operationalizing the R2P, the AU intervened in Burundi to build peace and enable the establishment of a more robust UN peace operation. The AU peace operation in Burundi in 2003, also known as the African Union Mission in Burundi (AMIB), was the AU's first operation wholly initiated, planned, and executed by its members. In this regard, it represents a milestone for the AU in terms of self-reliance in operationalising and implementing peacebuilding. The AMIB was effectively mandated to build peace in a fluid and dynamic situation, in which the country could relapse into violent conflict.

The UN was reluctant to enter a situation in which there was the potential for a relapse into conflict. The role of AMIB in this case was crucial in creating conditions through which peace, albeit a fragile one, could be built in the country. By the end of its mission, AMIB had succeeded in establishing relative peace in most provinces in Burundi. In this case, the AU's Doctrine of Non-Indifference Conditions was appropriate to establish a UN PKO in the country. This was later exercised in other conflict areas across Africa.

Further progress towards transformation could be credited to the Constitutive Act, which created an enabling environment that progressively engaged its human security cum-development issues. These are now enshrined in its Agenda 2063. The 1999 Sirte Declaration in Sirte, Libya, signalled that the OAU leadership intended to transform the OAU into the AU, and positioned the latter to function competitively within the global economy (Kongwa, 2002:13).

This shows that the AU became the new paradigm of African integration. The AU's principles, protocols, and mandates are predicated on the promotion of good political and economic governance, democratic principles, and the strengthening of institutions in pursuit of economic growth, shared values, and comprehensive equitable development. The NEPAD emerged from these principles and has come to play a pivotal role in the development of the continent.

iv. The New Partnership for Africa's Development

The DTRP/centre-periphery prism problematises the limited neo-functionalist policy of the AU through its NEPAD prorgamme. The NEPAD has positioned Africa to participate meaningfully in the global economy by competing and timeously taking advantage of the opportunities presented by globalisation. The NEPAD is a pledge by African leaders, based on a common vision and a firm and shared conviction, that they have a pressing duty to eradicate poverty and to place their countries, both individually and collectively, on a path of sustainable growth and development, while at the same time actively participating in the global economy and body politic. The programme is anchored in the determination of Africans to extricate themselves and the continent from the malaise of underdevelopment and exclusion in a globalising world. The poverty and backwardness of Africa stand in stark contrast to the prosperity of the developed world.

The conditions of the Washington Consensus (democracy, human rights, and free enterprise) affected the treaty establishing the AEC. The AEC Treaty confirmed that "Any Member State, which persistently fails to honour its general undertakings under this Treaty or fails to abide by the decisions or regulations of the Community, may be subjected to sanctions by the Assembly" (Article 5).

This section examines the further changes made in the approaches to African development after the failures of the LPA and the Abuja Treaty. It also argues that Africa's socio-economic failures and problems are the result of both historical endogenous and exogenous factors. Given the state-centric, top-down vertical formations of the LPA and the Abuja Treaty, NEPAD suffered from the same malaise.

It also earned criticism due to the lack of public participation from non-state actors and the claim that it reinforced the neoliberal orthodoxy.

The NEPAD was the result of a merger between the Millennium Africa Recovery Plan (MAP) and the Omega Plan, the creation of President Abdoulaye Wade of Senegal. Gelb (2002:1) recounts that the MAP originated with the former presidents Thabo Mbeki (South Africa), Olusegun Obasanjo (Nigeria), and Abdelaziz Bouteflika (Algeria) when addressing the G8 summit in Japan in July 2000. The New Africa Initiative (NAI) was later renamed NEPAD in October 2001 in Abuja, Nigeria (AHG/235(xxxviii). According to NEPAD documents (NEPAD/HSGIC/03/2003/MOU), "it [NEPAD] is a comprehensive and holistic integrated strategic framework for the socio-economic development of Africa" and is predicated on an assessment of the reality of globalisation, its dominant neoliberal edifice and the parallel failures of the LPA's ISI programmes. The NEPAD's architects understood that the military balance of power exercised by the West was unmatched by Africa. While the LPA stated that Africa's socio-economic problems were rooted in the Global North's desire to maintain it as an extractive export-dependent enclave, the NEPAD maintained that internal conflict and bad governance have been the cause.

The NEPAD was constructed to set Africa on a path to peace, security, democracy, and good political and economic governance, as well as respect for private property and the rule of law (NEPAD, 2001; Postumus, 2003; Nwonwu, 2006). The NEPAD and the AU subsequently created the AfCFTA, which was successfully ratified on 30 May 2019. This is a legal framework that integrates Africa's industrial and trade policies to affect a competitive and structural manufacturing economy.

Taking into consideration the dynamics of globalisation, the NEPAD instituted three key frameworks: peace and security governance, economic and regional governance, and political and democratic governance (UNECA, 20120). These areas are seen to be inextricably intertwined and mutually reinforcing. These frameworks enable Africa to take responsibility for influencing both the endogenous and exogenous dynamics to realise its aims and objectives towards development. Wiseman Nkuhlu agrees with this approach, remarking that: "We accept that as African leaders we have not been accountable to the African people over the years and that we also share responsibility for the wars in the continent, for the poverty over the years, but the time has come for things to change."

The NEPAD Initial Action Plan (July 2002) endorsed 'peace and security governance' as critical and imperative to create a conducive, enabling environment in pursuit of socio-economic development in Africa. As part of a three-pronged strategy, peace, security, and governance will provide for sustainable development by unlocking investment capital, both locally and foreign. To this end, the AU Summit adopted a protocol establishing a PSC on 9 July 2002 (Adopted by the 1st Ordinary Session of the Assembly of the African Union; Durban South Africa.

The PSC is the collective security mechanism for the continent and responds timeously to conflict and crises. The PSC upholds the common values of the Constitutive Act and its principles for democratic governance. These include the adoption of and respect for a democratic constitution, separation of powers, political pluralism, protection of human rights, and the organisation of free and regular elections. The AU declaration states that non-adherence to these common values and principles often causes a political and institutional crisis, which then culminates in an unconstitutional change of government, namely: (i) a military coup d'état against a democratically elected government; (ii) an intervention by mercenaries to replace a democratically elected government; (iii) the replacement of a democratically elected government by armed dissident groups and rebel movements; or (iv) the refusal by an incumbent government to relinquish power to the winning party after free, fair, and regular elections.

The PSC, in conjunction with the chair of the AUC, can institute sanctions whenever an unconstitutional change of government takes place in a member state. For example, the PSC has exercised sanctions against unconstitutional changes of government (coups d'états) in the [ECOWAS region] following countries: Guinea-Bissau (2009 and 2012); Guinea (2008), and Burkina Faso (2010 and 2015). Constitutional governments and democracy were reinstated successfully within the region. Cilliers (2004:25) also argues that peace and human security governance is now more broadly defined and involves non-state actors, such as civil society groups.

Cilliers further explains that security is no longer only about territorial integrity and national sovereignty, but also about public participation in all facets of development policies, which are underpinned by transparency and accountability within security sector reform (SSR). The AU and its organs – including the PSC – suffer from the same malaise, as the LPA, including an absence of or late member state contributions.

Of the total budget, 38% is to be collected from member states while 61% is from partners. The operating budget will be fully funded by member states while the programme budget will be funded by member states (41%) and solicited from international partners (59%). From 2018 to 2022, with the exclusion of peace support operations (PSOs), the AU budget decreased by 30% from $529M to $372M. The operating budget decreased by 16.4% from $195M to $176M, while the program budget decreased by 41% from $333M to $195M.[14]

The PSC's operational effectiveness is compromised because over 90% of the AU budget is provided by foreign donors. The continuing conflicts are due to lack of resources, which would enable the AU to mount a sustainable development policy, leading to peace and security and actioning the aims of Agenda 2063 (Nwonwu, 2006:10). The continuing conflicts in Sudan, Somalia, Ethiopia, and the DRC are due to Africa being under-resourced to effectively engender a sustainable development policy of peace and human security governance towards Agenda 2063. Nwonwu

(2006:10) argues that this is why NEPAD looks to foreign partners, such as the EU and NATO, for funding.

While Africa exhibits a semblance of peace and democracy, its lack of independent funding compromises its policy formulation and implementation is left to the dictates of foreign donors. Against this backdrop, the DTRP/centre-periphery framework confirms the AU as the periphery dependent on foreign donors (the centre) rendering its neo-functional integration programmes unimplementable. As a result, there are varied interpretations of NEPAD as a framework. Its critics see it as outward and externally oriented, lacking in policy independence. Its supporters liken it to its predecessor, the LPA.

The NEPAD's reliance on Western donor support has forced it to gravitate towards neoliberalism, characterised by a democratic, deregulated free-enterprise market space, with a separation of powers and the rule of law to protect individual rights and private poverty. Similarly to the LPA, the primary objectives of NEPAD are to eliminate endemic underdevelopment and poverty. It seeks to bring about competitive human resources, training, and development, which will stimulate complementarities in factor endowments and a GDP of 7%, coordinated to the continent's population growth.

Sustainable peace and security governance will help to unlock (and hopefully) attract both local and foreign direct (productive) investments, which are imperative to modernising economic designs to be globally competitive (NEPAD, 2002: paragraph 153). The hitherto – and ongoing – unfavourable ToT that have consigned Africa, under colonialism and neo-colonialism, to the role of an extractive, primary resource appendage of the Global North, encourages financial speculation and resource outflow (NEPAD, 2002: paragraph 34).

Given the primacy and hegemony of Western institutions, such as the WTO, UNSC, NATO, and BWIs, Africa may not be able to muster investment capital (either local or foreign) to replicate and rival both the Global North and China. A group of anti-globalisation researchers has criticised the gravitation of NEPAD towards embracing neoliberalism and globalisation.

These sceptics argue that the benefits that Africa receives from neoliberalism and globalisation, reinforce the rent-seeking and neo-patrimonial structures within the African postcolonial state, thereby depleting its natural resources and polluting Africa's environment without any structural benefit for its wider population (Bond, 2003; Onimode, 2004; Taylor, 2006). This is further confirmation of the DTRP/centre-periphery framework, indicating that neo-functionalist integration programmes of the AU aimed at achieving self-reliance and sustainability are ultimately unachievable.

The NEPAD also recognises that Africa's debt of over US$220 billion is an invidious trap, which militates against its socio-economic development. Africa's debt servicing amounts to (approximately) US$14 billion annually and is taken from its foreign export earnings. This is a structural impediment that keeps the continent underdeveloped. This structural debt deprives Africa of fiscal policy space and independence, and therefore the pursuit of a neo-functionalist integration project of the AU remains elusive.

The debt instrument constitutes a BWI conditionality for any advancement of poverty reduction strategy paper (PRSP) loans and balance of payment support. This translates into minuscule debt relief for heavily indebted poor countries (HIPC) in the short-term but does not contribute to long-term sustainable structural and productive development (Zulu, 2004:5). The debt system is therefore a pivotal component of the neo-liberal-dominated foreign exchange control mechanism.

The NEPAD, under the aegis of the AU, does not challenge the illegitimate nature of this debt. It could be argued that this debt was incurred by the transatlantic slave trade, colonialism, neo-colonialism, and unrepresentative postcolonial governments.

Similar to the LPA, the NEPAD recognises the imperative of intra-regional economic development, taking into consideration the small and fragmented (and unattractive) nature of Africa's economies and their paths towards long-term sustainable development.

The creation of the SAPP in 1995 by 12 national utilities, was a major step for SADC in exploiting the Southern African region's numerous energy resources (SADC, 2010). Against the backdrop of increased donor dependency, the AU and NEPAD continue to formulate and implement self-financing strategies to become self-reliant and globally competitive. The AU Assembly adopted the AU's 0.2 % levy on all eligible imported goods into the continent to finance its projects, in July 2016, in Kigali, Rwanda. This would encourage full membership by member states and bring about budgetary sustainability and predictability (AU, 2016a).

The 0.2% import levy is intended to fully fund the AU's projects.

The AU needs adequate, reliable, and predictable resources to implement its programmes to achieve its development and integration goals. Since 2015, successive AU summits have taken financial reform decisions, to ensure there are sound and predictable finances to address the historical challenges the AU has faced. These are:

a. Unpredictability and volatility of its revenues;
b. Dependence on external partners;
c. Reliance on a few member states;
d. The need to demonstrate the value for money and probity; and
e. The growing budget.

The adopted financial reform decisions were, therefore, intended to achieve the following key objectives:

· Timely, adequate, reliable, and predictable payment of all Member State assessed contributions and partner contributions to the AU;
· Financial autonomy and reduced dependence on external sources;
· Equitable burden-sharing of the AU's budget and reduced dependence on a few countries;
· Improved budget, financial oversight, and governance to achieve high fiduciary standards, value for money, and probity; and

· Predictable and sustainable financing of the AU's PKOs through the revitalization of the AU Peace Fund and the pursuit of strategic partnerships.

The Kigali Decision on financing of the AU resulted in the implementation of the 0.2% import levy. Since the adoption of the Kigali Decision (Assembly/AU/Dec.605 (XXVII)) in July 2016, there has been unprecedented momentum gathered around its implementation. As of 16 June 2020, there were 17 countries representing about 31% of AU membership that were at various stages of domesticating the Kigali Decision on Financing the AU (Kasaija, 2019: 77-91).

Collectively, these countries are obliged to provide US$73,761,008 towards the regular budget and US$15,307,159 for the AU Peace Fund, accounting for 30% of the total amount allocated to the regular budget and AU Peace Fund. These countries still owe the AU US$41,735,749 (US$30,761,020 for the regular budget and US$10,974,729 for the AU Peace Fund) for previous budgets and US$33,359,115 (US$22,095,806 for the regular budget and US$11,263,308 for the AU Peace Fund) for the 2019 budget. As of 16 June 2020, US$7,419,039 had been received from these member states (US$6,417,102 and US$1,001,938 as contributions to the regular budget and AU Peace Fund, respectively).

All 17 countries have made either partial or full remittances to the AU for the 2020 budget. As of the date of this publication, an amount of US$25,135,107 (US$12,767,675 and US$8,833,571 for the regular budget and AU Peace Fund, respectively) was in arrears. All of it is attributable to Sudan because the economic embargo imposed on them and other considerations have made it impossible to remit the funds to the AU on time.

Kasaija asserts (2019:77-91) that the flexibility built into the implementation of the 0.2% levy appears to have been embraced by many member states. This flexibility allows member states to determine the appropriate form and means they will use it to implement the Kigali decision on financing the AU in line with their national and international obligations, provided the principles of predictability and compliance are adhered to. This is in addition to several member states expressing their intention to continue paying using the current arrangement. There are several advantages to the way the AU levy is implemented.

a. The levy provides extra revenue to member states. The excess collection over and above the amount assessed to a member state is used to finance other purposes of importance to the member state.
b. The levy mechanism makes it easier for member states to pay to the AU because it is not subjected to time-consuming budgetary procedures and parliamentary approval.
c. Sixteen of the levy-collecting countries cleared all arrears they had before implementing the levy.

However, there are several challenges faced when implementing the 0.2% import levy. Only 17 of the 55 member states are collecting the levy. Although funds are being collected, they are not remitted in full by some member states. There is no enforcement mechanism to ensure that the money collected is actually transmitted. Some countries, such as the Seychelles and Mauritius, have undertaken a zero tariff commitment at the WTO on almost 95% of their imports. Imposing the levy on the remaining goods would yield less than is required to pay the AU. Similarly, doing so would be in breach of GATT Article II on the schedules of commitments.

Similarly, some small island states have raised concerns that their economies are small and not diversified, depending mainly on tourism. These countries have indicated that an increase in the tariffs on small quantities of their imports could potentially weaken their economies. Other member states are constrained by legal implications under their obligations to the WTO, especially under the Most Favoured Nation (MFN) principle.

The MFN principle requires that WTO members apply the same tariffs on a similar product imported from other WTO members. Some countries, such as the Saharawi Arab Democratic Republic, do not have a tangible productive industry or an export sector. Their imports are mostly for humanitarian purposes and are used for sustaining their refugee status.

On 7 December 2016, the USA and Japan raised the issue of the AU's 0.2% levy on imported goods at the General Council of the WTO. It was reported that the levy's implementation was contrary to and inconsistent with the WTO agreement and the MFN principle (WTO, 2017). The USA and Japan argued that the levy imposed on imported goods to Africa would discriminate against WTO members outside of Africa, while African WTO members would not be affected by the levy. This would be incompatible with Article I of the GATT on MFN treatment, which states that all WTO members are to be treated equally (WTO, 2017). In response, the AU has policy options within the WTO legal regime to counter the USA charge of inconsistency and the implied discriminatory 0.2% levy on imports to Africa.

Under the Marrakesh Agreement, Africa may apply for a waiver to implement the 0.2% on imports to Africa. Its motivation as the world's least developed region and the use of the revenue from the levy for peace, security, and development initiatives, would make a waiver highly likely. By January 2018, 21 of the 55 AUMS had passed national draft laws establishing the 0.2% levy on imported goods, and 14 of the member states had already started collecting the levy.

The collected funds are deposited into a special account held in the Central Bank of each member. Countermeasures to curb illicit financial flows out of Africa are continually and robustly administered by the NEPAD. The UNECA estimates that Africa loses as much as US$50 billion annually, twice what it receives in foreign donor funds (ECA, 2015; AU, 2015). Among other remedial measures, prudent capital account controls are imperative to moderate the spaces conducive to speculative capital and unfavourable exchange rate policies.

The ongoing lessons learnt serve as valuable insights into global best practices in TNCs, emphasizing the importance of their full disclosure, tax information, and declaration of countries in which they operate. This would globally standardise best practices in financial systems, thus addressing corrupt transfer pricing, trade miss-invoicing, and tax avoidance and evasion. The ongoing training and upskilling in regional projects would engender savings, bring about cost-effectiveness, and higher margins of productivity and efficiency.

The political economies of African countries are unevenly developed. This results in regional programmes affecting countries differently, as their development priorities vary. Coordinated interventions and policy deliverables with compensation for revenue losses are imperative. This is advantageous to countries at different developmental levels, as the process of variable geometry can sequentially align them to the AfCFTA's continental policies. As a result, Aid-for-Trade is more effective where standards are intra-regionally equivalent, which boosts the AfCFTA (IEG, 2011; WB, 2011; UNCTAD, 2013; Dube; 2016). A distinguishing and key feature of the NEPAD has been its role in taking responsibility for and ownership of Africa's development, as well as finding 'African solutions to African problems' (Landsberg, 2008; Dersso, 2012a: 8; Kasaija, 2012: 127).

Ronald Kempe Hope has argued that "ownership of policy reforms matters because it directly affects programme acceptance and implementation." This is similar to the role of the APRM, which was designed to monitor and assess the progress made by African countries in meeting their commitments to achieving good governance and sustainable development.

The APRM is an innovative governance instrument targeted at domestic issues and "presents opportunities for strengthening democracy to ensure that the basis of governance transcends the narrow confines of personal rule, patron-client relations or ethno-religious politics" (Akokpari, 2004:253; Hope, 2005:289; Mathoho, 2003:1). Submission to the APRM review process is voluntary and to date it has a membership of 39 member states.

The peer review process is conducted by a seven-member IPEP, which guides the countries through the various stages of the review process, which entail commitment to good governance, political stability, economic growth, and sustainable development (NEPAD, 2003). As with the LPA, the APRM lacks a non-compliance sanction provision This institutional weakness is exacerbated by its voluntary membership structure, which opens space for 'free-riding' without constitutional obligation. This major limiting factor has been the bane of all Africa's institutional reforms even under the aegis of the AU in the new millennium (Akokpari, 2005:6).

Another contending school of thought supports the voluntary membership of African countries, given the duplicity and double standards applied by donor governments. Bekoe and Landsberg (2002:2) express fears that the APRM might be used selectively to punish the non-compliance of particular countries declared to be pariahs by Western governments. This was the case with the USA's Zimbabwe Democracy Economic Recovery Act of 2001(107th Congress Public Law 99), which applied punitive sanctions against Zimbabwe. Simultaneously, the rise of parallel horizontal non-state actor activism by civil society organisations (CSOs) continues to grow, exerting influence across various aspects of political and democratic governance, helping with policy formulation and its implementation. This is in contrast to the state-centric LPA initiatives (Verwey, 2005:20).

v. African Development Initiatives Agenda 2063[16]

This section undertakes a historical and comparative study of the relevant literature, encompassing Africa and its international regional development experiences. This was approached as regional development experiences to compare and contrast the impacts and influences between them. First and foremost, Agenda 2063 is a shared strategic framework for inclusive growth and sustainable development.

It was developed and adopted in January 2015, in Addis Ababa, Ethiopia, by the 24th AU AHSG with all the formations of society in attendance. Agenda 2063 encapsulates the aforementioned socio-economic policies of the LPA, the Abuja Treaty, and the normative continental aspirations of Africa constituted in the Constitutive Act. It has also benefited from the recommendations of the 2007 AU Review Report and the 2017 Kagame Report, all of which are relevant to the study of the progress, problems, and progress of the AU.

---

16   Personal Interview with Professor Tola Odubajo. Lecturer
      Department of Political Science, University of Lagos, Nigeria. 2023.

Agenda 2063 is a strategic framework, for the development of Africa. It was created by the AUC at the celebration of the OAU and the AU golden jubilee in 2013. Hitherto, it is a work in progress, with measurable and quantifiable project outcomes. However, it has experienced weaknesses and gaps in policy implementation. It is therefore imperative to iron out the persistent challenges and offer recommendations on how to deal with them. Although pragmatic, Agenda 2063 may well be confronted by similar challenges and setbacks to the ones that have frustrated previous African plans from realising their self-reliant objectives and aims. These include a lack of global military hard power to leverage into daily politico-economic power relations; limited finances; lack of ownership; lack of political will; conflicting interests; and a lack of ideological longevity to sustain the vision.

These challenges still constitute either catalysts (to attain the goals of Agenda 2063), or worse, will remain its Achilles heel and stagnate Africa's plans for politico-economic self-reliance. To its credit, the AfCFTA, which is a flagship of Agenda 2063, was adopted and ratified in July 2019.

Other complimentary projects are still outstanding, such as the Investment Bank and Pan-African Stock Exchange (neither of which met their ratification deadline of 2016); the African Monetary Fund (AMF) (its deadline of 2018 was unmet); the ACB (whose deadline of 2028–2034 will hopefully be met); a single African air transport market (SAATM: a painstakingly slow work in progress), and the African passport and FMP and residence, which has shown little traction.

The aforementioned projects, together with the Programme for Infrastructural Development in Africa (PIDA) infrastructure development, constitute the drivers of Agenda 2063 (AUC, 2015a:16). The recently ratified AfCFTA (2019) is the vehicle and framework that will enable the boosting of intra-regional trade and welfare gains for Africa's citizenry (UNCTAD, 2015). Against the background of the economic global slowdown and unfavourable international capital markets for Africa, the alternative is domestic resource mobilisation. The establishment of African continental financial institutions is a sine qua non for continental resource mobilisation.

The finalisation of the African passport is commendable, notwithstanding its slow-paced rollout, and the empty rhetoric towards FMP and residence has neither been matched in implementation nor in practice. The AU member may state still lack the political will to cede their sovereignty to enable these provisions. The AUMS fear economic losses as a result of forgone customs revenue and the compromising of their national patronage networks (Draper, 2010:15; Duthie, 2011:139; Biswaro, 2011:415).

The eight officially AU-recognised RECs, as the pillars of continental integration, are under-resourced and weak. They receive little legitimacy or support from Africa's citizenry (Corrigan, 2015). The acceleration of the projects that underpin Agenda 2063 is imperative, thus the rhetoric should be matched by implementation (Qobo, 2007:11–13; AUC, 2015b: 89–92; 2016:94). Therefore, drivers, such as education and training, incentivised incomes, FMP and place of residence, and continental infrastructure development, need to be accelerated.

The Agenda 2063 First Ten-Year Implementation Plan provides for the accelerated establishment of an African Virtual and E-University, thus increasing access to ongoing human resource development. This will be reinforced by Open Distance and e-Learning (ODel), and the ability to access the university from anywhere in the world, at all times (AUC, 2015; Mabasanyinje et al., 2016).

A highly skilled labour force will generate competitive incomes, which will contribute to inclusive growth and higher levels of GDP, increasing continental savings as a source of domestic mobilisation and investments. Greater savings and investments will ensure financing for urban development, facilitating spatial planning and enhancing the productive base of urban economies (AUC, 2015a).

Agenda 2063 has infrastructural continent-wide projects that are currently underway with measurable progress. Among these are the Integrated High-Speed Train Network, the Grand

Inga Plant, the Pan-African E-Network, and the Africa Outer Space Strategy. These continental projects have weaknesses and deficiencies, especially a lack of funding and investment capital and a deficit of local specialised skills.

It could therefore be argued that the linear model of regional integration as espoused by Trudi (2011:4–5) – the FTA, customs union, common market-monetary and fiscal matters (economic union) and political union – is demonstrably not feasible. Africa, given its history and multi-varied cultures and dialectics, forges ahead with its own eclectic and pragmatic integration processes towards an integrated AEC. As Agenda 2063 is premised on inclusive participation and growth, this normative ideal of social overhaul and engineering is also beset with intrinsic conflict.

Clearly, within the multi-stakeholder edifice, others will want to maintain the elitist patronage network disadvantaging those who seek a much more transformed, accountable, and equitably beneficial institution (AUC, 2015a: 122; De Ghetto et al., 2016: 98).

To realise a transformed and inclusive economy, Africa's economy will need to be structurally transformed, moving from one that is extractive to one that is value-added. As argued by Acemoglu and Robinson (2012: 106–413) and Boldrin et al. (2012:1), value-added institutions are an impetus for research and development, enhanced savings, investments, innovation, and competitiveness. They are the antithesis of extractive institutions, which are only the supply end of raw materials and patronage networks.

Agenda 2063 attempts to treat Africa as a single unit of analysis (Geda and Kibret, 2002:12; Qobo, 2007: 6; Chingono and Nakana, 2009: 397; Trudi, 2011:19; De Ghetto et al., 2016 98). Notwithstanding the dialectics intrinsic to human interactions, Agenda 2063 allows for norm subsidiarity and variable geometry because it has been informed by the different stages of development, and the cultural and political outlooks of its nation-state members.

For example, the AU APRM for democracy and good governance is voluntary. However, through norm entrepreneurship and peer persuasion it has garnered 39 nation-states, which have domesticated its provisions and they have been harmonised with country-specific National Programmes of Action (NPoA).

Despite the challenges that have beset Agenda 2063, there is evidence of measurable traction in its projects. Furthermore, Acemoglu and Robinson (2012:64–83) note in their book 'Why Nations Fail', that poor countries are poor because those who have power make intentioned choices that create poverty. This binary configuration of haves and have-nots, however, remains exploitative and combustible. This is because power is not given but fought for and governance is not the preserve of the elite. Non-state actors like trade unions and ECOSOCC should continually engage in governance and power relations to realise their aims and goals in the same way that elites do (Adogamhe, 2008:21).

Agenda 2063 also outlines a financing strategy. This is imperative to regional integration, especially in areas such as infrastructure, science, technology, and innovation-based industrialisation, which prioritises agriculture, food security, and the production of local resources in alignment with environmental sustainability.

As argued by (Adoghame, 2008:19; Boldrin, 2012:5; Eyster, 2014:1; AUC, 2015b:134) to rid themselves of neocolonial domination by TNC's, the AUMS should muster the political will to domestically mobilise resources and finance their own projects. In this regard, Africa's CSOs should demonstrate greater creativity, courage, and imagination in terms of governance, thus overtly and covertly applying pressure on all institutions. This could be accomplished through a constant demand for viable and dynamic SSR, the representativity and full participation of the public in all financial institutions, and formulation and implementation of the Reserve Bank's monetary and fiscal policy. Governance of all institutions should cease to be the preserve of the elites, although non-state actors appear to be ineffectual thus far and activism is uninspiring.

Geda and Kibret (2002:2) and Trudi (2011:5-18), critique the bulwark of global regional groups, which they see as marginalising Africa's nation-states. Fifteen sub-Saharan countries have small economies and are landlocked with small populations that render their sovereignty incapable of advancing Agenda 2063. One of the authors' recommendations is that ECOSOCC should encourage these smaller states to cede their sovereignty to the AU.

Freedom of movement, residence, and compensation for loss of revenue should be encouraged to enable erstwhile landlocked countries to create an enabling continental environment towards Agenda 2063 and the AEC. The establishment of a unified African currency and the convergence of macroeconomic planning under a regional authority could be achieved sooner rather than later, following the successful examples set by the PAP and AfCFTA. The participation of Africa in both intra-regionalism and multilateralism is imperative and unavoidable, its extractive economy is inextricable and inseparable from the global economy. Agenda 2063 demands democratic representation in global institutions, such as the IMF, WB, and UNSC, which could not be achieved in the previous era of colonisation.

Jennifer Brinkerhoff (2002), in her book 'Partnership for International Development: Rhetoric or Results', explains that the concept of a development partnership is a means of applying effective, efficient processes and systems towards the public commons and delivery of services.

Brinkerhoff further explains that international organisations, such as the UN, AU, WB, IMF, and WTO, employ contrary processes and systems, such as paternalism and neo-patrimonialism, along with empty rhetoric. These have eroded public trust in the institutions of governance. This is applicable, for example, in the case of UNSC membership, which is not democratically reflective of the present-day world. It is dominated by five world hegemons (UK, France, USA, Russia, and China) and thus has eroded partnerships and exacerbated mistrust and paternalism. This in turn has had an impact on Africa's development and the attainment of the global Millennium

Development Goals (MDGs) and now the Sustainable Development Goals (SDGs).

Other authors, such as Cloete et al. (2001), have argued that the imposition of a neoliberal development orthodoxy on Africa's development initiatives, is nothing short of exploitation and that the unpayable debt entrapment policies are destructive. The authors argue for a transparent and equitable involvement of CSOs in development policy and planning processes to achieve sustainable outcomes. The IFIs have responded to this global critique by instituting a policy of civil society involvement in the PRSPs. Some development researchers still see the PRSPs as essentially structural adjustment policies disguised in new and misleading forms, as the terms and conditions of the IFIs still make access to human and financial capital conditional and difficult.

In 'Policies for African Development from the 1980s to 1990s', Patel (1992) presents a collection of papers from a conference held in Africa. The theme of the book covers the Washington Consensus, SAPs, and the neoliberal agenda of the BWIs (the IMF and WB). The first section of the book explains the deleterious effects of SAPs on Africa. Of relevance to this study, the book covers themes that would be potentially imperative to catalyse Africa's development, such as regional integration; partnerships of developed nations with Africa; and ownership of development initiatives by Africans themselves. The book lends support to Africa's development frameworks evidenced by the LPA, the Abuja Treaty, AU–NEPAD, and Agenda 2063.

The second section of the book deals with Africa's debt problem and the way it is serviced to the IFIs and its creditors. The book further argues that IFIs structurally keep Africa as an extractive appendage, supplying resources for highly developed Western countries. The third section focuses on financing, growth, and development in Africa as well as outlooks and other issues. The book explains how the issue of debt is reinforced, and privatisation and deregulation of public assets and utilities are demanded of Africa's governments to attract FDI.

According to Patel (1992), FDI is speculative capital. Its conditionality of no capital account controls allows for the unfettered repatriation of profits, further systematically subjugating Africa to structural dependence. This results in Africa's trade, investment, and growth prospects being supported by the neocolonial paradigms of privatisation, deregulation, and unfettered FDI.

In 'The Quest for Good Governance and Development in Africa: Is NEPAD the Answer?' Chabel (2002) critiqued the NEPAD and its APRM as well as Africa's development trajectory. Chabal's critique is informed by Africa's lack of hard power (military capability) as a deterrent to leverage its development initiatives. This renders Africa donor-dependent, militating against its independence and ability to find 'African solutions to Africa's problems.' He further proposes that the inadequacy of self-financing by the AU signals a lack of robust political will to attain the aims and goals of Africa's development.

In 'The Brexit: A Massive Setback for European and a Lesson for African Integration Aniche (2019) critiqued the neo-functionalist approach of the AU. The 23 June 2016 Brexit Referendum for African integration has implications for African integration. For example it has intensified agitations for a referendum on self-determination among ethnic nationalities in Nigeria and encouraged Zanzibar's separatism in Tanzania (de Vries, 2019).

Aniche (2020) explains the failed neo-functionalist approach and offers a postneofunctionalism solution towards Africa's integration. This confirms the DTRP/centre-periphery critique of the failed neo-functionalist integration self-reliance programmes of the AU. The AU is structurally dependent on the centre to fund its programmes; hence, it will not realise integration. History calls for post-neo-functionalism as a strategic approach to regional integration in Africa. If neo-functionalism could not work in Europe, it cannot work for Africa, either. Given the low level of national integration among the African states, neo-functionalism is likely unviable from the start. There is a need for Africa to adopt a theory that transcends neo-functionalism translating to a paradigm shift from neo-functionalism to post-neo-functionalism. Post-neo-functionalism is a blend of neo-nationalism, post-nationalism, and humanism. Therefore, post-neo-functionalism is a composite of neo-nationalism, post-nationalism, and humanism (Aniche, 2015). This requires further explanation. For example, neo-nationalism is a new form of nationalism mixed with protectionism. Therefore, neo-nationalism is a composite of political nationalism and economic nationalism. In other words, neo-nationalism is a revival of the nationalism that characterised the struggle against colonialism or the fight for decolonisation in Africa.

The current neo-nationalism in Africa is geared towards the struggle against neo-colonialism, rentierism, and dependency and operates as a basis for tackling the extreme inequality in the world and the pervasive protracted, intractable, and perennial conflicts in Africa that have rendered it a troubled region (Okafor and Aniche, 2017). Therefore, there are two main elements of neo-nationalism, namely; modern political nationalism and economic nationalism. Political nationalism is predominantly the political sphere of neo-nationalism; while protectionism or economic nationalism is the economic aspect. Modern political nationalism is targeted at facilitating national integration through nation-building to eliminate internal conflicts or reduce civil wars in Africa. This entails solving the problems of ethnic chauvinism and religious bigotry or resolving the national questions of ethno-religious violence that pose serious or enormous security challenges in Africa (Aniche, 2014).

The point being made is that a country which cannot achieve unity and integration at the national level cannot logically pursue, advocate or promote integration at the regional level because charity begins at home. African leaders, however, seem inclined to prioritise external initiatives over domestic cohesion, posing a significant obstacle to African integration efforts.

Therefore, neo-nationalism is an aspect of post-neo-functionalism, which proposes that integration should proceed from the national level (national integration), then gradually and naturally extend to the regional level (regional integration), and probably ultimately move to the global level (global integration or globalisation) (Aniche, 2015). Put simply, African economies as presently constituted have nothing to protect because the present situation reinforces the international division of labour or relationships of dependence and inequality, rather than relationships of interdependence and equality. As such, those who do not manufacture have nothing to protect (Okafor and Aniche, 2017), thereby contributing to the enormous security challenges in various states in Africa.

Aniche (2020) also examines the implications of the 23 June 2016 Brexit Referendum for African integration. It was concluded that the Brexit Referendum has tremendous implications for African integration. It has influenced agitations for a referendum on self-determination and restructuring among ethnic nationalities in member states. This has intensified the centrifugal forces of sub-nationalism among the AU member countries. These deepening centrifugal forces of disintegrative nationalism are potential threats to the recently ratified African Free Trade Agreement (FTA).

Therefore, arguably, post-neo-functionalism might be a way of avoiding or preventing the defects inherent in the neo-functional approach to European integration. As demonstrated already, the neo-functionalist approaches impede the AU's integration towards self-reliance and sustainability. Post-neo-functionalism will foster national unity through state-building to eliminate or lessen agitations for self-determination, separatism, secessionist movements, civil wars, centrifugal forces of sub-nationalism, and disintegrative nationalism in Africa. In contrast, Aniche (2020) does not indicate how a post-neo-functionalist approach will be funded. The policy implications of abandoning the current neo-functional strategy and adopting a post-neo-functional approach to African integration are enormous, profound, fundamental, and over-reaching. This is in addition to the perennial lack of funding, as underscored by the DTRP/centre-periphery framework, that traps Africa in dependency in all its developmental programmes.

In their article 'Grand theories of integration and the challenges of comparative regionalism' Borzel and Pizze (2019:1231-1252) depart from the grand traditional theories of integration developed from the European experience. Instead, they share a commonality with Aniche (2020) in engaging the post-functionalist approach that prioritises security interdependence and the quest for regime stability, whether democratic or authoritarian. This resonates with the AU's peace and security policies and its PSOs and reinforces the DTRP/centre-periphery framework that is metatheoretical in its critique.

These findings challenge the standard theories of integration, such as liberal intergovernmentalism or even neo-functionalism, which assume economic interdependence is the major driver of integration. However, from a comparative regionalism perspective, extra-regional economic relations, security interdependence, and the quest for regime stability (whether democratic or authoritarian) appear to be more important drivers for regionalism than intra-regional economic interdependence. I argue that the Latin American, Sub-Saharan African, Southeast Asian, and even the European experiences can be explained on these grounds. This resonates with the AU, which displays a greater bias for PSOs in comparison to intra-regional economic pursuits.

In their article 'What to expect from regional integration in Africa', Thonke and Spliid (2012:42-66) state that European integration was born out of the two world wars, with the ambition of making future wars in Europe unthinkable through economic interdependence. Thus, neo-functionalists in European integration theory argued that cooperation in 'low politics' (e.g., economy) would in time 'spill over' into 'high politics' (e.g., security and foreign affairs). The DTRP/centre-periphery framework shows that the neo-functionalism in Europe cannot be replicated in Africa's integration. Therefore the much desired goals of self-reliance and sustainability continue to be elusive. The African trajectory is different because the threat of conflicts between states is limited. In contrast, integration in the area of peace and security has to a large extent developed as a response to intra-state conflicts.

The original rationale for most African integration has been economic, but in some regions such as West Africa, intra-state conflicts have necessitated that the peace and security agenda be developed first as a prerequisite for economic development. Still, instability and conflicts remain the single biggest challenge to successful regional economic integration in Africa. The history and characteristics of the eight RECs in Africa are very different. The drivers and prospects are very different and are characterised by multi-causality. Each REC has followed a particular path of development.

With regard to peace and security, further advances and improvements have been observed. The softening of the principle of non-interference, which arose with the transition from the OAU to the AU, bears witness to a much more responsible and self-confident Africa. This has also paid off in terms of international recognition and influence. At the REC level, the peace and security architecture has come a long way in a short time, although again with large regional variations. Most African countries have common security interests due to the nature of transboundary intra-state conflicts and also have an interest in avoiding their negative spill-over effects.

It should also be noted that regional integration in Africa is still intergovernmental in nature and is likely to remain so in the decades to come. The division of labour between the RECs and the AU needs to be clarified, i.e., the question of whether the AU can call upon an REC to mobilise its standby force, or whether it is the other way around. The most successful regional organisations seem to be the EAC and ECOWAS and to a lesser extent SADC. This can be explained by the existence of a regional hegemon, a common history, and shared security and/or economic interests.

It has been realised that the APSA is dependent on the political will of regional hegemons. Anchoring the APSA in the RECs may be unsuitable for some conflicts, especially if they involve the regional hegemons directly. The international response to regional ambitions in Africa has been positive. It is clear that significant support is needed if Africa is to realise its regional ambitions as suggested by a post-neo-functional approach (Aniche, 2020)

In their article 'Theorising the rise of Regioness', Hettne and Soderkaum (2000:457-472), claim that regionalism has "been brought back into international studies after some time of almost complete neglect". The DTRP/centre-periphery framework factors in the 'new regionalism ' that began to emerge in the mid-1980s in the context of the comprehensive structural transformation of the global system. Similarly to the 'old regionalism', which began in the 1950s and stagnated in the 1970s, the new wave must be understood in its historical context. It needs to be related to the structural transformation of the world, which encompasses various aspects such as:

1. the move from bipolarity towards a multipolar or perhaps tripolar structure, with new divisions of power and labour;
2. the relative decline of American hegemony in combination with a more permissive attitude on the part of the USA towards regionalism;
3. the erosion of the Westphalian nation-state system and the growth of interdependence and 'globalisation'; and
4. changed attitudes towards (neoliberal) economic development as an associated political system in developing countries, as well as in post-communist countries.

The 'new regionalism' is a truly worldwide phenomenon that is taking place in more areas of the world than ever before. Thus the renewed trend of regionalism is a complex process of change, simultaneously involving state as well as non-state actors and occurring as a result of global, regional, national, and local level forces. It is not possible to state which level is dominant, because actors and processes at the various levels interact and their relative importance differs in time and space. In the widest sense 'regionalism' refers to the general phenomenon under study, i.e., the 'new' or 'second wave of regionalism' arising more or less all over the world today. In an analytical, operational sense it refers to the current ideology of regionalism, i.e., the urge for a regionalist order, either in a particular geographical area or as a type of world order. Regionalism in this particular sense is usually associated with a programme and strategy and may lead to formal institution-building. 'Regionalisation' denotes the (empirical) process that leads to patterns of cooperation, integration, complementarity, and convergence within a particular cross-national geographical space.

It is important to distinguish formal regionalism (as an ideology and programme) from the process of regionalisation. For example, with the 2016 Brexit of the UK from the EU there is a strong anti-regionalist ideology in the form of neo-nationalism, which does not necessarily prevent regionalisation on the ground from taking place. The empirical study of regionalisation has been neglected due to an excessive focus on regionalist projects and regionalism as an ideology. Regionalisation implies increasing 'regionness.' Thus the latter concept is a way to investigate the state of regionalisation in various dimensions and contexts, and to compare various situations. Hence, in Africa, there are eight officially recognized REC's but there are overlaps in membership with other regional organisations. This overlap of mandates and multiple memberships has resulted in the stagnation of self-reliance and sustainability of the AU.

Because the 'new regionalism' is closely linked to global structural change and globalisation it cannot be understood merely from the point of view of the single region in question. What we are looking for specifically is a global theory that considers regional peculiarities. The DTRP/centre-periphery approach combined with the post-neofuctionalist approach suggested by Aniche (2020) might be a global social theory that makes sense of ongoing events. It explains where we are, how we got there, and where we are going (without necessarily being able to forecast everything along the way).

Good theory also makes it possible to act to improve our situation; however, because we are not all sitting in the same boat, it also differentiates between different 'we-categories' and facilitates a dialogue between different worldviews and standpoints. Global social theory is a comprehensive social science that abandons state-centrism in an ontologically fundamental sense. Social processes must be analysed and delinked from the national space. Such a merger may ultimately strengthen an emerging 'new' or 'critical political economy' by considering historical power structures and emphasising the contradictions in them, as well as expressing change and transformation in normative terms (i.e., development). This much-needed focus on history represents a departure from unchanging transhistorical theories that are artificially imposed on an ever-changing reality, which is a characteristic that continues to define mainstream international theory (i.e., IR and the international political economy (IPE)).

Global social theory must overcome the missconceptions of the concept of globalization, distinguishing the new aspects from the old and specifying what concrete dimensions are involved and how they are related, *if* they are related. Globalisation cannot just be taken for granted, and neither should the privilege of defining the phenomenon be left to the ideological 'globalists.' Furthermore, global social theory has to come to terms with the micro–macro relationship because the distinction between international and domestic is being transcended.

Conventionally, analysts within the field of IR/IPE and international economics have been concerned mainly with the 'big' processes of macro-regionalism, primarily in and between the three core regions, Europe, North America, and Asia Pacific, often with a focus on the EU, NAFTA, and APEC or other regional organisations, such as the Association of Southeast Asian Nations (ASEAN), Mercado Común del Sur Mercosur (MERCOSUR), SADC, and ECOWAS.

In their article 'Theorising the rise of regioness' Hettne and Soderbaum (2000) complement the post-neo-fuctionalist approach of Aniche (2020) to understand the failure of the neo-functional approach to Africa's integration and self-reliance. This may be a workable theoretical approach. In this way, a geographical area is transformed from a passive object to an active subject capable of articulating the transnational interests of an emerging region in constant flux. The DTRP/centre–periphery framework definitively offers a critique of Africa being structurally trapped as an extractive economy supplying the centre, hindering the AU's ability to achieve self-reliance systematically.

Ernest Toochi Aniche (2020:70-87): 'From Pan-Africanism to African regionalism: A chronicle.'

Historical imperatives and an interdisciplinary application are necessary to underscore a much more objective analysis and pathway towards Africa's self-determined post independent development. Against this backdrop Aniche's (2020:70-87) papers are important as a peer-reviewed benchmark to extrapolate comparative historical themes that are relevant to contemporary African Union's Agenda 2063 Pan Africanist programmes. In this regard the DTRP/centre-periphery approach clarifies and complements Aniche's Pan-Africanism as a catalyst for African regionalism(2020).Just as the DTRP/centre-periphery approach factors in historical and present-day ongoing variables, Aniche (2020) traces the history of Modern African regionalism derived from the pan-Africanist philosophical foundations of Kwame Nkrumah, Julius Nyerere, and Nnamdi Azikiwe, culminating in the establishment of the OAU in 1963, which then became the AU in 2001.

This Pan-Africanist sentiment was instrumental to African integration agendas, such as the 1979 Monrovia Strategy, the 1980 LPA, and the Abuja Treaty of 1991 that gave birth to the AEC. African regionalism is thus rooted in Pan-Africanism (Aniche, 2015). However, Pan-Africanism and regional integration in Africa have come a long way. Historically, integration in Africa preceded European colonialism and European integration as well. Africa has a long tradition of regional cooperation, with its trade and monetary integration schemes being the oldest in the developing world. Thus, over the years, both diaspora and modern Pan-Africanism have served as strategies for decolonisation, anti-colonial and neo-colonial struggles, and continental unity, as well as a means of solving African developmental challenges. Modern African regionalism has been a means of collective cooperation, a strategy for economic transformation, or a development framework but to date, self-reliance has remained elusive for the AU.

Despite decades of Pan-African integration, some researchers have noted that numerous obstacles remain, making it difficult for Africa to achieve successful economic integration Other researchers have emphasised the benefits, opportunities, potentials, and prospects of Pan-African regionalism (Okafor and Aniche, 2017). African regionalism as presently constituted cannot achieve its objectives but there is still hope for African integration, although not with the current approach. Africa cannot be continually doing the same thing and expecting a different result. I, therefore, concluded that, given the realities on the ground and the strategies being applied, African regionalism has so far failed as a means of collective self-reliance, and it is not possible to talk of solving African developmental challenges.

Despite decades of contemporary phases of regional integration in Africa, African states still trade more with others than with themselves. This study has identified the numerous obstacles that make it difficult for Africa to achieve successful economic integration. It also noted the numerous benefits and prospects of regional economic integration in Africa. However, these opportunities have not been able to overcome the tremendous constraints impeding regional integration in Africa.

As a result, it is very unlikely that Africa will be able to achieve its aforementioned regional integration targets. As expected, the RECs have not been able to meet most of their targets. Therefore, even the AEC is very unlikely to achieve most of its goals within its stated timeline. Thus, it can be inferred from this study that so far African regionalism has failed as a strategy for achieving economic transformation and establishing a development framework.

The solution to the predicament of African integration should not be sought in the existing Euro-centric strategies or theories, but in a new theory of post-neo-functionalism or post-neo-nationalism that is suitable for the African situation and is capable of solving its problems. Post-neo-functionalism advocates for people-centred, human-centric, or bottom-up integration rather than a top-down approach to integration, or the state-centric or inter-governmental integration of neo-functionalism. Integration should be people-driven or private-sector-led rather than state-driven or public-sector-led. The role of the state should be regulatory or facilitative. Given the enormous security challenges in Africa, post-neo-functionalism suggests that African integration should begin with regional security integration. This entails creating a regional security organisation in Africa. I contend that despite the aforementioned solutions, the DTRP/centre-periphery framework remains pertinent in highlighting the argument that might be offered by any theory that self-reliance of the AU has failed due to its structural entrapment as a dependent extractive appendage of the 'centre.' Furthermore, the AU still lacks the military capabilities of the 'centre' to shift the power dynamics effectively, thereby impeding its ability to competently enforce self-reliance policies.

De Ghetto, Gray, and Kiggundu (2016:93-116): 'The African Union's Agenda 2063: Aspirations, Challenges, and Opportunities for Management research.'

Seven primary aspirations comprise Agenda 2063, which stem from the eight priority areas. Derived from these seven aspirations are 18 goals which are further expanded into 44 priority areas and finally expressed as 161 different national-level targets (see Agenda 2063, 'The Africa We Want', Draft Document, May 2014 for the complete national-level results matrix and a regional-level matrix).

Agenda 2063's vision is comprehensive, covering issues of identity, self-determination, political independence, and socio-economic development in the context of globalization. In addition, other research questions have arisen within participating countries of the AU at different levels of development, awareness, or commitment to the Agenda 2063 vision and aspirations.

For example, the larger and more developed African economies, such as South Africa, Nigeria, and Egypt, may see Agenda 2063 differently than smaller, less well-developed, or fragile countries, such as Swaziland, Burundi, or Guinea. Although the vision and action plans are promising, several key issues related to the implementation of the proposed agenda should be noted and addressed. This difference in perspective by different member states has resulted in free-riding and disinterest in ratifying protocols for fear of sovereignty and revenue loss. This has contributed to the stagnation towards integration and self-reliance of the AU. This confirms the analysis of the DTRP/centre-periphery framework regarding the failure of neo-functionalism as applied by the AU. Some member states only share in normative pronouncements but are not willing to lose sovereignty and revenue without statutory enforceable compensation.

Against this backdrop, Agenda 2063's authors recognise that new institutional arrangements are required to effectively move the agenda toward actual change, development, integration, and transformation. However, the exact nature, structure, and composition of these 'institutional arrangements' remain unclear. This is important because, as Acemoglu and Robinson (2012) show in their work on why nations fail, Africa needs to develop inclusive political and economic institutions. It should be noted that although Agenda 2063 calls for inclusive growth and sustainable development, these goals are not achievable without inclusive institutions. As experience elsewhere in developing countries shows, it is not sufficient to simply change "institutional arrangements". Africa must build effective institutions capable of balancing and protecting competing interests without conflict or open warfare while also avoiding state capture or fragility. An area of particular importance is effective governance and management under conditions of revolution.

Acharya (2012:3-15): 'Comparative Regionalism: A Field whose time has come.'

In the past two decades, there have been some important shifts, one might even say 'advances' (although not everyone would agree), in the study of regionalism. Most regionalism researchers today would have little problem in accepting that regionalism is no longer the monopoly of states but also encompasses interactions among non-state actors and between states and non-state actors within a given area.

First, integration by definition implies loss of sovereignty, either voluntarily or through pressure. Regionalism does not. This does not make regionalism less important, as some suggest, but it does call for different concepts and approaches to the study of the phenomena. This leads to the second difference. Integration studies have always been heavily influenced by the EU's history and experience. The founding theories of integration studies, especially neo-functionalism and transactionalism draw heavily from the early stages of what is called the EU today. In this regard, the DTRP/centre-periphery framework has demonstrated how neo-functionalism has perennially failed in Africa's pursuit of integration programmes towards self-reliance and sustainability. Alternatively, Aniche (2020) offered a post-neo-functionalist approach, which still remains to be tested.

In contrast, the main argument of this article is that regionalism or comparative regionalism has a much more diverse beginning and global heritage than regional integration and comparative regional integration studies. Regional integration is a distinctively Western European idea and is limited in scope. The ideas and literature that constitute comparative regionalism originate from and have been enriched by contributions from many regions, including Latin America, Asia, North America, the Middle East, Africa, and Europe. It is this multiple and global heritage of comparative regionalism that supports the post-neo-functionalism concept in Aniche (2020) and the DTRP/centre-periphery shows a visible zero-sum dominance by the 'centre' of the 'periphery' (Africa). This results in the constant failure of all of Africa's self-reliance integration programmes as they are dependent on the "Centre.'

Ndzendze and Monyae (2019:38-49): 'China's Belt and Road Initiative; Linkages with the AU's Agenda 2063 in Historical Perspective.'

The BRI is China's global infrastructure programme and is arguably the face of its IR and diplomacy. In this regard, this article aptly examines the African interface of the BRI, identifying synergies between it and Africa's development agenda. Its capacity to converge with the AU's Agenda 2063's Aspirations 2, 4, and 5 is assessed in particular detail.

Clearly, if Agenda 2063 is aptly leveraged towards the BRI there will be value and economies of scale that can be derived in terms of industrialisation and infrastructure roll-out, and by extension boosting intra-continental trade, the APSA, and intra-continental people-to-people exchange. To assess the competence of Africa, it is imperative to maintain an ongoing strengths, weaknesses, opportunities, and threats (SWOT) analysis toolkit to extract maximum value from this bilateral-cum-multilateral relationship across all stages of the value chain engagement processes.

In this regard, the document denotes that there are nine strategic partnerships in place, signed between the AU and six countries (USA, Japan, China, India, Turkey, and South Korea), as well as with the Arab League of States, South America, and the EU (African Union, 2015b: 31). The partnerships with China and the EU have accrued the most activity. However, the implementation document argues that "the full potential of the financial pledges and technical assistance pledges embedded in these partnerships are yet to fully leverage from the African side" (African Union, 2015b: 31). The implementation of the AU Agenda 2063 and BRI offers an opportunity for the direction of Chinese investment along appropriate, AU-determined, channels as set out in its Aspirations. The paper argues that the most congruent of the Aspirations to the BRI are Aspirations 2, 4, and, peripherally, 5. I argue that the problems of much-needed investment capital accruing to Africa favourably in a zero-sum game of geo-political and geo-economic interests, impact adversely on integration and self-reliance.

This is the position of the DTRP/centre-periphery framework, with zero-sum power relations at play as potential funders of Africa jostle for hegemony and to the first-amongst-equals to the detriment of Africa's self-reliance integration programmes.

Van Hoeymissen (2011:91-118): 'Regional Organisations in China's Security Strategy for Africa: The Sense of Supporting "African solutions to African problems.'

African regional organisations play a significant role in maintaining peace and security on the continent. This article investigates how China, as an emerging power in Africa, has incorporated these organisations into its policies on African security crises. It asserts that China has explicitly endorsed regional conflict resolution mechanisms, which it perceives as having a less intrusive impact on third-world countries' sovereignty than the initiatives taken under the global collective security system led by the UNSC.

The policy stance of China of non-interference in the internal affairs of nation-states, and specifically in Africa has earned it better investment traction compared to Africa's traditional investors in the Global North (Centre), with their intrusive and exploitative conditionalities. To enhance the ease of business and a peaceful climate for business, investment must be enabled to ensure a conducive environment. In this regard, the AU's APSA is at the coalface of conflict resolution in Africa, and China takes a cue from Africa's lead in conflict resolution and peacebuilding. As indicated by the DTRP/centre-periphery framework on the neo-functionalist failure in realising self-reliance in Africa's integration, still there is notable agency amongst AUMS in collaborating against rising transboundary conflicts, terrorism, and organised crime that threatens their regimes be they democratic or autocratic states.

Unlike the West (Centre), which dictates conditionalities of democracy to Africa to qualify for investments and loans, China has won traction and huge investments in Africa with their non-interference policy.

Vusi Gumede (2021:470-483): 'The African Continental Free Trade Agreement and the future of RECs.'

To implement the AfCFTA, the main areas of tension relate to instances where different RECs may hold or have different positions to those being proposed or implemented at the continental level. One example highlighted is with respect to the TFTA whereby each of the participating RECs (COMESA, UNECA, and SADC) have a different position on the issue of ROO for products. This is going to be one of the critical issues for the implementation of the AfCFTA. Another potentially contentious issue relates to a situation where one REC has signed bilateral agreements either with other RECs, and especially in the case of an external partner such as the EU or China whose positions differ from that of the AfCFTA.

The continuing bilateral arrangements of AUMS contribute to the failure of Africa's self-reliance in pursuit of their integration. I argue that as long as the AU remains an intergovernmental organisation, then there is no continental supra-authority to enforce compliance. How else can the objectives of AU's self-reliance goal be attained if nation-state members operate bilaterally in silos? A macro-economic platform for Africa would enable a much more efficient implementation of self-reliance programmes and policies, for example, integrating the TFTA and AfCFTA. The DTRP/centre-periphery framework uncovers all these variables that inhibit Africa's integration and self-reliance.

Fe Doukoure Charles (2021): 'African continental free trade area: Is there a trade potential for Cote d'Ivore?'

The AfCFTA, a flagship of Agenda 2063 has been ratified, adopted, and has been operationalised. Its full potential will only be realisable through the comprehensive integration of a people-centred agency and trajectory, which stands as one of Africa's most recent trade challenges.

Previous assessments have shown that the AfCFTA will catalyse intra-African trade. The cumulative impact on Côte d'Ivoire was considered as a case study, and its exports in the long term were found to be positive for other African countries and their RECs. Among them were four ECOWAS countries (Niger, Benin, Gambia, and Guinea). These countries could be prioritised when designing a national strategy for implementing the AfCFTA by conducting an in-depth market analysis. I argue that this study does not demonstrate how it will respond to the warnings of the DTRP/centre-periphery framework, i.e., that it is structurally trapped in the 'centre's' exploitative financial system of value extraction to the detriment of the majority of Africa's population (Amin, 1976:194; Amin, 2014). Without tackling this problem the evolution of the AfCFTA will be dictated to by the 'centres' financial processes and once again Africa's exploitation will persist.

Moorosi Leshoele (2020): 'AfCFTA and Regional Integration in Africa: Is African Union Government a Dream Deferred or Denied?'

The DTRP/centre-periphery analysis debunks neo-functionalist attempts at Africa's integration for self-reliance especially after the end of WWII in 1945 with the formation of the 'centres' IMF and WB. Regional integration, as espoused by Leshoele (2020) and Aniche (2020), has been the goal of Pan-Africanism to date, in its attempts to bring about a self-reliant integrated Africa. This was to be preceded by a political unification of Africa, but this remains elusive to date. This is evident in many historical attempts at unification, such as the Casablanca Group under the leadership of Dr Kwame Nkrumah, and the Monrovia bloc which was led by Nnamdi Azikiwe, the first President of Nigeria. The former argued for a wholesale and once-off comprehensive political and economic unification of Africa, from Cape to Cairo, the Horn of Africa to the West of Africa. The latter considered Nkrumah's approach to be unfeasible; therefore, a gradualist and more cautious approach was necessary, first by forming RECs, then later an AEC, with a politically integrated Africa emerging as the final step. The Monrovia bloc won the debate.

The central argument of this paper is that almost all of these regional integration efforts and agreements (from the LPA 1980, Abuja Treaty 1991, TFTA 2015, AfCFTA 2018, and the eight official RECs in Africa) disproportionately focused on trade and economic integration, while lacking consideration of the crucial integration aspects concerning the political unification of Africa in the form of a centralised union government.

History might be repeating itself in the efforts to comprehensively integrate Africa because the divisions among African leaders during the 2007 Accra Declaration that sought to resuscitate the roadmap to the realisation of a union government were reminiscent of the divisions that led to the formation of the OAU. This culminated in the Monrovia school of thought/perspective prevailing in the late 1950s and Africa still remains with that same gradualist pact. However, there is a silver lining expressed in this paper, which is the enormous potential and opportunity brought about by the ratification of the AfCFTA, even though this regional body too is devoid of the political, cultural, and epistemic levers needed for the comprehensive unification of Africa, and rather just focuses on the economic dynamics.

The paper further showed that most RECs primarily focus on the economic integration of their regions, with less focus on an equally important aspect of African unification, namely the political integration of regions and the continent at large. Furthermore, the paper attempted to show that FMP throughout the African continent is equally important as the free movement of goods, services, and capital, and that this must also be prioritised because socio-cultural integration is as important as economic integration because it will foster a bottom-up, people-to-people integration. This is more organic and sustainable than the conventional top-down approach of state-to-state integration.

It would seem that Nkrumah's dream for a union government has been deferred for now, or perhaps indefinitely if one looks at the growing trend of secession in Africa, exemplified by the secession of South Sudan from Sudan and growing calls for cessation in Cameroon and, to some extent, Nigeria emanating from the 1967–1970 Biafran civil War. As though to reinforce this notion, a banned underground organisation called the Indigenous People of Biafra has to date been mobilising through Radio Biafra to resuscitate calls for the Biafra region to secede from Nigeria.

Samuel Kehinde Okunade and Olusola Ogunnubi (2021;119-137) "Humanitarian Crisis in North-Eastern Nigeria:Responses and Sustainable Solutions."

Established in 1975, the ECOWAS was conceived, primarily to facilitate free trade and movement of persons, goods, and services within the subregion. The EU is the 'centre' underpinned by the Schengen Treaty and the ECOWAS represents the 'periphery' with its attempts at self-reliance enshrined in the ECOWAS Protocol. The comparison between the two as equals is not consistent with the DTRP/centre-periphery framework (Kvagraven, 2018 and Amin, 2014). The position of the 'periphery' renders it small, disarticulated, fragmented, and unwilling to surrender sovereignty and revenue loss. The consequential outcomes of ongoing political instability, poverty, corruption, and a plethora of social ills, do not encourage the political will for integration and self-reliance. Although it preceded the widely lauded Schengen Treaty, which created a single external border for the EU in 1985, the ECOWAS Protocol on the Free Movement of Persons and Goods established in 1979 aimed to convert borders from walls into 'bridges'. This paper examines the implementation of the ECOWAS Protocol by member states to establish whether the Protocol has strengthened or weakened the porosity of West African borders.

In addition, the study explores the recurring challenges that impede the successful implementation of the Protocol as an expression of Africa's agency for regional integration. The authors conclude by making suggestions regarding what is required to address these impediments to the fulfilment of ECOWAS' aspiration of an open border system.

Specifically, this study considered how the implementation or non-implementation of the ECOWAS Protocol on free movement has facilitated or hindered the porosity of the region's borders. The analysis of the implementation of the ECOWAS Protocol on Free Movement of Persons by member states showed that the loss of agency of member states could be attributed to a lack of political will, incessant political instability, and interstate border disputes and wars, as well as countries' reluctance to surrender national sovereignty to a sub-regional organ, severely limiting the effectiveness of the ECOWAS Protocol. Conscious efforts must be taken to address these challenges for the ECOWAS to fulfil its open border aspiration. In light of the preceding, it is suggested that to fulfil its mandate, the ECOWAS Court first needs to impose stricter sanctions on member states that violate the provisions of the Protocol. Doing this would serve as a deterrent to others. If Nigeria, as a leading country in West Africa, were to be sanctioned by the Court if found to be in violation of the provisions of the ECOWAS Protocol, this would prompt stronger compliance among other member states.

Second, to actualise the ECOWAS vision of a borderless West Africa, member states have to adopt a more pragmatic attitude by discarding the notion of security defence, which emphasises territoriality, and embrace border security, that is all-encompassing and more concerned with citizens' welfare, as envisaged by the Protocol. This calls for a clear distinction between open and closed borders.

Although the ECOWAS Protocol precedes the Schengen Treaty, the latter represents a good example of an open border system that guarantees freedom of movement of goods and persons to all citizens, providing an example for the ECOWAS. The role of the armed forces is diminished given that there are no borders to patrol, nor are there any border crossings between EU member states. Finally, ECOWAS member states should not simply pay lip service to the Protocol but take steady actions to implement its provisions. Political will is thus called for to ensure that African borders become bridges and not barriers that are detrimental to member states.

Ernest Toochi Aniche (2020): 'African Continental Free Trade Area and African Union Agenda 2063: the roads to Addis Ababa and Kigali.'

The AfCFTA was initiated in 2010 and adopted in 2019, while Agenda 2063 was initiated in 2012 and adopted in 2015. The objectives of the AfCFTA and the aspirations of Agenda 2063 are closely related, mutually inclusive, and reinforcing. In line with the strategic objectives of the AU's Agenda 2063 initiative, the AfCFTA provides a lever that can be used to strategically position the continent to exploit its numerous trade and investment opportunities and contribute positively towards the structural transformation of African economies and poverty eradication.

The Agenda's Aspirations 1, 2, and 7 are explicit in the objectives of the AfCFTA while Aspirations 3, 4, 5, and 6 are implicit in the objectives of the Agreement. For example, among the Seven Aspirations of the AU Agenda 2063, Aspiration 2 is most directly related to the objectives of the AfCFTA. Aspiration 2 seeks to achieve a politically united and integrated continent based on the ideals of Pan-Africanism and the vision of Africa's renaissance, which continues to remain unattainable (Leshoele, 2020). This is one of the objectives of the AfCFTA. It proposes the creation of a single continental market for goods and services with free movement of business persons and investments, and ultimately Pan-African political and economic regionalism.

The next aspiration of Agenda 2063 that is directly linked to the objectives of the AfCFTA is Aspiration 7. This Aspiration strives to realise a strong, united, and resilient Africa that will be an influential global player and partner. This is in tandem with the objectives of the AfCFTA in Africa. The AfCFTA aims to achieve an economically strong and politically united Africa that will become an influential global economic player and political actor.

Aspiration 1

Aspiration 1 aspires to attain a prosperous Africa based on inclusive growth and sustainable development. This aligns with one of the objectives of the AfCFTA that targets industrial development to generate employment, reduce poverty, and achieve sustainable economic growth and development.

Aspiration 4

By aiming to engender a peaceful and secure Africa, Aspiration 4 complements and reinforces the objectives of the AfCFTA, which aims to ultimately attain a pan-African security, economic, and political integration. Aspiration 5 of Agenda 2063, which tries to build an Africa with a strong cultural identity, common heritage, values, and ethics through socio-cultural integration is in line with the pan-African philosophy or ideology of regionalism in Africa, which is the ultimate objective of the AfCFTA.

Aspiration 6

Aspiration 6 plans to create an Africa whose development is people-driven. Relying on the potential offered by people fits into one of the objectives of the AfCFTA, which is to ensure private sector-driven development through the enhancement of industrial competitiveness through the exploitation of opportunities for large-scale production, continental market access, and better reallocation of resources to unleash the entrepreneurial prowess and proficiency across the continent.

Aspiration 3

Aspiration 3 seeks to establish good governance, democracy, human rights observance, a sense of justice, and the rule of law in Africa. It does not depart from the overall objectives of the AfCFTA in that it is indirectly or remotely related to these objectives. The strategic initiatives of the AU Agenda 2063 and the objectives of the AfCFTA are in harmony, reflecting a shared vision for progress and development. For example, the Agenda's strategic frameworks of ensuring a stronger push for African integration and unity and strengthening regional institutions, e.g., the RECs, are in accordance with the AfCFTA's strategic blueprints of bringing about a gradual elimination of tariff barriers and non-tariff barriers (NTBs) on intra-African trade, tackling trade and investment constraints, and fast-tracking trade and investment facilitations or infrastructures. It is therefore a means of achieving continental unity, collective self-reliance, economic transformation, and solving African developmental challenges.

Towards a new theoretical approach to African integration and free trade, current indicators caution against excessive optimism regarding the newly ratified AfCFTA. Generally, Africa's share of global trade in 2010 was very poor at about 4%. Despite the long evolution of the AU integration agenda, intra-African trade has consistently remained low averaging approximately 10%.[3] Over 80% of the imports and exports of African states are destined for markets outside the continent as non-value-added raw materials. This confirms the DTRP/centre-periphery analysis that structurally thwarts Africa's integration and self-reliance (Kvangraven, 2018 and Amin, 2014)

Alan Hirsch (2021:497-517): 'The African Union's Free Movement of Persons Protocol: Why has it faltered and how can its objectives be achieved?'

In January 2018, the AU agreed to establish the AfCFTA to enable the free flow of goods and services within Africa. Simultaneously, the AU adopted a protocol supporting the FMP between the countries of Africa. Both are considered necessary for the successful social and economic development of the countries of the African continent. As of January 2021, 54 countries had signed the AfCFTA and 35 countries had fully ratified it, whereas 33 countries had signed the FMP Protocol and only four countries had fully ratified it.

This article analyses the reasons for the slow adoption of the protocol within the DTRP/centre-periphery framework. This demonstrates how integration and self-reliance continue to fail.

Some institutional and procedural concerns restrict the commitment of some of the richer countries in Africa towards migration liberalisation. The key issues that undermine trust between African states include civil registration and identity documentation. Many countries in Africa have inadequate systems of civil registration and many have inadequate identity documentation systems. This makes it difficult for the home countries of migrants to vouch for their citizens to the satisfaction of host countries. Regional efforts to build civil registration and identity document systems to a common standard could reduce the current lack of trust between countries. Adequate systems require a considerable investment by government and aid partners in the development of the systems, as well as the development of the capacity to maintain and update such systems. These processes should be led by a competent technical committee of member states and experts at regional and continental levels. Countries with weak administration of their criminal justice systems must address this issue to avoid the untracked migration of criminals. Enhancing these systems and bolstering their maintenance capabilities would foster increased trust among stakeholders.

Many countries still do not have reliable border management systems. The EU (centre) for its own reasons has given considerable support to this function in West and North Africa (periphery) and in the Horn of Africa, which has seen positive outcomes that seem to not only serve the EU's interests but also regional interests. Dependence on the EU for such systems risks biasing them against migration northwards, rather than managing freer intra-Africa flows of people. Although it will be a long time before comprehensive border management is ubiquitous, it is possible to strengthen these systems in poorer countries with significant support.

This article considered the AU's FMP Protocol in the context of the recent adoption of the AfCFTA within the DTRP/centre-periphery framework. The reasons for the slow adoption of the FMP Protocol are complex, and include concerns about giving up sovereign protections regarding FMP in Africa, and lack of clarity about the implementation process. Previous analyses have noted how the free movement agenda is progressing despite these concerns, and ways of moving the protocol and its agenda forward have been suggested. These discussions have involved global, national, and regional initiatives on migration, and key issues to address have been proposed. These include improving systems for civil registration and identity documentation, the exchange of civil and criminal data between states, improved border management systems, stronger security monitoring systems, enhanced cooperation for the exchange of information on security matters, and repatriation agreements.

There has also been a proposal for the establishment of technical committees at continental and regional levels to facilitate the implementation of the FMP Protocol through conversations between governments. This will empower countries to address the preconditions for implementation and identify the challenges of implementation as a whole.

Ufiem Maurice Ogbonnaya (2016:185-199): 'Terrorism, Agenda 2063 and the challenges of development in Africa.'

The nobility of the objectives and aspirations of the AU's Agenda 2063 towards the developmental needs of the African people are laudable, as are the attempts being made to ensure collective action, despite the "shield of sovereignty behind which too many corrupt leaders have hidden". However, these noble objectives and aspirations may be undermined and threatened by the upsurge in militant Islamism and the spread of terrorism within and outside Africa, a fact that is not addressed by Agenda 2063. However, while Agenda 2063 does not seek to address the challenges posed by terrorist networks within the continent, which are threatening human security as well as the sovereignty, territoriality, legitimacy, and stability of political regimes, these issues are at the core of the agenda. This article argues for Agenda 2063 to step up its efforts to combat both the roots of terrorism and the threat to development that terrorism itself poses.

Assertions of global terrorism emanating from the Global North (centre) are also supported by John Perkins (2004) in his book 'Confessions of an Economic Hitman' and Nkruma (1965) in 'Neo-colonialism the last stage of imperialism.' This lends credence to the DTRP/centre-periphery framework, indicating that the 'centre' structurally and forcibly subjugates and subordinates the 'periphery' so as not to realise self-reliance and integration. The analysis points to the existence of some established and emerging terrorist organisations in Africa. From North to East and West Africa, with minimal presence in Southern Africa, terrorist organisations not only represent a threat to national, sub-regional and continental security in Africa, but in some instances have also emerged as powerful challengers to state security apparatuses. This has resulted in the protective function of the state and its monopoly on the use of force being increasingly undermined. At issue here is the trend in the escalation of terrorism and its implications for development in Africa.

A major trend in terrorist escalation in Africa is the establishment of linkages among groups operating on the continent, and their increased affiliation with international terrorist networks. For example, security operatives have established that there are linkages among Nigeria's Boko Haram, Somalia's Al-Shabaab, Mali's Ansa Dine, and Algeria's Islamic Maghreb (AQIM). Moreover, these are in turn affiliated, to varying degrees, with international terrorist networks such as Al-Qaeda and the Islamic State. For example, the Kanuri region of Chad provides Boko Haram with a corridor to Sudan and from there to Al-Shabaab in Somalia. Similarly, the Kanuri region of Niger provides Boko Haram with a northern corridor to the Touré region of Niger and the adjacent Touré regions of Mali, southern Libya, and Algeria.

These linkages enable transnational mobilisation by terrorist groups for operations with relative ease, as was witnessed in the coalition among AQIM, Boko Haram, and the Movement for Oneness and Jihad in West Africa (MUJAO) to support Ansa Dine in the Touré rebellion for the creation of the Azawad State in northern Mali in 2011 and 2013.[28] Second, they also enable the delivery of training and logistics supplies among terrorist groups. For example, the report of the UN Secretary-General. to the Security Council on 18 January 2012 indicated that seven members of Boko Haram were arrested while transiting through Niger to Mali. They were in possession of documents regarding the manufacturing of explosives, propaganda leaflets and lists of names and contact details of members of Al-Qaida in the AQIM, with whom they were allegedly planning to meet.

Finally, the affiliation of AQIM, Al-Shabaab, and Boko Haram to the Islamic State represents an attempt by the Islamic State terrorist network to spread its operational and human resource bases within Africa, as well as its vision of establishing a coordinating point in North and West Africa. Ultimately, the aim is to spread Islamic extremism and global jihadist movements within the continent. This is evidenced by the presence of the Islamic State in Egypt, Libya, and Tunisia already. The possibility of the successful execution of this vision by the group is enhanced by the fact that the North and West African sub-regions have many characteristics that make them increasingly vulnerable to exploitation by terrorist groups. This increase in instability and insecurity has restricted attempts to realise African integration and self-reliance.

Dennis Ndonga, Emmanuel Laryea and Murendere Chaponda (2020): 'Assessing the Potential Impact of the African Continental Free Trade Area on Least Developed Countries: A Case Study of Malawi.'

The agreement establishing the AfCFTA has been touted as an important pillar and driver of economic growth, industrialisation, and sustainable development in Africa. Among its expected key benefits is the promise to increase the level of intra-African trade by eliminating import duties and other tariffs among member countries, in addition to general trade expansion.

However, unlocking the AfCFTA's full potential will largely depend on how the continent is able to restructure its exports, which are poorly diversified and remain highly dependent on primary commodities. As explained by the DTRP/centre-periphery framework these primary commodities are a structural appendage supplying the 'centre' as determined by its pricing and intellectual property rights (IPR) structure (Amin, 2014 and Kvangraven, 2018). Therein lies the challenge to Africa's failed attempts at regional integration and self-reliance.

Moreover, intra-African trade remains dominated by a few large regional players. To this end, there have been growing fears that the AfCFTA's anticipated gains, and associated losses, are likely to accrue unevenly. Countries with large productive capacities in manufacturing or stronger supply capacities in non-manufactured products may reap more rewards than weaker landlocked and smaller economies, particularly the LDCs. These concerns have led to several countries, including Malawi, pushing for special and differential treatment in the implementation of the AfCFTA's provisions on the elimination of import duties and other tariffs. The DTRP/centre-periphery demonstrates that many LDCs, including Malawi (the periphery), rely heavily on international trade taxes as a source of government revenue. There is a legitimate concern that such economies are likely to be left grappling with the negative effects of tariff cuts in the form of substantial fiscal revenue loss. This article explores the potential impact of the AfCFTA on LDCs, with a focus on Malawi. It reviews Malawi's intra-African trade position in terms of its export potential and examines the likely impact that the AfCFTA agreement would have on the country's fiscal revenues.

To this end, there is a need to devise policies and measures that will ensure that the AfCFTA is mutually inclusive and beneficial to all member countries. The preferential treatment sought by the LDCs, in the form of an extended timeline within which to reduce tariffs, should be seriously considered. This would delay the impact of their likely trade revenue losses and enable them to implement appropriate policies, such as attracting investments for possible trade expansion, creating jobs, expanding their tax base, and enhancing economic growth. At the same time, the move towards establishing the AfCFTA should serve as a wake-up call to Malawi and other LDCs, ensuring that they actively create a substantial export base to reap some of the promised benefits of trade liberalisation.

Primrose Thandeka Sabela, Mfundo Mandla Masuku, & Victor H. Mlambo (2023): 'Unleashing the development potential of Africa's women through African Continental Free Trade Agreement (AfCFTA).'

This paper analyses the AfCFTA and its potential to unleash the development of women in Africa. The envisaged benefits of the AfCFTA include increased trade diversification, regional integration, enhanced human security, increased FDI, and technological advancement. The DTRP/centre-periphery framework indicates that the 'centres' FDI and technological transference and advancement is not automatic. As asserted by Amin (2014), not all FDI and technology arriving into Africa facilitates its pursuit of integration and self-reliance. Rather, the 'centres' investments and technologies seek to cement Africa's dependence and this has exacerbated gender policy inequalities towards self-reliance (Amin, 1976; 2014 and Kvangraven, 2018).

Despite optimism about the prospects of the agreement as a local innovation spearheaded by the AU, questions have been raised about the extent of stakeholder engagement. The agreement must be gender-responsive to enhance the outcomes for female cross-border traders.

The paper concludes that the lack of gender sensitivity confirms the need to address the specific needs of African women, especially those involved in informal cross-border trade. Hence, for the AfCFTA, the policy focus should be on ensuring the formalisation of women who participate in informal trade, thus helping increase access to markets, information, and growth opportunities.

More effort should be made to eradicate the patriarchal culture that impedes gender equality in the trade sector. This paper recommends focusing more on women, especially grassroots workers, whose participation in informal trade is considerable. In this way, the AfCFTA could have an important role in ensuring the formalisation of this informal trade and establishing greater access to market opportunities for women. This will ensure the eradication of existing inequalities in the sector. The AfCFTA has the potential to combat patriarchal economic systems and to safeguard inclusive intra-trade Africa, ensuring its sustainability. The paper further suggests that African governments should formulate practicable intra-trade policies that enhance the economic status of women in the industry. Issues impeding women's trade activities must be removed, policies that support trade should be entrenched, and inter-state government relations should share the same visions regarding trade integration.

vi. Peace and Security[17]

In 'The AU: Pan-Africanism, Peacebuilding and Development,' Murithi (2005), presents the historical background of Pan-Africanism, its evolution from the OAU to the LPA, and thereafter the emergence of the AU. According to Murithi, AU agency incrementally reinforces its raison d'étre in continental and global politics towards African unification under the banner of an African Renaissance. The AU, Murithi asserts, "provides a new opportunity for revitalising the Pan-Africanist agenda of united Africans and the Diaspora and encouraging them to work in solidarity with each other" (2005:36).

Over and above economic and structural development, the book also discusses human security and peace, the inclusion of civil society and non-state actors, which, according to Murithi, are required to participate fully and take ownership of Africa's development. Inevitably, Murithi argues that the AU will continue to experience significant challenges, which should be engaged successfully to achieve the aims and goals of Agenda 2063.

In 'The African Union's Evolving Role in Peace Operations: the African Union Mission in Burundi, the African Union Mission

---

17   Personal Interview with Dr. Dawn Nagar at the University of
      Johannesburg. 2022-2023.

in Sudan and the African Union Mission in Somalia', Murithi (2008), discusses the transition processes that led to the creation of the AU. He also highlights more contemporary, asymmetrical, and hybridised challenges, such as the AU's partnerships with the EU, UN, and China. The operationalisation of the APSA, for example, denotes a fundamental paradigm shift in how security is approached on the continent. For Murithi (2008: 82), "The AU will need to seriously orient the political leadership of the continent and take decisive action, without which the challenges of ensuring successful peace operations will not be met." Murithi goes on to highlight donor dependency and logistical incapacity as reasons for the AU's failure to implement its programmes with predictability and validity.

Although premised on the principle of subsidiarity, the evolution of the AU and its partnerships with the EU, UN, and other bilateral and multilateral institutions, encourage paternalism instead of partnership (Murithi, 2008:79).

In 'Peace and Security Policy of the African Union and the Regional Security Mechanisms', Klingebiel (2007) evaluates and audits the AU's approach to peace and security. The operationalisation of the AU's APSA with external partnerships, such as those with the EU, USA, and China, has enabled a definitive paradigm shift from the OAU. Despite the asymmetrical and hybrid multilateral partnering, the normative shift to emphasise the AU's raison d'être as the leading entity for human peace and security (in line with the 'African solutions to African problems' doctrine), marks the importance of Pan-African agency (Kobbie, 2009:25).

As was the case during the Cold War era rivalry between the USA and USSR, where superpower's and UN geo-strategic agendas in conflict management interventions in Africa took precedence, Klingebiel (2007:74) asserts that the AU's efforts to make it clear "that the involvement of other countries in this area is welcome only on condition that they are prepared to cooperate within the framework of African approaches and that they are invited to do so." However, Klingebiel shows that the AU's APSA institutional bottlenecks, such as donor dependency, and logistical and human resources incapacity, have hampered its effectiveness and efficiency.

Klingebiel concludes with recommendations, such as the AU funding its own programmes, thereby improving self-reliance and demonstrating commitment. Additionally, Klingebiel considers post-conflict peacebuilding to be imperative and integral in achieving a sustainable socio-economic polity of human security and peace. This predicates sustainable peacebuilding not only on protecting and preserving the state regime but also on being inclusive of the whole citizenry, with transparent accountable governance.

The diffusion of R2P as the norm is highlighted by Chizik (2007) in 'The Responsibility to Protect: Does the ASF Need a doctrine for Protection of Civilians?' Chizik comprehensively explains the stated goals of the APSA and outlines the ethical concerns of the R2P doctrine of non-indifference. The recommendation of the author is for the ASF to be premised on a multidisciplinary doctrine (Chizik, 2007:78; Däniker, 1995:93). This would entail ongoing security sector policy formulation and reform, as well as enhancing centripetal complementarities with human rights organisations, and civil society non-state actors in general. The complementarities between the ASF and non-state actors, according to Chizik, will result in the standardisation of 'rules of engagement for human protection.'

In 'The AU: Challenges of Globalisation, Security, and Governance', Makutu and Okumu (2007) share a somewhat Afro-pessimistic undertaking of the AU in the context of globalisation, history, law, and economic development. They assert that "African solutions are not adequate for all African problems" (Makinda and Okumu, 2007:93). This Afro-pessimism is reinforced by the failure of the AU in the deployment and operationalisation of the African Union Mission in Sudan (AMIS) and AMIS II between 2004 and 2007 in the Sudan. The double failure resulted from the AU's lack of self-funding, external knowledge dependency, and logistical and human resource incapacity.

This incapacitation has imposed limitations on the realisation of AU mandates. The recommendations from the author and others (Touray, 2005:651; Appiah-Mensah, 2005; Crupi, 2005; Chizik, 2007; Kobbie, 2009; Powell, 2005; O'Neil and Cassis, 2005) are that the AU should multilaterally strengthen relationships with other global organisations, such as the UN, EU, NATO, IMF, and WB. They argue that this institutional imperative would consolidate the continental security architecture, thereby favourably and incrementally leveraging its collective capacity. However, although multilateral partnerships are imperative they are not easily realisable because international organisations pursue their own geo-strategic realist agendas, which may not always align with the AU's vision and mandates.

In 'AU's Critical Assignment in Darfur: Challenges and Constraints', Appiah-Mensah (2005) highlights the AU's institutional weaknesses and restrictive mandates. These issues are considered to have reinforced the logistical inadequacy and planning shortfalls of the assignment. However, Appiah-Mensah bemoans Afro-pessimistic critiques that AMIS had failed because such an approach undermines support for the mission and escalates the risk to the lives of people in Darfur. The foregoing axiom that international organisations pursue their own geo-strategic realist agendas, finds resonance in Crupi (2005) 'Why the US Should Robustly Support Pan-African Organisations'. Crupi's assertion, as a US Army planning expert, is written from a USA foreign policy perspective. According to Crupi, the USA interest in stabilising West Africa, preferably via the ECOWAS rather than directly with the AU, is in securing, stabilising, and diversifying the global oil supply using West African oil production (Crupi, 2005:121).

The author's recommendation of preferably strengthening RECs, such as the ECOWAS, rather than strengthening the AU's APSA for continental consolidation, implicitly reinforces a deliberate divide-and-conquer stratagem, which serves to impede the AU's realisation of its Agenda 2063. The article, 'Military Responses to Mass Killing: The AMIS' by William (2006) is reminiscent of the international community's lack of response to the 1994 genocide in Rwanda. It critiques both the AU and UN (and other international organisations) for their disinterest and indifference towards a speedy response to the ongoing genocide in Sudan (Williams, 2006:170). As much as NATO had offered logistical support to the AU mission, Williams criticises them for their refusal to consider contributing troops on the ground despite being aware of the military, logistical, and doctrinal deficiencies within the AU's APSA (Williams, 2006:178).

Furthermore, notwithstanding the AU's lack of resources, Williams critiques the AU for the lack of robust political will in refusing to contribute timeously to the AU's APSA budget. It could be argued that this lacklustre response to a pending genocide – as was evident in Rwanda and Sudan – is the indifference of the global elite institutions, including those in Africa. In reference to the AU's APSA in particular, Williams (2006:172– 176) highlights its failure in neutralising the Janjaweed militia and its collaborative posture with Khartoum and coaching the government on how to "handle the whites" (2006:172–176).

3.2 The African Union 2007 Audit Review[18]

During the July 2007 AU Summit, the Chair of the AU, H.E. John Agyekum Kufuor, President of the Republic of Ghana, commissioned a High-level Panel to conduct an audit review of the AU. As a former UN Under-Secretary-General. and Executive Secretary of the UNECA, Professor Adebayo Adedeji from Nigeria was the Chairperson of this High-level twelve-member panel (Audit of the AU, 2007). Other High-level Panellists included technocrats and resource-persons from Cameroon, Kenya, Nigeria, South Africa, Uganda, and Zambia.

The subsections (3.2.1-3.2.3) will cover the specific points of the Audit report. Subsequently in section 3.2.4, an analysis of whether the report had fulfilled its terms of reference is conducted. Additionally, the strengths and weaknesses of the AU will be identified, with proposed remedies for the weaknesses.

---

18   Personal Interview with Professor Eddie Maloka, Exeuctive Director of APRM. "African solutions to African problems": the aphorism is a call for the continent and diasporic Africans for a coordinated and harmonized Pan African diplomacy to address common challenges faced by Africa and Africans both continentally and globally (AU Agenda 2063, 2014; Parker and Rukare, 2002; Murithi, 2009).

3.2.1 The Fulfilment of the High-Level Panel Mandate

From 10 September 2007 until 18 December 2007, the High-level Panel discussed the scope of its work with all the organs of the AU and other institutions and organisations (Audit of the AU, 2007). Meetings were also convened with other continental bodies and REC's. These included representatives from the UNECA, AfDB, COMESA, ECOWAS, EAC, and CEN-SAD (Audit of the AU, 2007). The engagements with members of the AUC were far more extensive given that this was the first continental performance review of the AU and all its organs. This entailed locating specific issues causing stagnation and proposing interventions and reforms to speed up Africa's integration (Audit of AU, 2007)

By engaging with individuals in key positions in the AUC and other structures, the Panel gained insight into the details of the challenges faced by the AU and its various institutions. However, there was no connection with the ordinary African citizenry in Africa's nation-states (Williams, 2013b).

The fact that the analysis of the interface between the AU and civil society was shown to be weak demonstrated that its research methods needed improvement. If proper sampling methods, surveys, and case studies had been conducted, a more valuable outcome would have resulted that enhanced the depth of analysis and the resulting insights.

3.2.2 Key Findings of the High-Level Panel as it Relates to the African Unions Key Decision-Making Organs

i. The Assembly of Heads of State and Government

The High-level Panel found that the AHSG, as the supreme organ of the AU, was wanting in a number of its critical leadership obligations. Hence, there were missed opportunities to provide leadership in terms of accelerating the processes of integration.

The Panel recommended that the AHSG should be timeous and more focused; therefore, the Assembly should hold one annual summit at the headquarters of the AU. The Extraordinary sessions were retained, to be used sparingly as exigencies arose. Institutional standardisation and harmonisation would accrue in the overall economies of scale, maximising production and efficiency through:

a.   improving cost-effectiveness;
b.   standardisation and harmonisation, thereby engendering efficiencies and the effectiveness of the operations of the AU;
c.   allowing sufficient time for the implementation of the decisions; and
d.   continuing with the current practice of delinking the hosting of the Summit from the Chair of the Assembly.

The Panel stated that it was imperative for the Chair of the Assembly to serve for two years because this would sustain policy continuity predicated on a definite thematic approach to integration. Thus, the theme of integration of the following annual meeting should be announced and recorded in the minutes at the closing of each ordinary annual meeting of the Assembly.

The findings and urgent recommendations made by the Panel highlighted a pervasive issue of implementation failures and crises, which were particularly evident at the upper echelons of AU decision-making and leadership. The norm for entrepreneurship, required by the Continent's leadership, was non-existent. It had not been put into practice or fully embraced, actions that could have enabled its supranational institutions to realise deeper integration. I argue there should be a robust nexus of activism, not only of the vertical top-down elite narrow agency but also of the horizontal and bottom-up participation of CSOs and the general African citizenry, which should be included at all times.

ii. The Executive Council

The Executive Council is another important organ, which is answerable to the Assembly. It was established as per Articles 10–13 of the Constitutive Act and details of its operations are contained in the Rules of Procedure. The Panel found that there was a strategic imbalance and disconnect within the Council, noting that while there was a focus on specialized commitments, there was a lack of engagement on crucial strategic issues, resulting in missed opportunities to engage on strategic issues. Under Article 13, the Council is responsible for coordinating and making decisions on policies in areas of common interest to the member states and that is its strategic aspect. Areas of common interest would be, for example, foreign trade, energy, industry and mineral resources, food security, and self-reliance. To effect traction and policy, sectoral synergies should be implemented to harness comparative advantages across the Continent.

In this regard, the High-level Panel advocated that the Executive Council should be redesignated the Council of Ministers and its composition aligned to Articles 10(1) and 14 of the Constitutive Act. The Panel's reason for this configuration was that it would enable sectoral ministers to pursue clear, appropriate, and optimally defined key tasks, which would have the maximum impact towards integration. The Specialised Technical Committees (STCs), therefore, would become obsolete. The sectoral Councils of Ministers would establish ad hoc committees of officials as a support service.

iii. The Permanent Representatives Committee

Article 21 of the Constitutive Act deals with the establishment of the Permanent Representatives Committee (PRC), a body of Permanent Representatives and other Plenipotentiaries of Member States accredited to the AU. It plays a significant role in liaising between the Commission and the member states. A serious criticism of the PRC, however, was that it abdicated its core business and duties and had become highly meddlesome and interventionist in AUC affairs.

The Panel made a comparative analysis under Rule 4 of its Rules of Procedure. The organ's powers and functions are to:

· liaise between member states and the Commission;
· exercise oversight over the Commission;
· facilitate and support the Executive Council in executing its powers and functions; and
· participate in the preparation of the AU's programme of activities.

Furthermore, Rule 26 of the Rules of Procedure of the PRC emphasise that 'decisions of the Committee shall be recommendations until adopted by the Executive Council.' The Panel found:

> "that the balance between oversight and advisory functions of the PRC needs to be adjusted. The emphasis on the role of the PRC should be advisory and the capacity of the PRC – its members and subsidiary – needs to be enhanced for an effective and informed advisory role to the Council of Ministers."

To enhance its capacity therefore, the Panel recommended that experienced ambassadors from member states should be posted to head their missions. Permanent Representatives should assume full control and be personally responsible for AU matters, eschewing the culture of delegating official responsibilities to their subordinates. This would further require that Permanent Representatives should attend PRC meetings in person, as this would instil professionalism and a seriousness of purpose.

A further recommendation was made for the AUC to issue a calendar of the PRC's meetings for the following year, three months before the end of each year and adhered to by both. The Panel noted that the then Sub-Committee system needed to be overhauled and streamlined to focus on substantive and strategic issues. This was to be accompanied by the employment of competently qualified technocrats to manage issues of strategic importance to the AU, such as finance, trade, the environment, and economic development. As and when necessary, ad hoc committees with clear terms of reference and periods were to add to the professionalism, work ethic, and delivery of outputs. Clear terms of reference and time limits were seen to be essential for ad hoc committees to minimise their unnecessary proliferation and reduce the risk of them becoming permanently institutionalized.

iv. The Specialised Technical Committees

At the time of the Panel's review, the STCs as proposed by the Constitutive Act had not yet been established. The purpose of establishing STCs was based on clusters of ministries that cover interrelated issues such as infrastructure, industry and trade, social affairs, education, health, social welfare, employment, and peace and security.

The Panel recommended the new commissioners in charge of the STCs to coordinate the work of the various sectoral ministries, meeting as STCs at the AU level. Each STC would draw up a common policy and programmes that member states would implement at national level. The outcome of STC meetings would be forwarded to the Executive Council through the chairperson of the STC or the appropriate commissioner. Furthermore, each commissioner would monitor the implementation of the STC programmes and projects in each member state and in the RECs. The Panel further recommended that the STCs configuration be subject to consultation among member states.

Through the STCs, the AUC will be able to coordinate and harmonise policies in all the AUMS. The Panel proposed that given the reluctance shown by most member states to cede aspects of their sovereignty to a supra-continental authority, there should rather be a focus on converging RECs and strengthening all AU organs and institutions, thereby establishing and operationalising the STCs. In this regard, it is hoped that the STCs will enable the AUC to coordinate and harmonise various policies as agreed to by member states and thus prepare the ground for the gradual formation of an AU Government.

3.2.3 The Recommendations of the 2007 African Union Review Report

The AU Audit made a total of 172 recommendations for the strengthening of the AU and "advancing the frontiers of African Unity and integration." One of the biggest problems that the AUC and its other departments have faced since their inception in 2002, is that they have been overwhelmed with unrealistic expectations and unattainable goals. These have been imposed on them, largely, by unaccountable actors and political principals. The central goal that underscores these recommendations is accelerated integration. The urgent institutional overhaul and strengthening of the AU's institutions are therefore imperative. To this end, a total of 159 recommendations have been made touching on all aspects of the work of the AU. It has also been suggested that each of the Organs of the AU should develop roadmaps that would guide their specific areas of work over the next few years.

The Panel put forward a set of measurable benchmarks to serve as a platform against which progress could be measured regularly and systematically. While the individual recommendations stand on their merit, the Panel emphasised that "their overall impact will, as emphasised earlier, reside in their implementation as parts of a coherent and integrated whole." The recommendations comprise elements of a plan of action, which should be carried out within specified timeframes. They are measures to be undertaken nationally, regionally, and continentally. This demands urgent mobilisation, not only of political will but also of the best human resources, such as competent technocrats able to pursue the AU's vision of unity and integration.

The Constitutive Act, as a beacon of continental unity, should enhance and enable centripetal factors and traction towards the attainment of the aims and objectives of integration. In this way, momentum in areas of consensus would be strengthened towards unity and integration. The AU's core values (as set out in Article 3 of the Constitutive Act) should be promoted, internalised, and domesticated in all African countries and AU organs. To promote the vision of Pan-Africanism further, issues of immigration within Africa and from Africa to Europe, should be engaged by the AU's organs. In its findings and recommendations, the Panel regarded the reform, strengthening, and efficient functioning of the AU's organs and institutions as 'a necessary precondition' (Momodu 2016)

Furthermore, it was recommended that the Chair of the Assembly should serve for two years, as this would maintain policy continuity and proactive leadership. Heads of states and government should endeavour to report to their populations, including parliaments and deliberative bodies, on the summit's proceedings and the decisions reached (Audit of the AU, 2007:31). The powers and functions of the PRC should be reviewed and properly streamlined so that they do not overlap into other institutional organs causing bottlenecks, inefficiencies, and stagnation in the implementation of policies.

The Panel also suggested that the PRC's oversight functions should be properly demarcated and conducted by the Advisory Sub-Committee on Administrative, Budgetary and Financial Matters, whose members would ideally be seconded from the ministries of finance (Audit of the AU, 2007:38). The institutional professionalisation and technocratic best practices should be appropriately allotted, which would enhance transparency and accountability. It was thought that this would engender a managerial and systematic performance that was oriented to measurable outcomes in line with the Pan-African vision of unity and integration, and the member states should be posted to head their own missions. In pursuit of institutional excellence, the Panel also advised that the heads of missions should personally attend the PRC's meetings, as they are endowed with political authority and decision-making powers.

Furthermore, they should assume full control and personal responsibility for AU matters and refrain from delegating their core duties and functions to other personnel, as this could result in bottlenecks and stagnation (Audit of the AU, 2007: 38). The Chair of the Commission, as the Chief Executive and Accounting Officer, should effectively uphold the chain of command and its functionality. In this regard, the STCs should be transformed into a Council of Ministers, some of whom may establish their own ad hoc technical preparatory committees, within the Chair's remit. It could be argued that this approach is based on professional performance, with a chain of command empowered to address the key result areas of unity and integration (Audit of the AU, 2007: 41).

The election of the Commissioners should focus more on core competencies. Each region should provide at least two, but preferably more candidates for the election. The election of the Commissioners should be de-linked from the portfolios that they will occupy. The portfolios of the departments should be rationalised and restructured by the Chair of the Commission in consultation with the Assembly and in accordance with the agreed chain of command to effect the strategies and priorities of the AU. The Secretary of the Commission should also be the head of the AUC staff and be responsible for interdepartmental and directorate coordination. Mandatory monthly meetings of the Commissioners should be chaired by the Chair and serviced by the Secretary of the Commission, who should prepare and circulate the minutes of the meetings in the working languages of the AU. The Secretary of the Commission should monitor the submission of mission reports and ensure that the Chair is regularly briefed and updated. A shared intranet system should be established for the exchange of non-public Commission documents and departmental folders for plans, budgets, and progress reports (Audit of the AU, 2007:75).

The Office of the Secretary to the Commission should be strengthened in terms of human resources and logistics to deliver efficiently and effectively, and to enable it to meet the new responsibilities assigned to it. The Council should further take a decision that in cases of failure to fulfil quotas allocated to specific member states, these member states should be duly informed through their representative mission at the AU in Addis Ababa.

The Gender Mainstreaming Strategic Plan should be finalised, disseminated, and implemented in all member states and the Commission. A programme to ensure Gender mainstreaming in all activities of the AU should be developed (Audit of the AU, 2007:56). The working languages of the Commission should be English and French, and a unit in the office of the Chair of the Commission should be established to liaise with the Chair of the Assembly.

Overall, the delineation of the chain of command in the AUC in this regard is essential. It will help to avoid the duplication of roles and overlapping spheres of authority, institutional ineffectiveness, and stagnation. On assuming the position of the Chair of the Assembly, the concerned member state should establish a corresponding focal point in the office of the head of state or government to coordinate with the AUC. The AUC, as the lifeblood of the AU, should be appropriately strengthened to serve as a secretariat of the PRC. As recommended by the Panel, the future management and administrative development plans should be internally driven on an inclusive and participatory basis.

A policy of information disclosure should be prepared in line with international best practice. Draft agendas and supporting documents, including the Commission Chair's report on activities, should be publicised on the AU website for summits and other meetings as soon as they are distributed to member states. The Citizens and Diaspora Organisation Directorate (CIDO) should continue to improve and strengthen its role as the Secretariat for ECOSOCC (Audit of the AU, 2007:92–93). The department should be strengthened in the areas of budgeting and staffing, thus enhancing competent human resources. A professionalised, competent, and institutionally structured AUC, after consultation, should comprehensively and authoritatively exercise its mandate. The AUC should take the lead in coordinating between African member states and the international world. It should also represent Africa in the global policy arena. This would entail member states leading African groups in negotiations, to work with the decisions of the Assembly and thereby uphold the collective interests of Africa.

The PAP should establish policy guidelines on its relationship with the other organs of the AU, in agreement with the other organs and the AU, and with approval from the Assembly (Audit of the AU, 2007:8).

The African Court of Justice should be established with the competence to function as the African Court of Appeal, and it should be accepted by all (Audit of the AU, 2007: 87–88). The AUC should establish a register for CSOs and professional associations based on the ECOSOCC statutes' criteria. The register should be updated periodically to serve as a database for the ECOSOCC in real-time, given the asymmetries of global change, which have an impact on the political economy of Africa.

The Peace and Security Department (PSOD) should be strengthened in respect of the personnel and operational personnel (Audit of the AU, 2007:107–108) and the Framework for Post-Conflict and Reconstruction and Development should be implemented. The PSC, in concert with the AUC should speedily and urgently implement the AU-UN Ten-Year Capacity-Building Programme (10YCBP) (Audit of the AU, 2007: 107–108). To improve the prospects for the 'African solutions to African problems' doctrine, African countries should contribute – substantially – to AU peace operations, thus underscoring the intent to cement Africa's ownership. The status of the Joint AU-UNECA-AfDB Secretariat should be enhanced to accelerate the integration process (Audit of the AU, 2007:112). The Assembly should adhere to its decision AU/Dec.112(VII), which recognises only eight RECs. In turn, the RECs should fast-track the creation of an African Common Market (Audit of the AU, 2007:137–138).

The NEPAD should be proactive in establishing processes for fast-tracking the integration of Africa (Audit of the AU, 2007:144) and the APRM process should be fully joined and supported by all member states (Audit of the AU, 2007). The ad hoc committee should include representatives of the Association of African Central Banks (AACB), the Commission, RECs, UNECA, and AfDB. It should submit a roadmap of the establishment of these institutions within a timeframe of up to three months.

However, to advance this extensive list of High-level Panel recommendations will add to the AU's already daunting challenges. Nonetheless, it is still incumbent on the AU and necessary to be comprehensively expedited as a historical imperative. It would herald the AU's 21st-century agency in a complex maze of global asymmetries and challenges. The subsequent institutional assessments and audits, which have been undertaken and are described in the following section, demonstrate a refined set of strategic and manageable continental goals.

3.2.4 An Analysis

The neo-functionalist nature of the AU is reflected in its key objectives (Article 3 of the Constitutive Act), which aim to: achieve greater unity and solidarity among African countries and the peoples of Africa; defend sovereignty, territorial integrity and independence of member states; accelerate the political and socio-economic integration of the continent; promote and defend African common positions on issues of interest to the continent and its people; promote peace, security and stability on the continent; promote democratic principles and institutions, popular participation and good governance; and promote and protect human and peoples' rights

The deployment of the DTRP/centre-periphery framework (Kvangraven, 2018; Amin, 2014) offers perspectives and explanations of the persistent failure of Africa to realise integration and self-reliance. The binary division of the dominant 'centre' (represented by the Global North countries) and the dominated, subordinated, subjugated 'periphery' (Africa) retains the latter structurally only as a supplier of raw materials. I argue that this is maintained through, amongst other means, IPR in the value chain of all processes of business and economics, and by force if necessary through its powerful military.

Against this backdrop the AU still faces several daunting challenges, including the stalemate over the Western Sahara question; seemingly intractable conflicts in the DRC, Darfur, and Somalia; a longstanding unresolved border dispute between Ethiopia and Eritrea that could erupt into another full-blown war; agile militia and rebel movements in the Niger delta and in the Uganda-DRC-Sudan-CAR-Chad region; piracy off the Somali coast and the Gulf of Guinea; the re-emergence of coups, transboundary global terrorism, and non-territorial climate challenges that threatens to spread throughout the Africa.

The AU was established as a neo-functionalist organisation, as the preamble of its Constitutive Act acknowledges, noting that "the scourge of conflicts in Africa constitutes a major impediment to the socio-economic development of the continent and of the need to promote peace, security and stability as a prerequisite for the implementation of our development and integration agenda." From 2004, it showed demonstratable agency in PKOs that recorded a modicum of improved peace and security but since 2021 there has been a re-emergence of coups, global terrorism, transboundary organised crime, and instability, which has overwhelmed the ability of the AU to maintain peace and security.

Although the AU borrowed the OAU's principles of sovereignty and non-interference in the internal affairs of member states, it also adopted a radical principle of intervention in failed and failing states on request. However, as explained later, this 'right to intervene' principle has largely been ineffective for several reasons, including a lack of political will. Additionally, subscription to the principle of territorial integrity and respect for colonial-era boundaries contradicts the objective of 'political and socio-economic integration of the continent.' The report of the High-level Panel of the Audit of the African Union (referred to hereafter as the Audit Report) aptly points out that the Constitutive Act "does not specify what steps need to be taken to accelerate the political and economic integration of Africa." The Audit Report further notes that if political integration is to be pursued, then "the ceding of sovereignty (is) inevitable."

These new ideas forced many authoritarian and dictatorial rulers on the continent to adopt political pluralism. Accompanying this trend of political pluralism was an effort to redefine Africa's identity through Thabo Mbeki's 'African Renaissance' idea. This movement to reclaim Africa's position in the new world laid the foundation upon which the NEPAD and AU were established. In addition to democracy, the AU and NEPAD embraced other norms such as good governance, the rule of law, and respect for human and people's rights. But other researchers argue that western dictated democracy with its conditionalities is unsuitable for Africa and only serves the 'centre' as a divide-and-rule ruse to maintain its dominance.

The NEPAD was conceptualized as an arrangement that would implement these norms through a monitoring mechanism, which would provide incentives for increased foreign investment and assistance. The DTRP/centre-periphery framework continuously warned that these were mere pledges and true foreign investment has never been realised. Other mechanisms such as the Charter on Democracy and the anti-corruption convention were later adopted to complement the Constitutive Act and NEPAD's APRM.

Unfortunately, the evolution of the AU has mainly been based on its neo-functional institutions rather than on the ideal of Pan-Africanism and norms such as democracy, good governance, rule of law, and respect for human rights as proffered by Aniche (2020). Halfway into its first decade of existence, the AU's vision has become blurred and its objectives remain largely unmet. In 2007, the AU embarked on yet another ambitious project of establishing a 'union government' even before the organisation had been fully established and was running efficiently. The establishment of a High-level Panel to audit the AU was based on the argument that a precondition for the formation of such a government must be "the reform and strengthening and efficient functioning of its various organs and institutions." The resulting Audit Report cautioned that unless these bodies "are dynamic, efficient and effective, they will constitute the Achilles heel of political and economic integration.

The AU is heavily dependent on external support to survive, as is explained by the DTRP/centre-periphery framework. Therefore, it remains weak because of financial dependence and cannot fulfil its objectives of integration and self-reliance.

In 1993, the OAU adopted the Cairo Declaration. A mechanism for conflict prevention, management, and resolution was later inherited by the AU and transformed into the PSC within the APSA. The AU has demonstrated agency in conflict resolution and peacebuilding in its PSOs in Burundi, Darfur, and Somalia. All of its PSOs are heavily foreign donor-dependent, which compromises its principle of independence and its resolution of 'African solutions to African problems'. Its track record reflects a mixed bag of successes and near failures, particularly in light of the re-emergence of coups and global terrorism. The AU Mission in Burundi (AMIB) is generally regarded as its most successful PSO. The mission was undertaken when the UN was reluctant to deploy troops to Burundi due to the UN's Brahimi guidelines, which required the deployment of forces only in situations where ceasefires had been signed and all the parties supported the presence of peacekeepers. In this regard, the AU must be complimented for demonstrating initiative and agency to secure peace on its own territory rather than waiting for a reluctant UN.

One of the most notable achievements of the AU is the introduction of the APRM to promote good governance in Africa. Initially, the APRM was conceived as a tool to hold African leaders accountable for the governance of their citizens in return for increased foreign assistance and trade. The process is meant to be voluntary and all-encompassing in the compilation of reports that are subsequently presented to the AU AHSG for evaluation. I argue that the voluntary nature of the APRM encourages free-riding and non-compliance because there is no supra-authority to enforce compliance.

Another achievement of the AU in the area of governance is the adoption of the Convention on Preventing and Combating Corruption, after which came the 2002 realisation that this issue costs Africa's development more than $148 billion annually. Antithetical to good governance, corruption significantly contributes to the high levels of poverty, insecurity, and underdevelopment in Africa. Despite the ratification of the anti-corruption convention, the destructive culture of misusing and abusing state resources is still prevalent in Africa. One of the reasons why the AU anti-corruption convention has had little impact in preventing, detecting, punishing, and eradicating corruption in Africa is the complicity of countries of the Global North (centre) that perpetuate and enable corruption with the ruling elite of Africa (periphery) (Amin, 2014).

For its part, the AU has come under constant criticism for not condemning grave violations of human rights and international law in Africa and for disregarding the African Commission on Human and Peoples' Rights (ACHPR) reports on Zimbabwe, Ethiopia, DRCongo, Uganda, and Sudan. It has never taken a strong position against impunity, one of the biggest causes of conflicts in Africa. Although the AU has made a commitment in Articles 3 and 4 of its Constitutive Act to protect human rights and reject impunity, the AHSG has blocked the extradition of Hissen Habré, former Chadian President and dictator, to Belgium to face accusations of torture and massive violations of human rights.

In January 2006, the AU Assembly made a decision that undermined the ACHPR's ability to work impartially by requiring that it first submit its findings on violations of human rights to the member states against whom complaints have been made. This inevitably rendered such reports unacceptable to the Assembly once governments rejected them. The AU Audit Report points out that member states have also placed enormous obstacles on the work of the ACHPR. For example "Some Member States do not grant the ACHPR authorization to undertake missions in their countries even though all Member States have ratified the Charter; the bulk of Member States do not submit their mandatory reports to the ACHPR; certain parties do not comply with the recommendations of the ACHPR; and National Human Rights Institutions do not participate regularly and actively in the ordinary sessions of the ACHPR."

This degrades confidence in the country amongst its citizens and globally as it does not inspire confidence in potential investors for the upholding of the rule of law. The resulting corollary is not a conducive environment to attract both domestic and foreign investors and against this backdrop self-reliance and integration are never attained.

For a strong, functional, and successful Pan-Africanist organisation to be built, it must overcome many daunting challenges. Among these are the AU's institutional incapacity, lack of resources, and a lack of Pan-Africanist ideology and leadership.

Building capacity is one of the largest challenges facing African institutions, from community-based organisations to state and regional organisations. The AU Audit Report strongly recommends that the AU "must grasp the decisive role of institutions in governance" and that these institutions can only "play decisive roles in the destiny of nations" with "good governance and leadership and peoples' participation."

Moreover, "good governance depends on the qualities of the men and women that deal with governance. It is institutions that guarantee good governance." For the AU to effectively deliver its ambitious agenda towards self-reliance and integration, its organs, institutions, and members, must be well governed, and be "untainted by corruption and arbitrariness." I argue that one of the fundamental aspects missing is the transference of sovereignty to a supra-authority to enforce compliance. Further, realising Agenda 2063 for self-reliance requires an abundance of capital that is self-resourced to own the whole process. The continued maintenance of the AU as an intergovernmental institution demonstrates the leadership's lack of interest in seriously pursuing Agenda 2063.

The 2007 AU Audit Report also found that there is a "fundamental lack of a full comprehension of the power, the function, the authority and the full responsibilities of the principal actors." This is because there is no mandated supra-authority with enforceable powers to enforce compliance. As long as member states sovereignty is not compromised and threatened, there is no reason or caveat to take the AU seriously in its programmes. This has resulted in the slow ratification of Protocols, and the timely delivery of assessed contributions.

For the AU to meet its ambitious development and integration agenda, it needs substantial financial resources. The AU has an annual budget of about $130 million. This financing is derived mainly from the following sources: membership contributions based on a formula that allows five countries (Algeria, Egypt, Libya, Nigeria, and South Africa) to contribute 75% of these funds and program funds from the voluntary contributions of member states, CSOs, individuals, the private sector, and foreign donors. Therein lies the challenge, where the greater part of the AU budget is dependent on foreign donors.

This analysis has shown that the AU's inability to run its programmes towards self-reliance and implement its ambitious agenda without external support flies in the face of Article 4(k) of the Constitutive Act that calls for the "promotion of self-reliance Article 4(h) that calls for "non-indifference," and of the much-heralded principle of African solutions for African problems." This lack of Pan-Africanist orientation and leadership results in the perception of the AU as being elitist-owned and driven and the African people remaining estranged and uninvolved in matters of the AU.

3.3   The Review of the 2017 Kagame Report

The Institutional Reform of the AU was adopted during the 27th Ordinary Session of the AHSG held from 17 to 18 July in Kigali, Rwanda 2017. President Paul Kagame of Rwanda supervised the implementation of the reforms. The AU's complex structure comprises many policy organs, technical bodies, and agencies that help to implement its Assembly decisions, but equally results in bottlenecks and inefficiencies, thereby impeding the core business of the AU to a certain degree. The following subsections (3.3.1–3.3.4) will present specific points of the Audit report. Subsequently, an analysis of whether the report had fulfilled its terms of reference is presented in subsection 3.2.4. Additionally, the strengths and weaknesses of the AU will be identified, with proposed remedies for the weaknesses.

3.3.1   Refocusing the African Union's Fragmented Structure and Systems

President Paul Kagame once remarked, "we have a dysfunctional organisation, in which member states see limited value, global partners find little credibility and our citizens have no trust." The breadth of the challenges confronting Africa is widening: modern slavery, conflicts, terrorism, resource contestations, rising inequality and poverty are some of the more notable manifestations of Africa's governance, development, and peace and security challenges. However, the continental body persists in being unfit for purpose, and is predicated on an unprofessional, fragmented, and unwieldy trajectory. This is the context of the decision on the Institutional Reform of the AU, which was adopted during the 27th Ordinary Session of the AHSG held from 17 to 18 July 2017 in Kigali, Rwanda. President Paul Kagame of Rwanda supervised the implementation of the reforms. The AU's complex structure comprises many policy organs, technical bodies, and agencies that help to implement its Assembly decisions, but equally they can result in bottlenecks and inefficiencies, thereby impeding the core business of the AU to a certain degree.

The complex structure of the AU has resulted in the overlapping of the responsibilities of the organs, in particular the AUC and NEPAD. While NEPAD has been incorporated into the AU as a technical implementation body, the programme implementation functions of both organisations have not been streamlined and continue to overlap. The NEPAD focuses on industrialisation and infrastructure, areas that are also inadequately distributed with the AUC, which already oversees political, security, economic, and social affairs. Clearly, coordination and communication between the two organs is disjointed. This management in silos creates bottlenecks and inefficiencies as they compete for the same financial resources.

Both the AUC and NEPAD work with individual countries. This duplication and overlap stagnates effective implementation as it cascades through the RECs and reaches the national level. The AUC and NEPAD have parallel reporting lines into the AU Assembly and the PRC. The Head of NEPAD reports to the NEPAD Heads of State and Government Orientation Committee at the AU Assembly level, but the AUC Chairperson does not report his/ her work directly to the same committee. It could be argued that such a blatant mismatch cannot be resolved only with managerial and technical expertise. An inclusive political mediatory factor is imperative to resolve this crisis, given that clearly different political cultures, outlooks, and national and regional interests are at play.

The Panel of the Wise (PoW) was established under Article 11 of the Constitutive Act and supports the PSC and the Chair of the AUC in optimising the AU's systems to materialise Agenda 2063 effectively. The expertise of the PoW should be leveraged to optimise the AU's delivery systems. This is a consequence of their experiences as 'highly respected African personalities of high integrity and independence who have made outstanding contributions to Africa in the areas of peace, security, and development.' Each member of the Panel is drawn from one of the AU's five regional groups. Failing to revise and streamline the PRC has led to it overextending its area of operation and authority enshrined in the Constitutive Act. The Constitutive Act limits the role of the PRC to that of an advisory organ, 'with the responsibility of preparing the work of the Executive Council and acting on the Executive Council's instructions.'

However, the PRC's Rules of Procedure are counterintuitive because its functions are more extensive. Rule 4, in contradistinction to the Constitutive Act, states that the PRC reviews the AU's "programmes and budget as well as the Commission's administrative, budgetary, and financial matters" (AU, 2018a).

This has resulted in some of the AU Assembly's decisions being delayed in the PRC or even reversed (Lisakafu, 2016:234; Okeke, 2017; Ukeje and Ako, 2017). The clear inference is that rather than "facilitating communication between the AUC and Member states capitals", the PRC interferes in the decision-making process. In the 'Final African Union Reform Combined Report', Kagame remarked that the only way to make the AU 'fit for purpose', was to amend the PRC Rules of Procedure to bring it in line with the mandate provided for it in the Constitutive Act.

This would "facilitate communication between the AU and national capitals, and act as the advisory body to the Executive Council, rather than a supervisory body of the Commission" (Kagame, 2017:9).

The PRC's interference, therefore, goes against the Constitutive Act, as its decision-making approach impedes other organs from expediting their agency in the division of labour processes to materialise the vision of the AU. The Rules of Procedure should be correctly located as a derivative and subset of the Constitutive Act. Preventive diplomacy should prevail in this regard, with the political assistance of the PoW (among others) to correct this anomaly. For the AU to successfully fulfil its continental vision of unity, integration, and global multilateralism, it should first and foremost organise itself by aligning the AU's institutions to deliver its chosen priorities. This section assesses the AU's priorities and its effectiveness in implementing its current and future mandates. Its recommendations build on past reports, most notably the AU's Audit Review 2007, which constituted an in-depth examination of the AU's Constitutive Act and assessed the mandates and execution of statutory functions of all AU organs. It also provided recommendations on how to reform the organs, mandates, and key staff roles.

There has been some progress but most of the recommendations remain unimplemented. In 2013, the AU's Agenda 2063 set out seven aspirations for the next fifty years. These aspirations were divided into 39 priority areas under 20 goals to be accomplished through 12 flagship projects. The First Ten-Year Implementation Plan for Agenda 2063 was published in 2015 and determined the priorities that the AU would pursue for the first 10 years of the report being published. To prepare the AU for its agenda, supporting studies were conducted on its operations, working methods, and organisational structure. In this regard 'The Comparative Study on the Working Methods of the AU and other similar International and multilateral organisations' benchmarked the AU's operations against those of similar institutions. It identified gaps and recommended a review of the AU's legal instruments, institutional architecture, working methods, decision-making, monitoring, evaluation processes, and sources of funding.

It also recommended that the AU review its Constitutive Act to confirm that its organs delivered the integration agenda, clarified their roles and responsibilities, and revised its leadership appointment and resource allocation process.

To date, many of the recommendations have not been implemented due to poor stakeholder buy-in at all levels, insufficient monitoring and evaluation, and critically the deficit of a structured implementation process within the AU. Some of these issues include:

·   the AU is highly fragmented with too many focus areas;
·   the AU's dense, complex structure and a deficit of managerial capacity that continually engenders inefficient systems and working methods, poor decision-making, and a lack of transparency, participation, and accountability;
·   the external donor dependency of the AU, which renders it financially dependent and unsustainable, fundamentally contradicting its ideal of 'African solutions to African problems';

- the limited coordination between the AU and the RECs, thereby being unable to realise supranational institutional authority to effect workable principles of norm subsidiarity.

In line with the aforementioned reviews, several reform recommendations have been made to build a more relevant, efficient, and effective AU. The AU's agenda should be focused on key priorities with a continental scope. There should be fewer and thus a more manageable number of priority areas. This will enhance the identification of comparative advantages and enable the division of labour and roles between the AUC/AfCFTA/AGA/APSA/APRM/RECs and regional mechanisms (RM's), the member states, and continental institutions.

The AU's institutions should be realigned to deliver against the identified priorities. An audit of the AU's bureaucratic bottlenecks and inefficiencies should be performed. The AUC's structures and capabilities should be resized. The structure of key organs and institutions should be regularly reviewed along with their mandates.

These reforms are imperative to keep the structure of key organs and institutions adaptable, efficient, and effective within international agreements and partners. The AU should enhance its connection with its citizens by promoting continental global goods and services, exemplified by initiatives such as the SAATM, the AU Protocol to the Treaty establishing the AEC concerning FMP, and the Rights of Residence and Right of Establishment. Additionally, the AfCFTA, adopted and ratified in 2019, will bring about welfare gains to the citizenry only if it is effectively implemented.

Both CSOs and other non-state actors need to take ownership of horizontal, bottom-up activism to robustly and urgently work towards achieving the aims and goals of Agenda 2063. The AU must ensure merit-based and optimal management performance of the AU at both political and operational levels.

Regarding political reform, the working methods of the AU Summits must be reconsidered to determine the appropriate African representation at Partnership Summits. Ceding of certain aspects of sovereignty to a continental supra-authority will enable the enforcement of sanctions mechanisms. This is imperative for greater institutional integration and reinforces legitimacy. Furthermore, for the continuity of policy and operations, a troika of the outgoing, current, and incoming AU chairpersons should be established. Regarding the operational management of the AUC, it is essential to implement a merit-based competitive, and transparent recruitment and selection process for the key roles within the Commission, such as the Commission Chair, Commission Deputy Chair, and the rest of the Commissioners.

It is necessary to reframe the role of the Deputy Chair and change the titles of the Chair and Deputy Chair to be more and specifically reflective of their job descriptions and authority without any overlap and duplication of power and duties. To mitigate the brain-drain of the high staff turnover at the AUC, an intermittent review of the structure, staffing needs, and conditions of service of the AUC must match the best practices adopted in its peer organisations, such as the UN and WTO.

The AU should be financed sustainably with the full ownership of the member states and the Kigali Financing Decision should be implemented with complementary measures. This should be based on an enforcement principle of the AUMS 'obligation to pay' their assessed contributions based on a periodically agreed upwardly revised Scale of Assessment. A structured high-level supervision arrangement for the AU reform process should be established, with an attendant unit within the AUC to drive the implementation of reforms within specified timeframes for key result areas. This should be a binding mechanism supported by sanctions for non-compliance.

3.3.2 The African Union's Financial Reforms

Kasaija (2019:77-91) explains that the AU hitherto is largely donor dependent and this renders its mantra of 'African solutions for African problems' hollow. By extension, its integration agenda is externally determined and controlled. The UNECA made a similar observation that Africa's integration was unsustainably donor-dependent, which 'was inimical for the Continent's integration agenda.' In 2014, the AU's budget was US$308 000 000 and more than 50% was funded by foreign donors. In 2015, it rose by 30% to US$393 000 000, 63% of which was funded by foreign donors. In 2016 donors contributed 60% of the US$417 000 000 budget. In 2017, member states contributed 26% of the US$439 000 000 budget and donors contributed 74%. From 2018 to 2022, with the exclusion of PSOs, the AU budget has decreased by 30% from US$529 million to US$372 million. The operating budget decreased by 16.4% from US$195 million to US$176 million. The program budget decreased by 41% from US$333million to US$195million (AfDB, 2022).

The AU's programmes, inclusive of peacekeeping, health, and education, are 97% donor-dependent. Donor dependency goes against self-reliance as enshrined in the Constitutive Act, presenting a challenge to the establishment of consistent and sustainable projects. At the AU summit in June 2015 (Johannesburg, South Africa), a proposal was adopted to finance 100% of the AU's operating budget, 75% of the programme budget, and 25% of the PSO budget. Subsequently, at the Kigali Summit in 2016, the AU leaders agreed on a 0.2% levy on imports from outside Africa (Kasaija, 2019:77-91).

This will initially raise US$325 million from the five regions of Africa and will be used to finance the AU's operational programmes and PSO budget. Member states will automatically pay the amounts collected from the levy into an account opened in the name of the AU within the Central Bank of each member state for transmission to the AU headquarters per the assessed contributions. In addition to the 2016 Kigali Summit, in January 2016, Dr Donald Kaberuka former president of the African Development Bank (AfDB) was appointed as the High Representative for the AU Peace Fund, and was tasked to underwrite predictable and flexible funding mechanisms to support AU led peace operations (Kasaija, 2019:77-91).

With the adoption of the 0.2% levy, a total of US$400 million was envisaged by 2020. Dr Donald Kaberuka's proposals were adopted by the 29th Assembly held in Addis Ababa in July 2017 but donor dependency still persists. For example, the total budget for 2018, two years after the 2016 Kigali Summit, was US$769 381 891, with member states contributing US$318 276 795 (41%) as assessed contributions, while US$451 105 099 (59%) was raised from international partners. Kasaija (2019: 77-91) and Engel (2015) argued that AUMS pay their assessed contributions throughout the year making it difficult for the organisation to budget properly as the amounts contributed are rather small.

The consequences of member states failing to timeously honour their financial commitments have contributed to the ineffectiveness of the AU. Although the aforementioned 0.2% levy has been successfully operationalised with some member states, uncertainties still abound with others. Primarily, this is an issue in developing domestic legislation to administer the new tax regime as others enjoy free riding (Kasaija, 2019:77-91 and Kagire, 2017). The Institute of Security Studies (2017) and Kasaija (2019:77) warn of pervasive corruption in administrative processes and NTBs that continue to intermittently impede the effectiveness and efficiency of achieving the African Union's self-reliance in this context. As the AU recognises eight official RECs, it still has several integration arrangements that result in overlaps, which makes it unaffordable for all member states to commit to the levy.

3.3.3 The Implementation of the New Financial Proposals

The Committee of Ten Finance Ministers was a body established to oversee the implementation of the new funding mechanisms for bolstering self-reliance in funding (Kasaija, 2019:77-91). At the end of May 2017, Dr Donald Kaberuka reported to the AU's PSC that 14 member states had made contributions to the AU Peace Fund (Kasaija, 2019: 77-91). As of 2024, a total of US$327 million had been collected for the AU Peace Fund (AU Peace Fund Secretariat, 2024). By January 2018, 21 of the 55 AUMS had moved to implement the 0.2% levy. Several AUMS have passed legislation establishing the levy on imported goods, including Rwanda, Cameroon, Chad, Ethiopia, Ghana, Kenya, Senegal, Morocco, Gabon, Gambia, Mauritius, and the Seychelles. The collection of the levy has started and the funds are being deposited into the central bank.

This demonstrates the AU's agency and the seriousness with which it takes the purpose of materialising its integration objectives. However, the 28th AU Assembly, "expressed concern that some member countries were slow to nationally domesticate its laws in order to effect the collection of the levy."

The commitment to the collection of these levies also demonstrates the maturing of the AU's institutional monitoring and evaluative mechanisms. They are now able to statistically identify gaps and non-contributions by other member states to effect remedial solutions. For example, although corruption is pervasive in several African countries (as indicated by Transparency International), foreign MNCs are also involved.

Their financially engineered transactions engender the perennial malaise of illicit financial flows (IPSS, 2018:103). Checks and balances are in place in the AU's organs to ensure the payment of the levy and the strengthening of financial and structural processes and systems to mitigate corruption and illicit financial flows. Of course, there will be short-term costs and pain to some poorer member states in the form of increased prices of imports but arguably these will be outweighed by the medium to long-term, benefits of an AU that is self-financing. The institutionalisation of the levy has raised concerns from some non-African countries, such as Japan and America. They have argued that the levy "is not compatible with WTO rules and obligations, is discriminatory in nature and a violation of the MFN principle."

In the preamble to the WTO Agreement, a relevant extract from the objectives for its establishment states the following:

"Recognizing further that there is need for positive efforts designed to ensure that developing countries, and especially the least developed among them, secure a share in the growth in international trade commensurate with the needs of their economic development. The AU's attempt to achieve self-reliance and independence is important to Africa as a whole. For as long as the AU is dependent on donor funding for its basic operations, it will not be able to make objective decisions to the benefit of Africa without fear of losing the funding."

Hence, it is imperative for the AU to pursue its objectives through self-reliance, ensuring that the strategies employed to attain self-reliance are WTO-compatible. To address this need for self-reliance, the AU proposed a self-financing mechanism (SFM) in the form of a 0.2% levy on all eligible goods imported into the territory of the AU. The SFM in its current form can be considered to be WTO-incompatible. The AU needs to consider actions to make the SFM compatible with the WTO rules and regulations, and therefore avoid any disputes that might arise.

The current WTO-incompatible status of the SFM could severely undermine the intention of the AU to become self-reliant. Even though the SFM might not have been officially challenged by a WTO member yet, it is better to be compliant with the WTO rules and regulations than to trust in the goodwill of the other WTO members. The SFM is, in the authors' view, a significant step towards the pursuit of independence and self-reliance and ultimately the greater good of Africa.

With reference to the opening quotation, the authors conclude their paper with the following statement, "Independence cannot be achieved without a significant measure of self-reliance and this independence cannot be conferred by anyone. It can be developed only from within those who seek it." This is very much the scenario in which the AU finds itself. Bravery and technical acumen are required from the AU's leadership to bridge the gap between the AU's independence and the technical requirements of the WTO.

The SFM of the 0.2% levy imposed by the AU is definitely a step in the direction of achieving the goals as set out by the AU in respect of self-reliance and economic growth. In its current form, the SFM may not be WTO-compatible, giving rise to the possibility of disputes being filed against AU/WTO members. However, the GATT 1994 provides for exceptions to the general rules that can be used by the AU as a means to defend the SFM and render it WTO-compatible. All the AUMS are either developing countries or LDCs in terms of the WTO classifications.

These classifications of the AUMS allow for certain exceptions to the WTO rules. As previously indicated, the COVID-19 pandemic has highlighted the need to be financially self-reliant and an SFM as envisioned by the AU that is WTO-compatible will significantly assist the AU in achieving that objective. As of 20 December 2018, 25 of the 55 AUMS were at various stages of SFM implementation. Of the 25 AUMS, 16 have implemented the SFM and except for two the remaining 14 AUMS fully or partially paid their 2018 contributions to the AU through the SFM. Currently, a further six AUMS are in the process of domesticating the Kigali Decision (Adams, 2018). Furthermore, Adams (2018) and Apiko and Aggad (2017) argue that based on the application of the relevant WTO rules and principles before considering the operation of the Enabling Clause, it would appear that the SFM in its current form is WTO-incompatible from both the MFN principle and mega-regional trade agreement (MRTA) perspective because Articles I and XXIV of the GATT 1994 respectively are not being adhered to. However, considering the Enabling Clause and its consequential effects on the MFN principle and MRTA, special and differential treatment can be sought for the SFM, given the WTO's general classification of the AUMS.

The possible corrective actions can be grouped into temporary short-term and permanent long-term suggestions, considering any possible future reclassification of any AUMS status as developed countries. Most of the AUMS are either developing countries or LDCs in terms of the WTO classifications and the preamble to the WTO Agreement recognises the responsibility to try to raise their standard of living.

However, it has been noted that no application for a special waiver has been sought to activate the Enabling Clause for developing countries or LDCs. An application under the provision of paragraph (2)(a) of the Enabling Clause for the AU's SFM to be WTO-compatible would be a short-term solution. This is because other WTO Members can apply to the WTO for the classification of developing country or LDC to be changed to developed countries, which would render the provisions of the Enabling Clause inapplicable.

As a long-term suggestion to the SFM's possible WTO incompatibility, the AU should apply to the WTO to have the AfCFTA Agreement registered as an FTA in terms of Article XXIV of the GATT 1994. If successfully registered, the AUMS would have the flexibility to apply varying rates among themselves, as necessary, while also being able to levy charges on charge WTO members who are not part of the FTA. The successful registration of the AfCFTA Agreement as an FTA would fundamentally allow the AUMS to implement the AUs SFM without contravening the rules and regulations of the WTO anti-discrimination principles. As a temporary short-term measure, the AU should apply to the WTO for the AfCFTA Agreement to be registered as an RTA under the non-restrictive requirements of the Enabling Clause, which would allow for the circumvention of the MFN principle in terms of Article XXIV of the GATT 1994. By having the AfCFTA Agreement registered as an RTA under the Enabling Clause, the AUMS would be able to eliminate trade barriers within the FTA group and still implement the SFM, which would be considered WTO-compatible.

The support for the AfCFTA Agreement was echoed by Deputy Director-General Alan Wolff of the WTO in a speech delivered at Addis Ababa University on 11 February 2020, in which he congratulated the African leaders on the signing of the AfCFTA Agreement and considered it a significant step towards achieving the SDG of peace and prosperity in Africa.

The long-term problem that could ultimately affect the registration of the AfCFTA Agreement as an FTA under the Enabling Clause is that other WTO members can apply to the WTO for some of the AUMS' classifications to be changed from developing countries or LDCs.

Therefore, as a permanent long-term suggestion, it is imperative that the AU work towards meeting the requirements of Article XXIV of the GATT 1994 to have the AfCFTA Agreement registered as an FTA with the WTO without the provisions of the Enabling Clause. This should be a priority whilst the AUMS are generally all classified as developing or LDCs.

In light of the above, the adoption and ratification of the AfCFTA in July 2019 have effectively addressed this issue. However, the optimisation of comparative advantages, exploitation of economies of scale, harmonisation of standards, and streamlining of RVCs with the imposition of levies "must be applied in a manner that preserves international agreements of member states", as cautioned by the AU Committee of Ten.

3.3.4 Reforming the African Union-Regional Economic Community Nexus

Kasaija (2018:149-182) explains that RECs/RMs are the building blocks of the AU and are recognised in the PSC Protocol as part of the comprehensive security architecture of the AU. This is further underpinned by a memorandum of understanding (MOU) on cooperation in the area of peace and security signed in January 2008 between the AU, RECs, and the coordinating mechanisms of the regional standby brigades of Eastern and North Africa.

This relationship has strengthened the linkages between the AU and the RECs/RMs, improving communication and deploying the principle of subsidiarity in areas of peace and security. Kasaija (2018:148-182) reports that under this principle, sub-regional organisations should be the first responders for problems transcending national borders. Against this backdrop the PSC Protocol designates the AU hierarchically as a superior body to both the RECs/RMs and this has engendered organisational tensions and friction. For example, during the Mali crisis of 2012-13, ECOWAS seized the initiative without the authorisation of the AU and insisted on taking the lead, thus impacting organisational development unfavourably. From the lessons learnt, the PSC in its communiques has reiterated the importance of collaborative synergies in policy execution and implementation.

Centripetal reforms are gradually gaining momentum. The division of labour between the AU and the RECs should take place as a matter of urgency, which would enable the RECs to enforce their role as the building blocks and pillars of integration. Higher degrees of convergence and cohesion are required to ensure that the discussions and consultations are frank. This is especially important in a global milieu made up of asymmetrical and marginalising power relations, in which Agenda 2063 needs to be materialised effectively and creatively.

The reform of the relationship between the AU and RECs is central to the AU's overall reform. For the AU to be fit for purpose, the role, responsibilities, and position of the REC's Secretariats and their Chief Executives should be factored in and made explicitly clear. There is a need to establish a Board of AUC/REC Chief Executives as a management body to ensure joint decision-making, financing/resource mobilisation, implementation, monitoring, evaluation, reporting, and accountability to the policy-making organs of the AU and RECs. There are already institutional reforms underway to enable the functions and mandate of this board. The current AU, RECs, UNECA, AfDB, and African Capacity Building Foundation (ACBF) Chief Executives' coordination meeting is being upgraded to a statutory Joint Management body. This will ensure the institutionalisation and sustainability of the AU and RECs with clear lines of authority and responsibilities to avoid duplication, overlaps, and stagnation.

In line with the pronouncement of the AUC Chair at the AU Executive Council on 25 January 2018, it was recommended to enhance and reinforce the AU Liaison offices to the RECs and vice versa, transforming them into fully operational permanent Representative Offices. This will reflect the enhanced, more robust, and higher level of responsibilities within the reformed AU/RECs nexus. Invariably, further streamlining and harmonisation are ongoing for the proposed REC Permanent Representatives to the AU to enable their participation in the AU PRC meeting and activities.

This will result in faster turnaround times in the decision-making and implementation of AU decisions between the AU and RECs. Further enhancement and strengthening of the AU's institutions will demand elevated levels of self-financing, with the new 0.2% import duty being fundamental to the AU's reform. The reformed joint roles and responsibilities of the AU and its RECs will remain inactive unless they are statutorily supported by joint financing and resource mobilisation mechanisms.

(i)   An Analysis of the Kagame Report

The AU relies mainly on two sources of funding: annual contributions of African member states and aid from foreign donors. The latter still makes the largest contribution to the AU budget. This confirms yet again that the DTRP/centre-periphery framework explains why the AU remains unable to become self-reliant in its integration programmes. Therefore, an analysis of the Kagame Report would identify the margins of manoeuvre for reformers and donors to resolve money and governance matters in the broader context of the ongoing institutional reforms of the AU. It deals with a particular group of donors, i.e., those that are at the core of purposefully cooperating to improve the partnership with the AU's operations and its high level of dependency rate on its former colonisers and current main donors, the AU is probably the world's largest and most complex regional partnership configuration.

The AUs organisational processes and systems remain wanting, which impedes transparency and accountability. Following the money trail is therefore a trying task because there is a lack of reliable, comparable, comprehensive, and publicly available data on how much African member states contribute to the AU, what donors exactly provide to whom, what gets spent on-budget, and what remains outside of the AU budget. This may partly explain why the problem of the financing of Africa's regional organisations has not been diagnosed and discussed more widely and more comprehensively. The figures presented by the AU on expenditure, cash flow, and other financial metrics must be taken with a pinch of salt. In July 2018, for the first time the AUC made its external financial audits publicly available from 2014 to 2017. This was a concrete step to improved transparency.

The AU relies on the annual contributions from 55 member countries and support from bilateral and multilateral donors to finance its operational costs, programmes, and PSOs. Each source of funding is problematic in different ways. Although African member states have agreed to resource the AU reliably and predictably since its creation, they only contributed approximately 27% of the spent budget in 2017. Donors, for a variety of reasons and in a variety of ways, have increased their contributions to an ever-increasing volume of projects, programmes, and pan-African organisations. Problems with the funding of the AU result in governance problems with the spending of funds and implementation of projects, but also affect the reliability and volume of future funding.

Unallocated annual 'assessed contributions' from African member states to the AU budget constitute one source of AU funding. These planned contributions are calculated based on three-yearly assessments and are meant to be paid upfront, at the start of each budget year (1 January - 31 December). However, some member states never pay upfront but only throughout the year, while some pay only a fraction of the total or nothing at all (AU 2016B). This impacts on the AU's ability to attain its self-reliance and sustainability.

It is likely that the degree of AU dependence on donors will only diminish slowly. The Global North (centre) who are the main donors have a vested interest in Africa (periphery) from slavery, through colonialism, and present-day neo-colonialism and with their domiciled MNCs in Africa. Given the dependent position of Africa as a supplier of raw materials, it is advisable to caution against overambitious, best-practice reform models. In the past, announcements of comprehensive AU reforms and experiences from the failed efforts to implement them have put reformers and their supporters on the wrong footing. Such experiences confirm the lessons from political economy literature on complex, institutional reforms and the tendency to overload the reform boat. It may be possible that the AU finds the foreign donors' policies of transparency and accountability unacceptably intrusive to the core. It might be best for the foreign donors to take the lead from the AU even though it will impact on AU's attainment of self-reliance.

3.4 Conclusion

This book has used the DTRP/centre-periphery framework to understand why the AU's neo-functionalist framework has not resulted in successful integration and self-reliance and sustainability for Africa. This investigation aligns with the study's objectives, providing thematic exploratory and explanatory perspectives. The related literature and international experiences in regional integration were considered. This enabled a benchmarking of global best practices that are relevant to the AU. The DTRP/centre-periphery nexus problematised the history of international financial systems from 1870 to the present day and determined how it further marginalised Africa. This resulted in the formation of the OAU that engaged the continental, global factors and actors, that inspired the LPA and the present Agenda 2063, which seeks to attain self-reliance and integration within the AEC.

Optimistically, a regional economic integration can be achieved that embraces all 54 AUMS endowed with the human resources of a growing and youthful population of over a billion people. If it succeeds in dismantling all trade barriers and NTBs to intra-African trade, will unlock the continent's immense development potential, boost its trade performance and integration into the global trading system, and reduce the continent's heavy dependence on aid for development. Thus, it has been noted that the achievement of a successful regional integration will require the removal of tariffs, the establishment of a common ROO, the harmonisation and simplification of customs regulations and procedures, and the elimination of NTBs to intra-African trade.

This will lead to significant growth and sustainable development just as the creation of the COMESA FTA led to a six-fold increase in intra-COMESA trade between 2000 and 2010. In summary, some of the benefits, opportunities, potentials, and prospects of regional integration in Africa include larger markets, economic cooperation, and trade facilitation (Okafor and Aniche, 2017).

Regrettably, out of the six stages of accomplishing the goals of Africa integration, the only one that can be said to have been achieved satisfactorily is the creation of regional blocs in regions where such do not yet exist. Other stages have passed their designated period for implementation within the AEC and some of the RECs (e.g., CEN-SAD) was unable to enforce an FTA in 2010.

COMESA was able to enforce an FTA (although all members are yet to participate) but was unable to establish a customs union in the proposed year of 2008, thus was not able to establish a monetary union in 2018 as proposed. The EAC claims to enforce an FTA and a customs union but was unable to meet the target of a single market and monetary union in 2009 and a political union in 2010. The ECCAS claims to have enforced a defence pact but was unable to enforce an FTA and a customs union in the proposed years of 2007 and 2011, respectively. ECOWAS claims to be enforcing visa-free movements and a defence pact but was unable to enforce a customs union in 2007. SADC was unable to enforce an FTA, a customs union, a single market, and a monetary union in the proposed years of 2008, 2010, 2015, and 2016, respectively. Not surprisingly, intra-African trade has consistently remained low approximately averaging 10%.

As problematized by the DTRP/centre-periphery framework, about 80% of imports and exports in African states are destined for markets outside the continent. This is a structural challenge for Africa that stunts its attainment of self-reliance in an integrated Africa. Intra-regional trade in other regions of the world is much higher than in Africa, e.g., the EU is over 60%, North America is 40%, and Asia is over 40%. The efforts of RECs in Africa, although substantial and laudable, have had limited or marginal impacts on intra-African trade.

It has been noted that Africa does not trade with itself because of the differences in trade regimes; restrictive customs procedures; administrative, bureaucratic and technical barriers; limited productive capacity; inadequate trade-related infrastructure, trade finance and trade information; lack of factor market integration; and an inadequate focus on internal market issues. However, it should be noted that Africa's share of global trade in 2010 was very poor at approximately 4%. This could be attributed to the binary division of the 'centre' that subordinates the 'periphery' (Africa) and prevents it from attaining self-reliance (Okafor and Aniche, 2017).

Africa is currently facing several trade-related challenges, such as a low share in world exports and low intra-African trade, poor trade infrastructure and supply-side constraints, lack of export diversification, and tariff barriers and NTBs. The share of Africa's exports among the total world exports is only about 4%. Essentially, African exports are directed outside the continent.

The structure of Africa's exports to the rest of the world reflects a market concentration in primary products to just a few partners, the EU and USA, who received 42.8% and 18.1%, respectively, in 2010. For example, the oil exporting African countries, i.e., Angola, Gabon, Libya, and Nigeria are among the least diversified African countries in terms of exports (Aniche, 2018). Even that exported oil is not refined in Africa, but in the global north (centre).

The production and export structures of most African economies are geared towards primary products, such as minerals, timber, coffee, cocoa, and other raw materials, for which demand is externally oriented. Inadequate infrastructure remains one of the chief obstacles to intra-African trade and investment, and private sector development.

This limits the range of products African countries can trade among themselves. Essentially, intra-African trade is weak, partially due to compromised foundational elements of trade facilitation, such as logistics, infrastructure including transportation, energy, information communication technology (ICT) (Okafor and Aniche, 2017).

Furthermore, multiple memberships has impeded economic integration in two ways. First, directly by generating inconsistencies and incompatibilities, and inhibiting the coordination and harmonisation of activities such as customs unions, free trade, single markets, monetary unions, and a single/common currency. Second, indirectly, by forcing member countries to dissipate scarce human and financial resources in seeking to service different regional communities and implementing differing, contradicting, and conflicting treaties. So far African regionalism has failed as means of collective self-reliance, let alone solving African developmental challenges.

Chapter 4

The African Union Self–Reliance And African Governance Architecture

4.1 Introduction

The DTRP/centre–periphery framework was explained in chapters 2 and 3. It was adopted to assess the AU's attempts at self-reliance through its governance, peace, and security institution initiatives. The AU is comprised of varied organs, such as the African Union Commission (AUC), its secretariat, APSA, and AGA. With the end of the Cold War rivalry between the USA and USSR, new asymmetric and hybrid security challenges emerged globally. Some continue to have an impact on Africa, such as neo-colonialism. The ongoing reforms of the AU and its organs reflect the evolving hybrid and asymmetric threats, and their complex regional and global interconnectedness. Among such threats are terrorism and global terrorist networks; transnational organised crime; the growth of illicit economies; climate change and food insecurity; the depletion of water and other energy resources; and global health threats, such as Ebola and COVID-19 (Gottschalk, 2004:138-158). The merging of both nation–states and external global imperatives have heightened the critical mass of global conflict and contestation (Aning, 2010b; Bond, 2014).

This chapter will broadly contextualise the discussion within the interrelated spheres of politics and security. This will provide a more nuanced and differentiated understanding of what adaptable strategies ought to be designed by the AU and its organs to proactively engage these threats (Aning and Salihu, 2013).

This chapter will also examine the progress of the AU's implementation of shared values by its member states in the following five areas of governance:

· transformational leadership;
· constitutionalism and the rule of law;
· global and multilateral interrelationships of peace, security, and governance;
· the nexus of development and governance.

It does so by providing a comprehensive assessment of the AU's pursuit of self-reliance and sustainability in the area of good governance under the AGA, comprising of the following 12 AU organs and institutions: The African Peer Review Mechanism (APRM); African court on human and people's rights (AfCHPR); African Committee of Experts on the Rights and Welfare of the Child (ACERWC); African Union Advisory Board on Corruption (AUABC); AUC on International Law; AUC; Economic, Social, and Cultural Council (ECOSOCC) ; PAP; PSC; and RECs.

4.2 Assessing the African Union's Pursuit of Good Governance Under the African Governance Architecture

The Constitutive Act established the AGA for its policy implementation. The establishment of the AGA arose from the adoption of the African Charter on Democracy, Elections and Governance (ACDEG) on 30 January 2007. The ACDEG is regarded as the AU's key normative instrument. It promotes and sets standards for good governance on the continent.

Figure 4.1 shows the number of AUMS that have ratified the major instruments for promoting good governance.

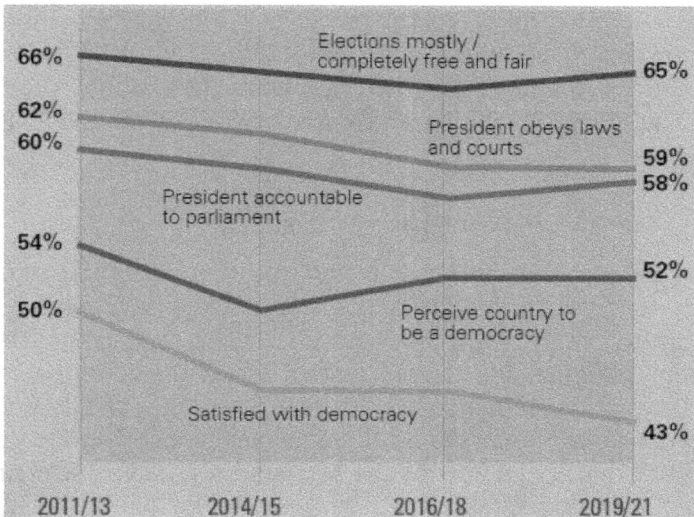

Figure 4.1: The Role of Citizen Polling in Building Democratic
Resilience

Source: (Afrobarometer, 2022)

The AGA platform is the institutional arm of the AU, and it aims
to enhance the ratification, domestication, and implementation
of AU shared governance values, particularly the ACDEG. The
AGA platform functions to facilitate stakeholder dialogue towards
the harmonisation and coordination of instruments, as well as
providing initiatives for promoting good governance, democracy,
the rule of law, socio-economic development, and human rights.

To ensure optimal and effective coherence and coordination,
the AGA is organised into five thematic clusters, which support
the substantive implementation of APSA (to be discussed in the
following section) and the AU's shared values:

·	governance;
·	democracy;
·	human rights and transitional justice;
·	constitutionalism and rule of law; and
·	humanitarian affairs.

The AGA platform is comprised of the following organs and institutions: The APRM; AfCHPR; ACERWC; AfCHPR; AUABC; AUC on International Law; AUC; Economic, Social, and Cultural Council; NEPAD Planning and Coordinating Agency; PAP; PSC; and RECs.

4.2.1 The African Peer Review Mechanism[19]

The APRM was established in 2003 by the AU as its primary institution responsible for facilitating the voluntary assessment of governance in the participating member states. The APRM monitors the member states adherence to, and conformity with, the Declaration on Democracy, Political, Economic, and Corporate Governance as well as the ACDEG. The mandate of the APRM was further expanded in 2017 by the AU Assembly, and its structures were integrated into the AU to oversee the monitoring and evaluation of all key governance areas on the continent.

This included monitoring the implementation of the AU Agenda 2063 and the UN's SDGs. The APRM was subsequently integrated with the APSA as an instrument to enhance its CEWS at the 30th Ordinary Session of the Assembly. This, together with the PoW, would bolster the AU's conflict prevention diplomacy capability. The APRM has become central to the promotion of African shared values and the tracking of the AU's Agenda 2063, as well as the UN's 2030 Agenda for SDGs.

The APRM works within the framework of the Constitutive Act to promote constitutionalism and the rule of law to reinforce democratic shared values in Africa. The Constitutive Act establishes several principles meant to guide member states in their endeavours to realise the objectives of the AU. These principles include the following:

- sovereign equality and interdependence among member states;
- the participation of the African citizenry in the activities of the AU;

---

19   Personal Interview with Professor McBride Nkalumba Head of Monitoring of NEPAD and statistical analyst of APRM. 2022.

- non-interference by member states in the internal affairs of other member states;
- promotion of gender equality; and
- the condemnation and rejection of unconstitutional changes of governments.

However, the principle of non-interference (in a member state) is counterbalanced by the principle of non-indifference, which is defined as:

> "[T]he right of the AU to intervene in a member state pursuant to a decision of the Assembly in respect of grave circumstances, namely: war crimes, genocide, and crimes against humanity, as well as threats to legitimate order to restore peace and stability."

Recognising the importance of governance as being of fundamental importance for Africa, the Sixth Summit of the Heads of State and Government Implementation Committee (HSGIC) of the NEPAD, held on 9 March 2003 in Abuja, Nigeria adopted the MOU on the APRM. The APRM is a mutually agreed instrument voluntarily acceded to by AUMS as an African self-monitoring mechanism. The objectives of the APRM are noted in Article 8 of the APRM MOU, which states that "...the primary purpose of the APRM is to foster the adoption of policies, standards, and practices that lead to political stability, high economic growth, sustainable development, and accelerated sub-regional and continental economic integration through sharing of experiences and reinforcement of successful and best practice, including identifying deficiencies, and assessing the needs for capacity building of participating countries."

The APRM is an open, inclusive, participatory, and broad-based process. Through its transparent processes, it has opened up the political space for citizen participation in policy debates, fostered national dialogue and innovation, demystified complex subjects for the public and increased the advocacy for good governance and better service delivery.

The APRM has achieved much since its inception and has made considerable progress in terms of the number of countries acceding. The achievements include: the roll-out of the structures, establishment of institutions, and deepening of the review process, as well as in the level of active participation and engagement of stakeholders, both nationally and continentally. To date, 33 countries have voluntarily acceded to the APRM. The APRM reviews have also assisted in identifying common challenges and in facilitating the sharing of good policies and practices among its member countries.

4.2.2 The African Court on Human and People's Rights[20]

This is evidence that human rights, democracy, and constitutionalism are gaining currency in Africa. The African Charter on Human and People's Rights is an instrument intended to promote basic human rights on the continent. Table 4.2 further shows the incremental entrenchment of constitutionalism and human rights in the 55 member states of the AU achieved by adopting the African Charter on Human and People's Rights.

A Protocol to the Charter, which was adopted in 1998 in Ouagadougou, Burkina Faso, resulted in the AfCHPR being founded in Arusha, Tanzania. The AfCHPR was established to complement the protective mandate of the Charter, thus further bolstering the African human rights system. The Protocol entered into force on 25 January 2004 and the court was operationalised in 2005.

The Charter was considered by the Panel to be purposed for Africa's socio-economic development and integration. The aims of the Constitutive Act are, among others, to "accelerate the political and economic integration of the Continent (Article 3(c)), and to 'coordinate and harmonise the policies between the existing and future RECs (Article 3(l))."

---

20   Interviews with former African Union officials. 2022-2023.

Table 4.2 African Charter on Human and Peoples Rights (August
2018)

Status	State Party
Up to date: 14	Angola, Botswana, Côte d'Ivoire, Democratic Republic of Congo (DRC), Eritrea, Kenya, Mali, Mauritius, Namibia, Niger, Nigeria, Rwanda, South Africa and Togo.
1 Report overdue: 10	Algeria, Burkina Faso, Djibouti, Ethiopia, Liberia, Malawi, Mozambique, Senegal, Sierra Leone and Uganda.
2 Reports overdue: 3	Gabon, The Sudan, and the Sahrawi Arab Democratic Republic (SADR)
3 Reports overdue: 3	Cameroon, Burundi and Libya.
More than 3 Reports overdue: 18	Benin, Cape Verde, Central African Republic (CAR), Chad, Congo, Ghana, Guinea Republic, Lesotho, Madagascar, Mauritania, Seychelles, Swaziland, Tanzania, The Gambia, Tunisia, Zambia and Zimbabwe.
Never submitted a Report: 5	Comoros, Equatorial Guinea, Guinea Bissau, Sao Tome and Principe, South Sudan and Somalia.

Source: African Commission on Human and Peoples' Rights, 'Information on the African Commission on Human and Peoples' Rights', submitted to the APRM in October 2018.

In the Accra Declaration, the African AHSG agreed to "rationalise and strengthen the RECs, and harmonise their activities towards materialising the African Common Market as enshrined in the 1991 Abuja Treaty that established the AEC." The harmonisation of RECs was seen as imperative because they have progressed at varying levels of integration with diverse institutional frameworks of engagement. The Panel also noted that the focus on peace and human security was an additional institution that was not envisaged under the 1991 Abuja Treaty with all RECs incorporating it except the AMU. The panel noted that this incoherence should be rectified for continental integration.

The diversity of legal regimes has a centrifugal tendency, hindering the courts from achieving the uniformity necessary for fostering a convergence towards the integration of a common African jurisprudence. The multiple legal systems and processes are costly for court users and the RECs, which may explain the default choice of affordable local judicial mechanisms.

An overview of the REC's progress indicated that some had not yet achieved the foundational stage within the envisaged timeframes. Their integration seemed to be proceeding more in pursuit of deadlines than tangible welfare benefits. The multiple memberships of RECs has caused overlap and stultified intra-REC trade with persistent tariff barriers and NTBs, and conflicting and overlapping standards, procedures and obligations.

This incoherent maze of multiple overlapping memberships deliberately satisfies an elite rentier class and its neo-patrimonial network. The uprooting of neo-patrimonial networks threatens the corrupt elite with loss of revenue and prestige, which accounts for the persisting lukewarm support for intra-REC integration. The Panel agreed with the view that this went against the main task of the AEC, which is to promote common sectoral policies ensuring policy harmonisation and coordination.

Furthermore, the Panel opined that without macro and sectoral converging policies within the RECs, harmonisation and coordination between the RECs and AU would be difficult.

The Panel advised that rationalising the RECs would require the AUC to provide the RECs with guidelines. These could be used for guiding and harmonising their sector policies aimed at integrating into continental sector policies. This neo-functional policy would facilitate the harmonisation of macroeconomic and monetary policy convergence through the establishment of continental financial institutions, such as the ACB and AMF. Adequate continental leadership by the AU is imperative to steer the work of RECs, in addition to a monitoring and evaluation committee within the AUC. The mobilisation of self-financing, calculated donor support and technical assistance may yield better results. This may also solve the problem of member states' disinterest in ceding significant aspects of their sovereignty to supranational, regional, and continental entities. The AUC was seen to be able to provide a leadership role on the continent.

From these findings, the Panel concluded that there was no coherence in the evolution of the decisions and treaties of the AU as they related to RECs. The AUC's evaluation committee was unable to bring about effective coherence or harmonisation throughout the continent, despite several attempts. This was because it had no follow-up mechanism with which to monitor implementation.

However, some shortcomings such as the lack of independent funding and technical expertise were noted by the Panel and it subsequently recommended an urgent merging of the Court of Justice of the AU with the AfCHPR. The Panel advised that supranational authority and the decisions of the Court should be followed by member states under the aegis and oversight of the Assembly and the Executive Council. There were concerns over what were seen as the ACHPR's over-dependence on foreign donor assistance. Consequently, it was recommended that its partnership arrangements with non-African actors should be reviewed.

In 2006 the protective mandate of the African Commission was complemented by the African Court on Human and Peoples' Rights (African Court). Significantly, the material jurisdiction of the African Court extends to all 'human rights instrument[s]' ratified by relevant States. The Protocol establishing the African Court has not yet been ratified by all States parties to the African Charter. I argue that this uneven progress and reluctance in the ratification of protocols by member states impacts self-reliance and demonstrates a lack of political will.

Cases may be submitted to the Court directly by individuals and non-governmental organisations (NGOs) or indirectly through the African Commission. If the court finds a violation of a human right, it is empowered to 'make appropriate orders to remedy the violation.' A remedy may be considered 'appropriate' if it is 'adequate, effective, promptly attributed, holistic, and proportional to the gravity of the harm suffered' This includes the payment of 'fair compensation' (whether provided in the form of money, goods, or services) or adequate 'reparation' (restitution or reinstatement).

Other possible remedies the Court may grant, based on the practice of other human rights bodies, include rehabilitation (medical and psychological care and other social services); orders of investigations and prosecutions of perpetrators when human rights violations have occurred in conflict or post-conflict contexts; mandating institutional reforms, repealing discriminatory legislation, and enacting legislation providing for adequate sanctions and guarantees of non-repetition. Judgments and orders of the Court in contentious proceedings are legally binding. Thus, a state's parties are required to "comply with the judgment in any case to which they are parties within the time stipulated by the Court and to guarantee its execution." The execution of judgments is monitored by the Executive Council of the AU on behalf of the AU Assembly.

4.2.3 The African Commission on Human and People's Rights

The Panel noted that the Danish Institute had been assisting the ACHPR with its Strategic Plan, even deploying experts on the premises of the ACHPR. The Panel argued that a strategic plan and its operation are the mandate of the organisation and cannot be outsourced to a foreign interest.

Furthermore, the Canadian NGO, Rights and Democracy, placed three technical advisors at the disposal of the ACHPR in January 2006. Another issue of concern raised by the Panel was the accreditation of non-African human rights NGOs for the attendance of ordinary sessions of the ACHPR. The Panel observed that some foreign NGOs, under the guise of promoting human rights, pursue their own geo-political agendas on the continent, influencing the behaviour of African states.

This drives a wedge among member states and enhances the divide and conquer stratagem. The Panel warned that the ACHPR should be sensitive to this reality in its interaction with non-African actors, lest member states continue to mistrust and question the legitimacy, credibility, and impartiality of the ACHPR's body of work. In terms of organisational improvement and knowledge transference, the Panel recommended the adoption of a non-renewable mandate for the Commissioners of the ACHPR, for one term of office of six years only. The current Charter neither promotes dynamism nor internal competition because it allows Commissioners to renew their tenure without limitation. Greater synergy and convergence of Article 19 of the Protocol establishing the PSC, alongside the enforcement of the recommendations of the ACHPR, will magnify the welfare advantages of the AU's efforts in promoting peace and human security.

The African Commission was established in 1987 following the entry into force of the African Charter in 1986. Its headquarters are based in Banjul, The Gambia. The Commission consists of "eleven members chosen from amongst African personalities of the highest reputation, known for their high morality integrity, impartiality and competence in matters of human and peoples' rights; particular consideration being given to persons having legal experience." Commissioners are nominated by States parties to the African Charter and elected by the AU AHSG but they are required to serve in their personal capacity on a part-time basis.

However, in the past, the independence of some individual commissioners has been questionable on the basis that they were senior civil servants and diplomatic representatives. For example, in 2003 a commissioner from Mauritania was appointed as a cabinet minister shortly after being elected to the Commission.

The Commission meets twice a year in regular sessions for up to two weeks. The functions of the African Commission include the promotion of human rights through research 'on African problems in the field of human and peoples' rights', dissemination of information, and cooperation with 'other African and international institutions concerned with the promotion and protection of human and peoples' rights.'

It is also empowered to 'ensure the protection of human and peoples' rights' under conditions laid down by the African Charter. In addition, the Commission has the mandate to 'interpret' all the provisions of the African Charter at the request of a State party, an institution of the AU or an African Organisation recognised by the AU. It also considers inter-state communications (complaints) by which one member state brings a complaint alleging violations of human rights in another member state. Furthermore, the Commission considers periodic State reports on the domestic implementation of the African Charter and its

Protocol on the Rights of Women followed by the adoption of concluding observations.

The main achievements of the Commission include the development of standards on the various provisions of the African Charter through: (i) decisions on the admissibility of communications mainly concerning the exhaustion of domestic remedies; (ii) decisions on the merits of communications; (iii) adoption of resolutions, principles/guidelines, general comments, model laws, and advisory opinions; (iv) special rapporteurs and working groups to deal with thematic human rights issues; (v) consideration of State reports and conducting on-site visits; and (vi) referral of communications (unimplemented interim measures, serious or massive human rights violations, or the Commission's admissibility and merits findings) to the African Court.

While there is much progress still to be made, the African Commission has contributed greatly to the regional protection of human rights in Africa. The Commission has exposed human rights violations in most authoritarian African States. Through its decisions on communications, it has developed human rights jurisprudence in Africa on several aspects consistent with the jurisprudence of other human rights bodies.

These include jurisprudence on the exhaustion of local remedies, State obligations concerning civil and political rights, economic, social, and cultural rights, as well as group rights, indigenous peoples' rights, and the right to development.

4.2.4 The African Committee of Experts on the Rights and Welfare of the Child

The ACERWC was formed in July 2001, 18 months after the ACRWC came into force. The ACERWC draws its mandate from articles 32–46 of the African Charter on the Rights and Welfare of the Child (ACRWC). It aims to protect and promote the rights enshrined in the ACRWC.

This essentially documents information and encourages national and local institutions to undertake initiatives towards this cause and also makes recommendations to member states. The ACERWC formulates and lays down principles and rules aimed at protecting the rights and welfare of children in Africa (Berger Levrault, 2014:29).

The Committee has among other actions; (i) adopted its Rules of Procedure; (ii) developed guidelines for the preparation of initial reports by member states on the implementation of the ACRWC; (iii) developed a work plan (iv) planned and undertook advocacy missions to selected states to lobby for the ratification and implementation of the ACRWC in Sudan, Burundi, Madagascar, and Namibia; (v) initiated partnerships with civil society organisations (CSOs) as well as other relevant institutions working in the area of children's rights; (vi) strong collaboration with NGOs; (vii) held thematic discussions on key issues and problems adversely affecting the rights and welfare of children namely; children and armed conflict, and the impact of HIV/AIDS; (viii) selected and disseminated annual themes for the celebration of the Day of the African Child; (ix) undertook investigative fact-finding mission in AUMS; (x) developed, together with the AUC, a reporting schedule indicating the dates by which States parties should have submitted their initial reports; (xi) prepared guidelines for considering communications, conducting investigations, and granting observer status; and (xii) coordinated reports by State Parties for the midterm review of the UN declaration on 'Africa Fit for Children', and (xiii) managed to put the ACRWC in the public fora. These achievements, are commendable and represent 'work in progress

The Committee is not self-reliant but is rather heavily dependent on foreign donors, with minimal support from the AU. The Committee is yet to establish a fully functional secretariat. There is a need for a functional secretariat because the Committee is expected to carry out its promotional activities as well as cater for its protective mandate by dealing with communications as well as member states' reports. This can only be achieved when the secretariat provides the necessary support to carry out this mandate. The Committee suffers from a serious lack of resources. and this has hampered the speedy work of the Committee, especially in consideration of state reports and the logistics of the Committee's work. It also affects efforts to follow up on the Committee's resolutions. The unenthusiastic manner and unwillingness of States parties to nominate persons to serve as Committee members is a recurring challenge for the Committee.

The constant resignation of Committee members is worrisome as it is always difficult to obtain sufficient nominations for membership of the Committee and to fill vacant seats when they occur. Financial incapacitation has besieged the work of the Committee. This has halted some lobbying visits for the ratification of the ACRWC, with sponsorship from the AU and other institutional partners not available.

4.2.5 The African Union Advisory Board on Corruption

The AUACB was established by Article 22 (5) (a) of the African Union Convention on Preventing and Combating Corruption (AUCPCC), adopted by the Second Ordinary Session of the Assembly of the AU in Maputo, Mozambique in July 2003. It entered into force on 5 August 2006, 30 days after the deposit of the 15th instrument of ratification. The main mandate of the Board is to "promote and encourage the adoption of measures and actions by States parties to prevent, detect, punish and eradicate corruption and related offences in Africa", and to "submit a report to the Executive Council regularly on progress made by each State Party in complying with the provisions of this Convention."

The Board has also been faced with the daunting challenge of the non-ratification of the AUCPCC by member states. To date, almost 10 years since the adoption of the AUCPCC, only 33 States have ratified the Convention, representing about 60% of the AU's total membership. This low level of ratification would seem to suggest a lack of political will in the fight against corruption in Africa. This has implications for our ethical culture and does not encourage self-reliance. The Board's mandate includes the coordination of activities among AUMS in their fight against corruption. The AU's normative excellence is undoubted. From its inception, the AU was committed to transparency, good governance, and the development of the African continent. This is clear from its objectives and principles.

The objectives of the AU include, among others, the promotion of democratic principles, institutions, popular participation, and good governance as outlined in the Constitutive Act (2000/2001), Article 3 (g) (Heyns and Killander, 2006). Additionally, the AU emphasizes the importance of respecting democratic principles, human rights, the rule of law and good governance (Article 4 (m) and the promotion of social justice to ensure balanced economic development (Article 4 (n). The AUPCC is the major instrument to prevent and combat corruption in the African continent.

This Convention is binding on AUMS that became parties thereto by signing and ratifying it. Finally, the Board remains committed to ensuring the full implementation of the AU Convention on Preventing and Combating Corruption, which entered into force in August 2006 and will fulfil its mandate as defined by the decisions of the Executive Council and the AU AHSG.

States met their obligations under Article 5 (1) which requires them to adopt the legislative and other measures necessary to define the acts provided for in the Convention, such as the establishment and strengthening of anticorruption bodies, enactment of the anticorruption Act and national anticorruption strategies, protection of witness and informants, and the declaration of assets by senior public officers. Furthermore, there is an active role for civil society and media to play, in addition to the confiscation and seizure of instrumentalities and proceeds of corruption.

There are many civic education and awareness programmes, as well as anti-money laundering laws that deal with the laundering of proceeds of corruption. This is in addition to the strengthening of accountability systems such as the Audit, Accountant General, and Parliamentary accounts committees

Challenges still exist because there have been delays in implementing these provisions, exacerbated by a lack of adequate funding. This results in uneven institutional processes with many not being fully independent and adequately resourced. Some are not rooted in the Constitution. Legislative and other measures are in place but actual implementation still needs to be improved. Access to Information is still a challenge for most State Parties, and many aspects of the actual monitoring of implementation is still not streamlined.

4.2.6 The African Union Commission on International Law

The African Union Commission on International Law (AUCIL) was established to codify and ensure the progressive development of international law in the African continent. The rationale behind the decision to establish the AUCIL according to Article 2(1) of its Statute, was for it to function as an independent advisory organ of the AU in accordance with Article 5(2) of the Constitutive Act. The Preamble to the Statute and Article 4 together further disclose the specific objectives of establishing the AUCIL. This includes establishing a body that works on: reviewing treaties; consolidating the principles of international law to remain relevant and update the development of international law, which compliments standardisation in important areas of international law; taking stock of the contribution of the AU, including the RECs, in advancing the codification of international law in Africa; promoting universal values and principles of international law in Africa, taking into consideration the historical and cultural conditions of the continent; promoting the culture of respect for international norms and rules; promoting peaceful settlement of disputes; promoting the value of research and norm diffusion of international law; and generally working to bring about the codification and development of international law in the continent of Africa (Kilangi, 2013:1-27).

The multilateral treaty-making process in the AU, as in other international organisations, is essentially a process of negotiation. Such negotiation may cover a wide range of initiatives and stages, both formal and informal, and may originate from proposals from a variety of actors. For example, formal proposals by individual Member States to elaborate a treaty on a particular subject may originate within the representative organs of an international organisation. Informal contacts and discussions (whether internal or external) can also lead to proposals to elaborate a treaty. Individual member states and external bodies initiating a proposal must submit it through the AUC, for consideration by the appropriate AU organs. Most OAU and AU treaties are initiated by the AUC (or formerly by the OAU General Secretariat), often as a result of a proposal from one or more member states. Following consultations with stakeholders, the AUC drafts the text for the proposed treaty, which it then submits to the AU's PRC, which is a standing committee of AUMS ambassadors accredited by the AU either at the subcommittee of full membership levels. Following debate in the recipient PRC body, the draft text goes to either a meeting of experts or a ministerial meeting where the sectors affected by the subject matter of the proposed treaty are represented. The AU's Executive Council (composed of Member States' ministers responsible for foreign affairs) considers any draft emanating from the experts or ministerial meeting and determines whether to recommend the draft to the Assembly for its formal adoption. If the treaty is adopted by the Assembly, it is usually immediately opened for signature. But in at least one case under the OAU, a meeting of relevant sectorial ministers adopted a treaty that was endorsed by the Council of Ministers without referral to the OAU Assembly.

The establishment of the AUCIL increasingly benefits Africa as international law supports most of its endeavours and engagements. This includes the need to improve relations among states within the continent by promoting peace and security and peaceful resolution of disputes relating to border conflicts in the continent, thus supporting the political and socio-economic integration of the continent. Both IR and international law are deemed necessary in the efforts to improve relations between Africa and the outside world by covering all engagements between Africa and the rest of the world. The experience in these two paradigms, namely the intra-Africa and extra-Africa relationships, has clearly shown a requirement to take both legal and political approaches, with a need to put international law at the forefront.

The establishment of the AUCIL was inspired by the common objectives and principles enshrined in the Constitutive Act, notably Articles 3 and 4 which underscores the importance of accelerating the socio-economic development of the Continent through the promotion of research in all fields. It was also inspired by the common goal to strengthen and consolidate the principles of international law, to agree on common approaches to international legal development, and to continue to work towards maintaining standards in important areas of international law.

In line with Article 4 of the AUCIL Statute, the AUCIL shall have the following specific objectives:

a. To undertake activities relating to the codification and progressive development of international law in the African continent with particular attention given to the laws of the AU as embodied in the treaties of the AU, in the decisions of the policy organs of the AU and in African customary international law arising from the practices of member states;
b. To propose draft framework agreements, model regulations, formulations, and analyses of emerging trends in the practices of member states to facilitate the codification and progressive development of international law;
c. To assist in the revision of existing treaties, assist in the identification of areas in which new treaties are required, and prepare drafts thereof;
d. To conduct studies on legal matters of interest to the AU and its member states; and
e. To encourage the teaching, study, publication, and dissemination of literature on international law, in particular the laws of the AU, to promote acceptance of and respect for the principles of international law, the peaceful resolution of conflicts, respect for the AU, and recourse to its organs, when necessary.

Through the AU, and previously the OAU, African countries have adopted multilateral treaties that have enriched the scope of international law by complementing the corresponding universal instruments with additional rules and principles. At the very least, these contributions signify the emergence of a regional African international law or a public law of Africa. Although often these rules and principles are only applicable among the African States parties to the particular treaties, they can make an impact on future developments in international law outside the African regional context.

African states are also incorporating their regional perspectives into international law instruments, mostly through conventions adopted under the auspices of the UN and by actively participating in the international discourses that lead to normative developments in certain areas of international law.

It is important to pay attention to the counter-narratives and norm-contestations opposing these emerging norms, and to the non-implementation of some of the norms by the norm-creators themselves. This might signify a certain ambivalence or caution. It is possible that the narrow specificity of the treaty rights discussed here, while laudable, will limit their effective implementation.

Moreover, the widespread failure among African states to incorporate these treaty provisions into domestic law creates a disjuncture between what the states have committed to under the treaties (institutional policy) and the practice that follows the adoption of these treaties. It may suggest a lack of opinio juris (i.e., *a belief that an action was carried out as a legal obligation*) in favour of the newly recognized norms.

Nonetheless, these developments, ultimately represent a rise, rather than a decline, of the international rule of law. The selected normative developments from the African multilateral treaty practice discussed here represent a positive contribution to the development of international law.

4.2.7 The African Union Commission[21]

The AUC, 'the nerve centre of the AU architecture', was set up under Article 20 of the Constitutive Act as the Secretariat of the AU. It was composed of a Chair, its Deputies, Commissioners, and other necessary staff. Article 3(2) confers the mandate and functions of the Commission to:

---

21   Personal Interview with Professor Khabele Matlosa former Head of AGA. 2022-2023.

- represent the AU and defend its interests as guided and mandated by the Assembly and the Executive Council;
- initiate proposals for consideration by other organs;
- implement decisions taken by other organs;
- coordinate and monitor the implementation of the decisions of the AU in collaboration with the PRC and report regularly to the Executive Council;
- coordinate common positions of the AU and its member states in international negotiations;
- prepare the AU's programme and budget for approval by its policy organs.

It was the Panel's view that the statutes vest clear powers, authority, and functions in the Commission to act not only as the Secretariat of the AU but to also provide the leadership and representation *of* the AU, monitoring and implementing the decisions taken by the policy organs. However, according to the Panel, the AUC was handicapped at three levels. First, the Panel members found that there was a lack of clarity in the setup of the Commission's leadership. There was a disjuncture, mismatch, and uncertainty over the Commission's role in policy-making versus policy execution and management. The Panel advised that this confusion should be addressed. Second, the Commission's activities were seen by the Panel to have been spread too widely, and thus its effectiveness was diminished. This in turn was seen to have harmed its financial and human resource base too much to realise returns on its investments. Third, the management needs of the Commission were viewed as critical and it was recommended that they should be urgently and constantly improved.

The relationships between the Commission and the PRC, therefore, needed to be improved, in the same way as the relationships between the Commission and the RECs were seen to require enhancement. The Panel also clearly expressed itself on the micro-policy and micro-management challenges faced by the AU. The election process for the Commission and the election of Commissioners (and other positions) needed attention and the Panel recommended that the 'collegiate culture of the Commission' should be strengthened.

Based on these points, the Panel proposed that the Chair should:

- exercise full authority within the Commission as the Chief Executive Officer and Accounting Officer;
- instigate a compulsory induction for all members and staff of the Commission, which would clearly define the Commission's modus operandi and code of conduct;
- take responsibility for assigning portfolios, and monitoring and managing the performance of the Commissioners;
- rationalise the portfolios of the departments in consultation with the Chair of the Assembly, following the agreed strategies and priorities of the AU.

The Panel also proposed that the tenure of office for elected posts should remain at four years. Furthermore, to avoid problems with the simultaneous election of all members of the Commission, the elections of the Chair and Deputy Chair should take place six months before the election of the Commissioners.

For subsequent elections, the Chair and the Deputy Chair should be elected one year before the election of the Commissioners. It was clear from the Panel's assessment that the Commission, until that point, had been dysfunctional. The overlapping portfolios, lines of responsibility, and limited understanding of their roles had led to false expectations. To counteract these issues, the Panel recommended a general streamlining and harmonising, as well as standardisation across the Commission (African Union, 2007a).

The Panel also considered the management of the Commission's finance and human resources and indicated that it required a complete overhaul. In that context, the Panel strongly recommended the establishment of an AU Staff Commission to be responsible for staff matters. It also proposed that the Council should appoint an African firm of international repute to perform regular audits of the Commission's accounts. Finding predictable and stable sources of funding was identified by the

Panel as crucial, not only for planning purposes but also for reducing its dependency on foreign financing (Ndulu, 2007; Williams, 2016:40-49). This would result in greater certainty and predictability of the planning and financial viability of the AU, making it less dependent on foreign funding.

On the important question of power dynamics related to gender, the Panel emphasised that while the AU had made major strides in mainstreaming gender in its activities, as evidenced by the gender parity found at the Commissioners' level, it expressed its disappointment on the state of gender parity at staff level. There was thus a disjuncture between the AU's stated commitment to gender empowerment at the macro-level, versus its gender empowerment at the institutional level. The Panel, as a result, recommended that the Commission should review its organisational design and culture and make appropriate gender-sensitive modifications.

In addition, the Panel reiterated the need to designate all AU positions as continental roles, irrespective of their region of origin. This was seen to be an important step towards developing a culture of Pan-Africanism within the AU's Commission itself. Any post holder in the AUC, furthermore, should have a "clear vision of Pan-Africanism and a personal mission, as well as total commitment to enabling the acceleration and fast-tracking of political and economic integration" (Oppong, 2010:92-103)

The ACDEG defines the term 'unconstitutional change of government' to mean the illegal means of accessing and maintaining power by:

· a coup d'état;
· the use of mercenaries to replace a democratically elected government;
· armed dissent and rebels replacing a democratically elected government;
· refusal by an incumbent to relinquish power to the winning party or candidate after free and fair elections; and
· amendment or revision of the constitution or the law, which infringes the benchmarks on the implementation of its principles and commitments,

The ACDEG also evaluates member states' compliance. In this regard, the AUC observes the conduct of elections in member states to ensure that the provisions of ACDEG and the Declaration on the Principles of Governing Democratic Elections in Africa are being implemented.

The AUC, therefore, not only observes elections but also intervenes if the relevant laws and standard procedures are being violated. The AU's observation of elections has widened the scope of its preventive diplomacy by encapsulating all stages of elections, namely, pre-voting, voting, and post-voting. This technical process entails issues such as constituency demarcation, voter and candidate registration, and post-election disputes (Aniekwe and Autobi, 2016).

The AU has the right to intervene militarily in its member states in circumstances of war crimes, genocide, and crimes against humanity. I argue that in demonstration of its agency and self-reliance, no matter how limited, to this end, the organisation has carried out PKOs on multiple occasions. African Union PKOs often work in coordination with UN missions.

The AU's efforts have helped avert catastrophes and protected people from violence in Burundi, CAR, Comoros, Darfur, Somalia, South Sudan, Sudan, and Mali. The AU's diplomatic efforts have resulted in success on multiple occasions. For example, in October 2022, the AU organised negotiations in South Africa that resulted in a peace deal between the Ethiopian government and the Tigray Peoples' Liberation Front.

The AU has also acted successfully to protect and promote democracy throughout the continent. For example, when violence broke out in Kenya following the 2007 elections, an AU-led mediation effort contributed to ending the violence and the creation of a coalition government.

Finally, AU health initiatives have achieved considerable results. For example, the African Vaccine Acquisition Task Team, established in 2020, secured over one billion doses of vaccines to be distributed among member states. Initiatives against aids and malaria have also resulted in fewer people being infected across the continent.

4.2.8 The Economic Social and Cultural Council[22]

The ECOSOCC is an advisory organ similar to the PAP, established under Article 5 of the Constitutive Act. It thus enables a voice for the CSOs within the AU institutions and in decision-making processes. The composition of the ECOSOCC is wide and varied, with a diversity of non-state actors, which includes the African Diaspora.

The Panel noted that against the ECOSOCC's struggle to fully operationalise, a practical and more complete evaluation of the ECOSOCC could only be made after the launch of its General Assembly, which was to take place in January 2008.

After its first year of operation, it was possible to realistically examine the adequacy of the organs process and spread of representation, the functioning of the sectoral clusters and the impact of their input on the work of the Commission. The Panel was of the view that more support should be provided to the judicial organs in the discharge of their duties.

It was also recognised that for the AU to deliver on its aspirations, it was important for it to put to use its diverse 'human and institutional resources at the grassroots level.' It was thus imperative to institutionalise the relationships between the various African governments and the different segments of society within the respective African states. Thus, through articles 5 and 22 of the Constitutive Act the ECOSOCC was established. The ECOSOCC provides a platform which the civil society could use to organise themselves and contribute to the workings of the AU. It provides a bridge through which African governments connect with the masses of the people on the ground for the AU to become truly people-owned, people-centred, and people-driven. Presiding over the launch of the First Permanent General Assembly in Dar es Salaam on 9 September 2008, Tanzanian President and then Chairperson of the AU, President Jakaya Mrisho Kikwete, noted in his keynote address that, "with the establishment of

---

22   Mutasa, C. (2008). 'A Critical Appraisal of the African Union-ECOSOCC Civil Society Interface.' In Akokpari, J., Ndinga-Muvumba, A., Murithi, T. (eds.) 'The African Union and Its Institutions.' Fanele. Aukland Park.

ECOSOCC we are creating a people-oriented, people-centred, and people-driven community in the AU, in which all stakeholders are effectively represented." He further added:

> "this event today has its uniqueness and significance in the annals of international organisations. This is the first time that an institution such as the AU that began as an intergovernmental organisation is incorporating non-state actors as full partners in the policy-making process. In, following this path, the AU has gone beyond the mere processes of consultation that other institutions still adhere to. Africa therefore, has given the values of democratization and inclusiveness, a more holistic and enduring meaning and significance."

I argue that the normative excellence of the AU vis a vis the ECOSSOC is not matched by an enabling environment for CSOs to thrive. This monopoly of agency and the lack of division of labour and talent by the AU prevents it from reaching organisational self-reliance and sustainability. Despite numerous commitments by African leaders to allow African CSOs to participate in the affairs of the continent, both at national and continental levels as demonstrated above, the praxis of these leaders on the ground has not been consistent with these pro-CSO participation commitments they have undertaken both at national and supra-national levels. It is therefore necessary to consider the extent of the involvement of CSOs in key issues, such as governance, within the continent.

The involvement of CSOs in the AU is almost meaningless. There is no involvement of CSOs in the key structures of the AU that determine the future of the people of Africa. In terms of the Constitutive Act, it is the AU's vision to establish 'a united and strong Africa', built on partnerships between governments and all segments of civil society.

The African states shun CSOs both within the AU and at the national level. As shown above, not only do African states shun CSOs within the AU, they also undermine their work and their territories through oppressive laws. For example, the funding of

CSOs is capriciously cut or arbitrarily and unjustifiably limited in many African countries. Their registration is purposely delayed or frustrated through intentionally complex bureaucracy. The practices and tendencies of African states clearly show that the political culture and value system of the continent do not currently foster the active- involvement of CSOs in public life, particularly in the areas of democracy and human rights. African leaders are merely paying lip service to the desirability of opening space for CSO participation in the continent's democratisation process. I therefore argue that CSOs must not expect everything to be handed to them on a silver platter, they must persistently fight for their rights.

4.2.9 The Nepad Planning and Coordinating Agency

At its first meeting on 23 October 2001, the AHSG Implementation Committee established the Steering Committee, which was mandated to develop a strategic plan for marketing the NEPAD at national, regional, and international levels (De Waal 2002). The Initial Action Plan of the NEPAD focused on three priority areas, namely, the preconditions for sustainable development (i.e., political, economic, and corporate governance), sectoral priorities (i.e., agriculture and market access, human resource development, infrastructure, and environment), and resource mobilisation.

For its sectoral priorities, NEPAD's Secretariat prepared a Strategic Action Plan for the period of 2004–2007. It consisted of the following:

· the Comprehensive African Agriculture Development Programme;
· the Short-Term Action Plan for continental infrastructure development;
· the science and technology consolidated action plan;
· the environment plan;
· the AU-NEPAD Health Strategy; and
· the Education Action and Tourism Action Plan

In its report, the Panel confirmed that these plans were being implemented through national governments and RECs. However, as the Panel recognised the active role played by NEPAD, it also advised that it should focus and concentrate its efforts in mobilising domestic resources, particularly from the African Private sector, and thus finance areas of transport infrastructure and energy.

The Panel recommended that the NEPAD should be one of the main instruments of the Commission in the injection of accelerators into the integration process, particularly the development of trans-continental and inter-regional infrastructure and the promotion of multinational companies.

The NEPAD successfully operationalised the APRM. As of December 2007, the Panel confirmed that 25 countries had voluntarily acceded to the APRM, and further encouraged all member states of the AU to follow suit. In addition, countries that have acceded to the APRM were encouraged to take measures to undertake the necessary processes to facilitate their review, as evidenced by Kenya, Rwanda, South Africa, Ghana, and Algeria. Finally, the Panel proposed that after the country reviews had taken place, follow-up actions should be conducted in an all-inclusive and transparent manner.

The Panel also proposed that the AU should endeavour to fully exploit its trilateral group, thereby fully engaging its joint AU-UNECA-AfDB Secretariat to make it more effective in accelerating the integration process.

This should include the publication of a joint annual report to the Assembly on the progress towards continental integration. Such a report should focus on cross-border trade and investment, the degree of the FMP across national and regional borders, the implementation of regional and continental projects, the level of effective supranational authority entrusted by member states to RECs, resource mobilisation efforts at the continental, regional, and national levels and finally the progress made in operationalising the continental financial institutions.

The NEPAD has also made some progress in the area of agriculture. Through the Comprehensive Africa Agriculture Development Programme (CAADP), NEPAD is slowly laying the foundation for greater agricultural productivity and output in

Africa. As a result of the CAADP, African countries are paying more attention to the agriculture sector. For example, eight countries have achieved the 10% target in their budget allocation to agriculture stipulated in the CAADP, and nine countries have achieved the target average annual growth rate of agricultural output of at least 6% (United Nations, 2011b). The NEPAD has also taken measures to develop infrastructure in Africa, which is crucial for agricultural development in the region. For example, the Programme for Infrastructure Development in Africa, launched at the 2010 summit of the AU in Kampala, presents a coherent strategy for the development of regional and continental infrastructure in Africa, thereby laying the foundation for higher agricultural productivity and output in the region.

Another achievement of the NEPAD is that it has compelled the UN to take action to enhance coherence in the provision of support to Africa. Since the endorsement of the NEPAD in UNGA resolution 57/7 of 4 November 2002, it has become widely accepted as the framework and mechanism through which the UN and the international community should support Africa's development efforts.

The UN has also established the Regional Consultation Mechanism (RCM), thereby enhancing coherence as well as coordination in the provision of support to Africa (Economic Commission for Africa, 2012).

It should be noted that membership of the RCM is not restricted to UN agencies. In particular, regional Organisations such as the AfDB and the African RECs are now members of the RCM. Despite the progress that has been made so far in the implementation of the programmes and activities of the NEPAD, it is becoming clear that African countries are far from achieving their ultimate goals of eradicating poverty, putting the region on a sustainable development path, and halting the marginalization of the continent in the global economy.

Against this backdrop, the following factors impact the self-reliance of the AU(NEPAD) and its integration programmes: (a) low levels of human and financial resources; (b) capacity constraints; (c) coordination problems between the NEPAD secretariat and the RECs; (d) inadequate involvement or a lack of involvement of important local stakeholders in the process; (e) weak infrastructure; and (f) the absence of quantifiable benchmarks for monitoring and evaluation (Economic Commission for Africa, 2007).

4.2.10 The Pan-African Parliament[23]

The PAP is an important representative body of the AU covered by the audit. The PAP is an advisory body of the AU, established in March 2004 based on Articles 7(c) and 14 of the Abuja Treaty. It is recognised under Article 5 of the Constitutive Act, reporting to the Assembly. Its budget is processed through the AU's policy organs.

According to the Panel's report, it has not performed as expected. Like many other AU organs at the time, the PAP found itself in a constant financial crisis and there remained confusion about when it could assume a legislative function and role.

During 2007, the PAP concluded its 8th Ordinary Session in Midrand, South Africa. This session effectively marked the fourth year of PAP's existence since its inauguration in 2004 and, more significantly, it marked the halfway point of PAP's first term. In terms of the Protocol to the Treaty Establishing the African Economic Community relating to the PAP signed in 2001 (PAP Protocol), the AU should evaluate the PAP's performance after the first five years and possibly review the PAP Protocol. Such an evaluation will determine the efficacy and effectiveness of the PAP and its Protocol. Currently, the PAP serves only as a consultative and advisory body, but according to the PAP protocol, it would be transformed or evolve into a full legislature after its first term, or by a date to be determined by member states. Obviously, this puts PAP in limbo because it is not clear exactly when and what will determine whether member states decide to vest PAP with legislative powers.

Given this, the stated vision for PAP remains that of providing a common platform for African peoples and grassroots

---

23   Personal Interview with Professor Garth LePere lecturer at the University of Pretoria former official of the African Union and African Development Bank. 2022.

organisations to be involved in discussions and decision-making regarding the issues facing the continent. Equally important are its stated objectives, which include the requirement to facilitate the process of regional/continental integration, the promotion of peace and security, human rights, democracy, good governance, and accountability, among others. However, several questions arise. Since its establishment in 2004, has PAP operated effectively and efficiently to realise the stated vision and objectives? If not, what challenges and problems has PAP been confronted with, what is the root cause of these issues, and how, if at all, has PAP sought to address them? Is PAP's role and mandate clear enough for it to effectively and efficiently discharge its responsibilities?

Clearly, PAP faces the challenge of demonstrating that it can facilitate continental integration and provide a common platform for African people and their organisations. To date, PAP has not meaningfully and significantly demonstrated its agency to integrate Africa cooperatively or otherwise, so that self-reliance is realised. This is critical in view of the general pessimism and criticism of Africa and its institutions because of their failure to realise their goals and objectives.

From this discussion, it should be apparent that the PAP is confronted with various challenges and obstacles. It has been noted that, given the traditional role of parliaments, PAP does not have a clearly defined role and position within the emerging APSA. As a result, this affects its ability to work and cooperate with other AU organs and structures. There is still an opportunity for innovation for the PAP to become a relevant, effective institution within the AU architecture but this depends primarily on the PAP exploiting the little space it has to its own advantage. In this regard, the PAP should utilise the space created by the various provisions contained in the PAP Protocol, Constitutive Act (Art 5, 17), and the Protocol relating to the PSC (Art 18). The PAP needs to fully engage with other continental institutions, especially AU organs and should request representation or the production of reports from AU officials and AU organs in line with the limited mandate it currently has.

Equally significantly, the body should effectively exercise its oversight function within the limited powers granted to it by various protocols and treaties. Doing so will ensure that the PAP contributes effectively and positively towards the vision and the objectives for which it was established. The PAP must be more visible to the citizens it hopes to serve. Unfortunately, neither the decision taken under the Sirte Declaration nor the processes towards integration of the continent can be reversed or wished away. Rather, the PAP must be given the capacity to carry out its objectives. What is required is the commitment by all member states, including officials of the AU, to practically demonstrate their political will to realise the continental vision.

Chapter 5

African Peace and Security Architecture

5.1 Assessing the African Union's Pursuit of Peace and Security under The African Peace and Security Architecture[24]

In his seminal work, Towards a Pax Africana, Mazrui (1967) offered the earliest analysis of the need for Africans to assume responsibility for the maintenance of peace and security on the continent.

Arguably, the most comprehensive effort towards achieving this ideal was made with the establishment of the APSA in the context of the transformation of the OAU to the AU (Mazrui, 1967; Nagar D. 2013). Most importantly, there is also the question of how far this ideal embodied in the APSA provides Africa with the means for achieving *Pax Africana*.

Against this backdrop, the APSA is a set of institutions, legislation, and procedures designed to address conflict prevention and promote peace and security on the African continent. The Constitutive Act 2000, Article 5(2) lays down the legal basis for the APSA (Kasaija, 2018:149-182). The Protocol Relating to the Establishment of the AU's PSC, adopted by the AUMS in 2002, defines its structure, objectives, and principles. Ten African sub-regional organisations (SROs), to which their respective member states have conferred a mandate to act in the area of peace and security, also play a role in the APSA. Eight are RECs, and two are RMs for conflict prevention, management, and resolution (Murithi, 2014).

---

24   Personal Interview with Captain Mariann Vecsey NATO military analyst specializing in African Affairs. 2022-2023.

Cooperation between these organisations and the AU under the APSA is subject to the principles of subsidiarity and complementarity. The principle of subsidiarity is founded on the idea that sustainable peace is possible if conflict resolution mechanisms are led by actors who are culturally, geopolitically, and/or strategically close to the crisis in question. In the African context, mediation should therefore be directly supported and, where appropriate, led by RECs.

Subsidiarity has been long recognized as a principle for organising divisions of labour. By one definition, subsidiarity is the principle that a central authority should have a subsidiary function in carrying out only those tasks that cannot be done effectively at a more immediate or local level.

Historically subsidiarity has been applied to organise relations between central and local authorities, but increasingly the principle has also been applied in international politics to govern relations between international organisations that have overlapping membership. In theory, the benefits of subsidiarity are clear. The advantages most commonly mentioned are:

- Better local awareness: local actors are considered to be more aware of nuances and the underlying issues of a situation. With a better analysis and understanding, their role can be more fitting to the task at hand.
- More interest in the outcome: due to proximity, local actors have more to potentially gain or lose from a particular outcome. Local actors are more interested in seeing sustainable and effective outcomes than a more distant actor might be.
- Greater flexibility and adaptability: all these factors are likely to come together to give local actors a more adaptable approach to the issue at hand, in that they can more quickly respond to changes on the ground.
- Greater legitimacy: actors that are closer are viewed as more legitimate than distant actors. Previous relationships and closeness thus also reflect positively on the ability of local individuals and bodies to act.

- Sustainability of peace processes: finally, due to all the above issues, the meaningful involvement of a sub-regional actor will increase the likelihood of a sustainable peace process.

However, there are also potential flaws and limits to the application of subsidiarity:

- Limited capacities: typically, smaller organisations have fewer resources, and may be less able to act than larger, international organisations. Institutional weakness can be an obstacle to effective interventions. In the worst case, weak interventions can even worsen the conflicts that they seek to resolve.
- Conflicts of interest: there are few guarantees that there will not be conflicts of interest between states and/or organisations. This can be particularly problematic if one state seeks to co-opt mediation efforts to further its own interests over internationally recognized principles.
- Bias: being close to actors does not always translate into fairness. A lack of objectivity sometimes means that outcomes can be biased in favour of incumbents or other elites, to the detriment of inclusive and non-partisan solutions. At times, this can create conflict between international/regional best practices and local sentiments.

As a principle, subsidiarity assists in determining ways to organise the division of labour in overlapping or asymmetric hierarchies. In and of itself, subsidiarity is not enough to achieve this. Instead, it is often linked to several other, mutually supportive principles. For example, within the APSA, subsidiarity is linked to the notions of complementarity and comparative advantage. These come together to support the effective implementation of the overall architecture.

The underlying elements of the idea of subsidiarity revolve around the relative effectiveness of more immediate levels, but also around organising relationships between the different levels involved in processes. As such, the effective implementation of the principle also involves linking to these mutually reinforcing notions, as opposed to notions of centralization.

In the African context, subsidiarity as a principle involves three different levels of actors: between the UN and AU; the AU and various RECs; and to a lesser extent the UN and RECs. All three organisations have a distinct and valid legal basis for acting in the realm of peace and security among their member states and present different views of how subsidiarity operates. The UN Charter Chapter VIII describes regional arrangements for peace and security, and encourages localized agency in conflict resolution. However, the Charter is also insistent in reaffirming the primacy of the UNSC and of its decisions over any potential alternative.

The Security Council and General Assembly have frequently endorsed the role of regional oin conflict resolution. The relationship between the AU and RECs is based on two key documents: the 2002 Protocol related to the establishment of the PSC, and the 2008 MOU on cooperation in the area of peace and security between the AU and RECs. The 2002 Protocol seeks to position RECs more clearly as part of a hierarchical arrangement for peace and security, with the AU having primacy, while at the same time encouraging cooperation and harmonization of activities. The 2008 MoU sought to elaborate on this relationship, and more explicitly describes subsidiarity as an operational principle. The wider framework of AU-REC relations is still under development, and each iteration of reviews has improved the possibilities for cooperation and coordination between the organisations.

The principle of complementarity is the basis of the relationship between the AU and its member states, RECs, and RMs concerning the application of its Constitutive Act. Protocols, and Agenda 2063. To 'complement', within the scope of this research, is defined as an act of enhancing the quality of one international institution by adding to it the features of another international institution. In this regard complementing implies a non-monopolistic attitude that one cannot function without the other. Therefore, the basic nature of the concept of complementarity reflects an interdependent relationship geared towards improving the attributes of various components as integral parts of a larger system. When used in conjunction with the principle of subsidiarity, these principles can be employed cooperatively and flexibly to enhance their mutual comparative advantages to gain maximum economies of scale and welfare gains for Africa's population.

At the centre of the APSA is the PSC, established by the AUMS as a "standing decision-making organ for the prevention, management, and resolution of conflicts". The APSA aims to provide the framework and tools for the AU and SROs to play an active role in preventing and resolving conflicts in Africa, all of which have different causes. The AU and the SROs intervened under the APSA framework in 28 of the 67 violent conflicts (42%) occurring in Africa during 2016.

The interventions took the form of diplomacy, mediation, and peace-support operations, or a combination of the three. Evaluations of these 28 interventions indicated that 21 were at least partly successful in either preventing or de-escalating conflicts. The AU and the SROs have guided APSA's development with roadmaps (Williams, 2018b:172-192). They adopted the current APSA roadmap covering the period from 2016 to 2020 in December 2015. It has five strategic priorities: conflict prevention; crisis and conflict management; post-conflict reconstruction and peace-building; strategic security issues[14]; and coordination and partnerships within the APSA framework.

I argue that, state weakness is the principal source of insecurity in Africa. State weakness also leads to weaknesses in regional security mechanisms. State weakness results in a fragile state where the government or region has no semblance of capacity in organs of government and no funding.

This has made it difficult for APSA to intervene in these areas. Against this backdrop, the principle of subsidiarity and complimentarity has become impossible to implement in some of Africa's most fragile states. Individual conflicts are caused by a complex mix of factors but three main triggers have been identified: government transitions, inter-state contestation, and violent extremist movements.

According to the Institute for Economics and Peace's Global Peace Index 2022, five of the ten least peaceful countries globally were in the region: the CAR, the DRC, Somalia, South Sudan, and Sudan. Additionally, Burkina Faso, Mali, Niger, Nigeria, and Somalia were ranked among the top ten countries worldwide most impacted by terrorism.

During the reporting period, a worsening trend of political instability and authoritarianism was apparent on the continent. Several coups were staged in 2020–22, including successful military coups in Burkina Faso, Chad, Guinea, Mali (twice), and Sudan, and failed coups occurred in the CAR, Djibouti, Guinea-Bissau, Madagascar and Niger.

Violence and lawlessness further escalated across the Western Sahel and Lake Chad Basin (LCB), where radical Islamist groups (both domestic and transnational) expanded their operations and reach to coastal countries. Inter-state tensions reignited in the Great Lakes Region, where ties between the DRC and Rwanda significantly worsened over protracted violence in eastern DRC. In East Africa, Ethiopia registered an uneasy ceasefire between the central government and the Tigray People's Liberation Front (TPLF), a truce that is deemed highly unstable given the multiple regional and identity-based conflicts taking place elsewhere in the country. At the time of writing, the Horn of Africa, particularly Somalia, is suffering from one of its worst droughts in living memory, a development that further strains the ability of newly elected President Hassan Sheikh Mohamud to address the country's compounding conflict and humanitarian issues.

The global trend of increasing intervention by third-party states in internal conflicts is long-lasting and well-documented. In Africa, this trend is even more pronounced. Twelve internationalised-internal conflicts (i.e., civil wars with external intervention by a state) were recorded in the two decades between 1991 and 2010 (counting each conflict that occurred across multiple years only once). In the following 11-year period (2011–21), 27 such conflicts were recorded. Most of these conflicts were recurring year after year. In 2021, there were 17 internationalised civil wars in sub-Saharan Africa – more than twice the number of internal conflicts without external intervention.

The current proliferation of third-party interventions in sub-Saharan Africa is related to a chaotic global order characterised by rising geopolitical competition. However, this situation is not a new phenomenon. Colonial powers historically exploited endemic conflicts by fomenting divisions among identity-based groups, Cold War era external intervention in African civil wars profoundly altered and complexified the dynamics of internal struggles, often deepening fault lines and escalating violence.

After the Cold War, the demise of inter-state wars led to competing sub-Saharan African countries also displaying their rivalries through their support for rival conflict parties in each other's domestic conflicts. This development resulted in an intricate web of alliances between state and non-state actors, with detrimental effects on domestic conflicts.

Multilateral interventions, including PKOs and ad hoc coalitions, represent another facet of the internationalisation of the current internal conflict in sub-Saharan Africa. Several PKOs on the continent are protracted, with no end in sight. Furthermore, the DRC, Nigeria, Mali, and Burkina Faso constitute the epicentre of complex regional wars engulfing multiple countries in the Great Lakes Region, the LCB, and the Western Sahel, respectively. In the Sahel, the decade-long French-led Operation Barkhane was reconfigured in 2021, while in 2022 the stand-off between France and Mali led to French troops pulling out of the country. Generally, Western actors, including France, the UK, and the USA, support stabilisation, train local forces, and fight violent extremists in several conflict theatres, such as Somalia, the Sahel, and the LCB.

Amid the ongoing war and political strife, urgent action is needed to avoid disaster in Africa's worst-affected countries. Libya, South Sudan, the CAR, northern Mozambique, Ethiopia, and Cameroon's north-west and south-west regions are six African conflict hotbeds to date. The Libyan situation has not improved significantly after years of instability and a major civil war from 2018 to 2019. The issue of the withdrawal of mercenaries, among others, has not been resolved.

The CAR has been embroiled in conflict for several years. Recent developments indicate that it remains trapped in an intractable cycle of violence. The political dialogue desired by the International Conference on the Great Lakes Region and others has been stymied largely by President Fausten-Archange Touadéra but also by armed groups. Touadéra oscillates between efforts to centralize power and launching military operations against armed factions that exploit the vulnerabilities of the state and its people. He also expresses a desire to implement the 2019 Khartoum Peace Accord. The CAR desperately needs a new approach to sustainable peace. Over the last five years, the conflict in north and south-west Cameroon has not received the attention it deserves from regional and continental actors. What began as protests over poor governance and marginalisation have turned into a deadly insurgency. This has caused many deaths, upended the lives of thousands and created a humanitarian crisis, all of which could have been avoided. The Cameroonian government's dogmatic stance and military approach to resolving the conflict have not helped, and are likely to persist.

Africa will also continue to face the threat of violent extremism and terrorism in the Sahel and LCB regions, East Africa, and the Horn, and Mozambique's northern province of Cabo Delgado. The menace will also hover over the coastal countries of West Africa. The situation in the Group of Five for the Sahel (G5) countries has not abated, causing insecurity and humanitarian crises.

Burkina Faso, Mali, and Niger have seen continuing attacks. The Liptako-Gourma border area among the three countries remains highly volatile, with a terrorist threat, intercommunal violence, and transnational organised crime. This is not expected to change significantly in 2025 The Burkinabè government has come under increasing public pressure to deal decisively with violent extremism. The focus in Mali and Chad on completing their political 'transitions' could also continue to detract from the fight against terrorism.

The situation is similar in the LCB, with terror attacks by Boko Haram, flare-ups in intercommunal violence, and organised crime. What appear to be local conflicts have also spilled over, adding to the region's insecurity. Government responses to the LCB security crisis have negatively affected women's livelihoods, which means that many families have suffered significant hardships. As with the Sahel, the trends in LCB are unlikely to change in 2025 as their reversal will require a shift in strategy from all stakeholders.

The Cabo Delgado extremist insurgency has been ongoing since the end of 2017. The slow response early on led to a deteriorating situation. Since then, a Rwandan troop deployment based on a bilateral arrangement and an SADC multilateral deployment, have helped quell the insurgency and restore humanitarian access to affected populations.

While the military response seems to have now pushed back insurgents, a more holistic approach is needed to address the socio-economic challenges of communities. The regional ramifications of Cabo Delgado's insurgency are also of concern, including links to countries such as Tanzania and the possible creation of a larger extremism axis along the continent's eastern flank.

The spread of the threat from the Sahel to West Africa's coastal countries is best evidenced by the resurgence of attacks in northern Cote d'Ivoire near the border with Burkina Faso. Cote d'Ivoire is now suffering repeated attacks, and the fear is that violent extremism could affect other parts of the country and neighbouring states such as Ghana, Benin, and Togo. The continent must heed the challenges posed by violent extremism and start to chart effective ways to address them at country, regional, and continental levels. It has to curtail and revert the spread of terrorism, which would devastate its aspirations for peace and prosperity.

These numerous challenges facing Africa require concerted regional and continental responses. While several response mechanisms exist, their implementation largely depends on the will and means of the states. Although such mechanisms and frameworks provide guidance, solving structural vulnerabilities will remain the primary responsibility of national governments.

The vision of the AU is to achieve "an integrated prosperous and peaceful Africa, driven by its own citizenry and thereby representing a dynamic global force" (Tieku, 2004:249; Tondi, 2005; Murithi, 2014; Nagar, 2020). The attainment of that vision hinges on incrementally materialising Africa's aspirations of integration.

These aspirations are predicated on three foundational imperatives: democratic governance, peace and security and sustainable development. To this end, the AUMS also established the APSA, which predates the AGA. The AGA's role is to support the APSA, whose role is to address the structural root causes and drivers of conflict on the continent.

The APSA, as an organ of the AU, is predicated on the AU's core peace and security organs: the PSC, the PSC Secretariat, the PSO division, and the Military Staff Committee. The APSA, as an organ of the AU, shares overarching mechanisms with the AGA in pursuing and entrenching democratic governance and peace and security.

As reiterated by the AU Assembly, there are centrifugal and centripetal forces to strengthen the synergy and complementarity operating between the AGA and APSA. This is evident in the APSA Strategy 2016–2020, where it is acknowledged that:

> *"linkages between APSA and AGA as well as the AU and the RECs in the domain of structural conflict prevention remain tenuous, partly due to a lack of communication and collaboration between different departments at the AUC, and between the AU and the RECs."*

Amid shrinking global resources and intensive global competition, Africa's singular nation-state has been rendered politically, economically, and culturally fragile and fails to meet the needs of its population, such as creating jobs and eradicating endemic poverty. Therefore, the three imperatives of democratic governance and peace and security are complementary and indispensable to Africa's socio-economic development and global competitiveness.

The AGA was established a decade after the APSA in 2012. It was designed to complement the communication and management deficits in the APSA, particularly in response to the rapidly evolving asymmetrical geopolitical dynamics. Both the APSA and AGA share their foundational basis in the Constitutive Act and the 2003 amendment, which established the PSC and PSC Protocol. This is another indication of a Pan-African converging agency.

The APSA's structures and pillars (Kasaija, 2018:149-182):

- The PSC
- The PoW
- The ASF
- The CEWS
- The AU Peace Fund
- Post-conflict reconstruction and development
- The AUC
- RECs/RMs
- Military staff committee
- PSOs

Assessing APSA's Five Pillars

i. The Peace and Security Council

The PSC is the organ of the AU in charge of enforcing union decisions. It is patterned somewhat after the UNSC. The PSC is also the main pillar of the APSA, and works with other pillars of the APSA to promote "peace, security and stability in Africa."

The specific goal of the PSC is the "prevention, management, and resolution of conflicts". To achieve these goals, it involves subsidiary organisations such as the Military Staff Committee and the Committee of Experts.

Members are elected by the African Union Executive Council and endorsed by the Assembly of the African Union so as to reflect the regional balance within Africa as well as a variety of other criteria, including the capacity to contribute militarily and financially to the AU, political will to do so, and an effective diplomatic presence at Addis Ababa.

The council is composed of fifteen countries, of which five are elected to three-year terms, and ten to two-year terms. Countries are immediately re-eligible upon the expiration of their terms.

ii. The Panel of the Wise

The PoW constitutes an advisory body of five highly respected African personalities supporting the PSC and Chairperson of the AUC and all its organs. The operationalisation areas are advice on conflict prevention and peacemaking, preventive diplomacy, and mediation (Article 11(2) PSC Protocol).

The PoW was developed from the OAU processes and was influenced by communal and traditional African peacemaking methods. The experience of the elderly was a form of social capital that lent credence in peacefully resolving conflict and engaging in peacebuilding. This approach is not a zero-sum game but rather a win-win method based on consensus and community building that the AU uses in its toolkit of mixed strategies.

It is the Chairperson of the AUC and the AUHSG-Assembly that appoint the members of the PoW in meeting the following criteria :

· well-known state or non-state African personalities;
· have made a noteworthy contribution to the advancement of peace, security, and development in Africa and globally;
· moral integrity, impartiality, and appeal to Africa's and global populations; and
· not an active statutory political incumbent.

iii. The African Standby Force and the African Capacity for Immediate Response to Crisis

To date, APSA has registered some achievements through its ad hoc ASF major military peace missions across Africa. Article 13.1 of the PSC positions the ASF to serve as a continental rapid-response team for PKOs, according to Article 4 (h) and (j) of the Constitutive Act, although it is not yet officially operationalised.

It consists of five standby brigades in each of the following five regions: the Eastern Africa Standby Force (EASF), ECOWAS Standby Force, North African Regional Capability (NARC), ECCAS (FOMAC-Standby Force), and SADC-Standby Force (Ndaguba, 2016:44; Alghali and Mbaye, 2008).

Thus, APSA ad hoc task forces were operationalised as building blocks for the ongoing and incremental formation of the ASF in the AMIB, the AMIS (which evolved and converged into the UN/AU Hybrid Mission in Darfur or UN-AU Mission in Darfur – UNAMID) and the AMISOM. The APSA has also sponsored an intervention in the Comoros, without the sanction of the UN – Operation Democracy in the Comoros was designed to overthrow an unconstitutional secessionist government on the island of Anjouan. To date, the ASFs have been fully operationalised, but rapid reaction still remains a challenging task. This is due to a lack of adequate independent funding and logistical supplies, such as strategic airlift and technical support personnel.

To minimise the rapid reaction gap, the AU AHSG declared at the 1st Extra Ordinary Ministerial meeting in Addis Ababa on 29 January 2016 that African Capacity for Immediate Response to Crises (ACIRC) capability is ready to rapidly respond to crises and contribute to PSOs mandated by the PSC pursuant to Article 4(h) and (j) of the Constitutive Act. The ACIRC has become complementary to the ASF in fulfilling its rapid response mandate. In light of the aforementioned problems faced by both ACIRC and ASF, this continues to be a work in progress (Brosig, 2015; AUC report, 2013 paragraphs 26-52; Esmenjaud, 2013:115-124).

Table 5.1: Africa standby force achievements by the end of 2010

Achievements	The five regional brigades				
	EASBRIG East Africa	**FOMAC** Central Africa	**ECOBRIG** West Africa	**NASBRIG** North Africa	**SADCBRIG** South Africa
Framework Documents	Done	Done	Done	Done	Done
Memorandum of Under-standing	Done	Done	Done	Done	Done
Planning elements	Done	Done	Done	Ongoing	Done
Brigade HQs	Done	Decided against	Done	Ongoing	Decided against
Pledged Units	MoU on troop allocation pending,[1] 5,500 troops pledged by member states	MoU pending, 'force catalogue' of 4,800 troops presented by member states	MoU pending, 6,200 unspecified troops pledged by member states	MoU pending	MoU pending, unspecified troops pledged by member states
Civilian Components	Ongoing		Ongoing		Ongoing
Centres of Excellence	Done	Ongoing	Done		Done
Standby Rosters	Delegated to AFDEM[2]				Ongoing

Notes:
1) Not identical with the MoU on the establishment of the ASF (see row two of this table).
2) African Civilian Standby Roster for Humanitarian and Peace Building Missions.

Source: Institute of Development Studies, April 2011.

iv. The Continental Early Warning System

As stipulated under Article 12 of the PCS protocol, the CEWS was established to enable preventive diplomacy in the anticipation and prevention of conflicts. It primarily monitors and reports on emerging crises.

It is also responsible for data collection and analysis and is mandated to collaborate with other concerned organs. Furthermore, it gathers information about potential conflicts or threats to the peace and security of member states and provides this information to the PSC, together with recommendations on courses of action. The CEWS receives reports on a daily or weekly basis from operational staff including field missions, liaison officers, and early warning officers. (Protocol relating to the establishment of PSC, 2002)

v. The African Union Peace Fund

The following section will examine the incremental ad hoc agency of the APSA-ASF against limiting and enabling factors. These include a lack of adequate predictable funding and logistical support, such as strategic airlift and technical personnel, which engender both intermittent divergences and convergences. This occurs within a milieu of actors that have an impact on both and includes its partners the UN, EU, USA, and AUMS. The most active agenda items of the UNSC concern Africa and as a result the UN supports centripetal policies to expand and enhance the effectiveness of the role of APSA (UN, 2011a:12). In a globalised and interdependent world, the UN equally supports the principle of subsidiarity and complementarity. It is in this regard that the APSA is more closely situated geographically and otherwise to better effect African solutions to African problems (UN, 2011b). Cooperation between the UN and AU has become the mainstay of converging diplomacy, as members of the UNSC and PSC hold regular joint consultative meetings in Addis Ababa and New York (UN, 2011c:3).

The African Union Commission

The Commission (Secretariat) is one of the main organs of the AU and provides bureaucratic support to enable the functioning of the AU. The AUC is composed of the chairman, a deputy, and commissioners. It is responsible for the organisations day to day executive and management functions as enshrined in the Constitutive Act.

Post-Conflict Reconstruction and Development Policy

This AU policy on Post-Conflict Reconstruction and Development (PCRD) is intended to serve as a guide for the development of comprehensive policies and strategies that elaborate measures that seek to consolidate peace, promote sustainable development, and pave the way for growth and regeneration in countries and regions emerging from conflict. Given the peculiarities of each conflict situation, this policy was conceived as a flexible template that can be adapted to, and assist, affected regions and countries, in their endeavours towards reconstruction, security, and growth. The imperative for this policy is derived from the reality of Africa making greater progress in resolving conflicts on the continent. The AU and RECs have put enormous efforts into the facilitation of negotiations for the peaceful resolution of existing conflicts and the effective implementation of peace agreements. As a result of these activities, there has been a steady decline in the number of active conflicts on the continent and an increasing demand for the consolidation of peace, reconstruction, and development.

However, experience has indicated that in the early phases of the transition from conflict to peace, peace processes remain fragile and the risk of the resumption of violence is high. This is because countries emerging from conflict are characterised by weakened or non-existent capacity at all levels, destroyed institutions, and the absence of a democratic culture, good governance, rule of law, and respect for human rights, as well as underlying poverty. Furthermore, responses to post-conflict situations have, in the past, remained fragmented and largely ineffectual.

This policy framework goes beyond such limited interventions, noting that post-conflict reconstruction and development activities do not stop with stabilisation but seek to achieve long-term sustainable development as underpinned by the African vision of regeneration and growth.

For these reasons, the AU is focusing more attention on measures that consolidate peace and pave the way for growth and regeneration. These AU efforts are informed by past practices of the OAU in reconstruction efforts, and all relevant OAU/

AU mandates and decisions. This includes Article 5(2) of the Constitutive Act, on the basis of which the PSC was established and the OAU/AU established a ministerial committee for the reconstruction of the Sudan.

The mandate proffered by the Protocol Relating to the Establishment of the PSC, which was specifically created to, inter alia, promote and implement peace-building and post-conflict reconstruction activities, and to consolidate peace and prevent the resurgence of violence (Articles 3a, 6). Thus, peace-building, post-conflict reconstruction, humanitarian action, and disaster management constitute the core activities of the PSC. Because of this, the PSC Protocol delineates several post-conflict reconstruction activities that require action, including the restoration of the rule of law, the establishment and development of democratic institutions, and, the preparation, organisation, and supervision of elections in the concerned member states (Article 14(1)).

This mandate is extended in countries affected by violent conflict to include the consolidation of the peace agreements that have been negotiated. This establishes conditions of political, social, and economic reconstruction of the society and government institutions; implementation of disarmament, demobilisation, and reintegration (DDR) programmes, including those of child soldiers; resettlement and reintegration of refugees and internally displaced persons (IDPs); and assistance to vulnerable persons, including children, the elderly, women, and other traumatised groups in society (Article 14 (3)). The Protocol also emphasises the link between the prevention of conflict and consolidation of peace and mandates the PSC to take all measures that are required to prevent the resumption of a conflict for which a settlement has already been reached.

Based on these experiences and mandates, the Executive Council Decision EX.CL/191(VII) in Sirte, Libya, of July 2005, mandated the Commission to develop an AU policy on post-conflict reconstruction based on the relevant provisions of the PSC Protocol and the experience gained thus far on the continent.

To fulfil this mandate, the AUC crafted a draft policy framework, which was subjected to many consultations for its review and improvement. These included the 4th Brainstorming Retreat of the PSC and other member states of the PRC on 4-5 September 2005, in Durban, South Africa, whose recommendations were endorsed by the PSC on 30 September 2005; a Technical Experts Meeting on PCRD on 7-8 February 2006 in Addis Ababa, Ethiopia; an AU-CSO meeting on the draft policy framework on PCRD on 5-7 April 2006 in Abuja, Nigeria; a Validation Meeting within the AUC on 31 May 2006 in Addis Ababa, Ethiopia; and a Governmental Experts Meeting on 8-9 June 2006 in Addis Ababa, Ethiopia. This policy is the result of the above-mentioned consultative process.

The objective of this Policy is to improve the timeliness, effectiveness, and coordination of activities in post-conflict countries and to lay the foundation for social justice and sustainable peace, in line with Africa's vision of renewal and growth. The policy is, therefore, conceived as a tool to:

a. consolidate peace and prevent a relapse of violence;
b. help address the root causes of conflict;
c. encourage and fast-track planning and implementation of reconstruction activities; and
d. enhance complementarities and coordination between and among diverse actors engaged in PCRD processes.

It is imperative that PCRD processes be viewed and used as an opportunity for the reconstitution and social, political, economic, and physical transformation of the affected state and society. The promotion of human security should be the basis of all PCRD activities, and this policy should be pursued within the global context of the search for peace and security; hence, complementing existing international initiatives.

This PCRD policy is a strategic and normative framework that elaborates, in a comprehensive manner, the entire spectrum of activity areas that are crucial for the consolidation of peace. It also provides guidelines to translate comprehensive strategies for PCRD into specific actions that empower affected countries to take the lead in the reconstruction and development of their societies.

The policy draws on lessons learned from past African reconstruction efforts, which indicate weaknesses from the conceptual to the strategic and operational levels. Most reconstruction models have been borrowed from outside Africa and lack comprehensiveness, favouring some aspects of PCRD to the exclusion of others, which sometimes risks the resumption of conflict.

Taking this into account, there is a critical need for PCRD processes to translate the commitment to peace into tangible benefits. This is dependent on the formulation of comprehensive integrated strategies and approaches that require substantial institutional and human capacities in the implementation of PCRD.

This policy will reduce the pressure on affected countries by providing a consistent and coherent strategy that will fast-track the planning and implementation of quick-impact programmes, consolidate peace in the emergency/transition phase, and hence increase the chances of successful long-term sustainable development.

Finally, this policy will provide parameters to improve the coherence and coordination of all actions between state and non-state actors operating at local, national, regional, and/or international levels, during all phases of PCRD.

Regional Economic Communities and Regional Mechanisms

Regional Economic Communities in Contemporary Times (Recognised by the African Union)

Since the formation of the earlier RECs, many have been formed and others have been dissolved, for various reasons. Despite the continued formation of the RECs, it is unclear how many exist in total. However, the AU made a decision specifying the eight RECs that it recognises namely: the SADC, ECOWAS, EAC, ECCAS, COMESA, CEN-SAD, IGAD, and AMU; and further stated that other RECs apart from those listed would not be recognised (AU Assembly, 2006).

Despite their identification as AU-recognised RECs, these eight RECs were created and have evolved separately from the AU. The RECs are independent and have structures, functions, missions, visons, and objectives that are not influenced by the AU. The major development in the purpose of contemporary RECs is that they are considered to be essential vehicles or 'building blocs' towards achieving continental integration.

Regional Mechanisms (Recognised by the African Union)

While discussing RECs that are recognised by the AU, RMs for Conflict Prevention, Management, and Resolution are also discussed under the same umbrella because they were officially recognised by the AU under Article 16 of the Protocol Relating to the Establishment of the Peace and Security Council of the African Union. Article 16 also states that RMs are essential for the promotion of peace, security, and stability in the continent, and they are a part of the security architecture of the AU (Djilo, 2021).

The focus of RMs on the 'peace and security' objective is what differentiates them from RECs, which are mostly focused on economic integration. There are three RMs recognised by the AU: "International Conference on the Great Lakes Region (ICGLR); Eastern Africa Standby Force (EASF); and North African Regional Capability (NARC)" (African Union, 2022). There is some criticism that the recognised RMs do not cover all five regions of the continent, with the focus being in the eastern and northern regions.

Regional Economic Communities and Regional Mechanisms (Unrecognised by the African Union)

In addition to the eight RECs that are recognised by the AU, there are other RECs that are active in the continent. The unrecognised RECs include: CEMAC; ECGLC; IOC; MRU; WAEMU; the Accra Initiative; the Liptako-Gourma Authority (LGA); and the Gulf of Guinea Commission (GGC) (European Council on Foreign Relations, 2023).

These unrecognised RECs are located in various regions of the continent. Their lack of recognition by the AU is justified given that other 'recognised' RECs already exist in these locations. Also, some RMs are not recognised by the AU, such as the Western Africa Standby Brigade; the Central African Standby Brigade; and the Southern Africa Standby Brigade, which together with the EASF and NARC form the ASF. The recognition of some but not all ASF members as RMs as defined by AU is interesting in terms of the new structures created within the AU (AU, 2022). The consequence of RECs and RMs not being recognised by the AU is that they exacerbate the duplication of efforts by these institutions as they work towards achieving similar objectives.

There are various reasons for the failure and delay of the RECs to meet their integration objectives. These include:

1. The overlapping memberships in RECs has been attributed as a major obstacle to regional integration because of the problems it creates, such as: duplication of efforts; misuse and/or abuse of the resources available to institutions; difficulties for member states to make sufficient contributions because they belong to several RECs and have to make contributions to all, among others.
2. The infrastructural, financial, and technical challenges facing RECs reduce their capability to meet their integration objectives. Also, they are forced to be reliant on external funding.
3. Hegemonic politics derail regional integration. The countries that are considered the most powerful in a particular region make decisions for the less powerful states, which impacts the level of commitment of the latter in implementing those decisions.

Military Staff Committee

The Military Staff Committee advises and assists the PSC in all questions relating to military and security requirements for the promotion and maintenance of peace and security in Africa. The Protocol enables the Committee to comprise senior military representatives from the 15 PSC member states. The Committee is chaired by the military/defence attaché of the member state chairing the PSC in any given month.

The Committee can invite any AUMS to its meetings to assist with its work. Rules of Procedure for the Committee are yet to be adopted.

Peace Support Operations

The PSC Protocol provides for PSOs to be a function and tool of the PSC and gives the Council powers to "authorise the mounting and deployment of peace support missions" and "lay down general guidelines for the conduct of such missions, including the mandate thereof, and undertake periodic reviews of these guidelines". PSC operations are also authorised by the UNSC in accordance with the UN Charter, Chapter VIII, Article 53(1)4

Nine AU-mandated PSOs have been deployed since 2003, as well as four AU-authorised missions. Each PSO has varied in nature, personnel strength, duration, and budget. Most operating mandates are renewed periodically and can be revised if necessary. Funding arrangements vary between missions and include a mix of sources, such as the AU Peace Fund, international bilateral and multilateral partners, and, in some cases, UN trust funds. The PSOs mounted to date include: African Union Mission in Somalia (AMISOM), African Union–United Nations Mission in Darfur (UNAMID); Regional Cooperation Initiative for the Elimination of the Lord's Resistance Army (RCI-LRA); Human Rights Observers and Military Experts in Burundi. In addition, sub-regional security arrangements have been rolled out including the Multinational Joint Task Force (MNJTF) against Boko Haram and the G5 Sahel Joint Force

Other bodies related to the PSC include the AU Police Strategic Support Group (PSSG) which) was launched in June 2013, under the PSOD of the AUC. It has a remit to provide strategic and technical advice and support to the PSC, AUC, and member states on police matters in the context of AU-led PSOs. The PSSG consists of two main levels: Chiefs of Police from the police in contributing countries and technical experts.

5.2 The African Union's Peacekeeping Missions

5.2.1 The African Union Mission in Burundi[25]

The AMIB was approved prior to the launch of the PSC by the seventh ordinary session of the Central Organ of the Mechanism for Conflict Prevention, Management and Resolution on the 3 February 2003 (AU, 2003a:1).

The AMIB comprised a total of 3 335 troops from Ethiopia, Mozambique, South Africa, Burkina Faso, Gabon, Mali, Togo, and Tunisia. Its mandate was informed by the following objectives:

- to supervise the implementation of the ceasefire agreement (Arusha Accords, the October 2002 Ceasefire Agreement, and the December 2002 Ceasefire Agreement);
- support the DDR initiatives of the combatants;
- create an enabling environment for the subsequent takeover by the UN peacekeeping mission;
- contribute to political and economic stability in Burundi. (AU, 2003b)

In partnership with the Multi-Country Demobilisation and Reintegration (MDRP) of the WB, the AMIB expedited the overseeing of the DDR initiative, which remained throughout the UN PKO and replaced the AMIB (Boshoff et al., 2010:54). The UNSC approved the deployment of the United Nations Operation in Burundi (UNOB), under Chapter VII, UNSC resolution 1545 on 21 May 2004. The UNOB had a military component of 5 650 personnel and its core component was provided by 2 612 AMIS troops. The AMIB's Force Commander, South Africa's Major General Derrik Mgwebi, remained in Burundi as the Force Commander of the ONUB (Jackson, 2006:13). The APSA troop-contributing countries (TCCs) executed a successful handover to the UN amid shortages of funding and technical expertise.

The involvement of the UN, EU, and other AUMS, underscored that this was a regional security problem that demanded a regional solution (Svensson, 2008a: 14; Williams,

---

25   Interviews with AU officials. 2022-2023.

2006: 354). The APSA also exercised its agency in Burundi as part of the AMIB, with South Africa leading the member states as a TCC together with the UN. The EU and its member states also significantly supported AMIB logistically, by providing airlift capacity to TCCs deploying to Burundi, as well as delivering food to the troops before the DDR exercise (Boshoff et al.,2010: 71). The DDR initiative was competently managed in Burundi by APSA, thus enabling APSA to handover to the UN (Svensson, 2008a:14; Williams, 2006:354).

5.2.2 The African Union Mission in Sudan·

The United Nations Mission in Sudan (UNMIS) collaborated closely with the AMIS to resolve the north/south conflict (United Nations, 2004:14, UNSC, 2005b:10). The R2P was a new norm adopted by the AU predicated on Article 4(h) "to intervene in a member state pursuant to a decision of the AU AHSG in cases of war crime, crimes against humanity and genocide" (Jibril, 2010:10).

In Sudan, the Human Rights Watch (HRW), Aegis Trust, and International Crisis Group (ICG) invoked the R2P framework to call for 'robust' international action over Darfur (Pace & Deller, 2005: 22.. For example, Grono (2006: 626-628) argues that those capable of acting failed because they did not put real pressure on the government of Sudan to disarm the Janjaweed or contribute their troops for a military intervention in Darfur. Others have suggested that NATO should have sent troops (AU, 2004f; Rice, Lake, and Payne, 2006; ICG, 2004:15). I caution against the assessment that the global commitment to R2P failed on the sole grounds that international forces were not rapidly deployed to Darfur. First, the principle of R2P has many unresolved tensions. As discussed above, the paragraphs on R2P in the World Summit Outcome Document are deliberately vague on when and how sovereign responsibilities devolve onto international actors.

Given the ambiguity of Paragraph 139 concerning the specific mechanisms and resources necessary to react to concrete cases, ignoring potential responses other than the use of force may have seemed possible. Also, selectivity was made part of the

R2P framework because R2P was not intended to be applied to all imaginable crises worldwide. Furthermore, the R2P advocacy turned protection into a question of intervention rather than support for the political process. According to de Waal (2007: 1043, 1045), in the absence of a workable political process, designing R2P in the guise of a large UN force under Chapter VII was an unfeasible plan for Darfur.

There is thus a clear need to guard against advocacy that narrows R2P down to a question of interventionism and military measures. A potential danger exists that such advocacy may overlook important questions about what intervention can actually achieve. Military civilian protection in an ongoing conflict should never substitute for the government's responsibilities, but should rather be done to reinforce them. Those who argued for NATO action did not explain fully to what extent they could have made a significant difference. Military experiences, such as those in Afghanistan and Iraq, highlight the limits of what 'robust' military power and presence on the ground can achieve (Weiss, 2007:135).

Second, it is important not to underestimate the complexities of the political conflict in Darfur. As Thakur (2006: 247) states, 'the size of Sudan, the historical roots of the crisis, and the ease with which any Western intervention can be exploited as yet another assault on Arabs and Muslims, means that the prospects of a successful outcome of the use of unilateral military force are questionable." Without Sudan's consent, unilateral intervention would probably have been met with sustained resistance, resulting in decreased security for large segments of Darfur's civilian population and diminished humanitarian access for the humanitarian agencies. Without a good strategy and sustained political support to bear the financial and human costs, such consequences would have neglected any global duty to care worth its name.

As de Waal (2007) has argued compellingly, the expectations were set too high regarding what PKOs could actually achieve in active conflicts such as the one in Darfur, especially in light of their vague mandates and the shortage of proper resources and troops on the ground. The lack of political will to implement the R2P principle was evident not only in Darfur but also in other situations around the time of the World Summit. This also raises questions about the distinction between success and failure in its implementation. Darfur received high levels of attention from R2P advocates and civil society, while the crises in Burundi and the DRC received considerably less.

The AMIB and the UN Mission in the DRC (MONUC) were both deployed before 2005. In different ways, they have had a bearing on the debates around R2P and civilian protection. A credible military response would have had to have been led by NATO or a coalition of Western states led by France, UK, or USA (Williams, 2006:171,173).

The UK also provided support to the AMIS by paying for the initial deployment of the observer mission (AU, 2004c:4). The UK further provided 143 vehicles in December 2004 and another 476 vehicles in 2005, including Thuraya satellite phones for the operability of AMIS military observers. The AMIS offices in El Fashir, Khartoum and Addis Ababa were connected to the UN communications network. The UN contributed to the map exercise in El Fashir and the training of the AMIS military was conducted at the tactical and strategic levels. The AMIS military observers and their Protection Force, collaborated closely with the UNMIS and the Office for the Coordination of Humanitarian Affairs in all three Darfur states (UNSC, 2005b:11; Ekengard, 2008:37). The adoption of UNSC resolution 1769, established the hybrid UNAMID, on 31 July 2007 (GoS, 2007:2; UNSC, 2007c:3; Ekengard, 2008:38). The resolution stipulates that the Force Commander must always be African, thereby asserting African ownership and maintaining APSA's role as an African-led organisation (Derblom et al., 2009:41). The Force Commander and Police Commissioner of UNAMID were appointed by the Chair of the AUC in consultation with the UN Secretary-General.

The United States Africa Command (AFRICOM) also supported the mission, contracting Pacific Architectural Engineers, an American subsidiary of Lockheed Martin, to construct camps, provide water, food, and other fundamental support services (Ekengard, 2008:18). Between June 2004 and August 2006, the US spent approximately US$280 million on building and maintaining the 32 camps that housed AMIS forces throughout Darfur (AU, 2005b:11; GAO, 2006:55; Ekengard, 2008:22).

It is clear that AU agency, in pursuit of 'African solutions to African problems', is bound to external partnering, especially with those that make up the permanent members of the UNSC (USA, UK, Russia, China, and France). Global hegemons, such as the US, UK, and France, have to operate with the AU within a limited political framework, given the rapid global changes and players (e.g., China, Russia, India, and Turkey) that are challenging their influence. This has become evident with China (infrastructure for the BRI), Russia (military hardware supplies in Central Africa), India (affordable pharmaceutical products), and Turkey (training of the Somali military) becoming the preferred investors of choice in Africa's political economy. This is because their model of investment does not demand intrusive conditionalities as is the case with investors from the Global North (Dollar, 2019; Devonshire-Ellis, 2021).

5.2.3 The African Union Mission In Somalia[26]

AMISOM proved to be both innovative and adaptive in its PKO, metamorphosising into the surrogate army for the Transitional Federal Government (TFG) against the Islamic Courts Union (ICU). The AU's flexibility and creativity was demonstrated through its ability to operate in a challenging, asymmetrical, and hybrid security environment. They had to engage with various warlords and their clan's militias, and the militant Islamic militia group Al Shabab who were all pursuing different agendas (AU, 2007i)

In 2006, the two most heavily armed groups in Somalia fought for the control of Mogadishu. In June of the same year, the ICU defeated the USA-supported Alliance for the Restoration of Peace and Counter-Terrorism. The ICU had significant

---

26   Personal Interview with Somalia Ambassador H.E. Mohammed Ali Mire in Pretoria South Africa. (2022-2023). See: Newman, E. (2001). 'Human security and constructivism.' *International Studies Perspectives*. 2(3). 239-251.

legitimacy and popular support from varied segments of society to the chagrin of the USA. The USA provided public health care, education, law and order, and road maintenance (AU, 2007i:2; Barnes and Assan, 2007: 159; Shank, 2007:92; Moller, 2009a:3). Despite the successes and the legitimacy of the ICU, the APSA reiterated its support for the TFG as the legitimate government of Somalia (African Union, 2007i:1). In July 2006, Ethiopian troops reinforced and protected the TFG, and this resulted in peace negotiations between the TFG and ICU.

In October 2006, a full-scale intervention by Ethiopia enabled the TFG to relocate to Mogadishu and become the unchallenged government (AU, 2007b:1-4). The APSA, in the meantime, prepared to bolster the TFG's legitimacy and governance, pending the eventual withdrawal of Ethiopian troops. Their position was officially adopted by the PSC on 19 January 2007.

The AMISOM was further supported by UNSC resolution 1744, which, through reference to Chapter VII of the UN Charter, authorised a waiver of the arms embargo permitting the supply of equipment to the AMISOM and the TFG (AU, 2007b; UNSC, 2007b). The first AMISOM troops, totalling 2 613 personnel (mostly Ugandans), were deployed to Mogadishu in March 2007 (UN, 2008e:5; Hull and Svensson, 2008:28). The fighting, however, continued unabated, with Ethiopian troops providing support to AMISOM against the Islamist insurgents (UN, 2009a:3).

By 15 January 2009, amid the heightened warfare, Ethiopia withdrew their troops from Somalia leaving the AMISOM to protect the TFG government as a militant armed force and not as a neutral peacekeeping force. The aim of the Ethiopian support for the AMISOM was to create space for a handover to the UN:

"AMISOM shall be deployed for a period for a period of six (6) months, aimed essentially at contributing to the initial stabilisation phase in Somalia, with a clear understanding that the mission will evolve to a United Nations operation that will support the long term stabilisation and post conflict reconstruction of Somalia."

(AU, 2007b:2).

"The long term stabilisation and post-conflict reconstruction of Somalia will require the strong involvement of the UN. In this respect, Council urges the United Nations Security Council to consider authorising a United Nations operation in Somalia that would take over from AMISOM at the expiration of its 6 months' mandate."

(AU, 2007b:4).

Almost a year and a half after the AMISOM's mandate was supposed to have ended, the APSA had still not been enabled by the UN. Against the worsening situation, the AU Chair, Alpha Konare, requested funding support totalling US$817 500 000 for AMISOM. The AU was still without a reasonable response nine months later as the Ethiopian troops were withdrawing from Somalia, potentially compromising the mission. The UN's delayed response to the AU's request for help highlights a lack of regard for African PKOs.

Funding, technical expertise, and planning have been a chronic challenge for the APSA (UNSC, 2009:2). The first US$716 000 000 of the AMISOM support package was approved on 7 April 2009 (UN, 2009b:6), thus institutionalising its partnership with the APSA in Somalia.

This resulted in the establishment of the United Nations Support Office for AMISOM (UNSOA) in Nairobi in April 2009 (AU, 2010c:2). By January 2010, the AU had directly received US$16 612 000 from the Trust Fund (AU, 2010i). The AMISOM's mandate in Somalia was renewed and extended by the PSC for a further seven months on June 15 2009.

Despite support from the UN, the armed conflict continued. On 11 July 2010, Al-Shabaab claimed responsibility for a bombing in Kampala, Uganda, which killed 79 people (Cilliers et al., 2010). Instead of this creating an impetus for the withdrawal of the Ugandan-AMISOM contingent, at the 15th Ordinary Session of the Assembly, held in Kampala on 25–27 August 2010, Uganda pledged a further reinforcement of two battalions (AU, 2010h:11). The same summit finally approved the changes to the AMISOM's rules of engagement. This permitted the APSA to perform an aggressive defence, employing pre-emptive attacks. By 15 October

2010, the AMISOM had routed the insurgents and consolidated the defence of the Mogadishu, Hiran, Galgadud, Bay, Bakool, Gedo, and Lower Jubba regions (AFP, 2010; AU, 2010h:11; AU, 2011c:5).

The UN support cost US$210 000 000 based on UN-assessed contributions (AU, 2010i:11). The same UN Resolution (1863) also authorised a voluntary Trust Fund to help pay for the AMISOM, which was managed by the UNSOA. To date, the APSA has been underfunded and under-resourced, with meagre contributions from the UN resulting in AMISOM troops going without wages (AU, 2010h:19):

> "The United Nations retains the primary role in the maintenance of international peace and security, and therefore there is an expectation that it must contribute to the role of regional and sub-regional organisations, which has in recent years been shown to be seminal, especially in the context of the AU. We are convinced that the interests of peace will be served if the requisite synergy and cooperation exist between the two organisations at both the strategic and operational levels (UN, 2011a:5)."

Other ad hoc external funding for AMISOM came from the UK, which contributed £8.5 million to assist in payment for AMISOM deployments and to provide support for the Support Management Planning Unit (SPMU).

The UK also provided £4 million to the TCCs for reimbursement of contingent-owned equipment. Furthermore, on 19 May 2009, the UK High Commission in Nairobi provided £75 000 for the purchase of medical supplies for the AMISOM clinics in Mogadishu (AU, 2008d:9; AU, 2009d:8; AU, 2011d:3). Other EU member states, including Sweden, provided the mission with a level-II hospital, with the facility made available to the AMISOM, UN agencies and local staff operating in Somalia (UN, 2008e: 5). France also assisted with a training programme for the first Burundian battalion to be deployed in Somalia, adding logistical and airlift support for troop movements to Mogadishu (AU, 2007j: 3). The EU also disbursed €5 000 000 for the AMISOM's SPMU and another €500 000 to cover insurance costs and technical assistance for budget-related matters (AU, 2008d:9).

The US State Department has programmes that facilitate the training of African armed forces in peacekeeping capacity. The training programmes range from peacebuilding and peacekeeping, involving conflict prevention and management as well as logistics training and support (Avant and Nevers, 2011:2). AFRICAP has also been involved in the AMIS and AMISOM in a variety of roles, from airlift logistical support, information technologies, and infrastructure to disaster relief and public relations.

The New York-based private security company, Bancroft Global Development, has contracted South African and European military advisors to train AMISOM troops on how to counter and neutralise Al-Shabaab without endangering the civilian population, which could potentially compromise public support for the mission. Bancroft Global have been retained by APSA at a cost of US$12 500 000, with the APSA reimbursed by the US State Department (Kelley, 2011).

Against the background of an asymmetrical, hybrid, and complex regional conflict, AMISOM has proven to be highly adaptable. It did not play the role of an impartial peacekeeper but instead supported the TFG government against the rebel groups, playing the role of a surrogate army as the Ethiopian army withdrew. The AUC's continuous agency over a period of four years finally resulted in UNSC resolution 1863. The resolution legitimised the AMISOM, which enabled it not only to remain active but also provided it with a source of funding.

5.2.4 The African Union's Mission In Comoros [27]

Between 2007 and 2008, the security situation on the Comorian island of Anjouan deteriorated, resulting in the involvement of the APSA under Operation Democracy. For the elections in Anjouan taking place on 10 and 24 June 2007, the AU's APSA authorised the AU Electoral and Security Assistance Mission (MAES) in May 2007 (AU, 2007k:2; Svensson, 2008b:19). Before the elections, Colonel

---

27   Interview with Professor Khabele Matlosa former Head of the African Governance Architecture at the African Union. 2022-2023.

Mohamed Bacar refused to cede his presidency of Anjouan despite his mandate having expired on 14 April 2007. Colonel Mohamed Bacar rejected the authority of the AU Government and the appointment of the interim president.

This resulted in the deterioration of relations between Anjouan and the AU Government and jeopardised the forthcoming elections (AU, 2007k:1-2).

The elections in Anjouan were originally scheduled for 10 June 2007, but were postponed to 17 June 2007 to allow for the thawing of tensions between Anjouan and the AU Government (AU, 2007e). However, Colonel Mohamed Baca disregarded the AU's PSC and unilaterally went ahead with the elections on 10 June 2007. Ajouan's Electoral Commission announced Bacar's victory, despite international condemnation of the illegitimate elections. Subsequently, on 14 June 2007, Colonel Mohamed Bacar was sworn in as President of Anjouan (AU, 2007k:5).

On 8−9 July 2007, the APSA held a meeting in South Africa in an attempt to resolve the Anjouan crisis peacefully. Colonel Bacar rejected the APSA's proposals to restore the legitimate authority of the AU Government (AU, 2007c). After many further failed attempts at peace, at the 10th Ordinary Session of the Assembly of the AU, the President of the AU of the Comoros requested support from APSA to re-establish the legitimacy and authority of the state on the island of Anjouan, including through the use of force, as peaceful means had failed (AU, 2008e:1). The Assembly acceded to the request by the President of the AU of the Comoros. This resulted in APSA's Operation Democracy, which was to retake the island militarily, if necessary, and restore the legitimacy of the AU Government.

The TCCs to the APSA were Tanzania, Sudan, Senegal, and Libya. The 1 500 strong APSA Coalition, including Comorian troops, invaded Anjouan on 25 March 2008 and were airlifted by a French carrier. All strategic areas came under the control of the APSA, which included the capital city Mutsmudu, the port, and Domoni, the western strategic part of the island. The following day, Colonel Mohamed Bacar escaped and sought asylum in France (AU, 2008e:5). Thereafter, the MAES arrived on the island under a new mandate (Svensson, 2008b:21). The presidential elections were successfully held in June 2008 and were won by Moussa Toybou (AFP, 2008).

The AU TCCs successfully developed a mandate, the Concept of Operations, (CONOPS), executed their military hard power strategies and successfully attained their objectives. The mission did not need to seek UNSC approval, but used Article 4(h) of the Constitutive Act to facilitate an intervention into a sovereign state to thwart an 'unconstitutional change of government.'

It could be argued that the dictates of realpolitik took precedence in the roles of the AMISOM and the AU-backed Operation Democracy in the Comoros, intervening effectively in both countries on behalf of the internationally recognised governments and fighting against illegitimate rebels. Clearly, the APSA has given currency and legitimacy to its role as both protector and enforcer of constitutional order. The following section explores AU diplomacy as a non-linear exercise in an asymmetrical global world of actors, particularly in the case of the EU, which has geo-strategic interests.

The African-led International Support Mission to Mali

In communiqué PSC/AHG/COMM/2(CCCLIII) adopted at its 353rd meeting, held on 25 January 2013, Council stressed the need to speed up the deployment of the African-led International Support Mission in Mali (AFISMA) and to ensure its effective operation, as well as to build the capacity of the Defence and Security Forces of Mali (FDSM).

In this regard, Council requested the AU and ECOWAS Commissions, in cooperation with the UN, EU, and other partners, to review the CONOPS of AFISMA, as approved by its 341st meeting, held on 13 November 2012 [PSC/PR/COMM.2(CCCXLI)]. This would increase the authorized strength of the AFISMA, including through the integration of troops provided by Chad and other contingents under preparation, and consequently better meet the needs on the ground. This clearly demonstrates the AU's agency in implementing 'African solutions to African problems' in conflict resolution and peacebuilding by engaging all partners, domestic and foreign, as enabled by the Constitutive Act. In this regard, I argue that self-reliance does not mean total independence but rather taking the initiative and ownership cooperatively within partnerships to find solutions to problems.

The present report takes stock of the deployment of the AFISMA and provides an update on the results of the review process of the Mission's CONOPS. The report also addresses the envisaged transformation of the AFISMA into a UN operation. It concludes with recommendations on the way forward.

The push of the armed groups towards the south and the subsequent Franco-Malian operation, which helped put an end to it and initiate the process for the liberation of the north, led to the acceleration of the deployment of the AFISMA and the adoption of other measures. Several member states of the ECOWAS and other African countries took steps to either announce troop contributions to the AFISMA and/or accelerate their deployment (Benin, Burkina Faso, Côte d'Ivoire, The Gambia, Ghana, Liberia, Niger, Nigeria, Senegal, and Chad). Additionally, the immediate neighbours of Mali (Algeria and Mauritania) further strengthened the monitoring of their borders, or even closed them, to prevent the movement of arms or fighters for the armed rebel, terrorist, and criminal groups. This clearly underscores the principles of subsidiarity and complementarity that emerged between the AU, UN, Mali, France, ECOWAS, and Africa's TCCs towards cooperatively implementing a solution.

Pursuant to the above-mentioned decision of the Council, a planning conference was held in Bamako from 15 to 21 February 2013. It prepared a revised joint CONOPS, based on the latest developments on the ground. The Conference brought together military and civilian experts of the AU and ECOWAS Commissions, Mali, and bilateral and multilateral partners. The revised CONOPS provided for an increase in the strength of the AFISMA from 3,300 to 9,620 troops, including 171 elements of the civilian component, 8,859 troops, and 590 police personnel.

In its new format, the AFISMA has the following strategic objectives: facilitate the mobilization of resources to support the MDSF; support the Malian authorities in the restoration of State authority and the preservation of national unity and territorial integrity; reduce the threats posed by the terrorist groups and transnational criminal networks in Mali and establish a safe and secure environment; and support the Malian authorities in the implementation of the Roadmap for the Transition and assist in the SSR.

The AUC provides strategic direction for the AFISMA. The Special Representative of the Chairperson of the Commission is responsible for the implementation of the Mission's mandate and exercises authority over all civilian, military, and police personnel in the Mission area. The Deputy Special Representative is responsible for managing the civilian organic units. The Force Commander and Chief of the Police component have operational control over the forces assigned to them. The CONOPS was endorsed by the 42nd Ordinary Session of the ECOWAS Authority of Heads of State and Government held in Yamoussoukro from 27 to 28 February 2013.

Multinational Joint Task Force against Boko Haram[28]

The MNJTF is an effort by the LCB states (Cameroon, Chad, Niger, and Nigeria) to pool resources against jihadists that threaten all four countries. The joint force has carried out periodic operations, often involving troops from one country fighting in the neighbouring country. Offensives have won victories and helped instil an *esprit de corps* among participating troops.

---

28   Interview with the Nigerian High Commissioner. 2022-2023. See: Francis, D. (2009). 'Peacekeeping in a Bad Neighbourhood, The Economic Community of West African States (ECOWAS) in Peace and Security in West Africa.' *African Journal of Conflict Resolution.* 9(3).
See: Mutanda, D., (2027). 'What Makes Terrorism Tick in Africa? Evidence from Al-Shabaab and Boko Haram.' *Jadavpur Journal of International Relations.* 21(1). 20-40. Olanrewaju, J. (2015). 'Globalization of Terrorism: A case study of Boko Haram in Nigeria. International Journal of Politics and Good Governance.' (6). 1-22. Radlicki, M. (2015). 'Back to Basics: What ISIS, Al-Shabaab and Boko Haram Have in Common, and How They Preach Water and Drink Wine.' *Mail and Guardian.* 11 June 2015 [Accessed 17 April 2021].

I argue that such a unity of purpose amongst AUMS engenders greater results in self-reliance and that this must be encouraged.

However, nimble militant factions have regrouped rapidly and the MNJTF's effectiveness has suffered from confusion over priorities, the four states' reluctance to cede command to the force itself, and funding and procurement delays. It is clear, that important aspects of the AU's delivery of duty are compromised by the lack of a supra-authority that can enforce compliance. Hence, members of the MNJTF have refused to act under one command and the effectiveness of the implementation of their CONOPS has been limited. This impacts the AU's self-reliance and is an aspect that must be improved.

A successful response to militancy in Lake Chad will depend not only on the joint force but also on whether states can improve conditions for and inspire more trust among residents of affected areas. An improved MNJTF could help deliver such a strategy. The LCB states should boost their planning and communications capacity, intelligence sharing, human rights compliance, and civil-military coordination. They should then reach a consensus with donors on financing.

The LCB states, plus Benin, created the MNJTF in its current form in late 2014 and early 2015. Together they committed just over 8,000 troops to the joint force. The AU authorised the force on 3 March 2015 and envisaged that a sub-regional body, the Lake Chad Basin Commission (LCBC), would assume civilian oversight. The MNJTF established a critically important multilateral framework to combat Boko Haram insurgents, who were increasingly launching attacks across borders. As the MNJTF was not mandated but rather authorized by the AU on 3 March 2015, this is a result of intergovernmentalism and not supranationalism. Therefore, member states can always default to their sovereignty status without fear of legally enforceable compliance. This is an urgent and important area that must be re-worked by the AU because it clearly has consequences in terms of the loss of lives.

The joint force has brought some dividends. Working together has enabled forces from different countries to learn from each other, promoted the idea of cross-border cooperation, and improved tactical coordination. Joint operations, mainly involving Chadian troops deploying into the other LBC states, helped stem Boko Haram's spread in 2015 and 2016 and contained the group, resulting in its split into at least three factions. Short MNJTF offensives in 2017 and 2018, along with a more sustained operation in 2019, also reversed militant gains, freed civilians captured by them or trapped in areas Boko Haram controlled, and facilitated the delivery of humanitarian aid. However, the advances made against Boko Haram and its offshoots have mostly been short-lived. Jihadist factions have consistently weathered offensives. Their resilience is due partly to their ability to escape to other areas and partly to the inability of the states themselves, particularly Nigeria, to follow military operations with efforts to rebuild and improve conditions for the residents of recaptured areas. The situation was further exacerbated by the lack of continuity in earlier operations, allowing jihadists to regroup and rebound even after more extended campaigns, such as the one in 2019. A March 2020 militant assault on a base on Lake Chad was one of the conflict's bloodiest yet, killing some 90 Chadian troops. A subsequent Chadian operation to secure the lake was conducted mainly outside the MNJTF's auspices and militants appear likely to regroup again.

The MNJTF also suffers structural limitations. Its chain of command is weak, even by the standards of multilateral forces, because it comprises units of national forces fighting mainly in their own countries. Many MNJTF troops rotate in and out of the force as national commanders see fit. The under-resourced civilian oversight body, the LCBC, has struggled to exert authority over the force or curb abuses by soldiers who remain accountable to national hierarchies. The AU authorises the force but also has little oversight over it, although the body has tried to forge common practice on the treatment of captured militants and their associates. Funding and procurement delays are prominent. The EU funds the force through the AU, but European money has been held up in Addis Ababa for long periods, delaying the arrival of critical equipment and feeding recrimination among the actors involved. However, the MNJTF's shortfalls only partly explain why militancy persists around Lake Chad. Efforts against jihadists depend mostly on the policies of the states themselves, of which joint operations are only one component. It is, however, clear that the force's flaws limit its effectiveness.

The Joint Force of the G5 Sahel

The Joint Force of the G5 (FC-G5S) is the latest initiative by African member states to reduce the threat of terrorism in the Sahel, a region that is often framed as an arc of instability. The FC-G5S — which includes Mali, Burkina Faso, Niger, Mauritania, and Chad — was authorised by the AU's PSC on 13 April 2017 for 12 months, and was later (20 June 2017) welcomed by the UNSC. It was re-authorised by the AU's PSC for a further 12 months on 12 April 2018. I argue that this evidently represents institutionalization processes taking effect, cooperatively, bilaterally, and multilaterally, under the AU's leadership towards conflict resolution and peacebuilding

The mandate of the force is to: (1) combat terrorism, drug trafficking, and human trafficking to create a secure environment by eradicating the actions of terrorist armed groups and other organised criminal groups; (2) contribute to the restoration of state authority and the return of displaced persons and refugees; (3) facilitate humanitarian operations and the delivery of aid to the affected populations, and (4) contribute to the implementation of development actions in the G5 space.

While the joint force does not have a common doctrine that elaborates a theory of change underpinning its operations, it has developed a CONOPs that was approved by the PSC on 13 April 2017. This mandate contains all the elements of a stabilisation strategy, combining counter-terrorism (CT) with softer (traditionally civilian-led) tasks, such as facilitating humanitarian assistance and development. Several interlocutors have conceded that these will not be the priority, and that the joint force is a purely military tool that will focus on CT. Other aspects of the mandate will be the responsibility of actors such as national governments or the United Nations Multidimensional Integrated Stabilization Mission in Mali (MINUSMA). Once again the AU's PSC is the epicentre of Africa's conflict resolution processes. even amidst challenges such as inconsistent funding and the need for enhanced command and control mechanisms to foster greater self-reliance.

The current priority is to "detect and neutralise all terrorist groups of concern", as well as to prevent trafficking and disrupt supply chains to cut off the groups from their sources of funding. Specific operations will seek to isolate terrorist and criminal groups to deny them a support base, neutralise these groups, protect the local population and control the area. The joint force also aims to make the national military presence on the border posts more permanent, by transitioning existing battalions into a more permanent, sedentary status.

Eventually, it is foreseen that a fully-fledged force could operate in the Sahel, although details of the scope, scale, command and control, and objectives are still in development. The categorisation of all jihadist groups as terrorist armed groups effectively group together a range of disparate actors with different agendas and depoliticises their aims, some of which actually respond to local social and political grievances

Regional Cooperation Initiative for the Elimination of the Lord's Resistance Army

Since the 1990s, the LRA has terrorised the communities of northern Uganda and the surrounding region of South Sudan, the CAR and DRC. In an attempt to eliminate this threat, the AU-led RCI-LRA was developed. This AU-authorised task force brought together the states directly affected by the LRA and represented an important example of security cooperation in Africa.

This analysis provides insight into less traditional forms of regional security cooperation in Africa through the case study of the RCI-LRA in Central Africa. It explores the progress and shortcomings of this task force. It argues that although its successes were limited by its militarised mandate and approach, the operation has been largely effective in downgrading the threat status of the LRA.

I argue that the downgrading of the LRA by the innovation of the AU demonstrates political will and self-reliance despite organisational shortcomings that still require urgent improvement. This example of regional cooperation offers important lessons for other arrangements which deal with similar threats. This type of innovative response represents an emerging trend in security cooperation in Africa and it is clear that task forces of this structure such as the MNFTJ and F-G5S are becoming more capable of dealing with transnational, asymmetrical violence as opposed to more traditional cooperative arrangements. The AU task forces effectively leveraged the innovative and cooperative synergies of the principles of subsidiarity and complementarity, taking into account the proximity to the threat and the impact of the threat on their operations. In this regard, these conditions created the commonalities among member states that facilitated the cooperation.

Analysis

The question of the AU fulfilling its mandate in self-reliance and sustainability is met with uncertainty, particularly over many aspects of the AU's planned troop deployment to fight terrorism in Africa's regions. Since 2019 there has been a reversal of fortune on the AU's gains in bringing about a modicum of peace in Africa. There was a significant resurgence of attacks and violence in several regions of Africa, such as Burkina Faso, Mali, and Niger. It was this observation, and the lack-lustre African support for the Sahel countries, that led Moussa Faki Mahamat, chairperson of the AU Commission, to tell African heads of state and government at the 33rd AU Summit in February 2020 that "the continent has not shown solidarity to its brothers and sisters in the Sahel."

I argue that leadership as demonstrated by Moussa Mahamat, is uneven and lacking in some member states of the AU, which adversely impacts self-reliance as an AU objective. It was also at this meeting, after Mahamat's speech, that African leaders asked the AUC to develop a framework for the possible deployment of a "force composed of the MNJTF and 3 000 troops for six months, to further degrade terrorist groups in the Sahel."

Months later and after several meetings and discussions, what has become of this decision and what can it really add to the already complex reality of the Sahel? The first meetings on the subject at the level of the PSC did not garner the support of all its members. Uncertainty persists over financing and troop contributions. I further argue that the AU demonstrates excellent normative achievements that are not matched by timeous action, implementation, and the impacts of self-reliance. To date, the AU is still largely foreign donor-dependent, hence potential TCCs are reluctant to become involved without predictable funding. If more funding arrives from foreign donors, then who really owns the AU's agenda?

Against this backdrop, the issue of predictable and sustainable funding also raises questions about the ASF and why it has never been mobilised, especially when it has supposedly been fully operational since 2016. Yet Africa continues to set up ad hoc military missions to respond to the very situations for which the ASF was designed. To date, there has been no clear answer to these questions, particularly the thorny issue of funding and self-reliance, which were one of the issues raised in the Kagame Report of 2017

At the same time, the AU Peace Fund, which is currently endowed with around US$150 million, has been touted for the financing of less costly peace activities, such as mediation and preventive diplomacy. Although the initial plan was for the fund to finance 25% of African-led peace operations, its current level and unpredictable contributions mean it is not a viable financing option for any peace support operation at this point in time. Yet again there has not been a fundamental improvement in self-reliance by the AU. Operational questions also remain unanswered, notably concerning the command and control of the force and its potential integration into existing systems. It is precisely this problematic overcrowding of the security space that the AU-proposed force will not resolve.

Finally, the AU must also make use of the peace and security architecture that it has worked hard to put in place, notably the ASF when it comes to mobilising soldiers and carrying out non-combat activities. The multiplication of ad hoc reactions makes efforts to set up long-term mechanisms obsolete and is a waste of resources that the continent cannot afford.

5.2.5 Assessing the African Peace and Security Architecture's International Partnerships

i.   *European Union Support to the African Peace and Security Architecture*

The Joint Africa-EU Strategy (JAES) exemplifies the importance of global multilateralism and interdependence within peace and security, which underscores the EU's approach to capacity training and building for the APSA.

The EU's approach to Africa is predicated on peace and security, which are recognized as crucial components that underpin sustainable trade and economic development. "It is now universally recognised that there can be no sustainable development without peace and security. Peace and security are therefore the first essential prerequisites for sustainable development" (Commission of the European Communities, 2005; EU 2007:3–7). The EU's support for the APSA is provided through the Africa Peace Facility (APF). At its second ordinary session in 2003, the AU Assembly requested that the EU disburse its aid funding through the AU, instead of to member states individually. This achievement by the AU cemented its agency (AU, 2006b).

By preventing the funding from going directly to individual member states, the AU secured funding for its operations, which it may not have been able to elicit from its member states (AU, 2003c: Decision 16). This resulted in the formation of the APF in April 2004 with a budget disbursed by the EU to the AU of €250 000 000.

Out of the total initial funding, €200 000 000 was earmarked for the APSA PSOs, €35 000 000 was for capacity training and building and the remaining €15 000 000 was to monitor and evaluate APSA programmes (Vines and Middleton, 2008:27; Mpyisi, 2009:7).

The APF has provided strategic support to the AMISOM, covering expenses for pre-deployment planning, troop allowances, payment for death and disability, and daily expenses (Pirozzi, 2009:27; AU, 2010:18). However, the APF funding is a double-edged sword. Although helpful to APSA, it comes with conditions that constrain APSA's freedom of operation, i.e., the funding is drawn from the European Peace Facility (EPF) and can only be used for 'non-lethal' purposes.

It therefore has a negative impact on the peace and security sector, where military engagement may be necessary to maintain peace:

> "Decision 2003/3 of the APC/EC Council of ministers of 11 December 2003 proscribes the use of APF funds for military and arms expenditure, military training, EU military technical assistance, or offensive military equipment for the ASF (Pirozzi, 2009:25)."

A 2010 AU report criticised the EU's 'one-size-fits-all conditionalities', where all RECs/RMs were to spend approximately 70% of their previous APF allocations before new funds could be disbursed. Before the 2007 EU-AU summit in Lisbon, the UK wanted to exert its influence to exclude the late President Mugabe's Zimbabwe from the summit. This prompted criticism from Alpha Konare of the AU, who admonished the EU to focus on summit agreements instead of interfering in African politics (Sicurelli, 2010).

These kinds of conditions compromise the APSA and RECs ability to flexibly manoeuvre because these bodies have varying levels of absorptive institutional capacity (AU, 2010g:10). Rene Kouassi, director of Economic Affairs at the AUC, expressed disquiet about the EU's conditions, parallel governance structures, and influence on APSA, suggesting that the Chinese policy of 'no strings attached' to development aid would be preferable for African states (Klingebiel, 2008:54; Franke and Esmenjaud, 2008:149; Sicurelli, 2010).

Until the AU is self-reliant in funding and other required resources, the operability of the AU will be limited. It will be subjected to the conditions of external funders, who have their own priorities and political agendas. However, no nation-state worldwide can sustain itself in isolation. Africa, the EU, and USA are inevitably becoming increasingly interdependent against the backdrop of shrinking global resources and intensive competition.

For example, China has surpassed the EU to become the second-largest global economy. This resulted in Africa benefitting from China's aggregated demand for its commodities, thereby positively impacting its GDP (IMF and WB, 2014)

For the AU to overcome this challenge, it needs to foster strategic partnerships on its own terms by leveraging its soft power influence effectively. The EU, under EURO RECAMP/Amani Africa, supports APSA's extensive training requirement. This programme is now run by the EU's Political and Security Council and implemented by an international team, involving European and African representatives (Bagayoko, 2007:9–19). The EURO RECAMP/Amani Africa programme is financed by the APF, as well as by €20 000 000 in voluntary contributions from Canada and USA.

The EURO RECAMP/Amani Africa promotes a global and multifunctional approach in police support training and capability, civil affairs, human rights, and areas of economic development (Bagayoko, 2007:5; Pirozzi, 2009:36). The overlapping roles of the AU, APSA, and all its organs, is reflective of the inescapable interdependence of nations within the context of globalisation. This is against a plethora of push and pull factors, including issues related to territorial disputes leading to dwindling resources, as well as transnational issues such as climate change, desertification, global terrorism, migration, and diseases.

Although external support from the UN, EU, and USA is sometimes disbursed reluctantly and unpredictably for their own political agendas, it nonetheless bridges many of the capacity gaps within the AU and APSA. This has been the experience of peacekeeping operations in the DRC, Burundi, CAR, Darfur, and Somalia (Kasaija, 2004; Aboagye, 2004; De Conning, 2005:126-132; Murithi, 2010:1). In some ways this catalyses Pan-African agency.

The external funding, planning, training, supplying logistical airlifts, military intelligence, counter-terrorism, and expertise in many technical and specialist areas, have functioned as push and pull factors between various partners of APSA's external partners to enhance Pan-African agency. Many of the

AU's reforms are now underway since the recommendations by the 2012 AU committee. For example, APSA's limited number of administrative staff and its capacity to absorb external support is a case in point. Although €6 000 000 from the APF was earmarked for reinforcing the PSOD in 2008, by 2009, APSA had only spent €1 600 000 due to major procedural obstacles, thereby limiting the extent to which external partners could bridge APSA's capacity gaps (Pirozzi, 2009:26).

The success of the AU's adopted 0.2% levy on all member states' imports, which has been ratified by 38 member states, has brought about minimal improvements in funding and budgeting but the AU is still largely foreign donor-dependent to cover priority areas. The ad hoc nature of external funding, which has not been institutionalised, still remains unpredictable and results in uncertainty. This continues to have an impact on coherent planning and policy implementation (Ekengard, 2008:37). APSA's partners are its capacity trainers and enhancers, with billions of US dollars spent on training and equipment for peace and security missions in Africa since the formation of the AU in 2002.

The AU has turned a zero-sum game, where Africa was a playground of unmitigated violence and strife, into a gradual, peaceful win-win game in a complex asymmetrical hybrid world. This was evident in the anticolonial struggles and immediate postcolonial states of Africa (Nkrumah, 1965; Murithi, 2014). The following section further demonstrates the inevitability of global interdependence and multilateralism, despite the asymmetry in power relations and contesting divergent geo-political interests between the developed Global North and the developing Global South as explained by the DTRP.

ii.   *The United Nations and African Peace and Security Architecture Partnership*

In 2005, a 10YCBP was launched by the UN, which declared its support for 'the development and implementation of capacity-building programmes' to enhance the institutional effectiveness of the APSA (UN, 2005:24) in the following areas:

·   institutional capacity and human resource development;

- peace and security;
- political, legal, and electoral matters;
- social, human and cultural development; and
- economic and environmental development (UN, 2011b).

Paragraph two of the Declaration on the Framework for the 10YCBP describes the programme's objective, which is '"to enhance the capacity of the AUC and African subregional organisations to function as effective UN partners in addressing the UN" (2010, a:6). Using the DTRP/centre-periphery/neo-functional framework to assess the AU PKOs, the following sections explore the ideals of the human security development nexus by way of intervention in the AMIB, AMIS, and AMISOM.

Although the ASF was not yet officially operationalised, the TCCs became the ad hoc building blocks of its evolution. Integral to this assessment was the feedback received from the interviews with peace and security experts. These were contextualised within a triangulated dataset of primary and secondary sources on African peace and security mechanisms and approaches. The UN has a wide-ranging operational and legal partnership with the AU. Under Chapter VIII of the UN Charter 1945 (UN, 2008c:13), the AU is considered a regional organisation by the UN. This makes the AU subordinate to the UNSC, to which it should report under Article 54.[29]

Furthermore, Article 53 of the UN Charter stipulates UNSC supremacy over AU in enforcement of action: "no enforcement action shall be taken under the regional arrangements or by regional agencies without the authorisation of the Security Council" (UN, 1945). This gives the UNSC the right of veto over AU policies in the areas of peace and security. But this is counteracted by AU Article 4(h), which gives the AU the right "to intervene in a member state pursuant to a decision of the Assembly in respect of grave circumstances, namely, war crimes, genocide and crimes

---

[29] Interview with UN officials in South Africa, August 2021. Interviews with Ambassador Matjila former permanent representative of South Africa to the United Nations and former Director-General of DIRCO. November 2022. Interview with Chief Director Mr Zaheer Laher at DIRCO. November 2022.

against humanity." Chapter VIII of the UN Charter neither extends nor proscribes such extensive powers to regional organisations. This is evident from the AU creating its own legal space and agency (Derso, 2010:82).

The precise legal status of regional organisations in relation to the UN is always evolving. The AU Article 4(h) attests and affirms the AU's norm entrepreneurship, highlighting its ability to successfully disseminate and influence the global body of jurisprudence. Furthermore, Chapter VII, Article 51 of the UN Charter, explains that member states have the right to "collective self-defence if an armed attack occurs against a Member of the UN, until the UNSC has taken measures necessary to maintain international peace and security" (UN, 1945).

Further analysis shows that there are loopholes in the provisions of AU Article 4(h).

Article 4(h) of the Constitutive Act establishes the right of the AU to intervene in a member state to prevent grave violations of human rights. It does not state whether the AU should request prior authorisation from the UNSC, leading to many interpretations of the Article. In principle, the AU needs authorisation in accordance with Article 53 of the Charter of the UN. Further analysis reveals that under certain circumstances, the AU could implement such intervention without prior authorisation by the UNSCl. The centralisation of force, in the hands of the UNSC, is crucial for the safety of the international community. Subsequently, any regional actor willing to use force should always request authorisation from the UNSC. This rule also applies to regional organisations such as the AU. Nevertheless, due to a lack of unanimity among its members, the UNSC cannot itself pronounce on whether to give or to refuse such authorisation, while grave crimes such as those mentioned in Article 4(h) of the Constitutive Act are taking place on the continent, the AU has a right to intervene and to put an end to genocide, war crimes, or crimes against humanity. Although there have been cases of Article 4(h)-type interventions in Africa (e.g., in Burundi and the Comoros), the AU Assembly as the highest decision-making organ of the AU has not yet explicitly invoked Article 4(h).

This is similar to the AU's Non-Aggression and Common Defence Pact (AU, 2005a), which legitimises the AU's right to respond in the interests of security. It is devoid of any guarantee of support from the UN for collective action, but after four years of the AU's proactive diplomacy of non-indifference, it forced UN participation in the AMISOM and Darfur (Ekengard, 2008:20).

Within the UN framework, this has catalysed the AU's proactive engagement and asserted its African voice, ownership, and independence. This was emphasised by the AU's policy of non-indifference in Somalia and Darfur. However, William (2006) criticised the AU's policy of intervention in Somalia and Darfur because it lacked the capacity to undertake the missions. Nonetheless, it could be argued that the AU's diplomacy created conditions for a peace agreement, and therefore the UN had no excuse not to fulfil its role in Somalia and Darfur. In the case of the AMIS, it took the AU four years of intensive diplomacy to finally get the UN to participate. This then resulted in a snowballing of diplomacy, forcing the issue of Darfur onto the UN agenda.

The global exercise of AU diplomacy and agency has brought about increased and inextricable interdependence between the AU and the UN. With the approval of the UNSC, the UN allocated a budget to support the AMISOM (Browne, 2011:11). One school of thought argues that the globalisation of the AU and its adoption of UN norms and values, has resulted in the AU's independence and ownership being compromised. This shift is often viewed as a consequence of the increasing interdependence among the world's nation-states and the fluidity of global political dynamics. In addition, hegemonic power does not rest in one nation-state or organisation alone. Global power is constantly and intermittently devolving around state and non-state actors in varied and unpredictable ways, as Klingebiel et al. explained:

> "The AU is not an isolated regime comprising only African actors: this evolving architecture forms part of an international context, and foreign actors are increasingly becoming involved in African peace and security matters (Klingebiel et al., 2008:65)."

Criticism abounds regarding the AU's dependence on UN support for its PSOs and other capacity-enhancement projects, which have allowed the UN to set the capacity-enhancement agenda. This was the case when the US, UK, and Mexico refused to support a UN office for central Africa. Instead, the office was supported by the African states, the UN, and other external partners (UN, 2010b:195). This was a demonstration of the AU's self-reliance. To consider the ability of the AU and its organs to exercise their agency and fulfil their obligations within the Constitutive Act, an institutional audit was deemed essential. The aim was to identify its achievements, shortcomings, and lessons learnt to enhance the performance of the AU towards continental unity and integration. In this regard since 2007 the AU has been unsuccessfully requesting UN assessed contributions to fund the AU PSOs.

The challenges to accessing support from UN-assessed contributions appear threefold: doctrinal (that UN resources cannot be used to fight counter-terrorism operations), accountability and oversight (that the AU meet the necessary financial, administrative, and accountability standards), and burden-sharing (that the AU contribute 25% of the cost of AU PSOs).

The UNSC members' positions have evolved with the enhancement of the UN-AU partnership and the AU's increasing operational capacity to respond rapidly to crises in Africa. There now seems to be a broader agreement in principle that the UN should provide adequate, predictable, and sustainable financing to AU PSOs. The objective of the three African members of the UNSC (A3) in 2018 and 2019 was to secure a clear commitment from the UNSC on the financing of AU PSOs and agree on the broader frameworks and parameters of doing so in the future on a case-by-case basis, as recommended by the High-level Independent Panel on Peace Operations (HIPPO report).

While the 2018-2019 efforts did not lead to a concrete result, future discussions and negotiations on a substantive resolution are likely to build on the work done in the past. Council members will need to come to an understanding on some of the outstanding issues, including burden sharing, which some Council members consider a red line. Additionally, the arrangement described in the consensus paper, whereby the AU would fund 25% of its peace and security activities as a whole, rather than each AU PSOs also needs to be resolved. Regarding accountability and oversight, the AU continues to work towards fulfilling the requirements set out in resolutions 2320 and 2378 with the support of the UN and other partners; some Council members are likely to insist on the AU taking further steps, while others may argue for the need for the Council to show flexibility.

The A3 may have the difficult task of taming expectations in Addis Ababa about UN support for regional operations in Africa. Council members could be willing to provide support bilaterally or through a multi-donor trust fund, but they do not seem ready at this stage to do so through UN-assessed contributions. In its consensus paper, the AU has already indicated its preference for the hybrid and the support office options, which have their advantages and disadvantages. The AU believes that the hybrid option guarantees predictable and sustainable funding, but it also requires a high degree of UN-AU coordination on planning, decision-making, management, and oversight, including a shared political analysis of the conflict situation. Some of these issues have created challenges for the sole hybrid experience in Africa to date, UNAMID. The Secretary-General's report on the lessons learned from the experience of UNAMID (S/2021/1099) notes that "achieving the necessary alignment on a common vision and political direction between the Security Council and the AU's PSC proved challenging because of diverging views among the membership of the Councils".

The support office option appears relatively attractive to both the UN and the AU. In the case of the AMISOM/African Transition Mission in Somalia (ATMIS), the UN provides a logistical support package, whereas the AU would also seek troop allowances. In his upcoming report, the Secretary-General. may share the UN's views on which of these options is the more feasible. In terms of future negotiations, the A3 may have to learn the lessons from the experiences of 2018 and focus on maintaining its unity and cohesion to be able to advance the discussion in the Council.

It would be helpful for the A3 to convene a series of formal and informal meetings to continue building momentum on the financing issue over the coming months ahead of negotiations on a substantive resolution. One possible option is for Mozambique, as chair of the Security Council Ad-Hoc Working Group on Conflict Prevention and Resolution in Africa, and Ghana, as Chair of the Security Council Working Group on PKOs, to jointly organise a meeting on the AU consensus paper and enhance the awareness of Council experts of the salient issues raised in the document.

Another option is for the A3 to convene an Arria-formula meeting through the African Union Compliance and Accountability Framework (AUCAF). The AUCAF is designed to ensure that the African Union peace support operations adhere to international human rights, humanitarian law and AU norms. They invite officials from the AU and the UN to brief members on the progress made and the work that lies ahead. Furthermore, the A3 may need to coordinate with like-minded members to convene a formal Council meeting to deliberate on the upcoming report of the Secretary-General.

These A3 efforts will have to be buttressed by the strong mobilisation of the African Group in New York, which may have to carry out advocacy work not only in the Security Council but also in the General Assembly's Fifth Committee, which is responsible for budgetary decisions. The need for the AU's PSC and the AUC to avoid contradictory messages that could potentially complicate the A3's position in negotiations is equally as important. Keeping Addis Ababa informed every step of the way might be critical for the A3 to avoid confusion and secure consistent support from the AU headquarters in Addis Ababa. The AU may also have to pursue high-level engagement with the USA, particularly with the relevant congressional committees, ahead of negotiations on a substantive Council resolution. It will be necessary to factor in sufficient time for these engagements to secure the necessary support.

The window of opportunity for advancing the discussion on the financing issue seems to be narrow because of the 2024 USA elections. The A3 also cannot take for granted the support from other Council members and will need to continue engaging at various levels over the coming months. What is likely to make the upcoming discussion different from that of 2018-2019 is the sharp shift in geopolitical dynamics in Africa and the prevailing tension among the major powers. This may require the A3 to maintain a difficult balancing act and tread carefully to secure the necessary support from all Council members.

5.2.6 Towards a Regional Security Framework

The APSA's emergence and evolution have been driven by the AU's pursuit of a normatively guided policy framework, promotion of peace, development, and the improvement of African livelihoods toward Agenda 2063 (M2013:267). According to (Murithi, 2016; Souare, 2014: 69-94) the relative successes of the AU in its endeavour for continental peace, have meant that it can now be viewed as a norm entrepreneur and the behaviour of its PSC is considered to be interventionist. Overall, the APSA exists due to the convergence of interests shared by most AUMS in pursuit of Agenda 2063. The AU's APSA is predicated on collective and human security issues, which in turn need to be operationalised by the AU's institutional organs: the CEWS, ASF, PoW, and AU Peace Fund (African Union Commission, 2015:10).

The PSC oversees the processes regionally and multilaterally (Engel and Porto, 2009). It is now a firmly established pattern that no conflict can be comprehensively addressed by the AU, UN, or any other actor alone. Each conflict will see the presence of many regional and multilateral actors, such as the UN, AU, EU, and the relevant RECs and RMs due to globalisation (Souare, 201469-94; Sturman and Hayatou, 2010:70).

A normative and multilateral framework will better equip and inform the AU and its Agenda 2063. Nkrumah's remarks on the historical ties with and influences of Europe and the West on Africa are pertinent in this respect:

"It is impossible to separate the affairs of Africa from the affairs of the world as a whole. Not only has the history of Africa been too closely involved with Europe and the Western Hemisphere, but that very involvement has been the driving force in bringing about major wars and international conflicts for which Africans have not been responsible. Africa has too long been the victim of disruptive aggression, which still attempts to make a hunting ground of our continent."

The words of Emperor Selassie I, on accepting the presidency of the OAU in 1963, are a call to action in response to these influences:

"If we permit ourselves to be tempted by narrow self-interest and vain ambition, if we barter our beliefs for short-term advantage, who will listen when we claim to speak for conscience, and who will contend that our words deserve to be heeded? We must speak out on major world issues, courageously, openly, and honestly, and in blunt terms of right and wrong. If we yield to blandishments or threats, if we compromise when no honourable compromise is possible, our influence will be sadly diminished and our prestige woefully prejudiced and weakened. Let us not deny our ideals or sacrifice our right to stand as the champions of the poor, the ignorant, the oppressed everywhere."

5.2.7 An African Model of Peace Operations

An African model of peace operations is emerging as a result of these developments and is at odds with the multidimensional assumptions that underpinned the original framework of the APSA and ASF. The evolving African model relies normatively on complex hybridity and mutual dependencies, which transcend and problematise neat categories such as regional versus global, vertical and dependency versus ownership.

The revision of APSA, ASF, and other AU organs should be dynamic and ongoing. The AU's transitory Rapid Deployment Capability (RDC) concept should be agile and adaptable to the changing regional and global challenges. It should also be able to adapt to the conflict patterns with which Africa is inextricably intertwined (Bachmann, 2014; AU, 2015b). This discussion has substantively contextualised the inseparability of the promotion of peace and development towards Agenda 2063. A one-size-fits-all framework is inoperable against the asymmetrical contesting global interests, which have an impact on Africa's policy space. The emergence of a new regionalism, is evident in the gradual convergence of COMESA-SADC-EAC, which is a complex mix of bilateralism and multilateralism against global limiting and enabling factors.

In contrast to the above, the doctrine of the AU PSOs is a codification of core principles, practices and approaches that guide the AU PSOs as part of the AU's objective to promote peace, security, and stability on the continent. This occurs within the framework of the APSA and in partnership with the RECs/RMs, the UNSC (as the ultimate authority in international peace and security), and other partners. This doctrine provides the strategic direction and guiding principles that inform how the AU deploys PSOs, as one of the tools for the prevention, management and resolution of conflicts, and as part of its larger contribution to sustainable peace and security in response to complex emergency situations on the continent.

The AU Doctrine on PSOs is informed by the history, experiences, and realities of the AU, RECs/RMs, and AUMS in addressing security challenges through the deployment of PSOs. It represents one of the contributions towards the goal of 'Silencing the Guns in Africa', reflecting the recent and ongoing experiences of the AU PSOs. It also serves as one of the AU's approaches to facilitate collective security, including through close collaboration with other relevant stakeholders, in addressing security challenges in Africa[30].

---

30   Alkire, S. (2003). 'A Conceptual Framework for Human Security.' CRISE Working Paper 2. Queen Elizabeth House, University of Oxford. Atanassova-Cornelis, E. (2006). 'Defining and Implementing Human Security: the Case of Japan.' In Debiel, T, Werthes, S. (eds.) 'Human Security on Foreign Policy Agendas: Changes, Concepts, Cases.' 39–51. University of Duisburg-Essen. Duisburg. See: CHS. (2003). 'Human Security Now.' UN Secretary-General's Commission on Human Security. New York. Available online: http://www. humansecurity-chs.org/finalreport/. See: Jolly, R., Basu R.D. (2007). 'Human Security: National Perspectives and Global Agendas.' *Journal of International Development.* 19(4).

Peace, security, and stability on the continent are key objectives of the AU, as part of efforts to facilitate the regional integration agenda. Within this context, the AU notes that AUMS can be subject to a variety of multifaceted and complex human-made and natural risks that are most times difficult to predict, prevent, and manage. In this regard, the AU has established mechanisms to prevent and address threats to peace, security, and stability on the continent. This is as a result of the improved understanding of possible threats within AUMS with some that also transcend state and regional boundaries (AU 2015b).

Some of these threats include political exclusion and oppression, identity-based conflict, the rise of non-state armed actors, economic decline, the collapse of political orders, and the proliferation of small arms, terrorism, and organised crime. These factors, coupled with accelerated technological developments, continue to contribute to an increase in the number of non-state actors. Together with new political settlements and political cultures, this gives rise to civic, national, and ethnic-based violence due to irredentist and secessionist aspirations and movements (Engel and Porto, 2009). This change in the nature of insecurity on the African continent has contributed to the emergence and re-emergence of many intra-state armed conflicts, which are responsible for the deterioration of security in Africa. As a result, the rise in the number and intensity of complex security challenges in the latter part of the twentieth century led to the development of relevant normative and legal responses

457–72. See: Lee, S-W. (2004). Promoting Human Security: Ethical, Normative and Educational Frameworks in East Asia.' Korean National Commission for UNESCO. Seoul. Lodgaard, S. (2000). 'Human Security: Concept and Operationalization.' Paper for the UN University for Peace.
Available online: http://www.upeace.org/documents/resources%5Creport_lodgaard.doc. MacArthur, J. (2007). 'A Responsibility to Rethink? Challenging Paradigms in Human Security.' Paper to Symposium on Resolving Threats to Global Security, Dalhousie University, Halifax, NS, Canada. MacFarlane, N., Khong, Y. F. (2006). Human Security and the UN: A Critical History. University of Indiana Press. Bloomington, IN. Mack, A. (2005). 'Human Security Report.' University of British Columbia Press. Vancouver. See: O'Brien, K.L., Leichenko, R.M. (2007). Human Security, Vulnerability and Sustainable Adaptation. Background Paper for the UNDP Human Development Report 2007. UNDP. New York, NY.

and frameworks by the AU. This was in an attempt to respond to instances of insecurities by addressing both the underlying causes and symptoms of conflict (AUC, 2015).

When crises arise, they are deeply complex and involve state and non-state actors at various levels. These complex conflicts consist of causes and symptoms which may be inter-state, internally focused, or transnational in nature. Often they are a combination of all of these levels and actors. Common to all these situations is the flagrant disregard for human life and the targeting of civilian communities and individuals for political gain that may result in gross human rights violations, war crimes, crimes against humanity and genocide (Nagar, 2013). These conflict situations can also involve cross-border and transboundary dynamics, such as the movement of refugees, as well as internal displacement and forced migration, which can occur as a result of a crisis and is also a cause for further conflict. Complex conflicts and transnational insecurity can be perpetrated by a variety of state and sub-state actors, such as non-state armed groups, militias, political party armed wings and paramilitary entities, criminal elements and armed civilians, and are not solely conducted by national or regular armed forces (Muruthi, 2014).

As a result, social cohesion and state institutions can collapse and law and order can break down even further, leading to increased violence and an exacerbation of conflict dynamics. Underpinned by the development and integration agenda of the continent, one of the fundamental reasons for the transformation of the OAU to the AU relates to the quest for peace and security and to prevent wars and genocide, such as the 1994 Rwanda Genocide (Kasaija, 2018:140). This determination of African leaders to ensure effective responses to situations of conflict and gross human rights abuses on the continent necessitated the shift from a 'state-centric' to a 'human-centric' approach to security as reflected in the Constitutive Act. In this regard, the adoption of the Constitutive Act marked an introduction of the principle of 'non-indifference' as adopted by the AU. Whereas, the Constitutive Act upholds the principle of national sovereignty and "the right of member states to request intervention from the AU to restore peace and security", it however also reserves the right of the AU "to intervene in a member state in respect of grave circumstances namely: war crimes, genocide and crimes against humanity" (Williams, 2018:172).

The Constitutive Act also emphasises the inseparable link between security and development. This inseparable link is reflected in its Preamble, where it is indicated "that the scourge of conflicts in Africa constitutes a major impediment to the socio-economic development of the continent". The Preamble also notes "the need to promote peace, security and stability as a prerequisite for the implementation of [Africa's] development and integration agenda". In this regard, the AU's PSC Protocol (2002) embraces an expanded and comprehensive agenda for peace and security that includes conflict prevention, early warning, preventive diplomacy, mediation, peacemaking, PSOs, post-conflict reconstruction, peacebuilding, and humanitarian and disaster management (Maluwa, 2003).

The APSA is the embodiment of this expanded agenda for peace and security with the PSC at its core, as a standing decision-making organ for the prevention, management, and resolution of conflicts on the continent. The APSA through the PSC is a collective security and early warning arrangement through which the AU, RECs/RMs, and AUMS have developed several tools, frameworks, mechanisms, and processes for the prevention, management, and resolution of conflicts on the continent, including support for the reconstruction and sof affected countries (Mutanda, 2017:20). This to ensure that the AU has its own mechanisms for the maintenance of peace and security on the continent. In implementing the objectives of the APSA and realising the aim of effective collective security and early warning, the AU's PSC is supported by the APSA pillars, namely: the CEWS, PoW, ASF, and AU Peace Fund (AUC 2019).

The ASF is the standby arrangement foreseen in the APSA through which forces and personnel are generated for the deployment to the AU PSOs, as contained in Article 13 of the PSC Protocol. The ASF was established in 2003 and was declared operational in 2016, after the AMANI Africa Field Training Exercise, was held in 2015 (Kasaija 2012:1-86). The ASF is drawn from three RECs and two RMs, with each expected to contribute civilian, military, and police capabilities, including an RDC. Each regional standby arrangement takes a turn to be on a higher level of readiness for six-months.

The APSA is further complemented by the AGA, which is based on the ACDEG adopted in January 2007. The complementarity between the APSA and the AGA is reflected in Agenda 2063 and the Master Roadmap on Silencing the Guns by 2020 (2017) which is critical to ensure the root causes of conflicts are addressed. This is pursuant to the AU's expanded and comprehensive agenda for peace and security that spans the periods from conflict prevention to post-conflict reconstruction and peacebuilding (Dersso, 2010:73).

It is also in line with the resolution of the AHSG "not to bequeath the burden of conflicts to the next generation of Africans" as outlined in the Solemn Declaration on the 50th Anniversary of the OAU/AU adopted by the 21st AU AHSG in May 2013. (Assembly/AU/Decl.3(XXI) The operationalisation of the APSA takes into account the significance of the relationship and strategic partnership between the AU's PSC and UNSC, pursuant to Chapter VIII of the UN Charter (Dersso, 2011). This is outlined in Article 3(e and f) of the Constitutive Act, indicating the need to encourage international cooperation, taking due account of the UN Charter and the Universal Declaration of Human Rights as well as the need to promote peace, security, and stability on the continent. As a result of this strategic partnership, the AU's PSC cooperates and works closely with the UNSC, which has the primary responsibility for the maintenance of international peace and security (Derso, 2012;4-23).

This also includes cooperation with other relevant UN Agencies in the promotion of peace, security, and stability in Africa. Article 16(2) of the AU's PSC Protocol (2002) also outlines that it shall consult with RECs/RMs, to promote initiatives aimed at anticipating and preventing conflicts as well as peacemaking and peacebuilding in situations where conflicts have occurred (Derblom, 2008). In this regard, consultation, coordination, and cooperation between the AU and RECs/RMs is paramount, in addition to cooperation with AUMS and their national early warning capabilities. The AU, UN, and the RECs/RMs will not be the only stakeholders in any PSO. Thus, effective partnership through consultation, coordination, and cooperation with all stakeholders in a conflict is critical for the success of the AU PSOs (Dersso, 2012:4-23).

This doctrine primarily sets out common fundamental principles, concepts, practices and approaches to guide the processes and policy frameworks for mandating, deployment and management of multidimensional AU PSO aimed at preventing, managing and resolving conflicts It forms the basis for the development of subordinate and subsidiary policy documents such as standards, guidelines and directives that form the overall guidance for the planning, force generation, deployment, management, command and control, support, and liquidation of AU PSO. This doctrine shall inform decision making, with respect to force/capability generation and preparation, force employment, and post-force employment including the training of all AU PSO personnel (civilian, police and military components) at continental, regional and national levels. All processes to mandate, plan, deploy, monitor, manage, sustain, and liquidate AU PSO must be informed by this doctrine (Aning 2010:87).

This doctrine is intended to guide the AU [inclusive of the PSC and/or the AU Assembly of Heads of States and Governments of the AU - as appropriate], RECs/RMs, and AUMS in assessing situations, as well as mandating, planning, deploying, launching, monitoring, managing, evaluating, sustaining and liquidating AU PSOs. The doctrine shall also be used, mutatis mutandis by the PSC when it mandates, authorises, endorses, or recognises a PSO, and when it considers the performance and continuation as well as the drawdown or withdrawal of an AU PSO.

An AU PSO is part of the APSA's expanded and comprehensive agenda that will be used by the PSC, the Assembly, and other AU policy organs, and which includes conflict prevention, early warning, preventive diplomacy, peacemaking (including the use of good offices, mediation, conciliation, and enquiry), conflict management, post-conflict reconstruction and development, humanitarian support, and disaster management (Araoye, 2014). The AU's PSO's are multifunctional and multidimensional operations in which the impartial activities of military, police, and civilian components work to restore or maintain peace within a specific timeframe and area of operations, in pursuit of AU principles and objectives, within the APSA and AGA frameworks (Kasaija, 2012:1-86)

The AU PSOs are intended to assist countries in conflict to create conditions or an enabling environment for political processes led by national and other stakeholders to prevent or resolve conflicts. If such conditions do not exist or are threatened, an AU PSO can be deployed to support efforts to re-establish or create such conditions through political processes aimed at preventing conflict and/or its escalation. In this regard, the AU PSOs may also be deployed to create space for peace to be kept and assist national actors for peace to be sustained. In addition, PSO capabilities will also be used to support humanitarian and relief efforts as well as the broader stabilization processes (Engel and Porto, 2009:82-96).

As this expanded and comprehensive agenda for peace and security indicates, the AU's PSO is not the first and/or only form of response available to the PSC to prevent and manage conflicts and complex emergencies. It also reinforces that when appropriate, the AU PSOs can be deployed as multidimensional and multidisciplinary operations that combine and integrate several elements of the APSA into one multifunctional AU PSO. The aim is to adequately address the interconnected causes and symptoms of conflicts, and support humanitarian and relief efforts, as well as the broader stabilization process (Hulland and Svenson, 2008)·

The AU PSOs can be required to support other complex emergencies, such as Humanitarian Action and Natural Disaster Support (HANDS). For this purpose, they can be mandated, authorized, endorsed, or recognized by AU Policy Organs (inclusive of the PSC and/or the AU Assembly) as appropriate. It is essential to appreciate the strategic context and the nature of the conflict that will shape the conditions within which an AU PSO is conducted, including the means that are used (Klingebiel 2007).

Whilst no two PSOs are the same, the use of fundamental concepts and principles at the strategic level will aid the initial planning and implementation of an AU PSO. Article 3(l) of the Constitutive Act and Article 16 of the PSC Protocol (2002) provide that the RECs/RMs are a constituent part of APSA. Additionally, the need to "coordinate and harmonise the policies between the existing and future RECs/RMs for the gradual attainment of the objectives of the AU" is highlighted (Kobbie, 2009).

These provisions also call for the regular exchange of information, close harmonization, coordination, cooperation, and effective partnership between the AU's PSC and the RECs/RMs with respect to conflict prevention, early warning, preventive diplomacy, mediation, peacemaking, conflict management, post-conflict reconstruction, peace-building, and humanitarian and disaster management (Murithi, 2008:70-82).

To facilitate these processes, the APSA framework and tools enable the AU's PSC to discharge its responsibility for the promotion and maintenance of peace and security on the continent. In enhancing conflict prevention, early warning, preventive diplomacy, and mediation, the AU and RECs/RMs have established collective security and early warning systems at the continental and regional levels to provide decision-makers with timely information, analysis, and recommendations to prevent and/or respond to conflict situations (Lotze, 2016:76-89).

In this regard, coordination between the CEWS of the AU and the early warning systems of the RECs/RMs and AUMS is critical for enhanced collaboration and cooperation for the prevention of conflicts and/or their escalation. They also assist with the planning, deployment, and ongoing management of the AU PSOs (Murithi, 2008:70). In respect of preventive diplomacy and mediation, the AU has established the Pan-African Network of the Wise (referred to as PanWise) and the Network of African Women in Conflict Prevention and Mediation (referred to as FemWise) to support the role and work of the AU. These tools help to bring together relevant mediation actors to support the work of the AU, RECs/RMs, and African civil society to enhance preventive diplomacy and mediation. In this regard, the AU PSOs can be deployed as an instrument to support conflict prevention and preventive diplomacy (Kobbie 2009).

The AU's PSO can further be deployed to create conditions conducive for mediation and negotiation, and can be employed to help implement cease-fires or peace agreements reached through AU-led mediation efforts. Once an AU PSO is deployed, it should continue to support the political process and facilitate further mediation as may be necessary (Komey and Nolawi, 2013).

In respect of conflict management, the AU, RECs/RMs, and AUMS are expected as per the Policy Framework for the Establishment of the ASF and the Military Staff Committee (2003) to continue enhancing the ASF, including other forms of multidimensional AU PSO capabilities to manage conflicts (Murithi, 2008:70).

This is in line with the evolution of the AU s and other subsequent guidance documents, including the need for all AU PSOs to take into account, the linkages between APSA and AGA in the implementation of their mandates. The Policy on Post-Conflict Reconstruction and Development (2006), also offers a framework to ensure effective linkages between the core mandates of AU PSOs, with efforts to assist countries to build resilient structures and systems for durable peace. This also includes efforts relating to Transitional Justice Disarmament, DDR, and SSR, with the latter being guided by the AU Policy Framework on SSR (2013). This provides a basis to support AUMS and the RECs/RMs in the formulation, implementation, monitoring, and evaluation of SSR processes (Mutanda, 2017:20-40). In contributing to a comprehensive approach to conflict management, including the deployment of PSOs, the AU Solemn Declaration on Gender Equality in Africa (2004) guides efforts to facilitate gender mainstreaming in peace and security initiatives.

This Declaration, in line with UNSC Resolution 1325, serves as a framework for ensuring the full and effective participation and representation of women in peace processes, including the prevention, management, and resolution of conflicts, as well as post-conflict reconstruction efforts in Africa (Murithi and Lulie, 2012). The AU Gender Policy (2009) also seeks to provide guidance for enhancing the role of women in creating an enabling, stable and peaceful environment for the pursuit of Africa's development agenda[29]. The AU PSOs are typically composed of multidimensional elements of both uniformed and civilian personnel.

The composition and structures of the mission and the components will depend on the mandate and context and are designed to ensure that AU PSOs are politically directed and that they operate in an integrated and coordinated manner. The APSA and AGA frameworks are mutually reinforcing and complementary.

The AU PSOs that are part of the APSA shall therefore support and incorporate as appropriate, all relevant elements of the APSA and AGA frameworks, to meet the objectives of the PSO that may be needed to prevent conflict recurrence and sustain the peace (Murithi, 2014).

The AU PSOs are distinct from special political missions, technical support missions, AU Representational offices, and operations in response to natural disasters and complex emergencies, all of which are deployed by the AU with their own mandates. In recognition of the importance of the protection of civilians in the AU's response to conflict situations and pursuant to the Communiqué adopted at the 326th meeting of the AU's PSC held on 22 June 2012, Protection of Civilians (PoC) must form part of the mandate of all AU PSOs. In this regard, all AU PSOs shall be conducted in full respect of the principles of International Humanitarian Law (IHL) and International Human Rights Law (IHRL). They should also take all relevant precautions to avoid the loss of civilian life, injury to civilians, and damage to civilian objects, including critical civilian infrastructure, as well as the environment (Nagar, 2013).

As a result, all AU PSOs must ensure compliance with IHL and IHRL, and operate strict standards of conduct and discipline. This is in line with the AU's objective to promote and protect human and peoples' rights, and ensure that all AU PSO personnel as part of the obligations of their member states, respect human rights. Furthermore, the AU and its member states shall continue to respect (Nagar, 2020).

This Doctrine is underpinned by eight core principles that constitute the fundamental values and standards that are the essential elements that guide all AU PSOs. These principles are derived from the foundational legal, policy, and normative instruments of the AU, including the Constitutive Act and other AU statutory provisions and relevant bodies of international law (Murithi and Gueli, 2008:70-82). These principles are interdependent, interrelated, and mutually reinforcing and will ensure that AU PSOs contribute to stability and create the conditions and an enabling environment for political processes and a sustainable peace.

The principles in the AU Doctrine on PSO are outlined and explained below: I. African Leadership; II. Primacy of politics; III. Non-Indifference; IV. Consent; V. Legitimacy; VI. Credibility; VII. Impartiality; VIII. Compliance with International Law and Standards for Conduct; and IX. Use of Force

African Leadership refers to the responsibility of the AU to provide political and strategic leadership and oversight to AU PSOs. This includes the commitment of all stakeholders involved in efforts to address and resolve continental issues, including peace and security challenges, and that all stakeholders undertake to respect the AU's leadership (Nagar, 2020).

This is pursuant to the provisions of Article 7(1) of the PSC Protocol (2002) and includes the authority of the AU Assembly, the AU's PSC, and other relevant organs and structures of the AU to provide decision-making and strategic direction, as well as the leadership, management, and oversight of its PSOs. This is essential to ensure that conflict analysis, prevention, and response efforts on the continent are in line with the strategic perspectives of the AU, RECs/RMs, and AUMS to guarantee durable peace. In this regard, the AU shall take the lead in providing political direction and developing the broader conflict management and resolution approaches, as well as developing contextually appropriate mission plans for all AU PSOs (Ndaguba, 2016).

The primacy of politics refers to the principle and commitment of the AU to ensure that all AU PSOs are deployed with the primary objective of facilitating a political end state as set out in its mandate. In this regard, the AU PSOs shall be geared towards contributing to the search for solutions to ending violence in societies affected by conflict. As a result, AU PSOs are deployed in support of political objectives set out by the AU in the mandate (Ndaguba and Okonkwo, 2017:140-153). Additionally, AU PSOs shall ensure that efforts to prevent, manage, and resolve conflicts are facilitated through dialogue to achieve peace. Dialogue and the peaceful settlement of disputes may however not always be subscribed to by all stakeholders. In such instances, necessary coercive measures may have to be used, which should be guided by IHL and IHRL, as well as strong principles of conduct and discipline, with a primary focus on safeguarding civilians.

Consequently, all AU PSOs shall be deployed as part of a political process for the prevention and/or resolution of a conflict and shall at all times be subordinate to the AU political process as reflected in the mandate.

Non-indifference means that the AU and its member states shall not stand by and not take action, and may deploy even where there is no peace to keep if there is a need to prevent and/or respond to grave circumstances namely: war crimes, crimes against humanity, and genocide. This is an obligation of AUMS derived from the Constitutive Act, which marked a radical shift from the cardinal OAU principle of non-intervention in the national affairs of AUMS to the principle of non-indifference as adopted by the AU.

In this regard, AU PSOs may also be mandated to deploy without the consent of the Host Nation in accordance with Article 4(h) of the Constitutive Act and in conformity with the Common Africa Defence and Security Policy (2004). They must always ensure respect for IHL and IHRL, and the guidelines for the Protection of Civilians. In such instances, the mandate of a PSO will be to intervene, based on the principle of non-indifference, to prevent or end gross violations of human rights, genocide, and war crimes, and to protect civilians, including where acts are perpetrated by state actors

Consent refers to the acceptance of the mandate and deployment of a PSO by the host nation and parties to the conflict in support of a peace process. If a cease-fire, political process or peace agreement is in place, consent will include the agreement of all or some of the signatories to the cease-fire or agreement. Consent therefore requires a commitment to a PSO by the host nation and parties to the conflict. If consent is given by the host nation but cooperation is withheld by other parties to the conflict, the PSO shall employ all efforts to resolve the conflict through dialogue with the other parties. In instances where other parties refuse to cooperate, necessary coercive measures may be used. This includes the degree of cooperation and willingness of the parties to a conflict and the local population to adhere to the terms of a peace process or agreement.

The promotion of consent and cooperation is fundamental to achieving the political end-state of all PSOs. If any of the parties withdraws consent after the PSO has been deployed but the need for an operation remains, the mandate, character, and posture of the mission will have to change accordingly.

The AU PSOs may also be mandated to intervene without the consent of the host nation in accordance with Article 4(h) of the Constitutive Act. In such instances, the mandate of the AU PSOs will be based on the principle of "non-indifference" to gross violations of human rights, genocide, and war crimes, including when perpetrated by state actors. The AU PSOs must strive to ensure that consent is managed and sustained at all levels, while at the same time assistance is given in the implementation of a peace agreement or supporting a peace process. The complete withdrawal of consent by one or more of the parties can challenge the rationale for the PSO and is likely to reshape the fundamental assumptions and parameters that form the basis of strategies employed by the AU, Host Nation, and the international community to support a peace process.

In this regard, a PSO should continuously manage the situation to sustain or further improve consent, by analysing its operating environment to detect and forestall any wavering of consent. However, concerns about consent should not prevent a mission from carrying out its mandate, such as the protection of civilians. Consent needs to be pursued in balance with the other principles highlighted in this doctrine

The legitimacy of an AU PSO is premised on the mandate issued by an appropriate policy organ of the AU as well as parties to the conflict for an AU PSO. The legitimacy of a PSO is a crucial factor for drawing support from AUMS, RECs/RMs, the UN, the international community, parties to the conflict, and the local population. However, the perception of legitimacy will vary among the stakeholders in a conflict situation. Perceptions of legitimacy may change over time, depending on political activity, the expectations of the population and conflict parties, local conditions, and the performance of the PSO. The manner in which an AU PSO conducts itself will have a profound impact on its perceived legitimacy on the ground.

The firmness and fairness with which an AU PSO exercises its mandate, the timeliness of the PSO in responding to emerging issues in the area of operation, the respect it shows to local culture, institutions, and laws, and how it engages with the population all have a direct impact upon the perceptions of the mission's legitimacy. The bearing and behaviour of all AU personnel must adhere to the AU's standards of conduct, IHL, and IHRL, and should meet the highest standards of professionalism, efficiency, competence and integrity. In instances of allegations of or actual violations of accepted standards of conduct, immediate and remedial responses shall be taken by the AU and TCCs to ensure redress and prevent the occurrence of similar instances in the future.

Credibility refers to the trust bestowed on a PSO by parties to the conflict that the PSO will deliver the expected objectives. Establishing credibility will also create confidence in the operation, not only amongst the parties to the conflict and the affected population but also with the international community and the relevant stakeholders working with and alongside the PSO. A precondition for the credibility of an AU PSO should include a clearly deliverable and achievable mandate and unity of effort by all stakeholders in the area of operation.

This includes being able to deploy and respond quickly to conflict situations with the requisite capabilities and operational effectiveness. Any loss of credibility will have significant negative consequences for a PSO, including reduced cooperation by parties to the conflict and support from the population, which is critical. Such loss of credibility can include actual or perceived failure to protect civilians and deter human rights abuses of the population. In this respect, effective promotion of and respect for human rights and IHL, in addition to fulfilling other applicable legal obligations, will help establish and maintain the credibility of a PSO.

Impartiality refers to the objectivity and fairness of a PSO, which is expected to not take sides in the implementation of the mandate. In this regard, in the implementation of their mandates, AU PSOs shall always be impartial and ensure that they do not favour one party over another.

In this regard, cooperation is expected from all parties to the conflict to enable AU PSOs to employ all efforts to resolve the conflict through dialogue. In instances where any of the parties to a conflict may refuse to cooperate, the AU PSO shall be mandated and authorised to use the necessary coercive measures to bring parties to dialogue to resolve the issues.

This may include the need to ensure the protection of civilians in line with the mandate and the responsibility and obligation of the AU and its member states to prevent or respond to war crimes, genocide, and crimes against humanity, and to respect international law more generally. Under these circumstances, AU PSOs shall not be indifferent but will act in accordance with their mandate to meet their responsibility and obligation to protect civilians under international law. The AU PSOs must implement the mandate without favour or prejudice to any party.

The effectiveness of AU PSOs may depend in part on how impartial, legitimate, and credible they are perceived to be by all parties involved. There is a risk that they may be viewed as favouring specific groups or even be seen as directly involved in the conflict. Impartiality is therefore crucial to maintaining the consent and cooperation of the parties, but should not be confused with neutrality or inactivity. The AU PSOs should be impartial in their dealings with the parties to the conflict, but not neutral in the execution of their mandate, including the use of force when required, and as stipulated in their mandate.

The use of force is the employment of lethal and non-lethal measures by AU PSO personnel to ensure or compel an unwilling party to comply with the political process for the resolution of a conflict, the mandate of the PSO, and international law. In this regard, the use of force must be guided by applicable IHL and IHRL provisions and standards, and other applicable guidelines. The framework governing the use of force is critical in the employment of lethal and non-lethal measures by AU PSOs. The details of how and when force will be used in each AU PSO will be specified in the AU Rules of Engagement (ROE) for the military component, AU Directives on the Use of Force (DoUF) for the police component, and other applicable guidance documents for the civilian component.

Misuse of force can have a negative effect on the ability of a PSO to achieve its long-term goal of contributing to durable peace, as well as the safety and security of mission personnel, premises, and facilities. Any use of force should be carefully managed, with the capability and willingness to use force applied prudently. All positive measures, including a risk assessment, should be taken to avoid or minimise casualties among non-combatants and the PSOs own mission personnel, as well as damage to installations and other collateral damage. Nonetheless, all necessary force shall be used when a PSO is at risk, to create an immediate impact, deter further acts of aggression, and maintain credibility and stability.

Whatever the circumstances, the use of force should be seen as a tool to set the conditions and create an enabling environment in support of a political process towards achieving peace in the long-term. Within the context of the principle of the use of force, AU PSO personnel shall abide by all requirements applicable under the AU Compliance and Accountability Framework, IHL,

IHRL, conduct and discipline standards, and other appropriate applicable international norms and standards.

In particular, AU PSO personnel shall ensure that all detainees in their custody, including disengaged fighters are treated in strict compliance with AU guidelines on detainees and disengaged fighters and the applicable obligations under IHL and IHRL. The AU must ensure that all AU PSOs have a protection mandate and are compliant with IHL and IHRL, as well as applicable international norms and standards of conduct and discipline. In this regard, a comprehensive framework for conduct and discipline compliance and accountability in AU PSOs guides the development and review of the required policies and guidelines.

This includes policies and guidelines that ensure adherence to applicable IHL, IHRL, and conduct and discipline principles, as well as the AU PSO Code of Conduct. This is done by taking into account the nature of the contemporary threats and contexts in which AU PSOs are deployed into. The AU Compliance and Accountability Framework, IHL, IHRL and conduct and discipline standards set out steps and approaches for policy development, as well as the review and effective implementation of IHL, human rights principles and conduct and discipline obligations.

This includes policies and processes for preventive measures during planning, training, and monitoring, as well as the response and accountability mechanisms at the strategic and mission levels to address allegations and violations of protocol should they occur. As part of these efforts, the Protection of Civilians norm characterizes the shift from 'noninterference' to 'non-indifference' as well as the shift from state-centric to human-centric approaches to security. The Protection of Civilians norm therefore underpins all AU PSO operations as emphasized by the PSC that all current and future AU PSOs shall have a Protection of Civilians mandate.

The AU has also developed a set of guidelines for ensuring the protection of civilians through a four-tier approach as follows: a. protection as part of the political process; b. protection from physical violence; c. rights-based protection; and d.

establishment of a protective environment. The harmonization and integration of international law and international PSO norms have been adopted into the strategic, operational and tactical policies, guidelines, approaches and activities of AU PSOs. Adopting and implementing the highest standards of these international legal and normative frameworks into AU PSOs is thus crucial for implementing the principle of 'non-indifference' and for the effective protection of all groups of people in an area of operation. This is also critical for enhancing legitimacy and credibility as well as improving and solidifying partnerships in PSOs, particularly with the UN. In this regard, the integration of compliance and accountability considerations must be prioritised and mainstreamed at all stages and levels of a PSO to contribute to mission effectiveness and success.

The AU and RECs/RMs have demonstrated the value of regional or sub-regional actors taking the lead in responding to conflict through the deployment of PSOs. However, the AU notes that it will not be the only stakeholder in a PSO environment. The AU PSOs are thus deployed within the context of larger international peace and security efforts and are expected to coordinate with and participate in international coordination platforms. In this regard, AU PSOs are expected to work closely with the relevant international and regional stakeholders, as well as with the host state, national and local institutions, and civil society. As a result, the extent of engagement of different stakeholders hinges on the specifics of each conflict situation, and therefore consultation and coordination with the relevant stakeholders is essential.

This will ensure coordination and cooperation throughout the duration of an AU PSO. The decision to deploy an AU PSO should therefore take into consideration the comparative advantages, synergies, and partnership with relevant stakeholders.

This approach is in line with the need for collective measures for the prevention and removal of threats to peace. It also enhances international cooperation to ensure effective partnerships in the promotion and maintenance of peace, security, and stability on the continent and the world at large.

Thus, partnerships in PSOs are essential for the AU but also the UN. Whilst the UNSC has the primary responsibility for the maintenance of international peace and security, the AU has the responsibility for the maintenance of peace and security on the African continent. The AU shall thus lead on a variety of peace and security initiatives on the continent in collaboration and coordination with the UN, EU, and other relevant partners. This shall be based on the AU and UN strategic partnership, comparative advantages, and synergies, in line with the shared vision of each institution.

The Assembly is the highest policy organ of the AU and is composed of the heads of state and government of all AUMS. The Assembly is also the highest decision-making body of the AU, including on matters relating to peace and security.

In matters relating to peace and security, the AU Assembly has delegated its powers to the AU's PSC to determine how to respond to conflict situations on the continent. The PSC Is a standing decision-making organ for the prevention, management, and resolution of conflict to ensure peace, security, and stability in Africa. In this regard, the PSC is the mandating authority for AU PSOs and is the main pillar of the APSA in its efforts to ensure timely and efficient conflict prevention and respond to conflict situations on the continent. It also authorises, endorses, and recognises PSOs undertaken by other entities. The AUC is the secretariat of the AU. It is responsible for planning, deploying, launching, monitoring, managing, sustaining, and liquidating AU-mandated PSOs. It also provides support to AU PSOs that are authorized, endorsed, or recognised by the PSC or appropriate AU policy organs.

The RECs/RMs are the building blocks of the APSA and the AU, and they have the responsibility for promoting peace, security, and stability in Africa. In this respect, the AU's PSC and the Chairperson of the Commission, shall: (a) harmonise and coordinate the activities of RMs in the field of peace, security, and stability to ensure that these activities are consistent with the objectives and principles of the AU; and (b) work closely with RECs/RMs, to ensure effective partnerships between them and the AU's PSC in the promotion and maintenance of peace, security, and stability. The modalities of such partnerships shall be determined by the comparative advantages and the prevailing circumstances.

The UN Charter states that the UNSC has the primary responsibility for the maintenance of international peace and security as spelt out in Chapter V, Article 24, of the UN Charter (1948). Chapter VIII, Article 53(1) of the UN Charter also outlines that the UNSC shall, where appropriate, utilise regional arrangements or agencies for enforcement action under its authority. AU In this regard, the AU and UN have prioritised the development of a systematic, predictable and strategic partnership, based on mutual respect, shared values, comparative advantages and complementarity

Ensuring a systematic, predictable and strategic partnership between the AU and the UN is based on the fact that no single entity or organisation can undertake PSO alone effectively and successfully. As a result, regular exchanges of information, coordination, cooperation, and effective partnerships between the AU's PSC and the UNSC is essential throughout the duration of all AU PSOs. Partnerships between the AU and the UN should be based on a strategic vision and objectives as well as the common goals of both institutions.

Host nations are those states in whose territory an AU PSO shall be deployed. This may be one or more nations depending on the scope and nature of the conflict and the mandate of the AU PSO. Host nations are essentially the entities recognised by the AU as the legitimate government and associated state apparatus. Host nations must consent to a PSO being deployed on their territory. However, this will not always be the case as there may be instances where the AU will mandate a PSO without consent, pursuant to Article 4(h) of the Constitutive Act.

Other partners also play vital roles in the success of PSOs. They include the EU, NATO, and other non-African states that have played important roles in support of AU PSOs. Coordinated and needs-based technical and financial assistance from these stakeholders will remain valuable in support of AU PSOs. These stakeholders provide essential funding but also crucial logistical support and training packages to AU PSOs. This comes in a range of training activities such as contingent pre-deployment training, mission headquarters training, police training, and support to regional training centres affiliated to the AU. The International Committee of the Red Cross (ICRC) notably provides support for IHL training. Engagement with the ICRC is of particular importance given the organisation's specific mandate and operational experience in situations of armed conflict. Other relevant partners can also enhance the legitimacy and credibility of AU PSOs.

Non-state armed groups is a broad category that can apply to a range of different stakeholders. Such stakeholders can be affiliated, aligned, or opposed to a state. In this regard, reference is made to rebel movements, militias, local/village defence groups, terrorist or violent extremist groups, and criminal gangs. This excludes private security organisations that possess arms under licence and operate within a state legitimately.

Populations refers to all non-combatant inhabitants in an area of operations. This is inclusive of citizens, permanent and temporary residents, IDPs, and refugees who are present within the area of operations. Populations are diverse, with many cleavages that include the urban/rural divide, vulnerability, identity and inter-communal tensions, and class issues. The Protocol to the African Charter on Human and Peoples Rights on the Rights of Women in Africa (2003) and the AU AHSG Solemn Declaration on Gender Equality in Africa, commits African governments and civil society, amongst others, to protect and respect the rights of women in situations of armed conflict.

In addition, the UNSC Resolution 1325 on Women, Peace, and Security (2000) highlighted the importance of incorporating a gender perspective, and ensuring women's participation in all decision-making processes throughout all stages of armed conflict and recovery. The AU instruments and this UN Resolution call for the inclusion of women and gender perspectives at all levels, and in all areas of conflict prevention, conflict resolution, peacekeeping, and peacebuilding. The AU recognises the gendered nature of conflicts, conflict management and post-conflict reconstruction and development. The consideration of gender perspectives is essential, especially concerning the gendered impact of conflicts on men and women, boys and girls, and the elderly. It is essential to address the specific requirements of various groups such as women, youth, children, and vulnerable populations, as well as to empower them to actively participate in conflict resolution of and build resilience. As a result, gender and the considerations of women must be mainstreamed in all stages of AU PSOs.

The Constitutive Act, and Article 20 of the Protocol Relating to the Establishment of the AU PSC, as well as aspirations 4 and 6 of Agenda 2063 reiterate the goal of a peaceful and secure Africa> They call for an Africa whose development is people-driven and reliant on the potential offered by people, especially its women and youth. The African Youth Charter adopted by the 7th Ordinary Session of the Assembly held in Banjul, The Gambia, on 2 July 2006, and particularly Article 17, also recognizes the important role of youth in promoting peace and security in Africa.

As a result, mainstreaming the issues of youth, including their participation and contribution to conflict resolution, is critical in ensuring a peaceful and stable Africa, and moving towards achieving the goal of regional integration. The AU notes that children make up a sizeable majority of the population in the conflict-affected countries of Africa. These children face serious abuses and violations of their rights and IHL needs to protect them in the context of armed conflict. The AU is also aware that annually, thousands of boys and girls are killed or maimed, recruited/abducted, and used by parties to participate in conflicts. Additionally, they are victims of sexual violence and are also denied access to humanitarian assistance.

In this regard, a series of decisions, including AU Assembly decision Assembly/AU/Dec.718 (XXXII) adopted by the 32nd Ordinary Session of the AU held on 10-11 February 2019 in Addis Ababa, Ethiopia, emphasize the importance of enhancing the existing AU and REC/RM mechanisms on child protection. In this regard, AU PSO's must continuously take the necessary steps to protect children in the implementation of their mandates to ensure full compliance with IHL, and in particular to ensure that schools are not attacked and used for military purposes. Additionally, AU PSOs are expected to guarantee the social and cultural rights of child refugees or IDPs, according to the ACRWC.

The AU PSOs shall coordinate, collaborate and cooperate with the Private Sector as well as traditional structures, and local and international Non-Governmental and Civil Society Organisations (NGO/CSO), in the area of operation, throughout the duration of an AU PSO. Local and international media are also part of this category and are always present in PSO environments to report on the conflict, including the actions of a PSO on a daily basis. The factors identified below are essential for the success of AU PSOs and apply to all components and all stages of an AU PSO.

It is essential that AU PSOs are grounded in the context of the conflict they are deployed to address. Operations and the personnel that constitute them must understand the causes and dynamics of the specific conflicts they are deployed to manage. Operations that are not tailored to or informed by local dynamics are unlikely to be effective. Appropriate and adequate capacities and capabilities should be provided and availed by the AU and its member states to guarantee the effective and successful implementation of AU PSO mandates issued by the AU's PSC and/ or the AU Assembly.

Partners may also assist in this regard and the AU should ensure that capacities and capabilities are determined by and linked to the mandate to enable an AU PSO to achieve its desired end state. In addition, the need for skilled and trained personnel in PSOs requires investment in the development of their capacities.

The AU PSOs should be adequately resourced and sufficiently financed. This is a fundamental prerequisite for the effectiveness and achievement of the mandate. The financing of an AU-mandated PSO is the responsibility of the AU. Funding of AU PSOs can also be sourced from other AU partners. The AU provides financial and other forms of support to PSOs based on a case-by-case assessment for operations that it authorises, endorses, or recognises.

The AU's force and capability generation for its mandated PSOs will prioritize the ASF as a timely, predictable, and dependable African standby mechanism. Through the ASF, the AU aims to efficiently prepare both uniformed and civilian personnel for its operations. If all the required personnel and equipment cannot be generated through the RECs/RMs using the ASF mechanism, the AU may enter into direct arrangements with AUMS who can provide the required capabilities.

The AU shall, in deploying an operation, consider the concept of a Lead Nation approach, wherein an AU Member State with the required capabilities provides the operational lead in coordinating the planning, deployment, and execution of an AU PSO. It can also be in the form of a coalition wherein a group of two or more AUMS agree to work together to achieve a common specific goal, as may be guided by the PSO mandate

This Doctrine forms the basis for the training of all AU PSO personnel (military, police, and civilian components). It also informs the issuance of strategic training directives, policies, standards, and guidelines by the AU. Personnel must be well prepared for the positions they fill and the Doctrine is applicable across all components. Training on core PSO activities and concepts as well as relevant legal obligations, AU policies, standards, and guidelines should also be part of all pre-deployment training. Training must therefore enhance skills and knowledge about how to perform a specific role in a specific mission as well as providing a broad understanding of PSO activities.

Understanding, interpreting, and translating mandates into tasks and functional activities as well as a detailed understanding of mission-specific regulatory frameworks, such as the CONOPS, must also be mandatory in any training for relevant personnel at appropriate levels. Pre-deployment should be augmented throughout the tenure of PSO personnel through in-mission training where possible. The responsibility for the conduct of training lies at different levels, with the AU, RECs/RMs, and member states having different responsibilities. In this regard, the AU shall provide strategic guidance for training, the RECs/

RMs shall provide operational guidance and training, whilst the member states shall provide tactical-level training. All training for AU PSOs must reflect the concepts, principles, and approaches outlined in this strategic doctrine. In addition to the three levels of responsibilities, AU PSOs shall facilitate additional training (in the mission area) to enhance the capacity of AU PSO personnel, including support from Training Centres of Excellence (TCEs), and other relevant training, research, and academic institutions.

An AU PSO must be flexible and its mission planning and execution of tasks should be adaptable to the context where deployed. A conflict is not static and can change at any time during its lifespan, as can the circumstances surrounding a PSO deployment. Operations must therefore be able to react and respond accordingly and effectively to changing conflict dynamics. It is critical to monitor and evaluate both the conflict and the responses and strategies.

An AU PSO is multidimensional in terms of its tasks and participation, and involves a multiplicity of actors who engage on a variety of issues. Inter-departmental cooperation at Strategic Headquarters and cooperation amongst all participating elements is essential to achieve the strategic objectives and political end-state specified in the mandate.

The multidimensional and multifunctional nature of AU PSO means that the Strategic Headquarters may have multiple, concurrent, and sequential engagements and lines of activity in the operation. When the Strategic Headquarters has more than one line of engagement and activity, there should be interdepartmental coordination at the Strategic Headquarters and in the field to ensure an AU system-wide coherent approach towards the realisation of the common objective. In relevant instances, there must also be coordination between AU PSOs and regional efforts within the same operation.

An AU PSO may involve various actors including the UN, international humanitarian agencies, multilateral development agencies, and bilateral partners. Collaborating with the various actors in an AU PSO offers an opportunity for the AU to provide strategic guidance to leverage resources, enhance complementarity, and minimise competition (Kouassi, 2007:50-62).

Unity of effort amongst components is essential for mission success. Military, civilian and police components must therefore be aware of each other's roles, responsibilities, and strategies as well as combining each other's expertise where relevant and required. An AU PSOs activities and tasks require integrated planning and operation. All components must be aware of all tasks and activities being carried out in the operation, including those that are predominately performed by one component (Lotze, 2016:50-62).

This Doctrine promotes the goal of 'Silencing the Guns in Africa' and is a manifestation of recent and ongoing PSO experiences of the AU. It also represents one of the AU's approaches to facilitating collective security, including through close collaboration with other relevant stakeholders in addressing security challenges in Africa. It is not exhaustive due to the fluid and dynamic nature of Africa's security environment. Efforts are therefore made to ensure periodic reviews and updates following directives by relevant AU decision-making organs and within the framework of APSA and the relevant stakeholders. Such coordination and partnership, as well as the provision of required capabilities, resources, and funding, will ensure the effectiveness and achievement of AU PSO mandates (Lotze and Williams, 2016).

The TFTA was launched in 2015 and brings together 29 countries to create a single market for the COMESA-EAC-SADC Tripartite region. It is expected to enter into force once it attains ratification by 14 member /partner states from the three RECs.

At the 9th meeting of the ministers who constitute the Tripartite Sectoral Ministerial Committee (TSMC) of the COMESA, EAC and the SADC in March 2023, the key agenda items were to consider the progress reports of the Tripartite Committee of Senior Officials covering the three key pillars of the TFTA namely; market integration, industrial development, and infrastructural development complemented by the cross-cutting issues of resource mobilisation and the FMP. The following objectives were set:

- promoting economic and social development of the Tripartite region;
- creating a large single market with free movement of goods and services to promote intra-regional trade;
- enhancing regional and continental integration processes; and
- building a strong TFTA for the benefit of the people of the three RECs of COMESA, EAC, and SADC.

The Minister of Trade and Industry of Egypt, Hon. Ahmed Samir, chaired the meeting and stressed the need to ensure that ratification of the TFTA was achieved. He said this will enable the agreement to enter into force and enable the member states to overcome the current challenges, such as the impact of COVID-19 and the global economic difficulties.

Currently, 22 tripartite member/partner states have signed the Agreement, of which 11 (Egypt, Uganda, Kenya, South Africa, Rwanda, Burundi, Botswana, Namibia, Eswatini, Zambia, and Zimbabwe) have ratified it. Only three more ratifications are required for the Agreement to enter into force.

Malawi and Tanzania have reported that their respective processes to ratify the agreement were underway and are expected to be completed soon. Kenya has reported that it is championing the ratification of the TFTA. The Kenyan Minister of Trade has conducted several missions, as the special envoy of his government, to lobby the remaining regional states to ratify the agreement.

A further key milestone of the TFTA reported at the meeting was the development of an online NTB reporting, monitoring, and resolution platform. Under this platform, individual RECs can effectively and expeditiously report NTBs, which can then be resolved.

5.3   Conclusion

This chapter used the DTRP/centre-periphery framework as explained in chapters 2 and 3 to assess the AU's efforts at continental integration. The chapter examined the AU's attempts at self-reliance through its governance, peace, and security institutions initiatives. It critically analysed the AU's various organs and programs, such as the AUC, its secretariat, APSA, and AGA, while pinpointing the gaps it aimed to address. It further argued that part of AU's challenges were both continental and geopolitical, such as the threats from terrorism and global terrorist networks; transnational organised crime; the growth of illicit economies; climate change and food insecurity; the depletion of water and other energy resources; and global health threats, such as Ebola and COVID-19 (Gottschalk, 2004:138-158).

The chapter further provides a comprehensive assessment of the AU's pursuit of self-reliance and sustainability in the area of good governance under the AGA, and through the operation of various AU organs and institutions, including the APRM; ACHPR; ACERWC; AfCHPR; The AUABC; AUCIL; AUC; Economic, Social, and Cultural Council; PAP; PSC; and RECs.

Furthermore, the chapter critically examines the AU's pursuit of self-reliance and self-sustainability in peace and security through the APSA. It does so by interrogating APSA's five pillars (PSC, PoW, ASF, CEWS, and Peace Fund), four of its peacekeeping missions (AMIB, AMIS, AMISOM, and the African Union in the Comoros), APSA's international partnerships, and the regional security cooperation spearheaded by the Tripartite bloc (comprising the SADC, EAC, and COMESA).

Chapter 6

The African Union's Pursuit of Socio-Economic Self-Reliance and Self-Sustainability: Towards the African Continental Free Trade Area and Global Multilateralism

6.1 Introduction

This chapter builds on Chapter 5, which focused on the AU's efforts at self-reliance, thus assessing its governance, peace and security institutions, and initiatives. This chapter aims to provide an objective examination of the implementation of the AfCFTA by the AU amidst global multilateralism and its institutions, namely the WTO; BRICS, NDB, BRI, FOCAC; G20; IMF; WB; and UN.

The AU's initiatives and development policies continue to be exercised within the legal frameworks of its past declarations, treaties, and constitutive documents. The functionalist and neo-functionalist role of the AfCFTA within the DTRP is outlined in pursuit of sustainable socio-economic policies of self-reliance.

In January 2012, 54 African countries agreed to establish the AfCFTA during the 18th Ordinary Session of the AHSG of the AU in Addis Ababa, Ethiopia. Thus, the AfCFTA became a flagship programme for deepening the integration of development policies among AUMS. The AfCFTA is a normative work in progress, which delineates the legal boundaries, flexibilities, and variable geometry enabling it to realise a better life for African people.

These flexibilities have enabled a comprehensive set of adaptable tools and institutions for the AfCFTA, thereby promoting continental economic integration towards the AEC, a flagship project of Agenda 2063. The AfCFTA is not a 'one-size-fits-all' blueprint for working in a marginalising asymmetrical global economy, it is a blueprint that has the freedom, pragmatism, and agility to operate in a variety of situations.

The chapter elaborates on the role of the AfCFTA and its contribution to the security-development nexus, which has the potential to foster cooperation on security among African institutions regarding transboundary and transnational violent extremism and terrorism. First, the AfCFTA has created and reinforced opportunities towards realising the AU's aims and objectives in materialising Agenda 2063. The AfCFTA creates an opportunity for high-impact entrepreneurship to improve complementarities and deepen integration, holistically, in the socio-economic and human security nexus. Second, the AfCFTA provides opportunities to scale e-commerce and ensure greater connectivity within the Fourth Industrial Revolution (4IR) ICT domain, thus enhancing intra-regional trade predicated on RVCs. Third, the AfCFTA creates opportunities to establish a more human-centred approach to trade through the effective integration of human rights. This compliments the more integrated approach that has been adopted to continental peace and security. The human security nexus will foster integrative development policies and security among African institutions.

The fostering of integrated development policies will enable robust civil society bottom-up activism, connecting to vertical top-down, and lateral intra-REC and RM collaborative agency for greater transparency and accountability. This will aid in expanding on the research objectives concerning the DTRP functional and neo-functional roles of the AGA, APSA, AfCFTA, and REC's. These roles are crucial for establishing an environment that fosters for setting an environment conducive to economic development in Africa.

The link between the AfCFTA and security cannot be understated. It is from a human security-development nexus angle that the AfCFTA will enable a more cooperative security regime to spur human security and development. Security and development are mutually reinforcing because without development the propensity for and conditions conducive to conflict emerge. Inversely, without security, development is restricted. As Collier (2008) maintains, "War retards development but conversely development retards war."

The AfCFTA[31], as a flagship of Agenda 2063, should enable horizontal and lateral linkages with APSA, AGA, and all AU organs. This will result in centripetal convergencies in intra-Africa trade and attract both continental investment and FDI. The human security development nexus of the AfCFTA will be explored later in this chapter, using its key aims and mandates as outlined in the treaty's framework.

The AfCFTA will therefore be considered as both a limiting and enabling factor in several situations, dealing with pull and push, centripetal intentions, and centrifugal factors to realise the aims of Agenda 2063. These dynamics have a further impact and contribute towards the evolution of AU initiatives and development policies.

6.2   The African Continental Free Trade Area

The AfCFTA is the world's largest FTA in terms of participating members. It was officially launched on 7 July 2019 during the AU Extraordinary Summit in Niamey, Nigeria. Its formation represented the incremental and cumulative effects of AU development policies, including the institutional reforms of the Audit Report (2007) and the Kagame Report (2017).[32] The AfCFTA came into force on 30 May 2019, after 22 countries had deposited their ratifications with the AUC and the minimum threshold had been reached. The vision of African continental integration to which the AfCFTA contributes has been a goal for over 50 years (Gerout et al., 2019). This aligns with the vision of Kwame Nkrumah, who surmised that political independence is inextricably linked to economic independence (Nkrumah, 1957). The is a milestone in this regard.

On 7 October 2022, the AfCFTA Secretariat launched the AfCFTA Guided Trade Initiative in Accra to allow for commercially

---

31   See Article 3(a) of the Agreement Establishing the AfCFTA.
32   AUC. (2019). 'Institutional Reforms of the African Union: A Review of Progress made in the Implementation of Decision Assembly/AU/ Dec.635(XXVII).'

meaningful trade under the Agreement to commence for eight participating countries: Cameroon, Egypt, Ghana, Kenya, Mauritius, Rwanda, Tanzania, and Tunisia, representing the five regions of Africa. This initiative is currently used to pilot the operational, institutional, legal, and trade policy environment under the AfCFTA.

As of August 2023, 47 of the 54 signatories (87%) have deposited their instruments of AfCFTA ratification (ordered by date): Ghana, Kenya, Rwanda, Niger, Chad, Eswatini, Guinea, Côte d'Ivoire, Mali, Namibia, South Africa, Congo, Rep., Djibouti, Mauritania, Uganda, Senegal, Togo, Egypt, Ethiopia, Gambia, Sahrawi Arab Democratic Rep., Sierra Leone, Zimbabwe, Burkina Faso, São Tomé & Príncipe, Equatorial Guinea, Gabon, Mauritius, Central African Rep., Angola, Lesotho, Tunisia, Cameroon, Nigeria, Malawi, Zambia, Algeria, Burundi, Seychelles, Tanzania, Cabo Verde, DRC, Morocco, Guinea-Bissau, Botswana, Comoros, and Mozambique (TRALEC, 2023).

The AfCFTA consists of a diverse range of countries. There are 15 landlocked countries and six small developing island economies. Several AfCFTA countries, such as Kenya, South Africa, Nigeria, and Egypt, have sizeable manufacturing sectors, while many others have largely undiversified economies, dominated by single unprocessed commodities (Economic Commission for Africa; AU Commission; AfDB, 2017).

The AfCFTA agreement has three layers. The first layer is a framework agreement, which defines the general terms, purposes, and intentions of the agreement. This framework agreement also outlines the institutional framework for implementing the AfCFTA as well as its procedures and processes for administration. Moreover, the first layer provides overarching guidelines on the principles of transparency and relates to regional and global bilateral and multilateral engagements (Abrego et al., 2019).

The second layer comprises the protocols to the agreement, which cover trade in goods, trade in services, rules and procedures on the settlement of disputes, investment, competition policy, and IPR. The protocols constitute the main substantive and operative components of the agreement, which are its obligations, intentions, objectives, exceptions, and institutional provisions. The first phase of the AfCFTA negotiations comprised the first three protocols; the other three were scheduled for the second phase of negotiations. The third layer contains the annexes, guidelines, lists, and schedules to the protocols, which describe the provisions of the protocol in detail. For example, while articles seven and eight of the Protocol on Trade in Services obliges State Parties to progressively eliminate import duties, Annexure 1 details the exact tariff schedules applicable to specific liberalisations (Saygili et al., 2018).

The three layers provide a balance of rights and obligations to progressively eliminate the barriers to trade and investment between State Parties and prepare the groundwork for mutually beneficial trade. Pan-African development policies and agencies therefore provide a rule-based legal system for governing the practices of preferential trade between State Parties in the AfCFTA. As the legal framework has been achieved continentally, attention now needs to be turned towards implementation. As Issoufou and Songwe (2018) reported, the AfCFTA institutional framework, as provided in articles nine to 13 of the framework agreement, is central to its implementation. The AU AHSG (the Assembly) is in charge of the implementing institutions. It provides oversight, and political and strategic guidance, and is the highest decision-making authority of the AU, comprising the Heads of State of all the AUMS.

The Assembly ensures that the AfCFTA institutions are firmly rooted within and aligned with the AU's institutions. After the Assembly, the Council of Ministers is the main decision-making institution in the AfCFTA. Its mandate is to establish and supervise the AfCFTA Secretariat and committees; issue directives and regulations; and to consider and propose legal, financial, and structural decisions for adoption by the Assembly (Sudip, 2019).

Various other AU instruments provide for sectoral liberalisation and the AfCFTA generally complements the existing AU structures and instruments in progress towards achieving an African single market and Agenda 2063. These include the SAATM, the Maritime Transport Charter, the Convention on African Energy

Commission as well as policy governance cooperation statutes, such as the Pan-African Intellectual Property Organisation Statute and the Convention on Nature Protection.

At the 2018 March Summit, another instrument, the Protocol to the Abuja Treaty on the Movement of Persons, Right of Residence, and Right of Establishment, was ratified. Its provisions allow for an integrated labour market framework, which complements the aims and objectives of AfCFTA. This instrument also provides a legal basis for a continental qualification authority and framework and further complements the aims of the AfCFTA member states to negotiate mutual recognition agreements. This continental regulatory body creates an impetus for the freedom of movement, labour, and capital, thus catalysing the attainment of a single continental market

The AfCFTA is therefore an enabling instrument that harnesses the principles of subsidiarity and comparative advantage to foster complementarities, which in turn engenders RVCs to compete profitably against global value chains (GVCs). Additionally, other institutions, such as the African Organisation for Standardisation and Pan-African Quality Infrastructure have become complimentary to the enabling AfCFTA framework. All of the AU's instruments contribute towards a centripetal regulatory body congruent to, and reinforcing of the AfCFTA's objective, which is to create a single continental market.

6.3 The African Continental Free Trade Area and the Regional Economic Communities: Centripetal Internal Trade Policies

The Abuja Treaty envisioned the establishment of an AEC, which entailed the creation of a common single market with the RECs as its building blocks (Ismail. 2017:139). Initially, the AfCFTA was conceived to consolidate the disparate pre-existing FTAs and multiple overlapping memberships of the RECs into a single Pan-African FTA. Only 12 African countries belong to a single REC; 33 belong to two RECs; eight belong to three RECs, and one belongs to four REC's (AU, 2015; UNCTD 2018).

The following four RECs operate FTAs (while the other RECs have deeper integration): the ECOWAS; EAC; COMESA, and ADC. They also have a monetary union and a CET (AfDB; AU; UNECA, 2016).

The overlap and duplication of trading arrangements in Africa create inefficiencies and bottlenecks in customs procedures and administration. This has prevented the realisation of deeper continental economic integration. The objective of the AfCFTA is to enhance the complementarities and economies of scale towards rationalised RVCs (Article 19 of the AfCFTA). This is in line with the objectives and principles enunciated in the Abuja Treaty during the 25th Ordinary Session of the AU AHSG held in Johannesburg, South Africa on 14–15 June 2015 (Assembly/AU/Dec. 569 (XXV).

However, Article 19 allows RECs to continue their trading arrangements alongside the AfCFTA. This provision facilitates a gradual negotiation process that aims to establish a mutually beneficial relationship, optimizing economies of scale and comparative advantages (Momodu, 2017).Variable geometry, which factors in the different stages of development in each country, is therefore a pragmatic part of the process towards a single continental market.

The provisions in the AfCFTA agreement on 'continental preferences' and MFN treatment counter the free rider problem. This occurs through the dispute settlement mechanism. The dispute settlement mechanism under AfCFTA addresses several challenges, allowing for cost-effective online dispute settlement procedures and reinforcing trade law capacity-building on the continent. Furthermore, as was the case during COVID-19 pandemic-related restrictions, court hearings in South Africa were conducted online through the use of video conferencing technology without compromising the quality of hearings or outcomes. Such adaptations have been mainstreamed and applied to state–state disputes under AfCFTA.

Depending on the ability of the other State Parties to reciprocate, they simultaneously risk creating multiple sets of market access conditions. In addition to the existing overlapping trade regimes within the AfCFTA, the MFN clause (where preferential trade links also pre-exist alongside those present under AfCFTA) will not be unconditionally and automatically extended to all State Parties, but will be considered under negotiated reciprocity. Although AfCFTA's pragmatic approach of variable geometry does not comprehensively consolidate the asymmetrical trading regimes of the member State Parties, it is a step in the right direction to address the challenge of uneven development and the overlapping trading regimes of its members in the short to medium-term.

If successfully managed, the intermediate stage of rationalising the AfCFTA could be used as a platform for later consolidation and coherence of the roadmap in pursuit of a single continental market (UNECA et al., 2019:55).

The AU Assembly, on behalf of the AfCFTA decided to negotiate global trade deals as a single entity on 10−11 February 2019. This was intended to avoid member states making external bilateral agreements, which would have impeded the objectives of the AfCFTA and the broader African integration of Agenda 2063 (Desta et al., 2019). By prying open Africa's tariff structure, the external partnership agreements (EPAs) would widen the divide between the tariff schedules of African countries and prevent the creation of an African CET. This would not only further thwart the realisation of the Continental Customs Union (CCU) envisaged in Article 3(d) of the AfCFTA Agreement, but also the aspirations of the 1991 Abuja Treaty, Constitutive Act, and 2012 Boosting Intra-African Trade (BIAT) Action Plan (UNECA 2019:56).

This challenge has precedents in the AU RECs, as ECOWAS and CEMAC have their own CET systems in bilateral agreements with the EU. The cases of ECOWAS and CEMAC should be resolved under the AfCFTA regimen. The failure of the 34-country Free Trade Area of the Americas (FTAA) in 2005 should serve as a warning in this respect: the US chose individual Latin American countries for the establishment of bilateral negotiations (Hereros, 2019; UNECA, AUC, and AfDB, 2017). The resulting bilateral FTAs split Latin America between the MERCOSUR countries in the east of South America and those in the west of South America. The latter were intent on strengthening links with the USA through the Trans-Pacific Partnership (TPP) negotiations. In the face of continued external interference, the AU Agenda 2063 continues to reiterate the importance of African 'unity and solidarity, with a single voice'. It believes that Africa can negotiate trade deals better and for more countries than the 55 AUMS could with their smaller disunited voices (Mutasa, 2018). The AU continues to undertake steps to enforce a coherent and unified external trade policy through the AfCFTA (Desta et al., 2019).

6.4 Optimally Operationalising the African Continental Free Trade Area

The AfCFTA embodies reforms that liberalise and facilitate trade along the export path. Phase I of the framework agreement, i.e., establishing the agreement, the protocols on trade in goods and services, and dispute settlement, has been completed. Phase II is dedicated to negotiations on investment, competition policy, and IPR. The institutional policies are linked to the key development reforms to the export path stemming from the AfCFTA agreement, indicating further synergies and complementarities beyond tariff reduction to create competitive RVCs[33]. For example, governments can create trade facilitation measures, such as a streamlined one-stop investment centre, within an enabling legal framework that promotes the ease of business and investments (ACBF, 2016; Karingi and Lisinge, 2017; Vickers, 2017).

The government's industrial and national production policies need to be coordinated with the AfCFTA, thus enhancing productive infrastructure and sector-specific policies. Government investment interventions, such as tax holidays and reduced tariffs for both domestic and global investors, are imperative to promote manufacturing and trade (UNCDP, 2016).

Among the trade facilitation measures are investment promotion agencies (IPAs), which assist in attracting and facilitating investments. The IPAs promote and empower physical and digital one-stop shops for investment, which enable investors

---

33   Smith, J., Johnson, A, (2020). 'Enhancing Regional Value Chains in Africa: Challenges and Opportunities.' *African Development Review.* 12(3). 45-62.

to register their companies with the necessary authorities in one place (UNCTAD, 2017a; UNECA, et al., 2019:72–73). The results in a reduction in time and transaction costs. This is already evident in several African countries, such as Ethiopia, Nigeria, and Rwanda (UNECA et al., 2019: 73).

The UNCTAD uses a range of investment policy tools, including policy investment reviews and online investor guides to AUMS with recommendations to improve their policies, strategies, and institutions for attracting FDI. As of February 2019, investment policy reviews had been conducted in 26 African countries: Algeria, Benin, Botswana, Burkina Faso, Burundi, Cabo Verde, Congo, Djibouti, Egypt, Ethiopia, Gambia, Ghana, Kenya, Lesotho, Madagascar, Mauritania, Mauritius, Morocco, Mozambique, Nigeria, Rwanda, Sierra Leone, Sudan, Tanzania, Uganda, and Zambia (UNCTAD, 2019:72).

There are also 'online investor guides' (iGuides) provided by AUMS with support from the UNCTAD, UNECA, and the International Chamber of Commerce. Investor guides provide prospective investors with enabling business information, thus facilitating ease of business.

As of February 2019, iGuides were available for 15 African countries: Benin, Burkina Faso, Burundi, Comoros, Ethiopia, Kenya, Mali, Morocco, Mauritania, Mozambique, Nigeria, Rwanda, Tanzania, Uganda and Zambia, and the EAC (UNECA, 2019:73).

The AfCFTA trade facilitation provisions align closely with the WTO Trade Facilitation Agreement. They are already being practised by Africa's RECs towards an incremental centripetal convergence, the AEC, and Agenda 2063. For example, NTBs build on the existing NTB reporting, monitoring, and elimination mechanism in AU RECs, i.e., the COMESA-EAC-SADC TFTA. This has been implemented through the online portal 'tradebarriers. org.'

All NTBs, such as licences, quotas, fees, and charges, are considered instruments that result in bottlenecks and inefficiencies. The AfCFTA-Tripartite NTB Trade in Goods (Annex 5) mechanism is now operational and allows private sector operators to report any NTBs they encounter in the region through their website or via email, fax, telephone, and SMS. As of October 2018, 532 of 616 complaints in the Tripartite area had been resolved.³⁴

This kind of consultation and collaboration between humans and ICT is suggestive of the rise of the 4IR. This is evident from the online system, which has leapfrogged bureaucratic barriers through a real-time NTB network, connecting government and private sector officials (Hove, 2015; UNECA, 2019:81). The AfCFTA Trade in Goods, Annex 5, further defines eight categories of NTBs: technical barriers to trade (TBT); sanitary and phytosanitary (SPS); charges on imports; clearing and forwarding; specific limitations; procedural problems and transport; customs and entry procedures; and government participation in trade and restrictive practices. While the AfCFTA is dedicated to TBT and SPS measures, which are considered instruments of commercial policy and procedural obstacles, they are implemented for legitimate and important reasons of food security and environmental protection. Both TBT and SPS measures are restrictive and create a distorting effect on global trade, but they are also coordinated with the SDGs. This coordination enhances international standards and best practice, regulatory cooperation, and transparency, ultimately mitigating the impact of rising costs. For the AfCFTA's trade in goods, TBT and SPS encourage intra-African productive systems, thereby enhancing cooperation and harmonising standards continentally.

This is evident in the areas of transboundary infrastructure, metrology, accreditation, management, and conformity assessment. Continental harmonised standards and technical regulations guarantee the quality of traded goods and promote development in the industrial policy of Africa.

The foundational institutional work done by the AfCFTA as a flagship of Agenda 2063, is incrementally streamlining all processes systematically to eliminate bottlenecks and other NTBs.

34   Ngwira, F., Kamndaya,A., (2018). 'Assessing the implications of Tripartite Free Trade Agreement on Regional Integration in Africa: A case study of COMESA-EAC-SADC.' *African Journal of Economic Review.* 7(2). 112-128.

Institutions, both governmental and private (such as the IPAs), serve to interface effective investment and business opportunities between the AfCFTA and global multilateral investors. The resulting multiplier effects include increased business confidence in Africa and inflows in FDI; cooperation contracts between local and foreign firms and the formation of research and development partnerships.

Within the AfCFTA framework, which both facilitates and enables development policies, the AUMS should optimise their productive capacities in natural, human, physical, and financial resources as well as entrepreneurial and institutional capabilities to be competitive and grow their economies (UNCTAD, 2006).

6.5   The Intellectual Property Rights Protocol

The creation of literary and artistic works, symbols, names, and images used for commercial gain results in the formation of IPRs. These IPRs confer the right to prevent others from using, making, and selling the subject of the protection (Ncube, 2021). The formation of IPRs on public goods, in particular in public health, can be controversial. For example, when South Africa wanted to source affordable generic anti-retroviral (ARVs) drugs for its citizens from alternative suppliers, the pharmaceutical fraternity of the Global North sued the government. This was also the case with the COVID-19 vaccines, which was a global public health issue, but the vaccines remained largely inaccessible to the greater public (Enhanced Integrated Framework, 2020; Lopes and te Velde, 2021). Through global non-state actor activism, the historical instances where IPRs have resembled the extension of property rights, especially the issues of public goods and the global commons, the current IPR system is an incentive to promote innovation and facilitate technology transfer.

The protection and enforcement of IPRs is critical for achieving the AfCFTA objectives. Particularly the objectives regarding sustainable and inclusive socio-economic development, structural transformation, industrial development, and the competitiveness of economies with the continent and global market. The ability to acquire IPRs provides incentives to inventors to generate new knowledge, and hold the patents of new inventions (de Beer et al., 2014; Ncube, 2021).

The AfCFTA will enhance Africa's cross-border trade. Consequently, authors, creators, designers, and inventors will require legal protection in other countries. Does the AfCFTA cover IPRs? When and how will the IPRs regime for the AfCFTA be negotiated? What will the regime look like? How can the IPRs regime achieve the AfCFTA objectives. Amongst several other questions these fall under the mandate of the AfCFTA secretariat headquartered in Accra Ghana mandate . In this regard the secretariat is responsible for overseeing the implementation of the AfCFTA agreement, which aims to create a single market for goods and services across Africa.

Trade in goods and services were negotiated in Phase II of the AfCFTA negotiations resulting in the Protocols on Trade in Goods, Trade in Services, and Dispute Settlement. Phase II negotiations will cover IPRs, and investment and competition policies (Ismail, 2017:119-146). More recently, African leaders approved the addition of digital trade on the AfCFTA agenda (Phase III negotiations), which will be negotiated concurrently with Phase II issues. There are also ongoing efforts to add women and youth to the AfCFTA agenda.

The Phase II negotiations will result in Protocols, which shall form an integral part of the AfCFTA Agreement, subject to their entry into force. The Protocols will enter into force 30 days after the deposit of the 22nd instrument of ratification (Article 24 of the AfCFTA Agreement). The Protocol will enter into force, i.e., become legally binding, only on State Parties (AUMS) that deposit their instruments of ratification or accession to the Protocols. With regards to the protection of IPRs, this means that only the inventors of intellectual property in the State Parties will be protected and entitled to remedies under the AfCFTA Protocol on IPRs (Owoeye et al., 2019).

How will AU member states negotiate the IPRs regime for the AfCFTA? Article 4 of the AfCFTA Agreement stipulates that the State Parties shall cooperate on investment, IPRs, and competition policy. The precise details of how the State Parties will cooperate on IPRs (investment and competition policy) are not yet known. Will this be limited to cooperation and coordination of IPRs? What will be the scope of the IPRs covered under the AfCFTA? The answers to these pertinent questions will only be clear once the modalities of negotiating the Protocol on IPRs are adopted. As the flagship of Agenda 2063, IPRs interface with several aspects of the AfCFTA. They do so in areas such as production and innovation, investment, entrepreneurship, and trade policies. Within the global multilateral system, the AU is a signatory to the international minimum standard, which was established by the WTO under the agreement on Trade-Related Aspects of Intellectual Property Rights (TRIPS) (Gathii, 2020; Erasmus, 2020).

The AU and some of its regional organisations, such as the African Regional Intellectual Property Organisation (ARIPO), the 'Organisation Africaine de la Propriete Intellectuelle' (OAPI), and the Pan-African Intellectual Property Organisation (PAIPO), cooperatively share norms on policies and ideas, and the way they should contribute to the development of an IPR protocol in the AfCFTA. The adoption of IPRs functions as a policy tool to promote and incentivise private investment and entrepreneurship, as well as competition and innovation (Helfer and Alter, 2013). This balanced cooperation allows for private sector incentives and innovation, while aligning with public policy objectives, in coordination with the AfCFTA and in line with the goals of Agenda 2063.

The promotion and protection of IPR are central to achieving the AfCFTA objectives. The Committee on Intellectual Property Rights was established in May 2021 by the Council of Ministers of Trade and State Parties to facilitate the negotiation of the Protocol on IPRs. At its first meeting in September 2021, the Committee adopted its Terms of Reference and the Modalities for Negotiating the Protocol on IPRs. The Committee also held capacity-building activities related to IPRs in preparation for the negotiations and development of the AfCFTA Protocol on IPRs.

In support of this, on 19 February 2023, the AU AHSG adopted three new protocols to the AfCFTA Agreement – on investment, IPRs, and competition policy. The significance of these protocols in deepening continental market integration is further expanded below.

The Protocol on Investment

The Investment Protocol aims to establish a "balanced, coherent, clear, transparent, predictable, and mutually-advantageous continental framework of principles and rules for the promotion, facilitation, and protection of investment". The objectives of the Protocol include the encouragement of intra-African investment flows by establishing a balanced, predictable and transparent continental legal and institutional framework for investment, complete with appropriate mechanisms for the prevention, management, and settlement of investment disputes (Sodipo, 2019).

A successful investment protocol will: (i) add the free movement of capital to the current AfCFTA portfolio already that contains elements of free movement of goods and services across Africa; (ii) allow African businesses to take advantage of investment opportunities beyond national boundaries; (iii) enable investors to take investment decisions based on the certainty that they can sell their products and services to a market of over 1.4 billion people; (iv) enhance Africa's capacity to produce the goods and services necessary to trade across borders under preferential AfCFTA terms; and (v) in the process, enhance the capacity of the AfCFTA to make a difference in the lives of Africans as business owners, workers, and consumers.

The Investment Protocol also establishes obligations on State Parties to promote and facilitate intra-African investment and to adhere to such traditional standards of protection as national treatment, MFN treatment, and freedom from expropriation without compensation. At the same time, these obligations are subject to exceptions that are designed to preserve a margin of regulatory space for State Parties (Article 26).

Finally, the Investment Protocol also has a dispute resolution mechanism under which disputes between State Parties, including cases of diplomatic protection under international law, are subject to the standard rules of the AfCFTA Protocol on Dispute Settlement (Article 44). The AfCFTA Investment Protocol is an expression of Africa's aspiration to materialise Agenda 2063, thus building an integrated continental market and fostering structural transformation in a competitive public and private sector (Articles 13.4 and 14.3).

The Protocol on IPR[35]

The AU and its member states are signatories to many international treaties and have established national IP regimes, which promote innovation and economic development in a knowledge-driven global economy. The AU IP thrust seeks to reconcile, harmonise, and standardise Africa's fragmented IP initiatives, which currently operate in silos (Adachi, 2019). This will enable the implementation of the AfCFTA, enabling African designers, artists, entrepreneurs, and innovators to reap the profits of their inventions, further inspiring a creative African continental economy.

The Protocol covers a comprehensive array of IPRs, including plant variety protection, geographical indications, marks, patents, utility models, industrial designs, undisclosed information, layout of integrated circuits, copyrights and related rights, traditional knowledge, traditional cultural expressions and folklores, as well as genetic resources (Article 31).

The Protocol on Competition Policy[36]

With the liberalisation of trade and development within the AfCFTA framework, fair competition and anti-competition policies are central to making market economies and the goals of Agenda 2063 attainable. These are structurally transformed

---

35   Adebola, F., Ncube, P. (2020). 'Intellectual Property Rights and Protection in Africa: Challenges and Prospects.' *African Journal of Intellectual Property*. 59(2). 87-104.
36   Ndiaye, M., Ofori, S. (2020). 'Competition Policy in Africa: Assessing the impact of the African Union Protocols.' *Journal of African Competition Law*. 3(1). 56-72. UN Secretary-General. (2013). 'Follow-up to General Assembly Resolution 66/290 on Human Security, Report of the Secretary-General, 23 December.'

economies that will enable sustainable and inclusive growth, science and technology innovation, manufacturing, industrialisation and value addition, economic diversification, and resilience.

Africa's role as a subordinate entity to the economies of the Global North is supported by MNCs such as Lafarge (Pty) Limited cement company and PPC (Pty). The economies of Africa are predominantly based on extractive industry and it therefore suffers from cross-border and transnational anti-competitive conduct. Various oligopolistic practices are practised by the MNCs, such as price fixing through cartels, predatory behaviour to eliminate local competition and other market-sharing agreements, and mergers and acquisitions resulting in abuse and dominance. With the fast-paced globalisation of ICT, the 4IR[37] has enabled modern investment, financialisaton, production, and trade across RVCs and GVCs. Competition policy solutions should therefore address cross-border practices (UNECA, 2000; Laprevote, 2015).

The decision by the AfCFTA to launch a continental competition policy chapter is a good sign, and will help member states overcome the asymmetries among them. This encourages centripetal forces among national competition authorities to cooperate to address the extra-territorial effects on anti-competitive MNC behaviour, which will have a negative impact on the realisation of Agenda 2063 aspirations and objectives. As the AfCFTA gains centripetal traction, the combined continental market, continental rules, and regulations should guide businesses, so that the liberalisation of Africa's market benefits the African population. Between 2015 and 2017, the South African Competition Commission addressed the cross-border impacts of the anti-competitive policies of the MNCs. For example, the cross-border anti-competitive behaviour of the cement cartel was uncovered by an investigation conducted by the Competition

---

37   Interview with Professor Everisto Benyera (4IR). 2022–2023.
      See: Mbeki, T. (2020). 'Neo-colonialism in the Fourth Industrial Revolution; Implications for Africa.' *African Development Review.* 12(4). 112–128.
      See: UNECA. (2021) 'Assessment of Neocolonial Tendencies in the Fourth Industrial Revolution.'

Commission of South Africa (CCSA) that began in 2008. The investigation targeted the southern African region's four main cement producers: PPC Ltd (PPC), Africa South Africa (Pty) Ltd, Lafarge Cement Company (Lafarge), and Natal Portland Cement Company (Pty) Ltd (NPC).

The investigative findings by the CCSA confirmed that cement prices had doubled since 2001, despite fluctuations in demand and input costs. Territorially, PPC mutually agreed with Lafarge that it would not compete in KwaZulu-Natal (South Africa) in exchange for the latter not competing with PPC in Botswana, while AfriSam would supply Namibia.

As from 2008, the harmful effect of the global financial meltdown coupled with Africa's burdensome debt repayments to the IMF and WB, caused rising unemployment and an untenable budget deficit (IMF, 2018, 2018a). With these circumstances in mind, an argument could be made for the laws to be amended so that boards of directors, chief executive officers, and participative shareholders could be criminally indicted for white collar crime. They should face the full might of the law for working against Africa's integration, development, and unity.

There are many other examples of anticompetitive behaviour across the regions. It could be argued that each MNC investigated by the CCSA has taken advantage of their particular environment, as the regions vary in the kind of support structures or institutions that are in place to follow-up on the anti-competitive behaviour. The diversity of national and regional competition laws is therefore not surprising given the varying levels of development that exist between the member states (UNCECA, 2019:143-150). The AUMS are at various levels of development and therefore there are divergences in their competition laws. This is detrimental to the agenda of regional and continental integration. A one-size-fits-all competition policy would be impossible in Africa given each member state's distinct economic and political imperatives. The multi-layered competition regulation landscape in Africa includes both national and subregional frameworks.

The AfCFTA IPR's protocols have enabled the Tripartite COMESA-EAC-SADC partnership to harmonise their competition laws. For example, they have established supranational regional competition authorities, while other RECs, operate through a cooperation framework (UNECA, 2018a). Given Africa's varying levels of economic and political development, cooperation using the principle of variable geometry would be the most feasible, pragmatic, and sustainable option.

These political and socio-economic development flexibilities in the varying levels of development are more disposed to policy convergences, which supports continental integration and the objectives of Agenda 2063. The flexibilities within competition provisions at the regional level function as instruments to develop an open rule-based and predictable non-discriminatory trading system with a fair distribution of benefits. The normative position that the AfCFTA has taken supports FDI, which in turn supports RVCs and the efficient allocation of resources, leading to competitive market prices (de Melo et al., 2020).

The AfCFTA authorities are gradually aligning and synergising competition among the overlapping RECs. This creates an enabling environment for cooperative coexistence and profitability, bridging the divergences towards sustainable competition laws in line with the objectives of Agenda 2063 (Shingal and Mendez-Para, 2020).

Anti-competitive conduct by corporations results in unfair trade practices and the AfCFTA Protocol on Trade in Services recognises consumer protection as a legitimate national and continental policy objective that parties must consider when liberalising services. Because competition and consumer protection are interlinked, interventions by authorities enhancing competition lead to improved consumer welfare. Consumer protection institutions across Africa differ considerably and the AfCFTA's member states are working cooperatively together to gradually harmonise their competition laws.

The adoption of the AfCFTA Protocol on Competition Policy constitutes a significant step forward in the process of continental integration and the realisation of Agenda 2063. The provision of safeguards in the regulation of anti-competitive practices by monopolies and oligarchies is imperative to prevent, mitigate, and penalise businesses that abuse their dominant productive and market positions through price-fixing cartels and predatory behaviour that eliminates competition among micro, small, and medium enterprises (MSMEs).

The protocol seeks to eliminate anti-competitive and other restrictive business practices for improved and inclusive economic participation, market efficiency, and the equitable distribution of income and wealth (Ncube et al., 2019:117-194).

In support of the DTRP/centre-periphery framework, that recognizes the polarization and disparities within the global economy, the AU's integration is continuously hampered by, amongst other factors, the lack of a continental supra-authority. The application of the neo-functional theory calls for significant devolvement to a supra-authority with enforceable sanctions and penalties enforced by the AfCFTA Competition Tribunal. In this regard, the AfCFTA Competition Authority will function as an autonomous body with the power to administer and enforce provisions of the Protocol, and decide on any undertakings, including approving mergers and acquisitions (Ncube et al., 2019:117-194). The adoption of the three protocols by the AU Assembly is a testament to the political commitment to underpin intra-African trade and realise Agenda 2063. The domestication and ratification of these three protocols by AUMS is imperative for the full realisation of the potential benefits of the AfCFTA.

6.6 Intra-African Investment: Convergences Towards Agenda 2063

Africa's investment policy landscape is fragmented. It is marked by 854 bilateral investment treaties (BITs) with 512 in force, of which 169 are intra-African with 44 in force. This spaghetti bowl of overlapping bilateral and regional treaties with inconsistent provisions, functions as a centrifugal force, further balkanising Africa's economy with no welfare benefits (UNECA, 2017a; Paez, 2017; UNCTAD, 2017b).

The 5th Meeting of the AfCFTA Negotiating Forum in March 2017, considered the draft proposal by the Pan-African Investment Code (PAIC), which suggested that the AfCFTA protocol on investment should be harmonised and binding. The PAIC was adopted by the Specialised Technical Committee on Finance, Monetary Affairs, Economic Planning, and Integration of the AU in October 2017 pending ratification by the member states. This confirms that Pan-African development policies and agencies are moving towards continental integration and reform of the exploitative investment treaty system.

The proposal for a harmonised investment treaty emphasises Africa's commitment to the MDGs and more recently the SDGs because it will redefine the obligations of the state and investors. The African BITs limit the right of other African host countries to regulate investment in their territories. The BITs that are unreformed expose African countries to investor-state dispute settlement with costly consequences (UNCTAD, 2015a; Mbengue and Schacherer, 2017; UNCTAD, 2018c; UNCTAD, 2019).

The PAIC has assisted African countries in articulating a common and innovative approach to redesigning the international treaty regime, such as the binding regional schemes on investment. These include the SADC Protocol on Finance and Investment (2006), the ECOWAS Supplementary Act on Investments (2008), the COMESA Investment Agreement (2007), and the EAC Model Investment Code (2006). African countries now maintain the right of host countries to regulate and adopt new laws governing FDI. This is because transfers resulting from investments can cause macroeconomic shocks. Balance of payments shocks, for example, can burden host economies due to the repatriation of capital and investment proceeds. Moreover, the increase in illicit financial flows, including tax avoidance, continues to pose a challenge to the AUMS fiscus (AU and UNECA, 2015).

Without controls, foreign investment can potentially crowd out domestic investments because they sometimes enjoy more favourable conditions than domestic investments (Agosin & Machado, 2005; Stiglitz, 2007). Capital account control on

FDI, within the AfCFTA's reformed finance, investment, and competition policy protocols, will direct capital to productive sectors of Africa's economies. This will discourage speculative FDI but encourage equity FDI, which will propel industrialisation and structural transformation on the continent (Tomi, 2015; Sutton et al., 2016; Zandile & Phiri, 2018). Because the targeted FDI will support the accumulation of productive investment assets, this results in higher factor productivity and resource efficiency.

Investment will provide an important source of development finance, as recognised in the Addis Ababa Action Agenda towards Agenda 2063 (AUC 2015a). The RECs, as the building blocks of intra-African trade towards Agenda 2063, continue to redesign their investment promotion and facilitation to create economies of scale and adopt world standard best practices. For example, under the COMESA Treaty of 31 October 2000, the member states agreed to several decisions promoting intra-regional investment (Kandelwal, 2004). This included the harmonisation of macroeconomic policies and the creation and maintenance of a predictable, transparent, and secure investment climate. Article 8 of the COMESA Common Investment Area stipulates that member states should cooperate in developing facilitation programmes and thus emphasise transparency and the simplification of investment rules (Karugaba, 2006; Sonu, 2006:57-73).

The COMESA Regional Investment Agency, launched in 2006, has become a one-stop clearing house in collectively managing the intra-regional investment database; promoting public-private partnerships (PPPs); and enhancing skills development and advocacy and investment opportunities (UNECA, 2012). The SADC Protocol on Finance and Investment compels member states to devise and implement strategies to attract both domestic and foreign investment and foster entrepreneurship. It further encourages the regional role of IPAs in facilitating investment flows into the SADC countries, thus supporting RVCs (UNECA, 2016). The role of the IPAs is to promote investment following national and regional developmental priorities in harmony with the AfCFTA.

In this regard, the IPAs advise the private sector, government, and other stakeholders on formulating and reviewing policies and procedures affecting investment and trade. In line with the rise of 4IR, a dedicated website (dev-www.sadc. int) lists all of the SADC IPA's individual investment regimes. This was further reinforced by the SADC Investment Policy Framework (2016), which outlines specific measures for investment policy reform across several dimensions.

This includes enhancing the transparency and coherence of the investment environment, as well as fostering regional and international cooperation through e-government, and the dissemination and realigning of trade and investment policies (Brauch et al., 2019). The norms which are being established in the AfCFTA framework seek to reform the BITs and enhance a common continental investment area, which can provide the joint benefits of investment and trade and enable comparative advantages and economies of scale (Fofack, 2018). This will reinforce RVCs, GVCs, and trade diversification, resulting in competitive economic growth, positive multiplier effects, and welfare benefits.

6.7 The Fourth Industrial Revolution: E-Commerce and Integration in a Digitalising Africa

Africa is digitalising. This offers a leapfrogging opportunity, by which the adoption of wireless and mobile technologies offerings are quicker and cost-effective when compared to the more expensive and time-consuming task of building fixed-line telephony. On a cost-benefit calculus, digital technologies are built on an easily deployable infrastructure. This advances economies of scale with far-reaching implications for economic development, integration, and structural transformation. Artificial intelligence, robotics, blockchains, drones, the Internet of Things (IoT), 3D printing, Big Data, and software enhance industrial platforms by changing the global systems of labour and production, requiring job-seekers to cultivate the skills and capabilities necessary for rapid adaptation to the needs of African firms and automation. By automating tasks, reworks, bottlenecks, waste, and other invisible costs that increase the final cost of the products are eliminated. This increased productivity, effectiveness, and efficiency is cost-effective and expands production, resulting in higher profits·

This is a globally inseparable environment where individuals straddle digital domains and offline reality with the use of connected technologies. According to Schwab (2015), the 4IR is a fusion of technologies. The technologies are blurring the lines between the physical, digital, and biological spheres enabled by the hybrid wireless interactive digital environments

For example, technologies such as augmented and virtual reality, cognitive computing models, and artificial intelligence, where the solutions interact with users and simulate their behaviour and characteristics are capable of making decisions. Their speed, velocity, scope, and their impact on systems and interconnectivity have no historical precedent. Every industry in every country that is affected demands a transformation in their systems of production, management, and governance.

The first industrial revolution changed people's lives and economies from predominantly agrarian and handicraft-based to a society characterized by the use of machinery and factory-based production within sector industries. Oil and electricity subsequently underpinned the second industrial revolution with its mass production and consumerism. The hallmark of the third industrial revolution was ICT, with its interconnectivity of automated production and distribution systems (Miller, 2015:3). Against a backdrop of global technology convergences, the AUMS have invested in a comprehensive digital transformation strategy to harness comparative advantages and economies of scale to upscale its RVCs to competitively interface with GVCs.

Based on the AU Executive Council Decisions related to ICT, at the UNECA Resolution (812–XXXI) on the African Information Society Initiative and the Smart Africa Board meeting held on the margins of the 32nd AU AHSG, the AUC undertook to develop a comprehensive Digital Transformation Strategy for Africa (DTSA) (UNCTAD 2015). This was in collaboration with the UNECA, Smart Africa, AUDA-NEPAD, RECs, AfDB, Africa Telecommunications

Union, Africa Capacity-Building Foundation, International Telecommunication Union (ITU), and WB (World Bank 2012). The DTSA addresses the objectives of the 4IR within the AfCFTA

The DTSA seeks to converge centripetal processes and systems within the AfCFTA frameworks, such as the Policy and Regulation Initiative for Digital Africa (PRIDA), PIDA, AU Financial Institutions, SAATM, and FMP. This will support the development of a Digital Single Market for Africa, further enhancing integration towards Agenda 2063.

E-commerce and the digital economy, as a constituent of 4IR, is already in use in Africa but at uneven levels of development. This results from low levels of both foreign and domestic investments, weak financial flows, poor levels of computer literacy and education, inhibitory cultural and socio-economic factors, inadequate access to the latest technology, and inadequate telecommunications infrastructure (Rademacher and Grant, 2018).

The terms e-commerce and digital economy cover both physical and intangible products and services that reach the end user digitally (Majama, 2018).

The e-commerce platforms operating in Africa include Jumia and Konga (Nigeria), Takealot and Bob's Shop (South Africa), and Kilimall (Kenya). These platforms bring together African consumers and entrepreneurs who also sell goods from outside the continent, including from China, which dominates cross-border sales (Kaplan, 2018). E-commerce entails placing and receiving orders over computer networks, using multiple formats and devices, including web and electronic data interchange and the use of personal computers, laptops, tablets, and mobile phones (OECD, 2011).

A well-known example is the M-Pesa mobile money solution, which first emerged in Kenya to extend banking services to people without bank accounts (UNCTAD, 2017b). The digital economy in Africa has reduced many barriers and has mitigated market concentration costs. Although market segregation remains due to the languages and specific characteristics of the different markets, one of the many objectives of the Digital Single Market in

Africa by 2030 is to harmonise standards and systems. Integrating existing and future digital policies at regional and national levels will enhance cooperation between institutions and bring RVCs closer towards the objectives of Agenda 2063.

According to UNCTAD (2022) estimates, worldwide e-commerce sales in 2023 will reach approximately US$6.3 trillion, with 90% in business-to-business (B2B) e-commerce and 10% in business-to-consumer (B2C) sales. China, the USA, and India lead in the global B2C segment. It is estimated that by 2050, Africa will have the largest youth population in the world. It is therefore important that its digital policies converge to carve a global niche for the continent in the lucrative global market (Benyera, 2021).

The SADC and COMESA, as AU RECs, have e-commerce strategy frameworks that continue to inform the DTSA towards Agenda 2063. In 2010, SADC developed a comprehensive regional strategy based on its members having national ICT strategies built upon four converging pillars: legislation; national and subregional infrastructure; skills development; and payment solutions and data collection (UNCTAD 2017b). In addition, in 2018, COMESA adopted a digital free trade area (DFTA) to enhance ICT comparative advantages and harness economies of scale in cross-border trade.

Other RECs, such as the ECCAS and CEN-SAD do not have comprehensive digital economy strategies but do have technology-related policies and tools, such as biometric passports, telephone roaming free areas, and regional payment systems to support cross-border payments and transfers (Bankole et al., 2013:12-28).

The SADC and COMESA digital free trade areas are suitable platforms to further converge and synergise e-commerce interoperability, with templates linking its programmes to similar initiatives in the TFTA and AfCFTA, and globally within the WTO protocols. Because e-commerce activities are predicated on the use of various technologies, such as internet services, the cloud and data hosting services of providers governed by regulatory systems across multiple jurisdictions have necessitated convergences of regulations and policies in ICT infrastructure and the 4IR. With the ratification of the AfCFTA and the adoption of various protocols (such as the manufacturing and trade policy protocol and the competition protocol), the AfCFTA DTSA must provide 4IR protocols that are interoperable and standardised.

With penetration rates in Africa standing at 43% by 2021, its digitalisation is supported by an active mobile broadband subscription. The adoption of e-commerce and digitalisation has demonstrated that Africa can overcome its challenges (UNCTAD, 2022f). This was the case with M-Pesa in Kenya, which afforded the unbanked the ability to e-transact nationally and regionally through systems innovation. The UNCTAD's B2C e-commerce Index 2021 indicated that online B2C shopping transactions had a global value of approximately US$27 trillion (UNCTAD, 2021c). This is an indication of Africa's gradual and growing capability ability to provide its data for comparative analyses on a global scale. This is also proof of Africa's integrated elements: relating to the web presence of the seller; internet access of users; availability of diverse payment methods, such as: credit cards, mobile payment, or cash on delivery; and the delivery of the product to the customers home or a convenient pick-up point.

As much as the UNCTAD B2C E-commerce Index 2021 confirms that Africa is lagging in comparison to the rest of the world, Africa also attracts both local and foreign investors. This is because the gaps are identifiable, measurable, and quantifiable (UNCTAD, 2021c). For example, the regional electronic payment systems that already exist have encouraged governments and the private sector to facilitate the interface of national banks. This will reduce the cost and time associated with cross-border payments. In this regard, the AfCFTA Secretariat and African Export and Import Bank (AFREXIM) has proposed a Pan-African payments and settlement platform to enable intra-African trade (UNCTAD, 2018i). The DTSA has also noted that data are the lifeblood of e-commerce.

The adoption of e-commerce legislation by countries will enhance trade facilitation measures and intra-Africa trade to meet the goals of Agenda 2063, including structurally transformed economies; enabling sustainable and inclusive economic growth; promotion of science and technology innovations; industrialisation and value addition that promotes economic diversification and competitiveness.

The free flow of data across borders has become imperative to firms engaged in e-commerce because it underpins many trade agreements. This is because data in e-commerce is quantifiable capital and inventory added onto a corporation's balance sheet. Additionally, when data is considered within the context of trade agreements, the issue of client privacy and confidentiality becomes paramount.

Cross-border data flows enable knowledge and data sharing, and collaboration on research and development across all sectors, including areas such as health technology and pharmaceutical development. It could also potentially provide solutions for climate change mitigation and adaptation

Another substantial advantage of cross-border commerce is brand awareness. Merchants who sell to customers in other countries develop brand awareness in the international market. In many African countries, many foreign products (especially those from the West) are believed to be of better quality. To support and protect the personal information used in e-commerce, the AU adopted the Convention on Cyber-security and Personal Data Protection in 2014. The aims of the convention further support the DTSA by establishing regional and national legal frameworks covering cybersecurity, electronic transactions, and personal data protection (AUC and Internet Society, 2018).

The following AUMS have enacted legislation in compliance with the Malabo Convention: Benin, Chad, Comoros, DRC, Mauritania, Sierra Leone, Djibouti, Gambia, Guinea-Bissau, South Africa, Sao Tome and Principe, Sudan, and Tunisia. The Malabo Convention formally known as the African Union Convention on Cyber Security and Personal Datra Protection, was adopted on June 27, 2014, in Malabo Equatorial Guinea. It serves as Africa's primary legal framework for cybersecurity, electronic transactions, and personal data protection. Other legal frameworks that apply include the EAC Framework for Cyberlaws, which was adopted in 2010, and the SADC Model Law on Data Protection (UNCTAD, 2016).

E-commerce legislation has become critical because access to and control over data represent intangible capital assets, which are key factors in competition. Taking this into consideration, the ECOWAS Commission developed a cybersecurity agenda in 2015, 'Enhancing Cybersecurity in ECOWAS region', to promote the convergence of policies by member states. This was a confidence-building measure and has attracted global partnering with the Council of Europe, ITU, and UNCTAD. The interest from global partners such as these affirms the importance of converging global cybersecurity legislation, which will be indispensable in the move towards 4IR and globalisation.

6.8 Fiscal Policy for Financing Sustainable Development in Africa: Agenda 2063[38]

The current pace and quality of economic growth in African countries is insufficient to achieve the SDGs and meet the aspirations of Agenda 2063. The key constraints to economic growth are inappropriate economic policies, inadequate human capital development, low levels of private investment, poor infrastructure, unreliable electricity power, low agricultural productivity, poor governance, and a lack of market competitiveness. As a result, the economic growth of Africa is predicted to weaken to 3.8% in 2023 from 4.1% in 2022 due to subdued investment and falling exports (World Bank, 2023). Africa's slow structural transformation and the value addition of its diversified manufacturing base need to be fast-tracked. Fiscal policy is a valuable tool to meet the goals of Agenda 2063 such as structurally transformed and inclusive economies. In addition, Africa's economic growth rate of 3.2% is insufficient to effect inclusive job creation and eradicate poverty, which are the goals of both SDGs 2030 and Agenda 2063 (WB, 2018b). However, under

---

38   Tetteh, E., Adegbite, E. (2020). 'Fiscal Policies for Financing Sustainable Development in Africa: A Comparative Analysis.' Journal of African Development. 12(3). 45-62.
See: AfDB. 920210. 'Fiscal policy strategies for achieving sustainable development Goals in Africa.'

the aegis of the AU, the five African regions have exhibited steady economic growth.

I argue that Africa's fiscal balance will continue facing challenges unless the AU moves quickly to create a single continental currency under one central bank, led by the stronger member states such as Nigeria, Egypt, South Africa, Kenya, and Angola. Provisions must be established and promoted to compensate for the revenue loss in weaker African economies. This will force homogeneity in macroeconomic planning and should also be accompanied by the simultaneous FMP and right of residence. A supranational authority should be enforced with the AU, AfDB, and PAP assuming these continental responsibilities. The CSOs, as constituents of the ECOSOCC within the AU, should exercise their horizontal and bottom-up agency to challenge the slow-paced vertical top-down governance of self-interested states.

6.9 Diversifying Africa's Economy for Development Goals

Since the formation of the AU in 2002 and its recognition of the RECs, there has been an improvement in Africa's collection of statistics. Statistics have been used to support the AU's development activities in line with the SDGs and Agenda 2063. Between 2021 and 2023 (UNCTAD, 2022), socio-economic development policies have been gradually improving the share of African merchandise exports to African partners. This has followed the impressive recovery from the shock of the COVID-19 pandemic in 2021. African economies stagnated amid significant headwinds in 2022 but they remain resilient with positive prospects. The deceleration in economic growth has been due to a confluence of reasons, such as climate change, persistent COVID-19 risks in Africa and globally, and the spill-over effects of geopolitical tensions, such as conflict and insecurity in Africa and the Russia and Ukraine war.

These domestic and external shocks have heightened the volatility in global financial markets, increased inflationary pressures, and the costs of capital and debt servicing, disrupted global supply chains (especially in food and energy markets), and reduced aggregate demand in the major export markets, such as Europe and China, Africa's main trading partners. The global appreciation of the US dollar has negatively impacted Africa's economy by increasing the cost of servicing existing debt and the cost of raising investments in the global capital markets (AfDB, 2022).

As expressed by the AU and its organs, the recovery and economic resilience of African countries in the short to medium term have generated cautious optimism given the considerable global economic uncertainty. The high dependence on exports of primary commodities with limited value addition could delay the structural transformation presented by the green transition as a goal of Agenda 2063. The AU has suggested policy actions to address the effects of rising inflation and subdued economic growth. A mix of monetary, fiscal, and structural policies has therefore been proposed (UNCTA, 2022).

It would appear that the efforts of the AU, and its organs are starting to yield some results, albeit at a modest pace. However, progress has been hindered by the sluggish growth of the global economy and the insufficient investment funding available to Africa. This has impacted Africa's self-reliance and has caused setbacks to its integration programmes. The AU as an intergovernmental organisation in its transboundary relations and pursuit of shared values is now prominent in the security and development nexus but it is still over-reliant on foreign donor dependency. The APSA peacekeeping efforts have created a stable, business-friendly environment leading to the implementation of the Pan African Payments and Settlement System (PAPSS). The PAPSS and other trade facilitation measures of the AfCFTA have enhanced cross-border RVCs thus leveraging expertise on the continent by creating more value chains in modern service sectors. This has enabled the comparative advantages and economies of scale to be fully exploited with realisable welfare benefits (De Melo and Twum, 2021)

6.10 Tax Policy and Performance in Africa[39]

An effective tax policy has become the cornerstone of the AUMS government's attempts to mobilise domestic revenue streams in all conceivable economic activities, be they formal, informal, in agriculture, e-commerce, or the digital economy converging towards the 4IR (ATAF, 2014; Dube and Casale, 2016). High levels of domestic revenue mobilisation are imperative to bring about Africa's structural transformation in supporting AfCFTA and Agenda 2063 (Kedir et al., 2017; UNDP, 2018).

Tax policy plays a crucial role within the broader African fiscal policy framework by generating revenue for use for strengthening AfCFTA and Africa's public industrialisation. In the competitive global economic milieu of FDI, the AUMS and RECs have focused on scaling up domestic revenue mobilisation in support of AfCFTA and Agenda 2063 (OCD/ATAF/AUC, 2022).

African governments are facing a dearth of capital and rising debt, as well as an increased need to finance AfCFTA and the Agenda 2063 goals. I argue that this negatively impacts their aspirations of integration and self-reliance. A dynamic and improved fiscal policy regimen is imperative, as are transparency and accountability in revenue collection activities. These are the hallmarks of good governance and inclusivity that will assist in actioning the goals of Agenda 2063. Public finance management incorporates public non-tax revenue planning into the budgetary process, ensuring allocation efficiency in revenue (Hodler and Raschky, 2001; IMF, 2018b). There should be transparency in terms of the unknown and miscellaneous sources of non-tax revenues, which are underpinned by volatile commodity prices. Due diligence, clear guidelines, and a regulatory system can help management systems buffer the impact of volatile non-tax revenue.

39   Adegbite, E., Abdulkadir, M. (2020). 'Tax Policy Reforms and Economic Development in Africa: A comparative analysis.' *African Development Review*. 12(4). 112-128.

6.11 The African Continental Free Trade Area / Africa Governance Architecture / African Peace And Security Architecture / Regional Economic Community Nexus in Human Security-Development: An Integrated Continental Approach

In addition to continental institutional reforms, greater transparency and broader collaborative participation by governments and citizens are required to provide the AfCFTA with the mandate to not only harness socio-economic gains but to also deal with the myriad of ensuing security challenges (Shievels, 2019). These include transnational organised crime groups, global and transnational terrorism, human trafficking, and xenophobic sentiments and attacks. The outlook for the AfCFTA, according to the current president of the AfDB, Akinwumi Adesina, is that "AfCFTA will stimulate the intra-African trade by up to US$35 billion per year, creating a 52% increase in trade by 2022, and a vital US$10 billion decrease in imports from outside Africa."

UNECA figures agree with this forecast, adding that the projected African population and market will increase from 1.2 billion to 2.5 billion by 2050. This translates into a 26% increase in the working-age population, which could be profitably leveraged towards economic growth and materialising Agenda 2063.

The Institute for Security Studies (ISS) PSC report proposes that the AfCFTA integrated 'human-security-development nexus' would institutionally bolster continental peace for the attainment of Agenda 2063. Multilateral collaboration on trade through the AfCFTA is inseparable from continuous development.

Furthermore, the improvement of a cooperative human security development nexus is necessary to effectively engage the anti-competitive behaviour of criminal elements and multinationals, which operate contrary to the rule of law. After the findings and recommendations of the 2017 Kagame Report, a Reform and Implementation Unit was established to institutionally improve and effect the working methods of the AU (AU PSC Report 2020). The Institutional Reform Unit was established within the Office of the Chairperson of the AUC and is tasked with implementing the daily activities to be delivered on the reform process.

In September 2017, Professor Pierre Moukoko Mbonjou and Ms. Ciru Mwaura were appointed as the Head and Deputy Head, respectively, of the newly formed Institutional Reforms Unit. Prior to his appointment, Mr. Mbonjou served in various ministerial roles for the Government of the Republic of Cameroon. He was Minister of External Relations from 2011 to 2015, Minister of Communication and Government Spokesperson from 2004 to 2006, and Minister Chief of Staff of the Prime Minister of Cameroon from 1996 to 2004. Ms. Ciru Mwaura, the Deputy Head of the AU Institutional Reforms Unit, served as the Chief of Staff to the African Union High Representative for Financing the AU and the Peace Fund and has also worked as a Senior Adviser with various organisations, including IGAD and the UK Department for International Development (DFID). The Institutional Reform Unit established within the Office of the Chairperson of the Commission consists of outstanding talent recruited from within and outside the AU. It is accountable to the AUC Chairperson who in turn is accountable to the supervising Head of State.

The synergy between AGA and APSA has long been an object of academic and policy debate. Neither the AU Assembly nor the Reform Implementation Unit has provided any clear guidelines on the matter throughout the consultation process that led to the institutional reform (ISS Policy Brief June 2021). To date, streamlined and rightsized linkages between the AUC, AGA, APSA, AfCFTA, RECs and RMs have been integrated for a bottom-up, vertical top-down, lateral collaborative, and transparent agency. This will enable the Specialised Technical Committee on defence, safety, and security to forge a common policy among its member states, thus avoiding duplication, overlap, and restricted mandates. Clearly, from the perspective of the human security development nexus, the AfCFTA fosters cooperation on security among the AU institutions.

In pursuit of progressive liberalisation, the AU is not a prisoner of dogmatic orthodoxy. The AfCFTA agreement has mandated the Council of Ministers with the authority to establish ad hoc bodies to evaluate the efficacy of policy, and thereafter to adopt them if they are deemed to be workable. In this regard, the AU Reform and Implementation Unit, together with the Council of Ministers, has identified the need for lateral collaboration between the RECs and RMs and the AUC. An MOU has been adopted to improve collaboration on economic matters.

This has inevitably necessitated law enforcement and the securitisation of the overall supervision of the AU's supranational authority through the APSA. The AfCFTA, through the security-development nexus, leverages the economic potential of Africa. Thus, it creates employment and better livelihoods, a business and entrepreneurial enabling environment, and de-escalates and mitigates factors that could be conducive to terrorism, criminality, violence, and undemocratic contestations of state power.

6.12 The African Union's African Continental Free Trade Area and Global Multilateralism

Africa's multilateral engagements with emerging powers such as BRICS, the NDB, the BRI, and the FOCAC have been significantly reinforced by AU instruments, such as the AfCFTA. These collaborations serve as a platform to advocate for reforms to global governance institutions, including the WTO, UN, IMF, WB, and G20.

The AfCFTA, which has been operational since 2021, is the largest FTA in the world in terms of the number of participating countries. It aims to create a single market for goods and services across Africa, enhance intra-African trade, and promote industrialisation and economic integration (UNECA, 2020). The AfCFTA strengthens Africa's bargaining power in multilateral negotiations by presenting a united economic front and consolidating the continent's fragmented markets. The AfCFTA also addresses one of Africa's historical weaknesses: low levels of intra-regional trade. By increasing intra-African trade, the agreement reduces the dependence on external markets, making the continent a more self-reliant and competitive player in the global economy (Edozie, 2021). This integration aligns with

Africa's efforts to strengthen its voice in multilateral platforms like BRICS, the NDB, and G20.

The BRICS bloc offers Africa an alternative partnership model to those of traditional Western-dominated institutions. Through South Africa's membership, Africa is already represented in BRICS. AfCFTA enhances this relationship by positioning Africa as a significant trading and investment partner within the block. The NDB established by BRICS, provides financial resources for infrastructure and sustainable development. African countries can pool resources through AfCFTA and collectively negotiate favourable financing terms for projects that align with the continent's priorities.

For example, AfCFTA-driven industrialisation projects could benefit from NDB funding, reducing reliance on Western institutions like the WB and IMF, which impose stringent conditionalities that are intrusive to Africa's sovereignty (Bhattacharya, 2020). Moreover, the AfCFTA enables Africa to speak with a unified voice in BRICS forums, advocating for reforms in global governance. By demonstrating the success of regional integration, Africa can influence BRICS to support its call for a more equitable global economic order, including increased African representation in the IMF and WB decision-making structures.

China's BRI complements AfCFTA's objectives by providing critical infrastructure investment across Africa. The BRI has financed large-scale projects, such as railways, ports, and highways, which are essential for boosting trade within the AfCFTA framework. Improved connectivity underpins the success of the AfCFTA by reducing transportation costs, thus linking Africa's markets more effectively (WB, 2021). The AfCFTA-BRI nexus strengthens Africa's bargaining position in multilateral negotiations. For example, as a significant beneficiary of BRI investments, Africa can leverage its partnership with China to advocate for reforms in the WTO that address imbalances in global trade rules. The collaboration also demonstrates the importance of infrastructure development in facilitating trade and economic growth, bolstering Africa's argument for increased investment from global financial institutions, such as the IMF and WB.

The FOCAC has been a cornerstone of Africa–China relations since its inception in 2000. It provides a platform for dialogue and cooperation on a range of issues, including trade, investment, and development. The AfCFTA amplifies the benefits of the FOCAC by providing a continental framework for engaging with China. Instead of fragmented bilateral agreements, African countries can negotiate collectively through the AfCFTA, ensuring that FOCAC outcomes align with the continent's integration agenda. Through the FOCAC, Africa can advocate for a more inclusive global governance system.

For example, the forum's emphasis on south–south cooperation aligns with Africa's push for greater representation in the UNSC and BWIs. By showcasing the AfCFTA as a model of successful regional integration, Africa can argue for similar reforms at the global level to enhance inclusivity and fairness.

Africa's participation in the WTO has often been constrained by limited capacity and fragmented representation. The AfCFTA addresses this challenge by uniting Africa's economies under a single trade framework, enabling the continent to engage more effectively in WTO negotiations. Through partnerships with BRICS and FOCAC, Africa can push for reforms that address issues such as agricultural subsidies, IPR, and special and differential treatment for developing countries (Adebajo, 2021). The UN remains a critical platform for advocating Africa's interests; however, the continent's marginalisation in the Security Council highlights the need for reforms. The AfCFTA, as an instrument of African unity, strengthens the AU's calls for permanent African representation on the UNSC. Collaboration with BRICS and China through the FOCAC can amplify this demand, given these partners' support for a multipolar world order (Tella, 2023).

The IMF and WB have faced criticism for their stringent loan conditions and limited representation of African voices. The AfCFTA provides Africa with a stronger economic foundation to negotiate reforms in these institutions. Partnerships with the NDB and BRI demonstrate alternative models of development financing, challenging the dominance of traditional financial institutions and pushing for more equitable lending practices (Bhattacharya, 2020).

To date, Africa's representation in the G20 has been limited to South Africa, but the AfCFTA strengthens the case for broader inclusion. By presenting a unified economic bloc, Africa can argue for permanent G20 representation, similar to the EU. Collaboration with BRICS and other Global South partners reinforces Africa's call for a more inclusive G20 that addresses the development needs of emerging economies (Edozie, 2021)

The AfCFTA is a transformative instrument that enhances Africa's capacity to engage multilaterally with emerging powers and advocate for global governance reforms. By fostering economic integration, the AfCFTA strengthens Africa's partnership with BRICS, the NDB, BRI, and FOCAC, positioning the continent as a key player in shaping a more equitable global order. Through these collaborations, Africa can push for reforms in institutions such as the WTO, UN, IMF, WB, and G20, ensuring that its development priorities are adequately addressed in the evolving global landscape.

Chapter 7

Regional Cooperation and Integration Towards Agenda 2063

7.1 The Tripartite Bloc and Regional Security Cooperation

This section assesses how the Tripartite bloc has managed the regional peace and human security development nexus towards materialising Agenda 2063, since its formation in 2008. Writing on regional security, Buzan and Waever (2003) state that "the possibility of systematically linking the study of internal conditions, relations among units in the region, relations between regions, and the interplay of regional dynamics with global acting powers.' This kind of interplay was seen during the proxy wars in Africa, where Jonas Savimbi of the National Union for the Total Independence of Angola (UNITA) movement in Angola was supported by the USA Government, and the MPLA – his arch-rivals – were supported by the USSR and Cuba.

The security dynamics at the inter-regional level, therefore, can override the regional dynamics through support gained from a single power or powers. This was also the case in the 2011 Libyan crisis with the ousting of Muammar Khadafy by NATO forces, following which an inter-regional level became a complex global configuration. The aftermath led to the emergence of a failed state, warlordism, and increased global terrorism spilling over into neighbouring countries (Winston, 2011). Low-intensity proxy wars and spheres of influence controlled by the USA, Russia, France, and China continue as hard power strategies to influence regional security and economics in Africa.

The theory of a regional security complex (RSC) in tandem with neorealist security convergence theory provides an understanding of the motivations of the Tripartite bloc's convergence in managing regional security. A reductionist analysis will also help to unravel the complexity of regional security, which is constituted by various components with military, political, social, and international dimensions.

Globalisation has had an impact on the interdependence of the African member states by engendering complex human security and development policy issues. This has inevitably forced African states to work together to mitigate their marginalisation from the globalisation process. The interdependence of member states' human security and development nexus is predicated on the Buzan and Weaver (2003) RSC theory, which states that:

> "A regional security complex cannot be applied to any group of countries, but in order to qualify as an RSC, a group of states or other entities must possess a degree of security interdependence sufficient both to establish them as a linked set and to differentiate them from surrounding security regions."

Resource-based conflicts, such as those in the DRC, Sudan, and Burundi, have varied dimensions and actors but are interlinked with national, regional, continental, and global interests. Actors such as MNCs, mercenaries, warlords, private security companies, and rebels accumulate wealth by gaining direct and indirect access to resource-rich areas. The DRC is a particular case in point, due to its resource-rich areas in diamonds, cobalt, oil, and titanium. Its resources have attracted belligerent forces, which have destabilised its regional peace and human security. These convergences negatively impact the AU's agency and development policies in materialising Agenda 2063. Moses Wetangula, former Kenyan Minister for Foreign Affairs, noted the lack of global interest – specifically from the UN – in supporting the AU's endeavours against atrocities (war crimes and genocide) in the DRC, Rwanda and other parts of Africa, remarking:

> "The practice in the past two years seems to indicate an undesirable trend that appears to be selective on the part of the United Nations Security Council and that seems to disregard full consideration of the position and/or recommendations of the AU or its organs."

It was only in April 2013, at the behest of the AUMS, that the UNSC authorised its first-ever offensive of the United Nations Force Intervention Brigade. This force numbered 19 815 troops and its key responsibility was to neutralise armed militias and rebels to restore peace in the Eastern Congo:

> "Resolution 2098 condemned M23 militia, the Democratic Forces for the Liberation of Rwanda, the Lord's Resistance Army, and all other armed group for their continued acts of violence and atrocities committed that impacted on the human rights of citizens. It tasked the new brigade with carrying out offensive operations, either unilaterally or jointly with the Congolese armed forces, in a robust, highly mobile and versatile manner to disrupt the activities of those groups."

In these conflicts, African militia groups have used civilians as tools of war. Children in their tens of thousands are forcibly recruited as child soldiers and women are targeted and raped. The REC member states are generally too dysfunctional to provide security for their citizenry. In these circumstances, the assistance of the UN is requested. In responding to these developments, the AU and the RECs/RMs continue to react to increasingly complex security environments, which implicitly display global traits and characteristics. In the context of the contemporary challenges facing Africa, this has resulted in the emergence of an African model of peace operations. In this regard, the activation of Article 4(h) and (j) of the Constitutive Act of non-indifference and the R2P[40] should be increasingly applied to peace and security interventions to asymmetric and hybrid security challenges, religious extremism, and transboundary criminal networks, which intersect within several of Africa's RECs (AUC, 2015:10).

---

40   Article 4(h) of the African Union Constitutive Act states: 'To promote and protect human and peoples rights in accordance with the African Charter on Human and Peoples rights.'

7.2 The Southern African Development Community-Common Market for Eastern And Southern Africa and the East African Community: A Tripartite Convergence towards Integration

Push and pull factors, both continentally and globally, continue to impact AU initiatives and development polices. The underlying asymmetrical and hybrid contributing variables are both divergent and convergent in nature. The realisation towards integration is therefore proceeding at a disappointing pace but at the same time is showing encouraging results.

The 2007 AU Audit report resulted in the TFTA, which was formed on 22 October 2008. The AfCFTA was ratified on 30 May 2019 in accordance with Agenda 2063. Constructed within a body of metatheories, the regional integration policies of the three RECs and their FTAs are premised on neoclassical economics and are linked to open markets and free trade. Against this backdrop of seeking converging policies, the unequal nature of intra-regional trade exhibits centrifugal forces resulting in a divergence of policies. The DTRP framework, as explained in chapters 2 and 3, explains the continued divergence or polarisation of policies within the global economy that continue to marginalise and Balkanise Africa's political economy.

This is evident in the case of the SADC and SACU, where South Africa as the regional hegemon dominates the Southern African economy, resulting in divergent regional integration policies. In turn, these policies have an impact on the COMESA, SADC, and EAC. Agenda 2063 operates in a global economy predicated on WTO principles; therefore, an imperfect economy with tariff barriers and NTBs is a reality. The economies of the three RECs and member states will inevitably diverge, given the distorted nature of the global economy and its trade, which is premised on neoclassical economics. In this case, poverty and underdevelopment will remain palpable challenges. This section builds on the DTRP/centre-periphery framework to consider the challenges in the tripartite alliance towards integration, self-reliance, and sustainability. In this regard, it proposes that the effective implementation of regional policies of the three RECs has the potential to converge regional trade policies in accordance with the aims and objectives of AfCFTA/AGA/APSA/Agenda 2063 through:

· deepening economic integration in Africa;
· creating a CCU;
· liberalising intra-African trade;
· resolving the challenges of overlapping memberships in RECs;
· enhancing competitiveness;
· contributing to the movement of capital and natural persons and facilitating investments;
· promoting sustainable and inclusive socio-economic development, gender equality, and structural transformation; and
· promoting industrialisation.

The institutional experience of the three RECs towards consolidation at the continental level, will be shared and benchmarked against other RECs and the AfCFTA. The regional security frameworks of the three RECs will also involve a convergence of the regional security mechanisms of its member states. This can be achieved within the Constitutive Act, which has transitioned from the archaic sovereign non-interference provision in the internal affairs of a member state, to non-indifference in matters of genocide, human rights abuse, war crimes, and crimes against humanity (AUC, 2015a:44–45).

According to the principles of new regionalism, COMESA, SADC, and the EAC are based on bilateral and multilateral relationships within the global economy. They can be seen as being part of a new regional dynamics, which forms the basis for the new regionalism. This presents challenges for trade creation and trade diversion, as the EU's Economic Partnerships Agreements and African Growth and Opportunity Act (AGOA), among other instruments, engender centrifugal trade diversion outcomes. Trade diversion is an anathema to the industrialisation of Africa and maintains the continent as an extractive economy of primary commodities for the Global North.

Africa's primary extractive industries, which are dependent on global price fluctuations, are negatively affected by the requirement for trade liberalisation set by the WTO and the BWIs. The UNECA has reported that it is more viable for Africa to do business with the countries of the Global North than trade inter-regionally or intra-continentally, due to poor African infrastructure, e.g., roads, ports, rail, water, and electricity shortages. Africa is compliant with the WTO regime and its drivers and architects, notably the USA and EU, have accelerated the pursuit of new inter-regional trade arrangements.

These agreements create a counterweight to those of the WTO in the face of uncertain global markets. An example of this is the Transatlantic Trade and Investment Partnership (TTIP) between the USA and the EU. The USA has also negotiated preferential trading agreements through the TPP, which comprises Asia, Latin America, and the Pacific.

The Southern African Development Community

The SADC has increased both intra-regional and international trade in fulfilment of its 2015–2063 Industrialisation Strategy and Roadmap. Specifically, enhancing SADC's global competitiveness in industrial and productive activities within the RVCs is imperative for intra-African trade and meeting the Aspirations of Agenda 2063. In 2018, during its multilateral exercise, the SADC, Germany, and the EU launched a €18 700 000 programme to enhance SADC's secretariat capacity to bolster its Regional Indicative Strategic Development Plan (RISDP).

This is meant to empower SADC member states' national structures to accelerate regional integration programmes. In 2017, 24% of imports into SADC countries were from African countries due to convergences in intra-regional trade. Of these imports, 92% came from FTAs such as SADC-FTA, COMESA-FTA, and EAC-FTA. Intra-SADC trade made up 72% of imports into the region, all of which were between FTA countries. An additional 9% of imports were from COMESA countries into SADC and 0.8% were EAC imports into Tanzania as a member of EAC (UNCTADStat, 2019).

The SADC aims to establish a common market, monetary union, and a single currency. In pursuit of these objectives, under the 2004 RISDP, SADC has identified key macroeconomic convergence criteria. These include fiscal policies, price stability, budget deficits, public debt, current account deficit, and debt-to-GDP ratios (Khadiagala, 2009; 2012). These will promote efficiency, public accountability, economic growth, and sustainable development to meet the goals of Agenda 2063. In 2017, SADC's average inflation decreased to 9.4%.

By 2018, seven of the SADC member states had achieved the convergence target of less than 5%, while only one member had achieved less than the 3% inflation target (Southern Africa Economic Outlook, 2018).

Many RECs, including SADC, have been able to demonstrate tangible statistical progress towards meeting the 2030 SDGs and Agenda 2063 goals. The RISDP also enables a cross-pollination of ideas, leading to better-informed decisions on ways to improve and integrate Africa's economies. In July 2018, Tunisia and Somalia joined the COMESA, increasing its membership from 19 to 21 states. As the largest REC in Africa, it contains a population of 590 million and has a combined GDP of US$796 billion.

The Common Market for Eastern and Southern Africa

Further centripetal convergences in trade facilitation have been of benefit to the COMESA. These are:

- A €15 000 000 cross-border trade programme (CBTP), which was signed in May 2018.
- The CBTP is an instrument of the Tripartite Transport and Transit Facilitation Programme. Its aim is to standardise and harmonise systems and regulations in the REC, thus creating comparative advantage and economies of scale to upscale the RVCs.

The COMESA is also pursuing a digital FTA to leverage e-commerce, the digital economy, and the 4IR, which is an AfCFTA objective (COMESA, 2019). Intra-COMESA trade has peaked, rising from US$3 billion in 2000 to more than US$21 billion in 2017.

These follow on from the converged trade facilitation measures and instruments, which are now operational, such as the COMESA Yellow Card Insurance Scheme and third-Party Motor Vehicle Insurance Scheme, which provide legal liability cover and compensation for medical expenses resulting from road traffic accidents (UNCTADStat, 2019).

The East African Community

The EAC is the most advanced REC in terms of regional integration, having already established a common market in January 2010. The common market supports the free movement of goods, services, capital, labour, and persons, including the rights to establishment and residence. The EAC has recorded and measured its trade facilitation measures and continues to attract FDI.

This is evidenced by the existence of a CET with standardised regulations and systems (Gasiorek et al., 2016; UNCTAD, 2018). Cross-border financial transactions have been improved due to the use of M-Pesa, a regional mobile telephone service platform, which has enhanced the EAC digital economy.

The EAC anticipates introducing a common regional currency for its member states by 2024. Centripetal imperatives towards this convergence will include:

· harmonising monetary policy frameworks;
· exchange rate operations;
· harmonising and standardising rules and practices governing bank supervision; and
· integrating payment systems, financial markets and financial reporting.

The convergence criteria adopted by the EAC shares commonalities with other RECs, such as a headline inflation ceiling of 8%, a reserve cover of four and a half months of imports, a 3% of GDP fiscal deficit ceiling, and a 50% ceiling of GDP on gross public debt (Trade East Africa, 2017). In 2016 and 2017, EAC members met the inflation target. The trend towards macroeconomic policy convergence is evident in all official RECs, including ECCAS; CEN-SAD; IGAD; COMESA, and AMU.

7.3 Region Building in West Africa Within The Agenda 2063 Framework

The AU officially recognises eight RECs. The ECOWAS· is the embodiment and driver of region-building in West Africa. It consists of 15 member states: Benin, Burkina Faso, Cape Verde, Côte d'Ivoire, Gambia, Ghana, Guinea, Guinea-Bissau, Liberia, Mali, Niger, Nigeria, Senegal, Sierra Leone, and Togo.

Ongoing complex asymmetric and hybrid security challenges have had an impact on the region and without peace, security, and a stable political environment, economic cooperation and integration cannot be achieved. As stated in the 2012 ECOWAS annual report:

> "Political instability hinders regional integration efforts. In this respect, problems, especially those that degenerate into armed conflicts, strongly disrupt production systems and the marketing of products, and thus hamper efforts to promote intra-regional trade and mobility of factors of production."

To counter the centrifugal forces resulting in destructive divergences, The ECOWAS has invested its political capital and resources to engender centripetal convergences for the process of regional peacebuilding in West Africa. This has created the foundation for regional integration in the subregion (Nagar, 2019; Murithi, 2014) and is contained in the AU's framework towards the attainment of Agenda 2063.

This section consists of an investigative assessment and validates the strengths and challenges of African agency thus far within the West African region. It will examine the basis, dynamics, and realities of the adaptive shifts made concerning the fast-paced asymmetrical hybrid regional security challenges. It will also examine the legal, policy, and institutional characteristics required to facilitate it, the challenges that have been confronted, and the opportunities created.

The section will begin with a historical background on why the ECOWAS was conceptualised and the way in which it was realised. It will be shown that it was imperative to establish peace and security as a fundamental prerequisite for socio-economic development and regional integration. With the final transition of the AU from the OAU in 2002, ECOWAS was officially recognised as an REC, becoming a member and signatory to its Constitutive Act.

The ECOWAS upholds the framework and protocols of the Constitutive Act, which contain the norms of human rights, security, democracy, and good governance. These are upheld in pursuit of Agenda 2063. The ECOWAS strategy for political investment in peace, security, and governance issues needs to be adaptable if it is to nurture and consolidate the realisation of regional economic cooperation and integration towards Agenda 2063. The ECOWAS will have to seek the right balance between economic and political region building to not only realise Agenda 2063 but also the goal of 'Silencing the Guns in Africa'. This has to be achieved among fast-paced, globalised, asymmetrical hybrid challenges and disparate conflicting interests.

7.4 The Formation of the Economic Community of West African States: The Convergence of the Security Imperative·

In the aftermath of the Biafran civil war, the multiple global OPEC oil crises and shocks of 1973 also had an impact on Africa. These came with additional cascading effects, which saw Africa's global ToT decline, debt deepening, a negative balance of payments, increased levels of illiteracy and unemployment, and endemic poverty.

These conditions led to heightened levels of social insecurity among the population of the region, and standards of living worsened. The ECOWAS was established on 28 May 1975, in response to these cumulative dynamics, with the ultimate aim of creating an FTA. This was calculated to mitigate these multiple negative effects and create space for cross-border economic activities within the region (Nagar, 2019). The normative ethos of ECOWAS is to promote economic cooperation and development for all its member states in all fields of economic activity. This includes the elimination of trade and non-trade barriers; the harmonisation and rationalisation of customs systems to create a CET, and improved trade facilitation interventions.

Such interventions have involved harmonising border systems by removing the duplication of inefficient border systems and restrictions; creating an enabling and conducive environment to promote a business-friendly environment; the free movement of goods and services, capital, and labour, and peoples' right to residence.

The ECOWAS was also established to provide integrated macroeconomic planning and implementation to better control inflation; encourage ISI; increase self-reliance in food production; address uneven development among member states to leverage comparative advantages to RVCs; and compensate countries that had lost revenue through the FTA or the regional integration process.

The converging ECOWAS framework was initiated by the late Nigerian UNECA executive director, Adebayo Adedeji, on 28 May 1975.

This was a cumulative soft power success for Nigeria, enabling it to regain the regional influence that it had almost lost in the preceding three-year secessionist Biafran civil war. At the time, global competitors such as France, the UK, USA, and China were vying for its oil resources. Francis (2010) poignantly captures this:

> "The Biafran civil war of 1967–1970 and the role played by neighbouring countries, in particular, how they were used by extra-regional actors and powers as a staging post for support to the secessionist group, drove Nigeria to take a leadership role in West Africa. This was viewed by the government as an attempt to "balkanise", the country, and it led to the realisation that the national security of Nigeria

cannot be divorced from regional security and stability. It marked an important turning point in the political history of the country as it led to a paradigm shift in its post-independence foreign and security policy from isolation to intervention in regional affairs."

The post-civil war foreign policy, therefore, focused on two interrelated tasks: the promotion of regional security and stability through regional cooperation; and integration and leadership roles in African and international affairs. An important aspect to consider was the intrusive role of France and its power politics with Nigeria for the dominance and control of West Africa. The motivation for the creation of the ECOWAS was, therefore, to provide an instrument with which to promote Nigeria's foreign and security policy in West Africa. It was also a way to limit the role of France in the subregion, which was considered by Nigeria to be its own political, strategic, and economic sphere of influence.

In hindsight, it could be regarded as ironic that Nigeria was nearly Balkanised by the Biafran civil war and is currently the main driver of the ECOWAS and Agenda 2063. At the time of the formation of the OAU in 1963, Nigeria was a member of the gradualist Monrovia Group (made up of the Côte d'Ivoire, Liberia, Togo, Benin, and Sierra Leone), which was sceptical and opposed Nkrumah's forceful call for an immediate United States of Africa. At that time, Nkrumah's vision was supported by Ghana, Ethiopia, Guinea, Egypt, Libya, and Mali, which were members of the Casablanca Group.

The Regional Peace Project

Four major documents define the regional peace project of ECOWAS: the 1993 Revised ECOWAS Treaty, the 1999 Protocol Relating to the Mechanism on Conflict Prevention, Management, Resolution, Peacekeeping, and Security, the 2001 Protocol A/SP1/12/01 on Democracy and Good Governance, and the 2008 ECOWAS Conflict Prevention Framework. The Revised Treaty commits member states to the "promotion and consolidation of a democratic system of governance as envisaged in the Abuja Treaty of 1991" as well as the "promotion and protection of human and people's rights in accordance with the provisions of the African Charter on Human and Peoples Rights." The ECOWAS has been regionally enhancing norm entrepreneurship in the areas of human security. The LPA is fully coherent with the ECOWAS project on economic development and human security

The Revised Treaty also established more (new) structures, such as the Community Parliament and Court. These are enabling centripetal converging organs, which are central to popular participation in decision-making and the adjudication of disputes among the member states and their citizens.

Considering the near Balkanisation of Nigeria, a result of the Biafran civil war, the new region-building project needed to be inclusive of the public. It therefore forestalls and pre-empts variables which could lead to civil war, secessionist tendencies, and further attempts at Balkanisation. The 2001 supplementary Protocol on Democracy and Good Governance reinforced the normative framework of ECOWAS, promoting democracy

There was a lack of devolution and democratisation of state power, which was dominated by the ruling elite. The key features missing included no: democratic separation of powers; holding regular elections, independent judiciary to uphold the rule of law; SSRs with inclusive participation and accountability of the security and armed forces to the public; freedom of the fourth estate 'media' and Chapter nine institutions that provide additional scrutiny of governments by the public to address corruption and abuse of power.

Against the backdrop of the Biafran civil war and the 1994 Rwandan genocide, which claimed the lives of approximately a million people, the ECOWAS was one of the main drivers behind the transitioning of the moribund OAU to the AU in 2002.

The Constitutive Act acknowledged the need to be relevant in the 21st century. Nigeria, South Africa, Senegal, Cote d'Ivoire, Libya, and Algeria acted as norm entrepreneurs in support of this new aim. The 2008 ECOWAS Conflict Prevention Framework echoes the Constitutive Act. It provides coherence and coordination in seeking to promote and consolidate democracy, popular participation, good governance, protecting and promoting human rights, and promoting peace, security, and stability across the continent, all of which are core objectives of the AU.

As one of the eight RECs officially recognised by the AU, the ECOWAS has been active in the realm of mediation and conciliation in Liberia, Guinea-Bissau, Niger, Mali, Côte d'Ivoire, Sierra Leone, Togo, and Guinea. For example, in the case of the presidential elections in Côte d'Ivoire in October 2010, ECOWAS stood firm in its decision that the incumbent. President Laurent Gbagbo, had lost the elections to Alassane Ouattara.

The AU, UN, and EU supported the firm stand taken by the ECOWAS. This action consolidated electoral legitimacy, recognition of sovereignty, and conflict prevention. ECOWAS overturned military coups in Sierra Leone (1998), Guinea-Bissau (2003), and Togo (2005). It also imposed sanctions after military coups in Guinea (2008), Niger (2010), and Mali (2012). Furthermore, advances were made in regional economic cooperation and development, which were complementary to the peace and security framework of the AU and Agenda 2063.

7.5 Region Building in Central Africa within the Agenda 2063 Framework

The ECCAS is officially recognised by the AU and is comprised of 11 member states: Angola, Burundi, Cameroon, the CAR, Chad, Congo-Brazzaville, the DRC, Equatorial Guinea, Gabon, Rwanda, and São Tomé and Principe. These states are members of more than one REC. This spaghetti-bowl configuration reflects a deeper problem for Africa and Agenda 2063. A history of varying and antagonistic political orientations and interests, coupled with the structural deficits inherent in the regional environment have exacerbated intra-regional deadly conflicts within and among member states (Collier, 2004:563-595).

Christopher Clapham argues that "The creation of effective systems of regional integration, depends on the success with which potential regional leaders are able to secure political stability and a reasonably working economy within their own territories.." The DRC, as a potential continental hegemon, holds a measure of normative influence; it could have played a leadership role in the regional integration of the continent (Dinka and Kennes, 2007). It is strategically located and endowed with a geographic space of 2 300 000 million km², a vast wealth of minerals, unlimited hydroelectric resources, and a rich agricultural base.

Compared to its neighbours, Rwanda and Burundi, it is better positioned and resourced to be a continental (and norm-setting) powerhouse, rivalling both Nigeria and South Africa. However to date, even after the overthrow of the late dictator Mobutu, the DRC has not functioned optimally as a state in terms of the efficient national levying of taxes; enforcing customs agreements; and securing its borders and expediting government regulatory decisions (Dibua, 2010).

By 2009, the DRC's economic performance had diminished as a result. Its public debt ratio having increased to 140% of its GDP. Ideally, a strong state, such as Nigeria or South Africa, acting as a hegemon, becomes a de facto driver of regional integration amid other small and vulnerable states (Duthie, 2011:37-40). The DRC is the opposite: it has the comparative advantage of immense geographic space and immeasurable mineral wealth but cannot translate and leverage its asset base to strengthen its nation-state to the level of South Africa. It could be argued that this would make it a competitive contributor to Africa's regional integration. I argue that in support of the DTRP/centre-periphery framework, Kvangraven (2018) and Amin (2016) lend credence to Francois Bayard's description that these circumstances are strategies of "extraversion which have at their heart the creation and capture of a rent generated by dependency; rather than promote integration, their immediate purpose is to instrumentalise dependency relationships with external donors." Under these imposed conditions of the 'periphery' by the 'centre', Africa's pursuit of integration and self-reliance is structurally and institutionally stunted.

Africa has been irregularly Balkanised, and its economies have been extractive appendages of Europe for centuries. Contemporary MNCs, which are entrenched across Africa, fundamentally sustain and are pivotal to the economies of the Global North. The 2011 invasion of Libya by NATO affirmed Europe's unrivalled military machinery compared to that of Africa's, which it leverages to coerce its neo-colonialism as Nkrumah forewarned (Kasaija, 2012:135-60). Africa lacks a military deterrent that matches NATO's (or any of the UNSC (P5) members), with which it could leverage and hedge its Pan-African integration programme towards Agenda 2063 without intrusion from the West.

Africa has managed to decolonise and continues to face global asymmetrical and hybrid challenges. Furthermore, under complicated circumstances, Africa has demonstrated agency, guiding the OAU through its transition to the AU to engage regionally and globally.

7.6 Region Building in North Africa within the Agenda 2063 Framework

The emergence of the North African regional union has been slow, as demonstrated by the AMU since 1989. The lack of political will to pursue intra-regional trade and deepen further trade with the rest of Africa, opens it to both rewards and risks.

Arab Maghreb Union[41]

The AMU was created by Algeria, Libya, Mauritania, Morocco, and Tunis in 1989 mainly as a consequence of the favourable sub-regional context. The Western Sahara conflict was in a period of détente and it was one year before Morocco and Algeria re-established contact after twelve years of non-existent diplomatic relations. Additionally, Libya and Tunisia established strong political ties following the ousting of President Habib Burguiba in 1987. Against this background, on 17 February 1989 in Marrakesh the five heads of state signed an agreement by which the organisation was formally constituted to guarantee cooperation

---

41   Personal Interview with Algeria Ambassador Mohammed Hacene. June 2022. Pretoria South Africa. Interviews with Prof Mammo Muchie; Prof Tim Murithi; Dr Hesphina Rukato. November 2022. Pretoria South Africa.

at different levels. The AMU intended to promote economic and social progress, inter-state peace, free circulation of persons and goods, and free transfer and movement of capital throughout North Africa (Hettne 2005:543-571). As the institutional treaty stresses, the AU aimed to reinforce the fraternal links, realise progress and prosperity, contribute to the preservation of peace, pursue a common political policy in different domains and work towards the progressive realisation of the FMP, services, goods, and capital.

Regarding the common political policies, the treaty defines four basic domains: international affairs, which aims to promote diplomatic cooperation founded on dialogue; defence, based on safeguarding the independence of each member state (the treaty also states that any aggression against a member state will be considered as an aggression against the other member states); economy, which aims to promote industrial, agricultural, commercial, and social development of member states; and cultural affairs bearing in mind the importance of Islam and the Arab identity (Moller, 2009).

The foundation and institutionalisation of the AMU can be understood as a top-down process or a regionalism "from above", where the government are the central actors. In this sense, it established agreements, rules, and institutions to reduce transaction costs and shape behaviours.

Despite the organisation's goodwill and common identity factors (the five countries share a common heritage, history, language, culture, and religion), sub-regional conflicts and competition between two sub-regional leaders have affected and continue to impede the advancement of the process.

The treaty establishing the AMU also created different bodies, resulting in this organisation being highly institutionalised. It is constituted by a General Secretariat in Morocco, a Secretary-General from Tunis, a Consultative Council in Alger, a Court in Mauritania, financial institutions in Tunis and an Academy of Sciences in Libya. However, the Presidency Council, which is composed of the heads of state, is the only body that has the right to make decisions, which are required to be made unanimously. This represents a constitutional obstacle to efficient decision-making. Following this supreme body, there is the Council of Foreign Ministers, which has to prepare the session of the Presidency Council and examine the questions submitted by the Monitoring Council and the Specialised Ministerial Commission (Brunnel 2008). The Consultative Council, composed of thirty delegates from each country, is also supposed to work for the Presidency Council, providing advice on any decision. Finally, the duties of both the General Secretariat and the General Secretary, also depends on the Presidency Council. Therefore, a block on the Presidency Council meetings not only impedes the decision-making process, but also the advancement of AMU institutions.

Despite being the supreme body of the organisation, since 1994, there has not been a sitting of the Presidency Council because of the border closure between Algeria and Morocco. The disputes between these two countries and their competition in leading the sub-region and the sub-regional process have represented a permanent block on the development of the AMU. Since 1994, the Western Sahara Conflict and political rivalries between Morocco and Algeria have impeded any advance of the AMU (Akhatar and Mustapha, 2010). Furthermore, the Algerian civil war and the international sanctions imposed on Libya cannot be overlooked as contributing factors to the distrust and instability in the sub-region. The political rivalry between Algeria and Morocco for the leadership of the sub-region is a block on any kind of sub-regional cooperation. Algeria and Morocco have a population that constitutes 77% of the sub-region and a GDP three times higher than the combined GDP of Mauritania, Tunis, and Libya. As Kindleberger (1986) argued, "leadership is needed if international public goods are to be provided, while in the absence of leadership, these goods will be under-produced, due to the free-rider problem".

Some analysts consider that the only hypothetical change in the leadership problem would involve the recognition of Egypt as the natural hegemon of the sub-region (Moller, 2009). However, despite being an organisation open to new members, AMU refused Cairo's application for membership in 1994. During

1999, the region entered into a new period of détente favoured by the election of Abdelaziz Bouteflika in Algeria and the accession of Mohammed VI to the throne of Morocco. Nonetheless, this period did not lead to the relaunch of the AMU.

The AMU has as a priority issue-area the economic cooperation. When it was created, the AMU aimed to reach a customs union by 1995 and by 2000 it was supposed to accomplish a single market (Brunel 2008). However, this cooperation has not been increased during more than 20 years of existence. The main facts that show the failure of this cooperation are intra-trade between the five countries, which is still around 3% of their total trade and intra-Maghreb trade which represents less than 2% of the sub-region's combined GDP (Akhtar and Mustapha, 2010).

The five countries' trade with the EU accounts for approximately 60% of the total sub-region's trade. Despite being bound by a common heritage, the five North African countries are economically diverse; they are at different stages of economic development and the endowments of natural resources also vary. They can be broadly classified into three groups: major oil producers (Algeria and Libya), a low-income country that recently became an oil producer (Mauritania), and two emerging market countries (Morocco and Tunisia) (Allain and Boileau, 2007). Moreover, high barriers to trade, logistical bottlenecks, and lack of production based on diversification added to various other political considerations are the explanatory factors of the low levels of trade.

In conclusion, the main obstacle to North African integration seems to be the unwillingness of rulers to achieve it, in combination with political differences and rivalries, protectionist commercial policies, the ineffectiveness of bilateral trade agreements, proximity to the EU trading bloc, the negligible absorption capacity of southern Mediterranean markets, and the supply structure of these countries, which is more competitive than complementary.

Despite these obstacles, the absolute benefits that could be obtained if the barriers to trade were eliminated would be worth US$4.6 billion dollars (Larramendi, 2008), which represents a deprivation of 2% to 3% of the annual GDP of North African countries. According to Bousset (2004:21-43), one of the solutions to boost intra-regional trade is the dismantling of tariffs. Thus, for Algeria, "a cut of 50% or 100% in taxes to farming imports from Morocco and Tunisia would lead to a progress of 20.9% and 47.9%, respectively in trade with these two countries (...) with regards to industrial trade it would amount to an increase in trade of 34.4% and 84.9%, respectively". In conclusion, despite there being many absolute benefits that should promote sub-regionalism, this process seems to be more affected by the states' interests.

In addition to economic issues, the AMU also deals with three more common policies: international, defensive, and cultural affairs. At the international level, member states are supposed to establish diplomatic cooperation based on dialogue while maintaining their sovereignty (Chourou, 2002:15-23). However, the AMU has only ever made one common declaration during the first Gulf War (1990-1991). The declaration asked for an Arab-led negotiated solution which should include the withdrawal of the Iraqi and foreign troops in the region (Seddon, 1999). Defensive affairs have also been considered by the AMU. Specifically, terrorism was brought to the agenda at the end of 1992, at the AMU summit in Nouakchott, where the chiefs of state committed themselves to fight against terrorism viewed as a product of religious fanaticism. Initially, the AMU countries, aware of the potential for and consequences of the spread of fanatic Islamism, strengthened their cooperation in security matters such as information exchanges and border surveillance.

Throughout the nineties, the Islamism threat has fuelled mutual suspicions between the AMU countries, especially between Morocco and Algeria and between Libya and the others (Larramendi, 2008). Since the 09/11 terrorist attacks and the rise of Al-Qaida in the Islamic Maghreb in the Sahel, the AMU countries' willingness to collaborate on defensive matters has increased, but with few concrete results.

Energy has also been an issue included in AMU's agenda. However, cooperation and agreements on energy issues have also been limited. The main achievement in this field was the inauguration in 1996 of the West African Gas Pipeline (WAGP), which connects Algeria with Morocco. The passage of time has proven how this achievement has not been sufficient for improving relationships between the two sub-regional leaders. These relationships are mainly determined by the Western Sahara conflict and their mutual mistrust

Since then, the AMU has been destabilised further, preventing closer regional integration. The AMU has become a hive of international terrorism (Kasaija, 2012), with warlordism in states such as Libya (Gottwald, 2012). The constant tensions between Algeria and Morocco over historical border disputes, together with the Western Sahara conflict, have undermined intra-regional trade and cooperation, thereby restricting efforts to build a more integrated AMU. The North African countries have individually sought a closer association with the EU and USA at the cost of the bargaining power that an integrated Maghreb might provide (UNCTAD, 2022f). These extra-regional agreements have individually helped each AMU member state increase trade in the global economy, but not with each other (World Bank, 2023). Intra-regional trade is limited among the members of AMU due to their member states similarities in trade structures, with each state being dependent on comparable produce. Against this backdrop, the attainment of Africa's integration and self-reliance is even further compromised.

These countries share a cultural outlook, religion, and language but significant strides are still needed to enhance their political relationships. The small market size of each member state coupled with the weak legal and bureaucratic investment environments has deepened the divide between them. There are also heightened tensions in the region, a lack of political will and disinterest among people sharing a common history, that works against the integration of the AMU to support AfCFTA/AGA/APSA towards Agenda 2063 goals. Africa's continental integration should not be dominated and dictated by a state-centric elite leadership. It is time for non-state-centric approach to be factored into continental integration.

Chapter 8

The African Union 2007 Audit Report and the 2017 Kagame Report on Reforming and Strengthening the African Union

The 2007 AU Audit Report and the 2017 Kagame Report on AU reform both highlighted critical issues and offered recommendations to address the systemic inefficiencies in achieving African integration and development goals. The reports converge on several key themes related to Africa's developmental challenges and opportunities. Below is an analysis of their findings and key recommendations.

8.1 Africa Mining Vision

The Africa Mining Vision (AMV) was established in 2009 and both reports noted Africa's wealth in mineral resources but emphasised the lack of value addition and beneficiation with the continent. They identified exploitative practices by foreign companies and weak governance structures as barriers to realising the AMV's goals.

The AMV aims to transform Africa's mineral sectors into an inclusive, integrated sustainable framework. This is consistent with the Pan-African development programmes within Agenda 2063. Africa should not be solely dependent on external capital to finance its programmes of Agenda 2063. An integrated extractive mining sector can be an instrument of domestic resource mobilisation. Against this backdrop, the two reports recommended the following:

· strengthen governance, transparency and accountability in the mining sector;

- develop local industries to process raw materials and promote value addition; and
- foster collaboration among member states for sustainable and equitable resource utilisation;

Additionally, Kagame's report emphasised the importance of aligning mining strategies with AU institutions for greater resource leverage and funding.

8.2   Human Peace and Security-Public Health

A comprehensive approach to human security and peace also constitutes public health. Under the auspices of the AUC, NEPAD, and the African Centre for Disease Control and Prevention, African countries are cooperating in the prevention and management of public health in diseases such as malaria, HIV-AIDS, ebola, and the recent global pandemic COVID-19. The five-year strategic plan was launched in March 2017 (AU, 2017a; AU, 2017b). Peacebuilding in areas of armed conflict is also integral to human security. Since the transitioning of the OAU to the AU in 2002, the number of armed and violent conflicts have substantially reduced in Africa (Williams 2015).

Against this backdrop, both reports stressed the importance of addressing persistent conflicts, weak institutions, and poor public health systems as obstacles to integration. The 2007 report highlighted the AU's limited capacity to manage PKOs and health crises. Furthermore, Kagame's report noted the duplication of efforts among AU organs and the lack of coordination in responding to crises such as pandemics.

Both reports recommended the capacity of the AU PSC be enhanced. It is imperative to increase investment in public health infrastructure and preparedness for health emergencies. The harmonisation of regional and continental strategies for security and health, including early warning systems and rapid response mechanisms, is a requisite enabling instrument.

8.3   Financial Integration and Convergence

Intra-African integration of macroeconomic and financial systems and their convergence are imperative towards an African monetary union (Karingi & Davis, 2017, COMESA, 2017). Both reports emphasised the lack of financial cohesion and dependency on external funding. Furthermore, the reports highlighted barriers to achieving a single African currency and the insufficient role of the AfDB.

In this regard, there are a growing number of African banks in multiple REC member states. This is a foundational basis from which to standardise and harmonise cooperative regulatory rules in facilitating ToT, finance, and improved macroeconomic planning and implementation. Among other measures, a single currency and an ACB are critical for macroeconomic management and stability, which would bring about a stable exchange rate regime. The aforementioned would be foundational to implementing AMF to facilitate financial integration, by strengthening regional monetary union as a precursor to continental financial integration.

The convergence, standardisation, and harmonisation of financial cooperative regulatory rules would enable a reduction in dependency on external donors by promoting self-financing mechanisms. For example the levy on imports to fund AU activities proposed in the Kagame report.

The ECOWAS has already stipulated the necessary criteria for a monetary union. The attainment of a monetary union in this REC would have a positive spillover and multiplier effect on other RECs, encouraging them to follow suit (West African Monetary Union, cited in EAC, 2017b). Integral to human security and integration is the FMP and the right of establishment.

8.4   Free Movement of Persons and the Right of Establishment·

Among the founding principles of the AEC (Chapter VI of the 1991 Abuja Treaty) is FMP, including their right of residence and establishment across borders. This basic human entitlement is also recognised in the 1948 Universal Declaration of Human Rights and the International Covenant on Civil and Political Rights (UNDP 2009). Free movement of people invariably paves the way for the free movement of labour. In an increasingly integrated world, international migration will continue. Therefore, migrant labour social security rights and their qualifications need to be recognised in other countries (Lloyd, 2000). Among the eight REC protocols, FMP across Africa is being recognised, albeit at a restrictive and inhibiting slow pace. The process is further inhibited by visa restrictions and border controls remain significant barriers to integration.

Factors such as security and high national unemployment levels have adversely affected the entire process. However, as Pritchett (2010) contends, enhancing the intra-African mobility of production resources could lead to an increase in GDP, despite the current global GDP standing at approximately US$65 trillion. Additionally, the FMP has an impact on a country's GDP by way of remittances, which migrants send to their countries of origin (Davis and Head, 1995:439–50; Ratha, 2011).

Remittance inflows to Africa quadrupled between 1990 and 2010 to nearly US$40 billion, equivalent to 2.6% of the continental GDP in 2009. Nigeria received US$10 billion in 2010, the highest in Sub-Saharan Africa.

The harmonised immigration and emigration regimen supported by the REC protocols must be promoted and implemented (Deacon, 2008; WB, 2011). Thus, to accelerate ratification and implementation of the Protocol on FMP, further simplification of visa regimes and regional agreements are required to build trust and mobility frameworks. Kagame's report highlighted the need for political will and legal reforms to ease the implementation of these measures. The ECOWAS, for example, has implemented progressive measures in this regard. Article 61 of the ECOWAS Treaty continues to enable the harmonising of labour and social security laws with the REC.

Approximately 3% of West Africans living in the region are not living in their country of origin. The harmonisation of policies is, therefore, beneficial for the FMP (ECOWAS Commission, 2007:3).

Other RECs. such as the ECOWAS and EAC, have taken steps to liberalise their visa regimes, especially to attract and facilitate the unencumbered free movement of skilled labour. Work permits and study visas are easily available in this regard. This has encouraged RECs to align their employment codes with REC protocols and to ensure that the rights of migrant skilled labour in host countries are protected. For example, as highlighted by Romans (2006) and Ndulo (2005), mining in South Africa has caused significant movement of people from central and southern Africa as semi-skilled labour. Since 1994, South Africa, as the most industrialised country in Africa, has attracted an influx of migrants continentally and globally. In this respect, South Africa could learn from ECOWAS by continuously improving its protocols towards FMP and residency to alleviate the xenophobic sentiments associated with the country.

8.5 The Movement Of Capital Goods And Services In Africa

Globalisation and shifting economic paradigms and conditions continue to influence Africa regarding the best ways to attract global investments. In response, the AU-NEPAD RECs continue to build and improve an enabling and conducive environment to boost intra-regional financial flows and investments (ECOSOC, 2017). This will attract both continental and FDI for strategic continental manufacturing development and the enhancement and diversification of its manufacturing base into RVCs. Linked cross-border infrastructures, supported by a developed financial sector within the RECs, function as the push and pull factors of FDI (Dunning, 2001:173–90). It is, therefore, imperative for Africa's RECs to continue to deepen their intra-regional systems (UNCTAD, 2009). According to a UNIDO (2005) survey, during the last decade, 29.4 % of FDI inflows went into Nigeria and 18.2% went into South Africa.

The bulk of portfolio inflows (87.6%) went to South Africa, which has a highly developed capital market. However, these FDI inflows supersede intra-Africa FDI, which vacillates between US$1.6 billion and US$2 billion annually. UNCTAD (2008) advises that intra-African FDI must be substantially improved in the intra-regional production sectors to create more value-added jobs than global FDI.

The refusal to cede aspects of sovereign authority to a continental supra-authority, such as the AU, will continue to have an adverse impact on Africa's integration prospects. Moreover, penalties for non-compliance, such as sanctions, are important to safeguard implementation. The following section will show that this results in the further entrenchment of neo-patrimonial systems of overlapping REC membership and disconnected trade policies.

8.6   A Comparison of Trade Policies and Multiple Memberships

Although the AUC recognises eight RECs, the problem of multiple memberships and overlap persists. Herein lies the challenge of developing a CET, as a member state cannot be a member of two customs unions (UNDP, 2011). The overlapping of multiple REC memberships undermines the binding commitments of intra-Africa mandates towards the AEC and prevents the aims and objectives of Agenda 2063 from being realised. For example, in 2000, COMESA launched an FTA aimed at reducing tariffs on intra-COMESA trade; however, implementation has rarely followed. Worse still, unlike the ECOWAS and SADC, the COMESA does not compensate its disadvantaged least developed member states for loss of revenue (Oyejide & Njinkeu, 2001; Nhara, 2006).

Ethiopia has the lowest commitment to the market integration of the COMESA-FTA because it fears revenue loss and has only reduced its tariffs by 10% (IGAD, 2009). The imposition of NTBs is also inhibitive towards intra-African trade because they impede the free movement of goods, encourage rent-seeking and other oligopolistic and corrupt patronage networks (Alaba, 2006; UNECA, 2008). To help mitigate and eliminate this anomaly, the COMESA, EAC, and SADC have developed a computerised online common reporting mechanism, which monitors and evaluates the removal of the NTBs.

8.7 Rules Of Origin

Rules of origin are the rules for determining the country of origin of goods. According to UNCTAD (2019), "rules of origin are like a passport for a product to enter an FTA and circulate without being imposed a duty." This is further described by the World Customs Organisation (WCO):

> "[T]he basic role of rules of origin is the determination of the economic nationality as opposed to the geographical nationality of a given good: the ROO are used as an important trade measure. They do not constitute a trade instrument by themselves and are not to be used to pursue trade objectives directly or indirectly or as a policy measure. The ROO are used to address different commercial policy instruments and they can be used to attain specific purposes of national or international policies (UNCTAD, 2016c; WCO, 2012)."

If the ROO within the RECs are costly and restrictive, they will have an impact on intra-African integration and trade as well as its international competitiveness. Rules of origin aim to ensure that products traded within the REC originate from a member country.

They also function as a preventive measure to discourage third-party countries, which are not members of the AfCFTA, from re-exporting through one AfCTFA member to another and thus illegitimately benefitting from trade preferences only exclusive to its members (Estevadeordal et al., 2014). As a trade policy, ROO define the scope of a preferential trade agreement. They provide industries with incentives to source from within the AfCFTA. Rules of origin, are costly to monitor and their enforcement would be detrimental to creating a business-friendly environment. It would be advisable to use them with flexibility and negotiated outcomes to fast-track the AfCFTA with a CET (Abdoulahi, 2005).

These contributions could then be used to further the continent's industrial and agricultural development and the emergence of RVCs. By defining the nationality of a product, the ROO stipulate the conditions for the application of tariff concessions and delimit the range of products eligible for preferential treatment.

In addition to the ROO, there are other trade-specific factors, which could optimally operationalise the AfCFTA, such as customs cooperation towards a CET and trade facilitation measures to improve skills and infrastructural efficiency.

The interactions between these factors are imperative to ensure AfCFTA meets the aims and goals of Agenda 2063, including – specifically – diversifying Africa's manufacturing and value addition base. This would enable Africa to delink from export dependency on primary commodities.

8.8   Analysis/Evaluation of the African Continental Free Trade Area's Current Status

Since 1 January 2021, African countries that had submitted their plans to reduce tariffs, or taxes on imported goods have been able to trade goods under the AfCFTA Agreement. The first trade using the trading preferences under the AfCFTA Agreement occurred a few days after its commencement. Many in the global trade community eagerly watched this initiation of trading as it marked a monumental step in support of the AfCFTA and its stated goal. However, as trading began under the AfCFTA, negotiations on many issues were yet to be resolved and as such the Agreement was and is not still in a position to be fully functional. The commencement of trading on 1 January 2021 is at most a symbolic mark, as the full impact and implementation of the Agreement are expected to take some time with predictions of its full effect being in place by 2035.

To fully understand the developments that have taken place in the lead-up to the commencement of trade, and the following developments, a review of negotiations under the Agreement is helpful. Generally, the negotiations can be divided into three phases:

- Phase I – Trade in Goods and Services
- Phase II – IPR, Investment, and Competition Policy
- Phase III – E-commerce

Each is discussed in turn below.

Phase I Regarding Trade in Goods and Services

Prior to the commencement of trading, a major part of the negotiations of Phase I had commenced, however, not all have been concluded. Some of the vital components that are still outstanding include the ROO, tariff schedules, and specific commitments on trade in services.

A crucial part of these components is the negotiation of ROO, the importance of which lies in the determination of products that are to be categorised as 'Made in Africa' and eligible for tariff concessions. The negotiations of the ROO were expected to be concluded by June 2021, however, as of 5 January 2022, negotiations were still ongoing, when according to the Secretary-General of the AfCFTA Secretariat, the parties had reached 87.8% agreement. As such, preferential ROO trade under the Agreement will be unable to take full effect until its conclusion.

Phase II Regarding IPRs and Investment and Competition Policy

While negotiations regarding Phase I remain ongoing, Phase II negotiations, focusing on IPRs, investment, and competition policy, also commenced in 2021. These negotiations were initially scheduled to be concluded in December 2020 and then rescheduled to conclude in December 2021. Indeed, contrary to what was originally expected, the draft legal text of the Investment Protocol was not submitted to the January 2021 Session of the Assembly for consideration. In the meantime, the fifth meeting of the AfCFTA Council of Ministers responsible for trade took place in Accra, Ghana, on 3 May 2021.

There has been much speculation and many recommendations regarding the proposed content of the protocols that are being negotiated, in particular concerning the Investment Protocol. It is expected that the Investment Protocol will bring with it unique changes in the investment disputes regime by replacing existing African BITs with a single treaty, which would be a noteworthy development because quite a number of them are yet to be ratified or utilized by African states but are still a work in progress.

Phase III Regarding E-Commerce

The interest in creating a protocol on e-commerce reinforces Africa's intention to capitalise on digital trade to contribute to the systemic transformation of African economies.

Phase III negotiations were to commence immediately after the initially proposed conclusion of Phase II negotiations in December 2020. To date, there is no publicly-known information regarding substantive developments in this regard and it is unclear what will be featured in the protocol on e-commerce. I argue that with all this uncertainty, the lack of investment funding does not inspire confidence in the realisation of integration and self-reliance.

As noted by the Secretary-General of the AfCFTA Secretariat, there is much more to be achieved with the AfCFTA. However, we must recognise that the AfCFTA is a very ambitious project which, despite the pandemic that hindered numerous global economic developments, is progressively moving to achieve its goal, albeit a little slower than predicted. Beyond the developments with ongoing negotiations as highlighted above, 2021 also saw an increase in movements towards ratification of the agreement by state parties. These include Malawi, Zambia, Algeria, and Burundi who have all deposited their instruments of ratification of the AfCFTA Agreement; Tanzania which has ratified the Agreement but is yet to deposit its instrument of ratification; and the Seychelles and Somalia who are both awaiting parliamentary confirmation of the ratification process. As of October 2021, a total of 41 of the 54 countries that signed the Agreement had complied with their domestic requirements for ratification of the AfCFTA Agreement and a total of 38 countries had deposited their instruments of ratification.

These developments occurred alongside the PAPSS, which was launched by AFREXIM on 13 January 2022. The PAPSS is expected to boost intra-Africa trade by transforming and facilitating payment, clearing, and settlement for cross-border trade across Africa. In light of these various developments, 2022 presented yet another opportunity for progressive developments regarding the AfCFTA and there is a strong basis to anticipate success going forward.

8.9 Conclusion

This chapter recognised Africa's progress towards political and socio-economic integration, a process that appears somewhat elusive and challenging, progressing slowly amidst cumulative asymmetrical global and transboundary marginalising challenges.

These challenges include: analysing the dominance of the ownership of structures of the global economy by developed countries; the polarising tendencies that result from such dominance and ownership vis a vis the marginalisation of Africa; and the uneven distribution of domestic and foreign investments. All these factors cumulatively resulted in a situation in which Africa's economies are conditioned by the development and expansion of the developed economies. The deployment of the DTRP/centre-periphery framework is a useful approach for understanding centre-periphery power relationships, transboundary state relationships, and non-state activism. Furthermore, the DTRP/centre-periphery framework explains the AU's persistent failure of its neo-functionalist pursuit of regional integration and attempts at supranationalism. At the 28th Ordinary Summit of the AHSG, held in Addis Ababa, Ethiopia, on 30-31 January 2017, the President of Rwanda, Paul Kagame, was designated as the Chair of the AU for 2018 to supervise the implementation of the reforms. To support the reform process further, previous AU chairholders, the Presidents of Chad (Idris Deby) and Guinea (Alpha Conde), were also designated by the Assembly to assist.

The three Heads of State, collectively, were referred to as the 'Reform Troika'. Their designation demonstrated the AU's political commitment towards institutional reform to achieve greater efficiencies and effectiveness in materialising Agenda 2063. The reform priorities, if successfully implemented, could be the drivers that catalyse and accelerate integration towards materialising Agenda 2063. Agenda 2063 aims to achieve a 'peaceful, prosperous Africa, driven by its own citizens and representing a dynamic force in the global arena.'

However, intermittent divergences and convergences have prevented a coherent regional peace and security policy from taking effect. A successfully integrated regional peace and security policy would support Agenda 2063 goals.

The AfCFTA entered into force on 30 May 2019. As a flagship of the AU Agenda 2063, it attests to the institutional centripetal convergence of AfCFTA/AGA/APSA/REC's, which has improved the enabling environment (regulatory and operational) for business and has attracted both domestic and foreign investment. The normative framework of the AfCFTA is evident because it seeks complementarities in policies to enhance inclusive economic growth through increased consumption, investment, and intra-regional trade.

Using the DTRP/centre-periphery framework, this chapter has exposed the marginalised position of Africa within the global economy. This has impacted domestic and foreign inflows for investments. The chapter has further explained the convergence of RECs and continental macroeconomic planning in terms of domestic capital mobilisation in; mining; monetary and fiscal policies; and the movement of capital goods and services. The deployment of functional and neo-functional approaches are supportive of bottom-up state and non-state activism, and possibly ceding certain aspects of sovereignty to empower a continental supra-authority. The chapter has argued that this will result in greater convergence between the AfCFTA, AGA, APSA, and the RECs to meet the Agenda 2063 goals. However, volatility in global commodity prices and dependence on commodity exports has restricted progress.

The chapter further argued that Africa's development trajectory will help to diversify its commodity-based industrialisation through value addition, raising productivity in agricultural and non-agricultural sectors in support of RVCs. Sectoral comparative advantages, competitiveness, and complementarities can be enhanced by raising the overall productivity of the RVCs. People's living standards are improved as a result, along with overall inclusive economic growth, which is necessary for structural transformation, self-reliance and sustainability.

The viability of the AfCFTA needs to be predicated on a sound continental infrastructure, with a reliable electricity supply and transport networks. This in turn would facilitate and enhance productivity and the competitiveness of factor inputs, such as labour and capital within the RVCs to compete effectively and globally. The AfCFTA/AGA/APSA/RECs, convergence, as problematised in this chapter, is a prerequisite for the human security-development nexus to progressively actualise Agenda 2063. This needs to be accomplished against global asymmetric challenges, such as transnational terrorism, organised crime, water scarcity, and climate change.

Chapter 9

Conclusion

9.1 Pan African Agency within the African Union Framework

This book has critically examined and analysed the progress, problems, and prospects experienced by the AU's organs and its initiatives and development policies in regional cooperation, integration, and self-reliance. Amongst the many organs and programmes that the book examined were the OAU, AUC, NEPAD, AfCFTA, Agenda 2063, PSC, APSA, AGA, APRM, REC's, PAP, AfCHPR, ACHPR, ACERWC, AUCIL, and ECOSOCC. The DTRP/ centre-periphery framework as explained in chapters 2 and 3 was deployed to problematise the AU's policies and programmes. The AU initiatives and development policies to materialise Agenda 2063 are underpinned by these analytical frameworks that problematise the AU's neo-functionalist approach towards integration and self-reliance. The DTRP/centre-periphery framework is suitable for examining the global asymmetrical transnational transboundary and unpredictable shocks, which have an impact on Africa's political economy and space. The AU is non-dogmatic in its approach to policymaking. In this regard, it is assisted by the DTRP, which is an ongoing research programme. This avoids rigidity in policy formulation and implementation but serves as the preferred framework to bring Africa closer to its integration goal.

The DTRP/centre-periphery uses historical research as a unit of analysis. The book therefore traces the transitioning of the OAU to the AU and the adoption of the Constitutive Act and its organs. The main discussions within the book addressed the findings and recommendations of the 2007 AU Review Report and the 2017 Kagame Report, which moved the AU towards materialising Agenda 2063. Both primary and secondary sources, interviews, and archival documentation were used to obtain the research data.

As a unit of analysis, the DTRP/centre-periphery framework (Kvangraven, 2018:1-55 and Amin, 2016) offers insightful perspectives that surpass those of other theoretical frameworks. It highlights Africa's historical limitations from having been rendered an extractive economy by colonialism and present-day neo-colonialism. Africa's economies are dominated, marginalised, and dictated to by the MNCs of the Global North and their capital. Intersubjective metatheories have offered thematic exploratory and explanatory perspectives to the marginalising global economy to which the AU is vulnerable. The 1972 global economic collapse following the OPEC oil crisis led to Africa's spiralling and unmanageable debt levels and the decision by the US government in 1973 to unilaterally delink from the global gold standard. These events trapped Africa deeper into unsustainable debt levels and to take conditional loans from the IFIs, WB, and IMF.

The book also highlighted pivotal factors in the establishment of the AU, such as the anticolonial struggles; Africa's further global politico-economic marginalisation; and the food insecurity that motivated the OAU to adopt the 1980 LPA, the 1985 FAL, and the 1991 Abuja Treaty. The assumptions of this research that Africa's leaders would automatically support the LPA and Abuja Treaty have been proved false. The further marginalisation of Africa within the global economy resulted in the transitioning of the OAU to become the AU predicated on its Constitutive Act. In July 2002, the AU was launched and operationalised in Durban, South Africa.

The establishment of the NEPAD and APRM were evidence of the normative successes and progress of the AU. The progress, problems, and prospects of the AU were assessed in the 2007 AU Review Report. The DTRP/centre-periphery framework has laid bare the failure of the AU's neo-functionalist programmes of integration and self-reliance. It further demonstrated that the analysis of AU progress and challenges cannot be confined to a one-size-fits-all neo-functionalist theoretical framework.

A consideration of a post-neo-functionalist framework to attain integration and self-reliance should be part of the reform processes.

In its discussions on security, the book noted the AU's peacekeeping agency in Burundi, Sudan, Somalia, Comoros, Mali and the Sahel, and Uganda, and the streamlining of RECs. However, problems remain due to the slow progress against the cumulative asymmetrical global and transboundary challenges.

9.2 Key Policy Recommendations for Enhancing AU Progress and Prospects in Materialising Agenda 2063

The following recommendations summarise the conclusions drawn from the aforementioned arguments, the observations and the key normative objectives. They aim to guide urgent and innovative strategies that can push subregional momentum in a positive direction towards the materialisation of Agenda 2063.

9.3 Increased Political Support and Accountability

Attaining the objectives of Agenda 2063 is largely dependent on strong political commitments, including capable and accountable institutions to support the implementation, monitoring, and reporting of Africa's 50-year development blueprint. With this in mind, a series of recommendations were developed.

1. Undertake multi-stakeholder collective reviews, joint reflection, peer learning, and mutual accountability on the implementation and reporting of Agenda 2063. Establish and operationalise institutional mechanisms for popularising, tracking, reporting, and discussing Agenda 2063 at national and sub-national levels. Work with national and regional agencies (and stakeholders) to implement policies and programmes that accelerate progress towards attaining the goals contained in National Development Plans and Agenda 2063 targets.
2. Demonstrate greater responsiveness to Agenda 2063 by the AUMS and their RECs. The political will and political dynamics

among AUMS will be one of the main factors to determine whether peace and security, stability, and good governance can be entrenched as a sine qua non to attaining Agenda 2063.

3. Innovation is imperative for enhancing supra-institutional authority to link country programmes and enhance RVCs to harness comparative advantages, complementarities, and economies of scale. This will help in overcoming institutional obstacles. Initiate processes to fill data gaps assessing and monitoring development dynamics at the subregional level. To achieve this, 'connectors', such as interfaith groups, women, youth, CSO, community-based organisations, and others, should be supported to build momentum for urgent positive change and traction across nation-state boundaries to attain Agenda 2063.

9.4 Strengthened Programming

As the First Ten-Year Implementation Plan of Agenda 2063 draws to an end and preparations begin for the commencement of the Second Ten-Year Implementation Plan, it will be important to undertake empirical studies (e.g., foresight studies) on the key interventions required across Africa's development trajectory, especially in the context of the COVID-19 pandemic. These interventions need to focus on COVID-19 recovery, and the stabilisation and revitalisation of African economies. The specific interventions will include the following:

- In the immediate and short-term, place greater focus and investment in specific priority areas that are more likely to trigger accelerated socio-economic recovery and growth.
- Include in the Second Ten-Year Implementation Plan a goal and priority area on building Africa's resilience to natural disasters and other widespread and high-impact events such as global pandemics.
- AU Continental institutions should leverage their core mandates to facilitate the development the utilization of innovative tools, methodologies, and institutional capacity building to assist AUMS towards improved integrated national policy development, planning, and implementation of Agenda 2063.

- Strengthen the capacity of AUMS and RECs to develop bankable projects and work closely with the AfDB and other African finance institutions to identify and design bankable projects for realising the targets in each Agenda 2063 individual Ten-Year Implementation Plan.
- Revise conceptual frameworks underpinning the development, formulation, and implementation of AU flagship projects, and ensure rationalisation, prioritisation, and recalibration with clear goals and targets against stipulated periods.
- Strengthen coordination mechanisms for deploying financial and technical support to AUMS based on expressed and implicit development needs, for example from AUMS' biennial reports on the implementation of each individual Ten-Year Implementation Plan.
- The lessons learnt and challenges faced during the implementation of the First Ten-Year Implementation Plan should guide the evaluation of the First Ten-Year Implementation Plan and the formulation of the Second Ten-Year Implementation Plan.
- Robustly enable the FMP and residence with added programmes seeking to advance a positive and pluralist subregional identity that celebrates diversity across identity groups and nations and forestalls any xenophobic proclivities.

The FMP and residence will be one of the many strategies that will force and deconstruct an elite neo-patrimonial polity, which serves the Global North neocolonial design. It should be noted that through Agenda 2063, Africa has reaffirmed the need for seamless borders. This has enabled an environment of free trade and FMP, thus inducing the African vision for a United Africa.

The CSOs and other non-state actors should demonstrate robust activism in this regard, as the current elite-driven processes in Africa lack momentum and a sense of urgency. This is because they benefit from neo-patrimonial policies to the detriment of the greater populace of Africa. Interventions to empower agents of change in all facets of the body politic of

African politics need to be improved, and a universal basic grant for all unemployed persons should be made available.

Support from external donors is indispensable towards achieving Agenda 2063, as Africa has been irreversibly locked into the global economy with geo-strategic interests. External political pressure on the AU, increased media attention and greater non-state actor activism, can have the necessary impact in realising the objectives of Agenda 2063. In this regard, added pressure for the reparations for slavery, colonialism, and neo-colonialism in the form of the cancellation of all forms of debt.

These proceeds could be used to benefit public goods, such as health, housing, education, and start-up grants for businesses.

In materialising Agenda 2063, Africa must continue to improve systems of good governance that are transparent and accountable to African people. The corollary is that good governance is intertwined with addressing insecurities arising from various factors, including neo-patrimonial states inciting discontent and conflicts to protect their narrow rentier class, and the collaborative attitude of some states to powerful counterparts, who engage in exploitative and destabilising agendas in the Continent.

A case in point is the DRC, which has been exploited by its African neighbours for the extraction of resources at a cost to civilian lives. In this regard, the AU should robustly use mechanisms such as the AGA, PAP, and APRM to drive the need for accountable people-centred governance. Africa has a critical mass of literate politicised citizenry. Both PAP and APRM are organs of the AU that contribute to public participation and accountability.

The PAP was inaugurated on 18 March 2004 in Midrand, South Africa, as a platform open to the public to exercise governance. To ensure that these organs remain true to their mandate of actualising good governance and materialising Agenda 2063, the citizens and CIDO unit of the AUC should be more proactive and robust in ensuring public and non-state actor participation in AU initiatives. It is imperative for Africa to continuously improve its resource base and be a powerful, significant actor in global relations. While thus far, the policy space developed by the AU is remarkable, greater self-reliance in independent resource capacity will much more effectively translate and materialise Agenda 2063 policies.

Africa should, however, robustly develop both its soft and hard power capability. Developing hard power is especially important if Africa is not to be continually marginalised and made vulnerable to the neocolonial dictates of powerful countries. The following instances are occasions that could have taken alternative paths if Africa had hard power capabilities: the disinterest of the UN in intervening to prevent the 1994 Rwanda genocide; the 2011 NATO illegal regime change war in Libya and the extra-judicial murder of Ghaddafi; and the military intervention of France in Mali in 2014 without the authorisation of the AU.

The materialisation of Agenda 2063 requires greater participation by the AU in multilateralism with international organisations such as the UN, EU, FOCAC, WTO, IMF, WB, AfDB, and NATO. The intrinsic interdependence of the global economy, although uneven, asymmetrical and predatory, behoves Africa to engage its capabilities with a cost-benefit calculus premise for greater welfare gains.

9.5 Data Management and Knowledge Capitalisation

The assessment of the continent's progress on the implementation of Agenda 2063 relies predominantly on the availability of data and information, therefore national statistical systems should be strengthened, along with the following:

- Devote more technical support to strengthening data and statistical capacities at national, regional, and continental levels.
- Strengthen the institutional architecture for national and regional data governance.
- Commit human and financial resources to strengthen statistical and data capacities to ensure data availability for accurate reporting and impact evaluation.
- Strengthen peer learning and mutual support through the identification, development, and dissemination of best

practices and the establishment of knowledge-sharing platforms.
· Work with national stakeholders to strengthen feedback loop mechanisms to understand the state of socio-economic systems to put in place and effect appropriate actions.

9.6   Resource Mobilisation

It is important to promote an integrated financing framework that minimises duplication, leverages economies of scale, and optimises the use of resources to finance the implementation of Agenda 2063. The specific interventions will include the following:

· Encourage AUMS, AfDB, and other African financing institutions to recommit to funding at least 75% of the Agenda 2063 programme budget.
· Fast track the roll-out of the Agenda 2063 Domestic Resource Mobilisation Strategy among AUMS and RECs, to mobilise resources in support of the implementation of Agenda 2063 programmes and projects at national and regional levels, respectively.
· Request AUMS to dedicate 0.1% of the national budget as financial support for reporting on Agenda 2063 implementation.
· Deepen collaboration and leverage political support on addressing illicit financial flows and financial leakages.

The AU and other international organisations do not hold a monopoly on ideas and expertise in materialising Agenda 2063. Its materialisation is complicated by a structure of global non-territorial challenges including climate change; global terrorism; transnational organised crime; and migrations and human trafficking.

Overall, the AU needs to robustly promote its indispensability in global affairs. There should be greater convergence between the AU and UN/UNECA in providing technical and planning expertise to the AU in terms of conflict prevention, mediation, SSRs, economic planning, and expertise in investment finance, manufacturing, and trade policies for welfare gains. The norm of subsidiarity in the recognition of the AU's leading role in the Continent as the referential body in all aspects of human security and peace, enhances mutual respect and not paternalism.

Despite this, it is incumbent on the AU and member states to attain international confidence by fulfilling its Constitutive Act mandate of good governance, human rights, upholding the rule of law and promoting an enabling environment for greater welfare gains. The greater public for their part should not always be led by the ruling elites to be participative; they should be continuously proactive in all manner of African and global governance.

9.7 The Imperative of Peer Benchmarking and Injecting Accelerators Towards The AU's Integration

Taking the range of aforementioned recommendations into consideration, it is possible to identify broad benchmarks-cum-accelerators, based on which, arguably, the project of African unity and integration will stand or fall in the foreseeable future (Audit of the AU, 2007:188). The benchmarks-cum-accelerators should thus be seen "as constituent elements of comprehensive package of policy and political measures that need to be implemented to advance the frontiers of African unity and integration" (Audit of AU, 2007:188).

The combined recommendations offer the people and leaders of Africa some of the most critical benchmarks-cum-accelerators. On one level they serve to signal progress in the march towards unification and integration. On another level, they will provide a yardstick against which the advances made can be assessed (Audit of the AU, 2007:188). During the process of implementing AU development policies, the actors driving continental statecraft should familiarise themselves with and embrace the benchmarks-cum-accelerators summarized in the following section. They are dependent on injecting a sense of urgency into the continent's integration project.

9.8 The Coherence, Effectiveness, And Efficiency Of Institutional Frameworks

This would involve institutional revamping because AU policy implementation cannot flourish in an environment of internal institutional incoherence and disarray (Audit of the AU, 2007: 189). The vision of a united and integrated Africa has been a part of Africa's recent history. If it is to be realised, this institutional crisis should be resolved speedily. The AU should focus on strengthening and improving coordination among the organs and institutions of the AU and the effectiveness and efficiency of the structures and processes that have been put in place.

9.9. Popularising and Internalisation of the Core Values Underpinning the Constitutive Act

The AU has been articulating a set of shared values that have come to constitute a key element among the imperatives for the unity and integration of Africa (Audit of the AU, 2007:190). In terms of the AU and the Constitutive Act that gave birth to it, the values are enshrined in Article 3. Both historically and contemporarily the values underpinning the quest for unity and integration remain contingent, on political will and adequate independent funding. What has been lacking is the constant momentum of urgent internalisation of the values, both in the actions of the governments involved and the conduct of the leadership. This politico-ideological deficit of the leadership has had a negative effect in popularising and materialising the shared values of the AU.

9.10. The Engagement and Mobilisation of the Peoples of Africa for the Unity and Integration Project

Historically and contemporarily the full mobilisation of the people is a condition for the pursuit of AU unity and integration, and this will remain so (AU Audit, 2007:191). The audit noted that central to the construction of the AU as a successor to the OAU, there was a conscious effort to optimally converge the nexus of vertical top-down and bottom-up horizontal activism of both state and non-state actors. It is in this regard that non-state actors should improve their activism without necessarily waiting for prompting from the political leadership.

Africa's political landscape has been plagued by elitist neo-patrimonial networks, which are a derivative of neo-colonialism. The lofty language of the political leadership is deceptive and ornate in the AU's sessions and literature. Rhetoric, however, does not necessitate sacrifices but rather focuses on enhancing benefits for the African citizenry.

9.11. The Free Movement of People Across Borders as Contained in Both the Abuja Treaty and the Constitutive Act

Africa's quest for unity and integration has been stymied by the restrictions placed on factor mobility on the continent, specifically the free movement of its continental citizenry (Audit of the AU, 2007: 192). Given that 2010 marked the golden jubilee of the independence of many countries in Africa, this represented a symbolic moment to commemorate the dismantling of restrictions on the free movement of African citizens, on the continent thus erasing the odious legacies of colonialism. A timetable to this effect is imperative, and a stage-by-stage removal of restrictions to culminate in the complete removal of all restrictions sooner rather than later with the possible introduction of a Union passport.

9.12. The Rationalisation of the Regional Economic Communities

The future of continental integration will, to a large degree, rest on changes made at the REC level (Audit of the AU, 2007:193). The rationalisation of the RECs has been on the agenda of the African continent since the establishment of the AU. The extent of attention that this issue has generated is a clear indicator of the necessity and urgency of the rationalisation exercise. The slow progress registered to date suggests that sufficient and concerted energies are not being devoted to the task.

The Panel has recommended that the eight RECs recognised by the AU should be maintained with a rationalisation of mandates along the lines detailed in the report. Therefore, benchmarking the rationalisation of the RECs has become an issue in the elimination of the unnecessary overlaps and duplication that have proven to be as diversionary as they have been energy-sapping.

9.13. The Development of Transcontinental and Inter-Regional Infrastructures, and the Continental Financial and Monetary Institutions Identified in Article 19 of the Constitutive Act (The African Central Bank, The African Monetary Fund, and The African Investment Code)

Political integration and political institution building are particularly important if Africa is to face its future with more confidence. However, Africa's integration efforts are often too politicised at the expense of economic integration (Mene, 2021).

If the continent is to become better at confronting its problems of economic underdevelopment and socio-economic crises, its leaders and institutions will have to become more serious about building economic institutions and prioritising economic integration. Because economic and financial challenges are so central to Africa's challenges, Africa needs to move forward as a matter of urgency to create common financial and monetary institutions on the African continent. These institutions can then foster intra-African cooperation, as well as strengthen the continent's abilities to engage with the outside world. The Panel suggests that the Assembly set a target date for launching the institutions, particularly as their locations have already been settled. The establishment of an ad hoc committee to move the process forward should be decided expeditiously, and the assignment completed within three months.

9.14. Fast-Tracking the Move Towards an African Common Market and African Economic Community Leveraging on Accelerators; the Multinational African Firms

The African Common Market and the AEC are longstanding items on the African integration and unity agenda, dating back to the 1980 LPA and FAL (Audit of the AU, 2007: 193). A detailed blueprint, with a complete timetable, was set out; regrettably, it was noted that it was not adhered to as intended. The Panel recommends a set of multi-prong accelerators that include major cross-border infrastructure investments and the formation of African multinational investment companies. The AUC, in collaboration with all other key players, should pilot the task of producing a comprehensive framework document.

This task should be completed in the shortest possible time, ideally 9–12 months, and should be followed with a phased pursuit of different accelerators, which should interface with the national, regional, and continental levels. Africa must fast-track the achievement of both the Common Market and the AEC. The RECs will have to play a pivotal role in this respect, and they should be invited to provide a roadmap towards this end. They should not be marginalised in the process.

9.15. Mobilising the African Entrepreneurial Elite for Unity and Integration

If there has been one area where the Pan-African project has been lacking, it is in regard to the mobilisation of the private entrepreneurial class to play a role in the attainment of the goals and aims of continental integration (Audit of the AU, 2007: 194). In both in its own right as an actor, and in collaboration with public institutions, the entrepreneurial elite could be mobilised to invest in Pan-African infrastructure and development projects that would underpin and advance the political goals of unity, the economic dynamics of integration, and the social ideals of full citizenship. In line with the recommendations already made in this report, it is deemed feasible for the AUC to take immediate steps to launch different measures to meet the demands.

9.16. Monitoring Mechanisms

Africa is urgently in need of monitoring and evaluation mechanisms (Audit of the AU, 2007: 196). According to the High-level Panel, "the history of African unity and integration efforts is littered with too many unrealised dreams, broken promises and unimplemented blueprints." This underperformance has serious implications for the AU and needs to be addressed to improve the potential for greater progress and success. Furthermore, a report should be sent to the Assembly biennially on the progress made towards implementing the benchmarks-cum-accelerators.

Chapter 10

Epilogue

Unraveling Africa's Neo-Patrimonial Dilemma and the Struggle for True Liberation

Africa's journey toward the realisation of Agenda 2063—a comprehensive blueprint for continental development—has been marked by both perseverance and persistent challenges. While some of the targets outlined in the First Ten-Year Implementation Plan (2014–2024) may not be fully realised by the projected 2024 deadline, the continent has nonetheless demonstrated commendable progress across various sectors, offering hope for the medium- and long-term achievement of these goals (AU, 2015). The efforts of civil society and youth activism are crucial to sustaining this momentum and catalysing the urgent action needed to address Africa's pressing socio-economic realities. However, this progress is heavily constrained by the deeply entrenched systems of corruption and neo-patrimonialism within Africa's political and economic leadership. These systems have become inseparable from the governance structures of many African nations, weaving themselves into the very fabric of power and obstructing the continent's true potential for self-determination and sustainable development.

The ruling elite's complicity in neocolonial systems of exploitation, often in collusion with foreign powers and MNCs, perpetuates the continent's underdevelopment. These leaders, many of whom are entangled in intricate patronage networks, have betrayed the aspirations of ordinary citizens in favour of personal and familial enrichment (Mkandawire, 2011). This nexus of corruption, authoritarianism, and international complicity has led to a disillusionment among the African populace, who increasingly see through the empty promises of the political class. As global systems of economic power, such as neoliberalism and financial imperialism, continue to shape Africa's political economy, it has become clear that the leaders who should be serving the people are instead complicit in perpetuating a system of wealth concentration and poverty.

The notion of black economic empowerment, which has been heralded as a solution to the legacies of colonialism and slavery, has, in many cases, only served to enrich a select few while the majority of the population remains marginalized. The reality is that economic reforms and policies designed to benefit Africa's people have often been subverted by those in power, leading to a widening wealth gap. In a continent rich in natural resources, Africa remains paradoxically poor, with millions trapped in endemic poverty while a few elites thrive. The refusal of African leadership to confront the historical and ongoing injustices of slavery, colonialism, and neo-colonialism is compounded by their reluctance to address the demands for reparations from their own citizenry, as well as from the global community (Pomeranz, 2000).

At the heart of this neo-patrimonialism is a political economy that thrives on corruption and cronyism. From the oil-rich deltas of Nigeria to the mineral-laden landscapes of the DRC, Africa's vast wealth has often been squandered, mismanaged, or illicitly extracted by local elites in tandem with foreign powers. Despite these resources, the majority of Africans continue to experience a life of deprivation, with millions subjected to violence from armed groups, and entire regions destabilized by conflict. Meanwhile, the international community, including organisations the UN and EU, frequently engage in rhetorical diplomacy while continuing to exploit Africa's natural resources, often turning a blind eye to internal political violence and human suffering (Dibua, 2010).

The global political economy in which Africa is situated cannot be understood in isolation. Africa's economic subjugation is intricately linked to the global system of capitalism, where the interests of wealthy nations, MNCs, and hegemonic powers, such as the G7, continue to shape the destiny of the Global South (Rodney, 1972). The recent shift toward a multipolar world order, with emerging powers challenging the hegemony of the West, offers both a challenge and an opportunity for African nations. However, it also highlights the contradictions within African leadership, where entrenched elites often seek to align with external powers that perpetuate exploitative practices, rather than challenging imperial structures (Shivji, 2008).

In this context, democracy in Africa remains a fragile and contested concept. While many African countries hold elections, the political processes are frequently undermined by authoritarian practices, the manipulation of term limits, and a lack of genuine accountability. Democracy in Africa, as in other parts of the world, has become a veneer that masks deeper systemic flaws. The realities of electoral fraud, state-sponsored violence, and the erosion of civil liberties point to a grim truth: true democratic governance is a far cry from the autocratic regimes that still dominate much of the continent (Herbst, 2000). Africa's political institutions often mirror the dysfunctions of the global system, where power and wealth are concentrated in the hands of a few, while the masses are left to endure the consequences.

Despite the grim political and economic landscape, there are glimmers of hope. Across Africa, the resilience of the people is manifest in the burgeoning movements for social and political change. From the protests in Khartoum, Mali, Niger, and Burkina Faso to the growing calls for justice in South Africa, ordinary Africans are beginning to demand accountability and reform (Neocosmos, 2010). The rise of pan-African solidarity, underscored by the Pan-African Conference in Accra in 2024 (despite its abrupt cancellation), reflects a renewed commitment to the ideals of unity, justice, and equity. The struggles for justice and reparations for the crimes of slavery and colonialism have found a new platform on the global stage, with brave countries like South Africa advocating for the recognition of genocide in global forums (Gonzalez, 2016).

The current global moment can be understood as a 'low-intensity' Third World War, where the battle is not only over material resources but also the control of narratives, power, and the direction of global governance. The hegemonic forces led by the West, particularly the United States and its allies, are losing their grip as emerging powers challenge their dominance. In this struggle, the rhetoric of democracy often conceals the naked ambition of the powerful, who use the language of human rights and democracy to perpetuate their own interests.

As the world confronts these contradictions, a growing wave of global activism is pushing back against the status quo. This activism, rooted in the collective will of ordinary citizens, is a force for social change and a reimagining of a more just global order (Chomsky, 2017).

As we reflect on Africa's journey and the challenges it faces, it is clear that the path to freedom, justice, and development is fraught with obstacles. However, the lessons learned from the past and the struggles of today offer a powerful reminder that the future is not predetermined. Africa's destiny will be shaped by the collective action and resolve of its people, not by the corrupt elites or the empty promises of international institutions. The philosophy of Ubuntu—I am because we are—reminds us that our shared humanity and collective will are the keys to overcoming adversity and building a just society for all (Tutu, 1999). It is only through genuine solidarity and an unwavering commitment to justice that Africa will break free from the shackles of neo-patrimonialism and reclaim its rightful place in the global community.

Bibliography

Abrahamsen, R. (2004). Review Essay: Poverty Reduction or Adjustment by Another name? *Review of African Political Economy 31(99)*. 184-87.

Acharya, A. (2004). How Ideas Spread: Whose Norms Matter? Norm Localization and Institutional Change in Asian Regionalism. *International Organisation,* 58, 239-275. https://doi.org/10.1017/S0020818304582024

Acharya, A. (2012) Comparative Regionalism: A Field Whose Time has Come? *The International Spectator.* 47:1. 3-15. https://doi.org/10.1080/03932729.2012.655004

Achen, C.H., Snidal, D. (1989). Rational Deterrence Theory and Comparative Case Studies. *World Politics* 41, 143-69. https://doi.org/10.2307/2010405

Addison, T. and Laakso, L. (2003). The Political Economy of Zimbabwe's Descent into Conflict. *Journal of International Development.* 15(4). 457-71. https://doi.org/10.1002/jid.996

Adedeji. A. (ed.) (1993). Africa Within the World: Beyond Dispossession and Dependence. Zed Books, London, in association with the African Centre for Development and Strategic Studies.

Adedeji. A. (ed.) (1982). Development and Economic Growth in Africa to the Year 2000: Alternative Features for Africa. West View. Boulder, Colorado.

Adedeji. A. (ed.) (2002). Indigenisation of African Economies. Hutchinson and Co. Publishers Ltd. London.

Adejumobi, S. (2009). Popular Participation and Africa's Development Agenda. Projecting a citizen-based United States of Africa. Politikon: *South African Journal of Political Studies.* Vol. 36(3). 405. https://doi.org/10.1080/02589341003600213

Adekunle, A.(198)3. The nature of African borders. *African Spectrum*, Vol. 18(20). 177-189.

Adjaye, J.K. (1985). Indigenous African Diplomacy: An Asante Case Study. *The International Journal of African Historical Studies,* Vol 18(3):487-503. https://doi.org/10.2307/218650

Adler, E. (1997). Seizing the Middle Ground: Constructivism in World Politics. *European Journal of International Relations* 3. 319-363. https://doi.org/10.1177/1354066197003003003

Adler, E. (2005). Communitarian International Relations: The Epistemic Foundations of International Relations. Routledge. New York. https://doi.org/10.4324/9780203022443

Adogamhe, P.G. (2008). Pan-Africanism Re-visited: Vision and Reality of African Unity and Development. *African Review of Integration.* 2. No. (2)1-34.

Agbeyegbe, T. (2008). On the Feasibility of a Monetary Union in the SADC. *International Journal of Finance and Economics.* (13). 150-157. https://doi.org/10.1002/ijfe.323

Aglionby, J., Mance, H. (2016). UK Ready to Shift Focus of Africa Aid to Trade. *Financial Times.* 18 October 2016.

Agosin, M.R., Machado, R. (2005). Foreign Investment in Developing Countries: Does it Crowd in Domestic Investment? *Oxford Development Studies* 33(2).142-162. https://doi.org/10.1080/13600810500137749

Agyeman, O. (1998). Pan-Africanism and its Detractors: A Response to Harvard's Race Effacing Universalitsts. *African Journal of Political Science.* 3, (1). African Association of Political Science.

Ahmed, I., Green, R.H. (1999). The Heritage of War and State Collapse in Somalia and Somaliland: Local-level effects, External Interventions and Reconstruction. *Third World Quarterly.* 20(1). 112 – 127. https://doi.org/10.1080/01436599913947

Ahmed, S.A., Diffenbaugh, N.S., Hertel T.W., and Martin W.J. (2012). Agriculture and trade opportunities for Tanzania: Past volatility and future climate change. *Review of Development Economics.* 16 (3). 429–447. https://doi.org/10.1111/j.1467-9361.2012.00672.x

Akinkugbe, O., Cham-Chiliba, C.M. Tlotlego, N. (2012). Health Financing and Catastrophic Payments for Health Care: Evidence from Household-level Survey Data in Botswana and Lesotho. *African Development Review.* 24(4). 358-370. https://doi.org/10.1111/1467-8268.12006

Akokpari, J.K. (1999). Changing with the Tide: The Shifting Orientations of Foreign Policies in Sub-Saharan Africa. *Nordic Journal of African Studies.* 8(1): 22-39.

Akokpari, J.K. (2001). The Debt Crisis, the Global Economy and the Challenges of Development: Sub-Saharan Africa at the Crossroads. *Journal of Social Development in Africa.* 16(2).147-169. https://doi.org/10.4314/jsda.v16i2.23877

Akokpari, J. (2003). The OAU, AU, NEPAD and the Promotion of Good Governance in Africa. Occasional Paper 14. Electoral Institute of Southern Africa EISA.

Akokpari, J.K. (2004). Ghana: Economic Dependence and Marginalised Foreign Policy-Making. East, M. and Robertson, J. (Eds.) Diplomacy in Developing Countries (Frank Cass) (Forthcoming).

Akokpari, J. (2005). The Challenges of Diplomatic Practice in Africa. *Journal for Contemporary History.* 41(1). 1-17. https://doi.org/10.18820/24150509/jch.v41i1.1

Akokpari, J. (2008). Dilemmas of Regional Integration and Development in Africa, in Akokpari, J., Ndinga-Muvumba, A., and Murithi, T. (Eds.). The African Union and its Institutions. Jacana Media. Johannesburg.

Akyuz, Y. (2005). WTO Negotiations on Industrial Tariffs: What is at Stake for Developing Countries? Third World Network. Geneva. https://doi.org/10.3848/iif.2005.232.4508

Alaba, O.B. (2006). Non-tariff Barriers to Trade Flows. Source: EU-ECOWAS EPA: regional integration, trade facilitation and development in West Africa. A draft paper for presentation at the Global Trade Analysis Project conference, United Nations Economic Commission for Africa, Addis Ababa, 15–17 June 2006.

Alden, C., Schoeman, M. (2015). South Africa's Symbolic Hegemony in Africa. London School of Economics, London, and University of Pretoria, South Africa. https://doi.org/10.1057/ip.2014.47

Alexander, L.G., Bennet, A. (2015). Case Studies and Theory Development in Social Science. Belfer Centre for Science and International Affairs. Cambridge University Press. New York.

Alghali, Z. A., and Mbaye, M. (2008). The African Standby Force and Regional Standby Brigades (Issue 3). African Centre for the Constructive Resolution of Disputes. Conflict Trends. South Africa.

Amaglobeli, D., E. Hanedar, G. H. Hong, G.H.,. Thévenot, C. (2022). Fiscal Policy for Mitigating the Social Impact of High Energy and Food Prices. IMF Notes 2022/001, International Monetary Fund, Washington, DC.

Amate, C.O. (1986). Inside the OAU. Pan-Africanism in Practice. Macmillan.

AMDC. (2016). Optimising Domestic Revenue Mobilisation and Value Addition of Africa's Minerals: Towards Harmonising Fiscal Regimes in the Mineral Sector. Economic Commission for Africa (ECA). Addis Ababa.

AMDC. (2017). Impact of Illicit Financial Flows on Domestic Resource Mobilization: Optimizing Revenues from the Mineral Sector in Africa. Economic Commission for Africa (ECA). Addis Ababa.

Amin, S. (1973). Neo-colonialism in West Africa. Penguin. London.

Amin, S. (1974). Accumulation on a World Scale. Monthly Review Press. New York.

Amin, S. (1976). Unequal Development: An Essay on the Social Formations of Peripheral Communities. New York: Monthly Review Press. New York.

Amin, S. (1990). Delinking: Towards a Polycentric World. Zed Books. London.

Amin, S. (1995). Africa and the Global System. In Bujra, A. (Guest Editor) African Development Review. A Special Number on Africa and the Future. https://doi.org/10.1111/j.1467-8268.1995.tb00070.x

Amin, S. (2010). The Law of Worldwide Value. Monthly Review Press. New York.

Amiti, M., Konings, J. (2007). Trade Liberalization, Intermediate Inputs, and Productivity: Evidence from Indonesia. *The American Economic Review* 97 (5). 1611–1638. https://doi.org/10.1257/aer.97.5.1611

Amjadi, A., Yeats, A.J. (1995). Have Transport Costs Contributed to the Relative Decline of Sub-Saharan African Exports? World Bank Policy Research Working Paper No. 1559. Washington, DC: World Bank.

Anadi, S.K.M. (2005). Regional Integration in Africa: The Case of ECOWAS. PhD Thesis presented to the Faculty of Arts of the University of Zurich. April 2005.

Aniche, E. (2014). Problematising Neo-functionalism in the Search for a New Theory of African Integration: The Case of the Proposed Tripartite Free Trade Area (T-FTA) in Africa. *Developing Country Studies.* 4(20). 128–142.

Aniche, E. (2015). The Calculus of Integration or Differentiation in Africa: Post-neo-functionalism and the Future of African Regional Economic Communities (RECs). *International Affairs and Global Strategy.* 36. 41–52.

Aniche, E. (2018). Post-neo-functionalism, Pan-Africanism and Regional Integration in Africa: Prospects and challenges of the Proposed Tripartite Free Trade Area (T-FTA). In State and Development in Post-Independent Africa, (eds.) Oloruntoba, S. and Vusi Gumede, V. Austin, TX: Pan-African University Press.

Aniche, E. (2019). Pan-Africanism and Regionalism in Africa: The Journey So Far. In Pan-Africanism, regional integration and development in Africa, (ed.) Oloruntoba, S. Palgrave Macmillan. New York. https://doi.org/10.1007/978-3-030-34296-8_2

Aniche, E., Ukaegbu, V. (2016). Structural Dependence, Vertical Integration and Regional Economic Cooperation in Africa: A study of Southern African Development Community. *Africa Review.* 8(2). 108–119. https://doi.org/10.1080/09744053.2016.1186866

Aniche, E. (2020). The Brexit: A Massive Setback for European Union and a Lesson for African Integration. *Chinese Political Science Review.* 5:13–30. https://doi.org/10.1007/s41111-019-00142-0

Aniche, E.T. (2020). From Pan-Africanism to African regionalism: A Chronicle. *African Studies.* 79:1. 70-87. https://doi.org/10.1080/00020184.2020.1740974

Aniche, E.T. (2020). African Continental Free Trade Area and African Union Agenda 2063: the roads to Addis Ababa and Kigali. *Journal of Contemporary African Studies.*41(4). https://doi.org/10.1080/02589001.2020.1775184

Aning, K. (2008). The UN and the African Union's Security Architecture: Defining an Emerging Partnership? The United Nations, Security and Peacekeeping in Africa Lessons and Prospects, Critical Currents no. 5. Uppsala: Dag Hammarskjöld Foundation, 8−23.

Aning, K. and Noagbesenu, H. (2010). The UN and Africa - Options for Partnership and Support. In de Coning, C. Atensland, A.Ø., Tardy, T. (eds) Proceedings from the UN Peacekeeping Future Challenges Seminar, 'Beyond the "New Horizon".' held 23−24 June 2010 at the Geneva Centre for Security Policy. Oslo: Norwegian Institute of International Affairs, 87−85.

Aning, E.K., and Pokoo, J. (2013). Threats to National and Regional Security in West Africa. WACD Background Paper No 1. Available at: http://www.wacommissionondrugs.org/wp-content/uploads/2013/05/DrugTrafficking-and-Threats-to-National-and-Regional-Security-in-West-Africa-2013−04−03.pdf (accessed12 December 2021).

Aning, K., Festus, A. Nancy, A., Fiifi Edu-Afful, F. (2013). Normative Changes in Peacekeeping Operations: How Much Are Current Norms and Practices Challenged?" Geneva Center for Security Policy. Accessed 23 July 2017.http://www.css.ethz.ch/content/dam/ethz/special-interest/gess/cis/center-for-securities studies/pdfs/Normative_Changes_in_Peacekeeping_Africa_s_Resistance.pdf.

Annan, K. (2000). "We the Peoples – The Role of the United Nations in the 21st Century", The "Millennium Report" by the Secretary-General of the United Nations, March 2000.

Appiah-Mensah, S. (2005). AU's Critical Assignment in Darfur: Challenges and Constraints. *African Security Review*. 14 (2). 7−21. https://doi.org/10.1080/10246029.2005.9627348

Araoye, A. (2014). Sources of Conflict in the Post-Colonial African State. Africa World Press. Trenton, NJ.

Aredo, D. (2003). The New Partnership for Africa's Development: Prospects and Challenges. *Organisation for Social Research in Eastern and Southern Africa (OSSREA) Newsletter*. 21(3). 24-30.

Arrighi, G. (1990). The Developmentalist Illusion: A Reconceptualization of the Semiperiphery. In Martin W.G. (ed.) Semiperipheral States in the World-economy, pp. 11–42. Greenwood Press. Westport, CT.

Arrighi, G. (2002). Global Inequalities and the Legacy of Dependency Theory. *Radical Philosophy Review.* 5(1/2). 75–85. https://doi.org/10.5840/radphilrev200251/26

Arrighi, G. (2002). The African Crisis. *New Left Review.* 15: 5-38.

Arrighi, G., Silver B.J., Brewer, B.D. (2003). Industrial Convergence, Globalization and the Persistence of the North–South Divide. *Studies in Comparative International Development.* 38. 3-31. https://doi.org/10.1007/BF02686319

Asante, Samuel K.B. (1997). Regionalisation and Africa's Development: Expectations, Reality and Challenges. Palgrave Macmillan. London.

Asante, S.K.B. (2003). The NEPAD: A Partnership of Unequal Partners. *New African.* June. pp14-16.

Asante, M.K. (2007). The History of Africa: The Quest for Eternal Harmony. Routledge. New York.

ASEAN. (1995). Framework Agreement on Intellectual Property Cooperation.

ATAF. (2017). African Tax Outlook 2017, Second Ed. Pretoria, South Africa.

ATAF. (2018). African Tax Outlook, Second Edition 2018. Pretoria, South Africa.

AU. (1991). The Abuja Treaty. Abuja.

AU. (2000). Constitutive Act of the African Union adopted by the Thirty Sixth Ordinary Session of the Assembly of Heads of State and Government. 11 July 2000, Lome. Togo.

AU. (2001). The New Partnership for Africa's Development. Addis Ababa.

AU. (2002). The Constitutive Act of the African Union. Addis Ababa.

AU. (2002). Declaration on Democracy, Political, Economic and Corporate Governance, [AHG/235(XXXVIII) Annex I], 8 July 2000.

AU. (2002). Protocol Relating to the Establishment of the Peace and Security Council of the African Union. Adopted by the Assembly at its 1st Ordinary Session, 9 July 2002. Durban.

AU. (2002a). Plan of Action of the African High-Level Intern-
    Governmental Meeting on the Prevention and Combating of
    Terrorism in Africa [Mtg/HLIG/Conv.Terror/Plan.(I)]. Adopted by
    the High-Level Intergovernmental Meeting on the Prevention of
    Terrorism in Africa, Algiers. 11–14 September 2002.

AU. (2002b). Protocol Relating to the Establishment of the Peace and
    Security Council of the African Union. Adopted by the First
    Ordinary Session of the Assembly of the African Union/ Durban.
    9 July 2002.

AU. (2003a). Communiqué [Central Organ/MEC/AHG/Comm.(VII)].
    Adopted by the Seventh Ordinary Session of the Central Organ
    of the Mechanism for Conflict Prevention, Management and
    Resolution at Heads of State and Government Level at Addis
    Ababa. 3 February 2003.

AU. (2003b). Communiqué [Central Organ/MEC/AMB/Comm. (XCI)].
    Adopted by the Ninety First Ordinary Session of the Central
    Organ of the Mechanism for Conflict Prevention, Management
    and Resolution at Ambassadorial Level, Addis Ababa. 2 April
    2003.

AU. (2003c). Decisions and Declarations [Assembly/AU/Dec.1 – 23(II)]
    [Assembly/AU/Decl.1– 5 (II)]. Adopted by the Second Ordinary
    Session of the Assembly, Maputo. 10-12 July 2003.

AU. (2003d). Policy Framework for the Establishment of the African
    Standby Force and the Military Staff Committee [Exp/ASF-
    MSC/2 (I)]. Adopted by the Third Meeting of African Chiefs
    of Defence Staff, Addis Ababa, 15-16 May; Approved by the
    Third Ordinary Session of the Assembly of the African Union
    [Assembly/AU/Dec.35(III)], Addis Ababa. 6-8 July 2004.

AU. (2003e). Protocol on Amendments to the Constitutive Act of the
    African Union. Adopted by the First Extraordinary Session of the
    Assembly of the AU in Addis 284 Ababa, Ethiopia, 3 February
    2003 and by the Second Ordinary Session of the Assembly of the
    AU in Maputo, Mozambique. 11 July 2003.

AUC. (2015). Services Exports For Growth and Development: Case Studies
    from Africa. Addis Ababa.

AUC and ECA (2016) Track it! Stop it! Get it! Illicit Financial Flows: Report to the High-Level Panel on Illicit Financial Flows from Africa. African Union Commission and ECA. Addis Ababa, Ethiopia.

AUC and Internet Society. (2018). Personal Data Protection Guidelines for Africa. Available at: https://www.Intersociety.org/wp-content/uploads/2018/05/AUCPrivacyGuidelines_2018508_EN.pdf.

AUC/OECD. (2022). Africa's Development Dynamics 2022: Regional Value Chains for a Sustainable Recovery, AUC, Addis Ababa/ OECD Publishing, Paris, https://doi.org/10.1787/2e3b97fd-en.

Avant, D., Nevers, R. (2011). 'Military Contractors and & American Way of War. *Dœdalus, the Journal of the American Academy of Arts & Sciences.* 140 (3). 1–12. https://doi.org/10.1162/DAED_a_00100

Avery, N. (1994). Stealing from the State. In 50 Years Is Enough: The Case against the World Bank and the IMF. Danaher, K. and Yunnus, M. (Eds). South End. Boston.

Axline, W.A. (1994). The Political Economy of Regional Co-operation: Comparative Case Studies. Pinter Publishers. London.

Ayangafac, C. (2008). Utilising the Management of Natural Resources to Forge a Union Government for Africa. In Murith. T.i (ed). Towards A Union Government for Africa: Challenges and Opportunities. Institute for Security Studies Monograph Series.

Ayinde, A.F. (2011). "Technical Cooperation and Regional Integration in Africa: A study of Nigeria's Technical Aid Corps. *Journal of Sustainable Development in Africa.* 13, 182-186.

Azmeh, S., Foster, C. (2016). The TPP and the Digital Trade Agenda: Digital Industrial Policy and Silicon Valley's Influence on New Trade Agreements. Working Paper Series No. 16-175. London School of Economics, Department of International Development.

Badmus, I.A. (2017). The African Mission in Burundi (AMIB): A Study of the African Union's Peacekeeping Success and Triangular Area of Tension in African Peacekeeping. *India Quarterly.* 73(1). 1–20. https://doi.org/10.1177/0974928416683038

Bah, A. (2005). West Africa: From a Security Complex to a Security Community. *African Security Review.* 14 (2). 77-83. https://doi.org/10.1080/10246029.2005.9627357

Baier, S.L., Bergstrand, J.H. (2000). Economic Determinants of Free Trade Agreements. *Journal of International Economics*. 64(1). 29-63. https://doi.org/10.1016/S0022-1996(03)00079-5

Baier, S.L., Berstrand, J.H. (2007). Do Free Trade Agreements Actually Increase Members' International Trade? *Journal of International Economics*. 71(1). 72-95. https://doi.org/10.1016/j.jinteco.2006.02.005

Baier, S. L., Bergstrand, J. H., and Feng, M. (2014). Economic integration agreements and the margins of international trade. *Journal of International Economics*, 93(2): 339-350. https://doi.org/10.1016/j.jinteco.2014.03.005

Balaam, D., Veseth, M. (2001). Introduction to Political Economy. Pearson Prentice Hall. Upper Saddle River.

Balaam, N.D., Dillman, B. (2014). Introduction to International Political Economy. Pearson Education Press. Essex. https://doi.org/10.4324/9781315663838

Balcerowwicz, L. (1995). Socialism, Capitalism, Transformation. Central European Press. Budapest. https://doi.org/10.1515/9789633864951

Baldwin, R.E. (1997). Reviews of Theoretical Developments on Regional Integration: In Oyejide et al. (eds.) Regional Integration and Trade Liberalisation in Sub-Saharan Africa, Vol. 1. Macmillan. London. https://doi.org/10.1007/978-1-349-25636-5_2

Baldwin, R.E. (2004). Openness and Growth: What's the Empirical Relationship?. In Challenges to Globalization: Analyzing the Economics. Baldwin. R.E. and Winters, L. (eds). Chicago University Press. Chicago. https://doi.org/10.7208/chicago/9780226036557.003.0014

Baldwin, R. (2006). Globalisation: The Great Unbundling. In Globalisation Challenges to Europe and Finland organised by the secretariat of Economic Council, Prime Minister's Office.

Baldwin, A. (2015). Africa's Political Economy: From the Past to the Future. Oxford University Press. Oxford.

Baldwin, R. (2013). Lessons from the European Spaghetti Bowl. Trade Working Papers 23411, East Asian Bureau of Economic Research. Canberra, Australia. https://doi.org/10.2139/ssrn.2255911

Baldwin, R. (2014a). The Impact of Mega-regionals: The Economic Impact. In World Economic Forum (WEF) (ed), Mega-regional Trade Agreements: Game Changers or Costly Distractions for the World Trading System? WEF. Geneva.

Baldwin, R. (2014b). The Impact of Mega-regionals: The Systemic Impact. In WEF (ed), Mega-regional Trade Agreements: Game-Changers or Costly Distractions for the World Trading System? WEF. Geneva.

Bandara, J.S. (1991). Computable General Equilibrium Models for Development Policy Analysis. *Journal of Economic Surveys.* 5(1). 3-69. https://doi.org/10.1111/j.1467-6419.1991.tb00126.x

Baran, P. (1957). The Political Economy of Growth. Monthly Review Press. New York:

Baran, P., Sweezy, P. (1966). Monopoly Capital. Monthly Review Press. New York.

Barnes, C., Assan, H. (2007). The Rise and Fall of Mogadishu's Islamic Courts. *Journal of East African Studies.* 1(2):150–160. https://doi.org/10.1080/17531050701452382

Barnett, M. (2005). Social Constructivism. In Baylis, J. and Smith, S. (eds.) The Globalization of World Politics: An introduction to International Relations, 3rd edition. Oxford University Press. Oxford. pp. 251-270.

Barnett, M.N., M. Finnemore (1999). The Politics, Power, and Pathologies of International Organisations. *International Organisation.* 53(4). 699–732. https://doi.org/10.1162/002081899551048

Barnett, M., Finnemore, M. (2004). Rules for the World: International Organisations in Global Politics. Cornell University Press. Ithaca and London.

Barron, I. (2013). The potential and challenges of critical realist ethnography. *International Journal of Research & Method in Education.* 36. 117–130. https://doi.org/10.1080/174372 7X.2012.683634

Battle, M.A. (2009). Ambassador Battle's Remarks at the UC/ECA Partners Dialogue Meeting. available from <http://www.usau.usmission. gov/ program-activities/ambassador battles-remark-on the- auc/eca-partners-dialogue-meetings.html > [10 December 2010].

Bauer, M. H. Lee-Makiyama, E., van der Marel, Verschelde, E. (2014). The Costs of Data Localisation: Friendly Fire on Economic Recovery. Occasional Paper No. 3/2014. European Centre for International Political Economy. Brussels.

Bekoe, D.A., Landsberg, C. (2002). Nepad: African initiative, new partnership. (In IPA workshop report. Inter-Continental Hotel, 2002. New York. 1-29.

Beneria, L. (1995). Response: The Dynamics of Globalisation (Scholarly Controversy: Global Flows of Labour and Capital). *International Labour and Working-Class History*. 47. 45-52. https://doi.org/10.1017/S0147547900012862

Benyera, E. (2021). The Fourth Industrial Revolution and the Recolonisation of Africa: The Coloniality of Data. Routledge, New York. https://doi.org/10.4324/9781003157731

Berg, B.L. (2003). Qualitative research methods for the social science (5th ed.). Allyn and Bacon. Boston.

Berger. S. (2006). How we Compete: What Companies Around the World are Doing to Make it in Today's Global Economy. Randon House. New York.

Bergholm, L. (2009). The African Union - United Nations Relationship and Civilian Protection in Darfur, 2004-2007, Unpublished PhD thesis. Aberystwyth: Aberystwyth University.

Bergstrand, J.H. (1985). The Gravity Equation in International Trade: Some Microeconomic Foundations and Empirical Evidence. *The Review of Economics and Statistics*. 67(3). 474–481. https://doi.org/10.2307/1925976

Bergstrand, J.H., Egger, P. (2007). A Knowledge-and-Physical-Capital Model of International Trade Flows, Foreign Direct Investment and Multinational Enterprises. *Journal of International Economics*. 73(2). 278–308. https://doi.org/10.1016/j.jinteco.2007.03.004

Berman, M. (1996). All That Is Solid Melt into Air: The Experience of Modernity. Yerso. London.

Berman, N., Couttenier, M., Rohner, D., Thoenig, M. (2014). This Mine Is Mine! How Minerals Fuel Conflicts in Africa. Research Paper 141. Oxford, UK: Oxford Centre for the Analysis of Resource Rich Economies. https://doi.org/10.2139/ssrn.2627073

Berman, N., Couttenier, M., Rohner, D., Thoenig, M. (2017). This Mine Is Mine! How Minerals Fuel Conflicts in Africa. *American Economic Review*. 107(6).1564–1610. https://doi.org/10.1257/aer.20150774

Bernasconi-Osterwalder, N. (2014). State-State Dispute Settlement in Investment Treaties. Best Practices Series, IISD, Winnipeg, MB.

Berry, J. (2005). Validity and Reliability Issues in Elite Interviewing. *Political Science in Politics*. 35(4). 679–862. https://doi.org/10.1017/S1049096502001166

Bhagwati, J. (1991). The World Trading System at Risk. Princeton University Press. https://doi.org/10.1515/9781400861590

Bhaskar, R. (1998). Philosophy and Scientific Realism. In Archer, M., Bhaskar, R., Collier, A., Lawson, T., Norrie, A. (Eds.), Critical realism: Essential readings (16–47). Routledge. Oxford.

Bhattacharya, A. (2020). South-South Cooperation and the New Development Bank. Brookings Institution.

Bilal, S., Rampa, F. (2006). Alternatives to EPAs: Possible Scenarios for the Future ACP Trade Relations with the EU, Maastricht: ECDPM, Policy Management Report 11.

Biney, A. (2008). The Legacy of Kwame Nkrumah in Retrospect. *The Journal of Pan African Studies*. (2)3. 139.

Biney, A. (2011). The Political and Social Thought of Kwame Nkrumah. Palgrave Macmillan. New York. https://doi.org/10.1057/9780230118645

Biney, A. (2012). The Intellectual and Political Legacies of Kwame Nkrumah. *The Journal of Pan African Studies*. 4(10). 127-142.

Bird, G. (1994). Changing Partners: Perspectives and Policies of the Bretton Woods Institutions. *Third World Quarterly*. 15(3). 483-505. https://doi.org/10.1080/01436599408420392

Biswaro, J.M. (2003). Perspectives on Africa's integration and Cooperation from OAU to AU: An Old Wine in a New Bottle. WIU. Washington.

Biswaro, J.M. (2011). The Quest For Regional Integration in Africa, Latin America and Beyond in the Twenty-First Century: Experience, Progress, and Prospects.

Biswaro, J.M. (2012). The Quest for Regional Integration in the Twenty-First Century: Rhetoric versus Reality: A Comparative Study. Tanzania: NkukinaNyota Publishers Ltd.

Biswaro, R. (2015). Reshaping the Financial Architecture for Development Finance: The New Development Banks. Working Paper Series, (31), 1.

Boas, M.H., Shaw, T.M. (1999). Special Issue: New Regionalisms in the New Millennium. *Third World Quarterly.* 20(5). 897-1070. https://doi.org/10.1080/01436599913497

Boateng, R.J., Budu, A.S., Mbrokoh, E., Ansong, S.L., Boateng, A.B., Anderson. (2017). Digital Enterprises in Africa: A Synthesis of Current Evidence." Development Implications of Digital Economies Paper 2, Centre for Development Informatics, Global Development Institute, SEED, University of Manchester, Manchester, UK.

Bogdan, R.C., Biklen, S.K. (2006). Qualitative Research in Education: An Introduction to Theory and Methods, Allyn and Bacon. Boston.

Boldrin, M., Levine, D.K., Modica, S. (2012). A Review of Acemoglu and Robinson's Why Nations Fail.

Bond, P. (2003). Can NEPAD Survive its Proponents, Sponsors, Clients and Peers? *Organisation for Social Research in Eastern and Southern Africa (OSSREA) Newsletter,* 21(3). 12-19.

Bond, P. (2004). South Africa and Global Apartheid: Continental and International Policies and Politics. Disscussion Paper 25, Uppsala: Nordiska Afrikainstitutet.

Bond, P. (2006). Looting Africa: the Economics of Exploitation. Zed Books. London. https://doi.org/10.5040/9781350221185

Bonizzi, B., Kaltenbrunner, A., Powell, J. (2019). Subordinate Financialization in Emerging Capitalist Economies. In Mader, P., Mertens. D., van der Zwan, N. (eds). The International Handbook of Financialization. 177–87. Routledge. London. https://doi.org/10.4324/9781315142876-15

Börzel, T.A., Risse, T. (2019). Grand Theories of Integration and the Challenges of Comparative Regionalism, *Journal of European Public Policy.* 26:8. 1231-1252. https://doi.org/10.1080/13501763.2019.1622589

Bossuyt, J., Sherriff, A. (2010). What Next for the Joint Africa-EU Strategy? Perspectives on Revitalising an Innovative Framework, European Centre for Development Policy Management Discussion Paper 94.

Bossuyt, J. (2016). The Political Economy of Regional Integration in Africa: The Economic Community of West African States (ECOWAS). European Centre for Development Policy. Maastricht.

Boshoff, H. (2005). The African Union Mission in Sudan: Technical and Operation Dimensions. *African Security Review*. 14(3). 57–60. https://doi.org/10.1080/10246029.2005.9627371

Bown, C.P., Kee. H.L. (2011). Developing Countries, New Trade Barriers, and the Global Economic Crisis. In Haddad, M., Shepherd, B. (eds), Managing Openness: Trade and Outward-Oriented Growth after the Crisis. World Bank. Washington, DC. https://doi.org/10.1596/9780821386316_CH06

Brauch, M.D., Mann, H., Bernasconi-Osterwalder, N. (2019). SADC– IISD Investment Facilitation Workshop. Report of the meeting in Johannesburg, South Africa, 21–23 August.

Brett, J. (2013).The Interrelationship between the African Peace and Security Agenda, the Global Peace and Security Agenda, and Regional initiatives. DANIDA.

Breytenbach, W. (2008). Peacekeeping and regional integration in Africa. In Monitoring Regional Integration. In Southern Africa, Yearbook Vol. 8. Bosi, A., Breytenbach, W., Hartzenberg, T., McCarthy, C., Schade. K. (eds). TRALAC. Stellenbosch.

Brinkerhoff, J.M. (2002). Partnership for International Development, Rhetorics or Result? Lynne Rienner Publishers.Boulder, Co.

Broda, C., Weinstein, D.E. (2004). Variety growth and world welfare. *The American Economic Review*. 94(2). 139–144. https://doi.org/10.1257/0002828041301443

Broda, C., Greenfield, J., Weinstein, D.. (2006). From Groundnuts to Globalization: A Structural Estimate of Trade and Growth. Working Paper No. 12512. National Bureau of Economic Research. Cambridge, MA. https://doi.org/10.3386/w12512

Brooks, J., Croppenstedt, A., Aggrey-Fynn, E. (2007). Distortions to Agricultural Incentives in Ghana. Report prepared for the World Bank. Washington, D.C.

Brooks, W.J., Pujolàs, P.S. (2014). Nonlinear Gravity. McMaster Univ. Work. Pap. 2014-15.

Brooks, W.J., Pujolàs, P.S. (2016). Capital Accumulation and the Welfare Gains from Trade. McMaster Univ. Work. Pap. 2016-03. https://doi.org/10.2139/ssrn.2826680

Brown, D., Kiyota, K., Stern, R.M. (2008). An Analysis of US-Southern African Customs Union (SACU) Free Trade Agreement. *World Development*. 36(3). 461-484. https://doi.org/10.1016/j.worlddev.2007.03.005

Brown, W., and Sophie Harman. (2013). African Agency in International Politics. Routledge. Abington. https://doi.org/10.4324/9780203526071

Browne, R.S., Cummings, R.J. (1984). The Lagos Plan of Action Versus The Berg Report: Contemporary issues in African economic development. Brunswick Publishing Company. Virginia, Lawrenceville.

Browne, M. A. (2011). United Nations System Funding: Congressional Issues [CRS Report RL33611]. Congressional Research Service.

Brunnée, J., Toope, S.J. (2000). International Law and Constructivism: Elements of an Interactional Theory of International Law. *Columbia Journal of Transnational Law*. 39 (1). 19-74.

Brynard, P.A., Hanekom, S.X., (1997). Introduction to Research in Public Administration and Related Academic Disciplines. Van Schaik, Academic. Pretoria.

Brynard, P. A. (2000). Policy implementation. In Cloete, F., Wissink, H. (eds). Improving Public Policy. 164-189. Van Schaik. Pretoria.

Budree, A. (2017). Policy Considerations for e-commerce in South Africa and other African Countries. Policy Briefing. Global Economic Governance Africa. Johannesburg.

Cadot, O., Carrere, C., De Melo, J., Tumurchudur, B. (2006). Product-specific Rules of Origin in EU [European Union] and US [United States] Preferential Trading Arrangements: An assessment. *World Trade Review*. 5(2). 199–224. https://doi.org/10.1017/S1474745606002758

Cadot, O., Estevadeordal, A., Suwa-Eisenmann, A., Verdier, T. (2006). The Origin of Goods: Rules of Origin in Regional Trade Agreements. Oxford University Press. Oxford. https://doi.org/10.1093/0199290482.001.0001

Cadot, O., De Melo, J. (2008). Why Organisation for Economic Cooperation and Development Countries Should Reform Rules of Origin. *World Bank Research Observer.* 23(1). 77–105. https://doi.org/10.1093/wbro/lkm010

Cadot, O., Asprilla, A., Gourdon, J., Knebel, C., Peters, R. (2015). Deep Regional Integration and Non-tariff Measures: A Methodology for Data Analysis. Policy Issues in International Trade and Commodities Study Series 69, UNCTAD (United Nations Conference on Trade and Development). Geneva.

Cadot, O., Ing, L.Y. (2016). How Restrictive Are ASEAN [the Association of Southeast Asian Nations]' Rules of Origin? *Asian Economic Papers.* 15(3). 115–134. https://doi.org/10.1162/ASEP_a_00461

Calì, M. (2014). Trading Away from Conflict: Using Trade to Increase Resilience in Fragile States. World Bank. Washington, DC. https://doi.org/10.1596/978-1-4648-0308-6

Callaghy, T. M. (1988). The State and the Development of Capitalism in Africa: Theoretical, Historical, and Comparative Reflections. In The Precarious Balance: State and Society in Africa, (ed) Rothchild and Chazan.

Campbell, H. (2013). Global NATO and the Catastrophic Failure in Libya: Lessons for Africa in the Forging of African Unity. Monthly Review Press. New York.

Caporaso, J. (1971). Theory and Method in the Study of International Integration. *International Organisation.* 25(2). 228-253. https://doi.org/10.1017/S0020818300017628

Caporaso, J. (1972). Functionalism and Regional Integration: A Logical and Empirical Assessment. Sage Professional Paper in International Studies Series. Beverly Hills. California.

Caporaso, J. (1973). The European and Regional Integration Theory. A Paper Presented at the Third Biennial International Conference of the European Community Studies. Istanbul.

Caporaso, J.A. (1977). Theories of Political Economy. Cambridge University Press. New York.

Caporaso, J., Marks, G., Moravcsik, A., Pollack, M. (1997). Does the European Union Represent An n of 1? *ECSA Review X* (3). 1-5.

Caporaso, J. (1998). Regional Integration Theory: Understanding our Past and Anticipating our Future. *Journal of European Policy*. 5(1). 1-16. https://doi.org/10.1093/0198294646.003.0012

Cardoso, F.H. (1973). Notas sobre Estado e depêndencia [Notes on Status and Dependence]. São Paulo: Centro Brasileiro de Análise e Planejamento.

Cardoso, F. (1977). The Consumption of Dependency Theory in the United States. *Latin American Research Review*. 12(3). 7–24. https://doi.org/10.1017/S0023879100030430

Cardoso, F.H., Serra, J. (1978). Las desventuras de la dialéctica de la dependencia' ['The Misadventures of the Dependency Dialectic']. *Revista Mexicana de Sociologí* XL(E). 9–55. https://doi.org/10.2307/3539682

Cardoso, F.H., Faletto, E. (1979). Dependency and Development in Latin America. University of California Press. Los Angeles, CA. https://doi.org/10.1525/9780520342118

Carlsnaes, W. (1992). The Agency-Structure Problem in Foreign Policy Analysis. *International Studies Quarterly*. 36(3). 245-270. https://doi.org/10.2307/2600772

Carmody, P. (1998). Constructing alternatives to structural adjustment in Africa. *Review of African Political Economy*. 25(75). 25-46. https://doi.org/10.1080/03056249808704291

Cassidy S. (2013). Acknowledging Hubris in Interpretative Data Analysis. *Nurse Researcher*. 20(6). 27-31. https://doi.org/10.7748/nr2013.07.20.6.27.e321

Chabal, P. (2002). The Quest for Good Government and Development in Africa: Is NEPAD the Answer? *International Affairs*. 78(3). 447-462. https://doi.org/10.1111/1468-2346.00260

Chang, H.J. (2002). Things They Don't Want You to Know About Capitalism. New York: Bloomsbury Press.

Chang, H.J. (2002). Kicking Away the Ladder: Development Strategy in Historical Perspective. Anthem Press. London.

Chang, H.J. (2011). Hamlet without the Prince of Denmark: How Development Has Disappeared from Today's "Development" Discourse". In Kahn, S.R., Christiansen, J. (eds) Towards New Developmentalism: Market as Means rather than Master. 47–58. Routledge. Abingdon.

Charalambides, A. (2005). SADC/EAC/COMESA and EPA Negotiations: Trade Policy Options to Overcome the Problem of Multiple Memberships. GTZ.

Charles, F. D. (2021). African Continental Free Trade Area: Is there a Trade Potential for Côte d'Ivoire?, *Cogent Economics and Finance.* 9:1. https://doi.org/10.1080/23322039.2021.1915932

Chauvin, D., Ramos. N., Porto. G. (2016). Trade, Growth, and Welfare Impacts of the CFTA in Africa. https://editorialexpress.com/cgibin/conference/download.cgi?db_name=CSAE2017&paperid=749.

Checkel, J. T. (2005). International Institutions and Socialization in Europe: Introduction and Framework. *International Organisation.* 59: 801-826. https://doi.org/10.1017/S0020818305050289

Checkel, J. T. (2001). Why Comply? Social Norms Learning and European Identity Change. *International Organisation.* 55(3). 553-588. https://doi.org/10.1162/00208180152507551

Checkel, J. T. (2000). Bridging the Rational-Choice / Constructivist Gap? Theorizing Social Interaction in European Institutions. ARENA Working Papers WP 00/11.

Checkel, J.T. (1998). The Constructivist Turn in International Relations Theory. *World Politics.* 50(2). 324-348. https://doi.org/10.1017/S0043887100008133

Chibber, B. (2004). Regional Security and Regional Cooperation: A Comparative Study of ASEAN and SAARC. New Century. New Delhi.

Chidede, T., Sandrey, R. (2018). Intra-African Trade: Focusing on Trade within Regional Economic Communities. Trade Law Centre. 17 October.

Chingono, M., Nakana, S. (2009). The Challenges of Regional Integration in Southern Africa. *Journal of Political Science.* 3(10). 396-408.

Chiziko, G.M. (2007). The Responsibility to Protect: Does the African Stand-By Force Need a Doctrine for Protection of Civilians? *Interdisciplinary Journal of Human Rights Law.* 2(1). 73–87.

Choi, A.H. (1998). Statism and Asian Political Economy: Is there a new paradigm?' *Bulletin of Concerned Asian Researchers.* 30(3). 50-60. https://doi.org/10.1080/14672715.1998.10411053

Chomsky, N. (2004). Hegemony or Survival: America's Quest for Global Dominance. Owl Books Press. New York.

Chomsky, N. (2017). Global Discontents: Conversations on the Rising Threats to Democracy. Haymarket Books.

Chossudovsky, M. (1997). The Globalisation of Poverty: Impacts of IMF and World Bank Reforms. Third World Networks.

Christian Aid. (2006). EPAs and Investment. Christian Aid. London.

Chuku, C., Kopoin, A. (2022). Debt Distress and Recovery Episodes in Africa: Good Policy or Good Luck? Working Paper Series 367, African Development Bank, Abidjan, Côte d'Ivoire. https://doi.org/10.2139/ssrn.3982165

Cilliers, J. (2003). Terrorism and Africa. *African Security Review.* 12. 91-103. https://doi.org/10.1080/10246029.2003.9627255

Cilliers, J. (2004). Human Security in Africa: A Conceptual Framework for Review. A Monograph for the African Human Security Initiative.

Cilliers, J., Boshoff, H., Aboagye, F. (2010). Somalia: the Intervention Dilemma. *Institute of Strategic Studies.* Policy Brief no. 20.

Cirera, X., Willenbockel, D., Lakshman, R.W.D. (2014). Evidence on the Impact of Tariff Reductions on Employment in Developing Countries: A Systematic Review. *Journal of Economic Surveys.* 36(3). 449-471. https://doi.org/10.1111/joes.12029

Clark, A. M. (2012). What are the Components of Complex Interventions? Theorizing Approaches to Parts, Powers and the Whole Intervention. Social Science & Medicine. https://doi.org/10.1016/j.socscimed.2012.03.035

Clarke, J.H. (1991). New Dimensions in African History. Africa World Press. New Jersey.

Cobham, A., Janský, P. (2018). Global Distribution of Revenue Loss from Corporate Tax Avoidance: Re-estimation and Country Results. *Journal of International Development* 30 (2). 206–232. https://doi.org/10.1002/jid.3348

Cochran, S. (2010). Security Assistance, Surrogate Armies and the Pursuit of US Interests in Sub-Saharan Africa. *Strategic Studies Quarterly.* (Spring) 111–152.

Coetzee, J. K., Graaf, J., Hendricks, F., Wood, G. (eds.) (2001). Development Theory, Policy and Practice. Oxford University Press. Cape Town.

Cohen, B.J. (1985). International Debt and Linkage Strategies: Some Foreign-Policy Implications for the United States. *International Organisation.* (39). 699-727. https://doi.org/10.1017/S0020818300027077

Cohen, B.J. (1990). The Political Economy of International Trade. *International Organisation.* (44). 261-81. https://doi.org/10.1017/S002081830003527X

Cohen, E. (2001). Globalization and the Boundaries of the State: A Framework for Analysing the Changing Practice of Sovereignty. *Governance,* 14 (1). 75-97. https://doi.org/10.1111/0952-1895.00152

Cohen, R. (2001). The Great Tradition: The Spread of Diplomacy in the Ancient World. *Diplomacy and Statecraft.* 12 1):23-38. https://doi.org/10.1080/09592290108406186

Coke-Hamilton, P. (2019). Accelerating Trade and Integration in the Caribbean: Policy Option for Sustained Growth, Job Creation and Poverty Reduction. World Bank Publication.

Collard-Wexler, S. (2006). Integration Under Anarchy: Neorealism and the European Union. *European Journal of International Relations.* 12. September 6. SAGE Publishers. 399-406. https://doi.org/10.1177/1354066106067349

Collier, P. (1979). The Welfare Effects of Customs Unions: An Anatomy. *Economic Journal.* 89. 84 95. https://doi.org/10.2307/2231408

Collier, P. (1991). Africa's External Economic Relations: 1960-1990. *African Affairs.* 90. 339-34. https://doi.org/10.1093/oxfordjournals.afraf.a098437

Collier, P., Gunning, J.W. (1995). Trade Policy and Regional Integration: Implications for the Relations Between Europe and Africa. *The World Economy*, Vol. 18. https://doi.org/10.1111/j.1467-9701.1995.tb00221.x

Collier, P., and Gunning, J.W. (1995a) Trade Policy and Regional Integration: Implications for the Relations Between Europe and Africa. *The World Economy*. 18. 387-410. https://doi.org/10.1111/j.1467-9701.1995.tb00221.x

Collier, P., Hoeffler, A. (1998). On Economic Causes of Civil War. *Oxford Economic Papers*. 50 (4): 563–73. https://doi.org/10.1093/oep/50.4.563

Collier, P. (1999). Why has Africa grown slowly? *Journal of Economic Perspectives*. 13(3). 4166. https://doi.org/10.1257/jep.13.3.3

Collier, P. (2002). On the Incidence of Civil War in Africa. *Journal of Conflict Resolution*. 46(1). 1328. https://doi.org/10.1177/0022002702046001002

Collier, P. (2004). Greed and Grievance in Civil War. *Oxford Economic Papers*. 56(4). 563–95. https://doi.org/10.1093/oep/gpf064

Collier, P., Sambanis, N. (eds.) (2005). Understanding Civil War: Evidence and Analysis. Washington, DC: World Bank. https://doi.org/10.1596/978-0-8213-6047-7

Collier, P. (.2007). The Bottom Billion. Oxford University Press. Oxford.

Collier, P., Hoeffler, A., Söderbom, M. (2008). Post Conflict Risks. *Journal of Peace Research*. 45(4). 461–78. https://doi.org/10.1177/0022343308091356

COMESA. (2011). Policy on Intellectual Property Rights and Cultural Industries. Council of Ministers, COMESA.

Commission for Africa. (2005). Our Common Interest. Report of the Commission for Africa. London.

Communications Authority of Kenya (2017). Sector Statistics Report Q3, 2017. Retrieved from https://ca.go.ke/wp-content/uploads/2018/07/SectorStatistics-Report-Q3-2017-18-2.pdf

Consultative Group to Assist the Poor (CGAP). (2011). Africa Financial Infrastructure Survey. Washington, DC.

Conway, P. (1994). IMF Lending Programs: Participation and Impact",
Journal of Development Economics. 45. 365-91. https://doi.
org/10.1016/0304-3878(94)90038-8

Corrigan, T. (2015). Regional Integration in Africa: Can Agenda 2063 be
Different? Retrieved from http://www.saiia.org.za/research/
regional-integration-in-africa-can-agenda-2063-be-
different/

Costa, O., Magnette, P. (2003). The European Union as a Consocation.
Western European Politics. *Frank Cass Journal*. 26(3). 1-18.
https://doi.org/10.1080/01402380312331280568

Cotelli, C. (1993). Limiting Central Bank Credit to Governments. IMF,
Washington DC.

Council on Foreign Relations (2008). Fact Sheet on Africa Contingency
Operations Training and Assistance (ACOTA). Council on
Foreign Relations [online] available from<http://www.cfr.
org/africa/fact-sheet-africa-contingency-operations-
trainingassistanceacota/p22318> [19 August 2012]

Coulibaly, B., Gandhi, D. (2018). Mobilization of Tax Revenues in Africa:
State of Play and Policy Options. Policy Brief. Washington, DC:
Africa Growth Initiative at Brookings Institution.

Creswell, J.W. (2003). Research Design: Qualitative, Quantitative and
Mixed Approaches (2nd Edition). Thousand Oaks, Sage, CA.

Cruickshank, J. (2004). A Tale of Two Ontologies: An Immanent Critique of
Critical Realism. *The Sociological Review*. 52(4). 567–585. https://
doi.org/10.1111/j.1467-954X.2004.00496.x

Cruickshank, J. (2012). Positioning Positivism, Critical Realism and
Social Constructionism in the Health Sciences: A Philosophical
Orientation. *Nursing Inquiry*. 19(1). 71–82. https://doi.org/10.1111/
j.1440-1800.2011.00558.x

Crupi, F.V. (2005). Why the United States Should Robustly Support Pan-
African Organisations. *Parameters*. 35(4). 106–123. https://doi.
org/10.55540/0031-1723.2275

Curran, L., Nilsson, L., Brew, D. (2008). The Economic Partnership
Agreements: Rationale, Misperceptions, and Non-trade
Aspects. *Development Policy Review*. 26(5). 529-553. https://doi.
org/10.1111/j.1467-7679.2008.00422.x

Curtin, P. D. (1990). The Atlantic Slave Trade: A Census. University of Wisconsin Press.

Däniker, G. (1995). The Guardian Soldier: on the Nature and Use of Armed Forces. SOS Free Stock.New York.

Davidson, C., Matusz, S. (2000). Globalization and Labour-market Adjustment: How fast and at what cost? *Oxford Review of Economic Policy.* 16(3). 42–56. https://doi.org/10.1093/oxrep/16.3.42

Davies, R., Head, J. (1995). The Future of Mine Migrancy in the Context of Border Trends in Migration in Southern Africa. *Journal of Southern African Studies.* 21(3). 439–50. https://doi.org/10.1080/03057079508708456

Deacon, B., Van Hoestenberghe, K. De Lombaerde, P., Macovei, M.C. (2008). Regional Integration: Decent Work and Labour and Social Policies in West and Southern Africa. Working Paper W-2008/13. United Nations University Institute on Comparative Regional Integration Studies, Bruges, Belgium.

de Beer, J. (2013). Applying Best Practice Principles to International Intellectual Property Lawmaking. *IIC-International Review of Intellectual Property and Competition Law.* 44(8). 884–901. https://doi.org/10.1007/s40319-013-0133-3

de Beer, J., Fu, K., Wunsch-Vincent, S. (2013). The Informal Economy, Innovation and Intellectual Property – Concepts, Metrics and Policy Considerations. Economic Research Working Paper No. 10 Geneva: World Intellectual Property Organisation. Retrieved from http://www.wipo.int/edocs/pubdocs/en/wipo_pub_econstat_wp_10.pdf.

de Beer, J., Armstrong, C. Oguamanam, C., Schonwetter, T. (2014). Innovation and Intellectual Property: Collaborative dynamics in Africa. UCT Press, Claremont, South Africa.

de Beer, J., Baarbé, J., Ncube, N. (2017). The Intellectual Property Treaty Landscape in Africa,1885 to 2015. Open AIR Working Paper 4. https://doi.org/10.2139/ssrn.3008743

De Coning, C., Cloete, F. (2000). Theories and Models for Analysing Public Policy. In Cloete, F. and Wissink, H. (eds). Improving public policy. Pretoria: Van Schaik.

De Ghetto, K. Jacob, R., Gray, M., Kiggundu, N. (2016). The African Union's Agenda 2063: Aspirations, Challenges, and Opportunities for Management Research. *Africa Journal of Management.* 2:1. 93-116. https://doi.org/10.1080/23322373.2015.1127090

de Melo, J., Sorgho, Z. (2019). The Landscape of Rules of Origin across African RECs in a Comparative Perspectives with Suggestions for Harmonization. Fondation pour Les Études et Recherches sur le Développement International, Clermont-Ferrand, France.

De Waal, A. (2002). What's New in the 'New Partnership for Africa Development'?" *International Affairs.* 78(3). 463-75. https://doi.org/10.1111/1468-2346.00261

Deng, F.M. (1996). Sovereignty as Responsibility: Conflict Management in Africa Brookings Institution Press.

Derblom, M., Frisell, E.H., Schmidt, J. (2008). UN-EU-AU Coordination in Peace Operations in Africa [FOI-R--2602--SE]. Stockholm: Swedish Defence Research Agency (FOI).

Dersso, S.A. (2010). The African Union's Mandating Authority and Processes for Deploying an ASF Mission. *African Security Review.* 19(1). 73–86. https://doi.org/10.1080/10246021003736666

Dersso, S.A. (2011). Reflections on the adequacy and potential of the APSA for responding to popular uprisings. in Sourare, I.K., Mesfin, B. (eds), ISS Conference Report: A critical look at the 2011 North African revolution and their implications. ISS. Addis Ababa.

Dersso, S.A. (2012a). The Adequacy of the African Peace and Security Architecture to Deal with Serious Democratic Deficits. *African Security Review.* 21(3). 4-23. https://doi.org/10.1080/10246029.2012.660491

Dersso, S.A. (2013). Annual Review of the Peace Security Council 2012/2013. ISS. Pretoria.

Dersso, S.A. (2014). Annual Review of the Peace and Security Council 2013/2014. ISS. Pretoria.

Desta, M., Gerout, G., MacLeod, J. (2019). Safeguarding the African Continental FreeTrade Area from Externally Imposed Threats of Fragementation". Retrieved from Afronomics Law: http://www.afronomicslaw.org/2019/03/14/safeguarding-the-african-continental-freetradeareafrom-externally-imposed-threats-offragmentation/

Devermont, J.,Olander, E. (2020). COVID-19 is an African Political Crisis as much as a Health and Economic Emergency. Retreived from: htpps://www.csis.org/analysis/COVID-19-african-political-crisis-much-healthand-econmic-emergency

Dexter, L. A. (2006). Elite and Specialized Interviewing. ECPR Press

DfID. (2017). Economic Development Strategy: Prosperity, Poverty, and Meeting Global Challenges. London.

Dibua, J. I. (2010). Africa's Democratic Republics: Transitions from Dictatorships to Democracy. Palgrave Macmillan.

Dinka, T., Kennes, W. (2007). Africa's Regional Integration Arrangements: History and Challenges, ECDPM Discussion Paper No. 74, September.

Dos Santos, T. (1970). The Structure of Dependence. *American Economic Review.* 60(2). 231–36.

Drahos, P., Braithwaite, J. (2002). Information Feudalism: Who Owns the Knowledge Economy? London: Earthscan Publications.

Draper, P., Halleson, D., Alves, P. (2007). SACU, Regional Integration and the Overlap Issue in Southern Africa: From Spaghetti to Cannelloni? *SAIIA Trade Report* (15), SAIIA.

Draper, P., Khumalo, N. (2009). The Future of the Southern African Customs Union (SACU). Trade Negotiations Insight, 8, SAIIA, July.

Draper, P. (2010). Rethinking the European Foundations of Sub-Saharan African Regional Economic Integration: A Political Economy Essay. *OECD Development Centre Working Paper.* 10(293). 1-34.

Draper, P., Lacey, S., Ramkolowan, Y. (2014). Megaregional trade agreements: Implications for the African, Caribbean, and Pacific countries. Occasional Paper No.2/2014. Brussels: European Centre for International Political Economy. https://doi.org/10.2139/ssrn.2984071

Draper, P., Chikura, C., Krogman, H. (2016). Can Rules of Origin in Sub-Saharan Africa be Harmonized? A Political Economy Exploration. Discussion Paper 1/2016. Bonn: Deutsches Institut für Entwicklungspolitik.

Dreyfus, P. (2017). Cote d'Ivoire: Le Brexit, un danger sur le cacao, previent Billon. Paris. Retrieved from www.afrique-sur7.fr, 9 November 2017.

Du Bois, W.E. (1964). The Souls of Black Folk: Essays and Sketches. Longmans. Green and Company Ltd. New York.

Dube, G., Casale, D. (2016). The Implementation of Informal Sector Taxation: Evidence from Selected African Countries. *eJournal of Tax Research*. 14(3). 601–623.

Dunne, T., Schmidt, B. (2008), Realism. In Baylis, J., Smith, S., Owens, P. (eds.), The Globalization of World Politics: An Introduction to International Relations (4th edition). 90-106. Oxford University Press. Oxford.

Dunning, J.H. (1981). Explaining the International Direct Investment Position of Countries: Towards a Dynamic or Developmental Approach. *Weltwirtschaftliches Archive*. 117(1). 30-64. https://doi.org/10.1007/BF02696577

Dunning, J.H. (2000). The Eclectic Paradigm as an Envelope for Economic and Business Theories of MNE Activity. *International Business Review* 9: 163-90. https://doi.org/10.1016/S0969-5931(99)00035-9

Dunning, J.H. (2001). The Eclectic (OLI) Paradigm of International Production: Past, Present and Future. *International Journal of Economics of Business*. 8(2). 173-90. https://doi.org/10.1080/13571510110051441

Dunning, J.H., Lunda, S. (2008). Multinational Enterprises and the Global Economy (2nd ed). Edward Elgar Publishing. Cheltenham.

Durst, M.C. (2016). Improving the Performance of Natural Resource Taxation in Developing Countries. ICTD Working Paper 60. Brighton, UK: International Centre for Tax and Development. https://doi.org/10.2139/ssrn.3120472

Duthie, S.R. (2011). African Integration: Many Challenges, Few Solutions. *Journal of International Organisations Studies*. 1:37-40.

EC. (2002–2007). External and intra-EU trade data. Eurostat pocketbooks, 2009 edition.

EC. (2022). The European Union and Africa: Partners in Trade. Factsheet, European Commission, Brussels. Retrieved from: https://trade.ec.europa.eu/doclib/ docs/2022/february/tradoc_160053.pdf.

ECA, Biannual Report of the Executive Secretary. (1979-1980). What Kind of Africa in the Year 2002? OAU. Addis Ababa.

ECA. (2004). Assessing Regional Integration in Africa (ARIA I). ECA Policy Research Report, United Nations Economic Commission for Africa. Addis Ababa.

ECA. (2005). Economic and Welfare Impacts of the EU-Africa Economic Partnership Agreements. ATPC Work in Progress no. 10. African Trade Policy Centre, ECA. Addis Ababa.

ECA and AU. (2006). Assessing Regional Integration in Africa (ARIA II): Rationalizing Regional Economic Communities. ECA, Addis Ababa.

ECA and AU. (2007). Economic Report on Africa 2007: Accelerating Africa's Development through Diversification. ECA. Addis Ababa.

ECA and AU. (2008). Assessing Regional Integration in Africa (ARIA III): Towards Monetary and Financial Integration in Africa. Economic Commission for Africa, Addis Ababa.

ECA. (2008). North-South FTAs after All? A Comprehensive and Critical Analysis of the Interim Economic Partnership Agreements. ECA. Addis Ababa.

ECA and AU. (2009). Economic Report on Africa 2009: Developing African Agriculture through Regional Value Chains. ECU. Addis Ababa.

ECA. (2010). Report of the Consultation Meeting of Cluster/Subcluster Coordinators and Co-coordinators (AUC and UN) on the Functioning of the Cluster System of the Regional Coordination Mechanism-Africa (RCM-Africa). Addis Ababa. 30 June.

ECA. (2011). Capturing the 21st Century: African Peer Review Mechanism (APRM) – Best Practices and Lessons Learned. ECA. Addis Ababa.

ECA. (2012). Assessing Regional Integration in Africa: Towards an African Continental Free Trade Area. ECA. Addis Ababa.

ECA. (2014). Economic Report on Africa: Dynamic Industrial Policy in Africa. Addis ECA. Addis Ababa.

ECA. (2015). Illicit Financial Flows: Report of the High-Level Panel on Illicit Financial Flows from Africa. ECA. Addis Ababa.

ECA. (2016). Brief for the Office of the Executive Secretary on Regional Integration and the Continental Free Trade Area, prepared by the African Trade Policy Centre. ECA. Addis Ababa.

ECA. (2016). African Economic Outlook, 2016: Macroeconomic Policy and Structural Transformation of African Economies. ECA. Addis Ababa.

ECA, AMDC, AUC. (2016). Optimizing Domestic Revenue Mobilization and Value Addition of Africa's Minerals. ECA. Addis Ababa.

ECA, AUC, AMDC. (2017). Impact of Illicit Financial Flows on Domestic Resource Mobilization: Optimizing Revenues from the Mineral Sector in Africa. ECA. Addis Ababa.

ECA. (2017a). Economic Report on Africa 2017: Urbanisation and Industrialisation for Africa's Transformation. ECA. Addis Ababa.

ECA (2017). Investment Policies and Bilateral Investment Treaties in Africa: Implications for Regional Integration. ECA. Addis Ababa.

ECA. (2018). Assessing Regional Integration in Africa VIII: Bringing the Continental Free Trade Area About. ECA. Addis Ababa.

ECA (2018a). Economic Report on Africa 2019: Fiscal Policy for Financing Sustainable Development in Africa Mauritania Case Study. ECA. Addis Ababa.

ECA (2018b). Economic Report on Africa 2019: Fiscal Policy for Financing Sustainable Development in Africa: Benin Case Study. ECA. Addis Ababa.

ECA (2018c). Economic Report on Africa 2019: Fiscal Policy for Financing Sustainable Development in Africa: Chad Case Study. ECA. Addis Ababa.

ECA (2018d). Economic Report on Africa 2019: Fiscal Policy for Financing Sustainable Development in Africa: Ghana Case Study. ECA. Addis Ababa.

Eckstein, H. (1975). Case Study and Theory in Political Science. In The Handbook of Political Science. Fred I. Greenstein, F.I., Polsby. N.W. (Eds.) 79-138. Addsion-Wesley, Reading, MA.

ECOSOC. (2017). Regional meeting on Innovations for infrastructure development and sustainable industrialization. New York. Retrieved from: https://www.un.org/ecosoc/sites/www.un.org. ecosoc/files/files/en/2017doc/summary_dakar_meeting.pdf.

ECOWAS. (1993). Article 7: Authority of heads of state and government establishment, composition and functions. Retreived from: http://www4.worldbank.org/afr/ssatp/Resources/HTML/legal_review/Annexes/Annexes%20VII/Annexe%20VII-02.pdf (accessed 2 October 2021).

ECOWAS and European Commission. (2004). Road Map for Economic Partnership Agreement Negotiations between West Africa and the European 290 Community. In Meeting of Ministers of Trade On the Economic Partnership Agreement Between West Africa and the European Community. Accra.

ECOWAS Commission. (1993). Economic Community of West African States (ECOWAS) Revised Treaty. ECOWAS. Abuja.

ECOWAS Commission. (2000). Ministers Review Progress On Free Trade Area. ECOWAS. Abuja.

ECOWAS Commission. (2006). Summit Approves Conversion of ECOWAS Secretariat into Commission. In The 29th ordinary Summit of Heads of State and Government of ECOWAS. Niamey.

ECOWAS Commission. (2008). ECOWAS Signs Agreements to Boost Trade, Investment with China. China.

ECOWAS Commission. (2009). ECOWAS Ministers Address Outstanding Issues in Negotiation of EPA with the European Union. ECOWAS. Abuja - Nigeria.

ECOWAS Commission. (2010). ECOWAS-Vision-2020: Towards a Democratic and Prosperous Community. (ed.) ECOWAS Commission- Office of the Vice President. ECOWAS Abuja.

ECOWAS Commission. (2011a). ECOWAS-Vision-2020-Thematictic Pamphlets. ECOWAS Abuja.

ECOWAS Commission. (2011b). West African Trade Ministers Meet on Negotiations with EU. ECOWAS Accra.

ECOWAS Commission. (2013). Economic Issues to Dominate ECOWAS Extraordinary Summit in Dakar.

ECOWAS Commission. (2014). Regional Experts Ready to Usher in the ECOWAS Cet in Early 2015. ECOWAS Accra.

ECOWAS and European Union. (2015). Economic Partnership Agreement Between the West African States, the Economic Community of West African States (ECOWAS) and the West African Economic and Monetary Union (Uemoa), of the one Part, and the European Union and its Member States, of the Other Part. European Commission ECOWAS Commission. Brussels. "ECOWAS : Basic Information." ECOWAS

ECOWAS Commission. (2016). West Africa-EU Prepare for Final Signatures Towards Implementation of the EPA. ECOWAS Abuja.

ECOWAS Commission and GIZ. (2012). Trading In The ECOWAS Free Trade Area ECOWAS Trade. ECOWAS Commission.

ECOWAS Heads of State and Government. (1979). Protocol A/P.1/5/79 Relating to Free Movement of Persons, Residence and Establishment. ECOWAS Dakar.

ECOWAS Heads of State and Government. (2003). Protocol A/P1/1/03 Relating to The Definition of the Concept of Products Originating from Member States of the Economic Community of West African States. ECOWAS Dakar.

ECOWAS Heads of State and Government. (2009). Final Communiqué, 36th Ordinary Session of the Authority of Heads of State and Government. ECOWAS Abuja.

ECOWAS Heads of State and Government. (2014). Forty-Fifth Ordinary Session of the Authority of ECOWAS Heads of State and Government: Final Communique. In Forty-Fifth Ordinary Session of the Authority of ECOWAS Heads of State and Government. Accra-Ghana. 291.

ECOWAS Heads of States and Governments. (1975). Treaty of Economic Community of West African States. Lagos.

ECOWAS Ministerial Monitoring Committee. (2011). Economic Partnership Agreement Negotiations Between West Africa and The European Union: Status of The Negotiations On the Text of the Agreement and The Protocol on EPADP. In Ministerial Monitoring Committee on the EPA Negotiations. Accra ECOWAS Ministers of Trade. 2011. West African Trade Ministers Meet On Negotiations with EU. ECOWAS Accra.

ECOWAS (2007). ECOWAS Annual Report: Consolidation of the Restructured Community Intuitions for the Effectiveness and Accelerated Regional Integration and Development. ECOWAS Abuja.

ECOWAS. (2008). The ECOWAS Conflict Prevention Framework (ECPF). Retrieved from: http://www.comm.ecowas.int/dept/h/h1/en/ecw_conflit_prevention.pdf (accessed 28 October 2021).

ECOWAS. (2017). 2016 ECOWAS Convergence Report. Abuja, Nigeria: ECOWAS. Retrieved from: http://www.ecowas.int/wp-content/uploads/2017/11/2016-Convergence-report_Clean-final final.pdf.

Edozie, R.K. (2021). The African Union and the AfCFTA: Enhancing Africa's Global Position. Routledge.

Egger, P., Larch, M., Staub, K. E., Winkelmann, R. (2011). The Trade Effects of Endogenous Preferential Trade Agreements. *American Economic Journal: Economic Policy*. 3(3). 113–143. https://doi.org/10.1257/pol.3.3.113

EITI. (2016). Progress Report 2016: From Reports to Results. Oslo, EITI International Secretariat. Norway.

Ekengard, A. (2008). The African Union Mission in Sudan (AMIS): Experiences and Lessons Learned [FOI-R--2559--SE]. Swedish Defence Research Agency (FOI). Stockholm.

Elder-Vass, D. (2012). The Reality of Social Construction. Cambridge University Press. Cambridge. https://doi.org/10.1017/CBO9781139169202

Elliot, R., Timulak, L. 2005. Descriptive and interpretive approaches to qualitative research. Retrieved from: http://nideffer.net/classes/GCT_RPI_S14/readings/interpretive.pdf [accessed 20 November 2021].

Elman, C. (2008). Realism. In Williams, P. (ed.), Security Studies: An Introduction. 15-28. Routledge. London and New York.

Elsayid, E. (2016). The Hidden Role of WB and IMF in Developing Countries. Egypt, Malaysia, and Turkey. AV Akadmikerverlag. Saarbrucken.

Engel, U., Porto, J.G. (2010). Africa's New Peace and Security.

Engel, U., Porto, J.G. (2009). The African Union's new Peace and Security Architecture: Toward an Evolving Security Regime? *African Security.* 2(2-3). 82-96. https://doi.org/10.1080/19362200903359774

Erasmus, G. (2015). The Tripartite FTA: Technical Features, Potential and Implementation. TRALAC. 18 June 2015. http://www.tralac.org/discussions/article/7568-the-Tripartite-ftatechnical-features-potential-and-implementation.html.

Erikson, M. (2010). Supporting Democracy in Africa: African Union's use of Targeted Sanctions to deal with Unconstitutional Changes of Government [FOI-R—3000—SE]. Swedish Defence Research Agency (FOI). Stockholm.

Erten, B. (2011). 'North–South Terms-of-trade Trends from 1960 to 2006', *International Review of Applied Economics.* 25(2). 171–84. https://doi.org/10.1080/02692171.2010.483469

Esedebe, P. (1978). The Emergence of Pan African Ideas: In Onigu Otite (ed.).Themes in African Social and Political Thought. Fourth Dimension Publishers. Ibadan.

Esedebe, P., Olisanwuche, P. (1994). Pan-Africanism: The Idea and Movement, 1776-1963. Howard University Press. Washington, DC.

Estevadeordal, A. (2000). Negotiating Preferential Market Access: The Case of the North American Free Trade Agreement. *Journal of World Trade.* 34(1). 141–166. https://doi.org/10.54648/267941

Estevadeordal, A., Suominen, K. (2008). Gatekeepers of Global Commerce: Rules of Origin and International Economic Integration. Inter-American Development Bank. Washington, D.C.

Estevadeordal, A., Suominen, K., Volpe, C. (2013). Regional Trade Agreements: Development Challenges and Policy Options. ICTSD and WEF. Geneva.

Estevadeordal, A., Blyde, J., Harris, J., Volpe, C. (2014). Global Value Chains and Rules of Origin. E15 Initiative. Geneva.

Evans, D. (1975). Unequal Exchange and Economic Policies: Some Implications of the NeoRicardian Critique of the Theory of Comparative Advantage. *IDS Bulletin.* 6(4). 28–52. https://doi.org/10.1111/j.1759-5436.1975.mp6004005.x

Evans, P. (1979). Dependent Development: The Alliance of Multinational, State and Local Capital in Brazil. Princeton University Press. Princeton, NJ. https://doi.org/10.1515/9780691186801

Evans, P. (1994). Class, State and Dependence in East Asia: Lessons for Latin Americanists. In Hall, J.A. (ed.) The State: Critical Concepts. 484–504. Routledge. London.

Evans, P. (1995). Embedded Autonomy: States and Industrial Transformation. Princeton University Press. Princeton, NJ. https://doi.org/10.1515/9781400821723

Evans, P. (2009). From Situations of Dependency to Globalized Social Democracy. *Studies of Comparative International Development,* 44(4). 318–36. https://doi.org/10.1007/s12116-009-9049-9

Evans, G. (2013). Commission Diplomacy. In: Cooper, A.F., Heine, G., Thakur, R. (eds), The Oxford Handbook of Modern Diplomacy. 278-302. Oxford University Press. Oxford. https://doi.org/10.1093/oxfordhb/9780199588862.013.0016

Fearson, J., Wendt, A. (2005). Rationalism v. Constructivism: A Skeptical View. In Carlesnaes, W. Risse, T. Simmons, B. (eds.). Handbook of International Relations. 52-72. Sage. London. https://doi.org/10.4135/9781848608290.n3

Fielding, N., Lee, R. (1998). Approaches to Qualitative Data Analysis. In Computer Analysis and Qualitative Research. Sage. London.

Fierke, K. M. (2006). Constructivism. International Relations Theory: Discipline and Diversity. Dunne, T., Kurki, M., Smith, S. Oxford University Press. Oxford (in press).

Fierke, K. M. (1998). Changing Games, Changing Strategies. Manchester University Press. Manchester.

Fierke, K. M., Wiener, A. (1999). Constructing Institutional Interests, EU and NATO Enlargement. *Journal of European Public Policy.* 6(5). 721-42. https://doi.org/10.1080/135017699343342

Finnemore, M., Sikkink, K. (2001). Taking stock: The constructivist research program in international relations and comparative politics. *Annual Review of Political Science.* 4. 391-416. https://doi.org/10.1146/annurev.polisci.4.1.391

Fischer, A.M. (2009). Putting Aid in its Place: Insights from Early Structuralists on Aid and Balance of Payments and Lessons for Contemporary Aid Debates. *Journal of International Development.* 21. 856–67. https://doi.org/10.1002/jid.1623

Fischer, A.M. (2015). The End of Peripheries? On the Enduring Relevance of Structuralism for Understanding Contemporary Global Development. *Development and Change.* 46(4). 700–32. https://doi.org/10.1111/dech.12180

Fischer, A.M. (2018). Debt and Development in Historical Perspective: The External Constraints of Late Industrialisation Revisited through South Korea and Brazil. *World Economy.* 41. 3359–78. https://doi.org/10.1111/twec.12625

Fischer, A.M. (2019). On the Origins and Legacies of Really Existing Capitalism: In Conversation with Kari Polanyi Levitt. *Development and Change.* 50(2). 542–72. https://doi.org/10.1111/dech.12480

Fofack, H. (2018). Economic Integration in Africa (AfCFTA). *IMF Finance and Development Magazine.* 55(4). 48-51.

Fosu, A., Mold, A. (2008). Gains From Trade: Implications for Labour Market Adjustment and Poverty Reduction in Africa. *Africa Development Review.* 20(1). 20-48. https://doi.org/10.1111/j.1467-8268.2008.00175.x

Fosu, A. K., Ogunleye, E. K. (2018). Neoliberalism and Economic Growth in Contemporary Africa. In Poku, N. and Whitman, J. (eds.). Africa under Neoliberalism. 23-47. Routledge. London. https://doi.org/10.4324/9781315565965-2

Friedman, B. (2002). Globalisation: Stiglitz's case. *New York Review of Books.* 49(13). 48-53.

Frank, A.G. (1967a). The Myth of Feudalism in Capitalism and Underdevelopment in Latin America. In Frank, A.G. Capitalism and Underdevelopment in Latin America: Historical Studies of Chile and Brazil, 221–42. Monthly Review Press. New York.

Frank, A.G. (1967b). Capitalism and Underdevelopment in Latin America: Historical Studies of Chile and Brazil. Monthly Review Press. New York.

Frank, A.G. (1972). Lumpen-bourgeoisie and Lumpen-development: Dependence, Class, and Politics in Latin America. Monthly Review Press. New York.

Frank, A.G. (1974). Dependence is Dead, Long Live Dependence and the Class Struggle: An Answer to Critics. *Latin American Perspectives.* 1(1). 87–106. The Relevance of the Dependency Research Programme 31. https://doi.org/10.1177/0094582X7400100106

Frank, A.G. (1978). World Accumulation 1492–1789. Macmillan. London. https://doi.org/10.1007/978-1-349-15998-7

Franke, B. (2008). Africa's Evolving Security Architecture and the Concept of Multi-layered Security Communities. *Cooperation and Conflict.* 43(3). 313–340. https://doi.org/10.1177/0010836708092839

Franke, B., Esmenjaud, R. 2008. 'Who Owns African Ownership? The Africanisation of Security and its Limits. *South African Journal of International Affairs.* 15(2). 137–158. https://doi.org/10.1080/10220460802614486

Franke, B. (2009). Security Cooperation in Africa: A Reappraisal. First Forum Press. London. https://doi.org/10.1515/9781626371200

Friedman, B. (2002). Globalisation: Stiglitz's case. *New York Review of Books.* 49(13). 48-53.

Gaisford, J. D., Leger, L.A. (2000). Terms-of-Trade Shocks. Labor-Market Adjustment, and Safeguard Measures. *Review of International Economics.* 8(1). 100–112. https://doi.org/10.1111/1467-9396.00208

Ga'le, S.F.B.T. (2002). Shaping a Southern free Sudan. Loa, South Sudan: Loa Catholic Mission Council.

GAO. (2006). Darfur Crisis: Progress in Aid and Peace Monitoring Threatened by Ongoing Violence and operational Challenges [GAO-07-9]. United States Government Accountability Office. Washington, D.C.

Garuda, G. (2000). The Distributional Effects of IMF: A Cross-Country Analysis. *World Development.* 28. 1031-51. https://doi.org/10.1016/S0305-750X(00)00002-4

Gasiorek, M., Winters, L.A.. (2004). What Role for the EPAs in the Caribbean?' *The World Economy.* 27(9). 1335-1362. https://doi.org/10.1111/j.0378-5920.2004.00655.x

Geda, A. Kibret. H. (2002). Regional Economic Integration in Africa: A Review of Problems and Prospects with a Case Study of COMESA. Retreived from: http://doi.org/10.1016/j.apgeog.2003.10.002. https://www.soas.ac.uk/economics/research/workingpapers/file28853.pdf

Geiss, I. (1974). The Pan-African Movement: A History of Pan-Africanism in America, Europe, and Africa. Translated by Ann Keep. Africana. New York.

Gelb, S., (2001). South Africa's Role and Importance in Africa and for the Development of the African Agenda. Paper prepared for the UK Department of International Development. Edge Institute. Braamfontein.

Gelb, S. (2002).Foreign Companies in South Africa: Entry, Performance and Impact. The Edge Institute. [Online]. Retreived from: www.the-edge.org.za.

Gelb, S. (2005). South-South Investment: the Case of Africa. In Teunissen, J.J., Akkerman A. (eds) Africa in the World Economy –the National, Regional and International Challenges. Fondad. The Hague.

Gelb, A. (2010). How Can Donors Create Incentives for Results and Flexibility for Fragile States? A Proposal for IDA. Working Paper 227, Center for Global Development. Washington, DC. https://doi.org/10.2139/ssrn.1817832

George, A.L. (1979). Case Studies and Theory Development: The Method of Structured, Focused Comparison. Diplomacy: New Approaches in History, Theory and Policy: 43-68.

Gerenge, R. (2015). Preventive diplomacy and the AU Panel of the Wise in Africa's Electoral-related Conflicts. Policy Briefing 136. South African Institute of International Affairs (SAIIA). Johannesburg.

Gerout, G., MacLeod, J., Desta, J. (2019). The AfCFTA as Yet Another Experiment towards Continental Integration: Retrospect and Prospect". In Inclusive Trade in Africa: The African Continental Free Trade Area in Comparative Perspective, Luke, D., MacLeod., J (eds). Routledge.London. https://doi.org/10.4324/9780429401121-3

Ghils, A. (2013). How to help women cross-border traders in Africa? Bridges Africa, 15 May.

Ghouri, A. (2018). Served on a Silver Platter? A Review of the UNCTAD Global Action Menu for Investment Facilitation. *Indian Journal of International Law.* 58(1). 139-170. https://doi.org/10.1007/s40901-018-0086-7

Gibb, R. (2006). Rationalisation or Redundancy? Making Eastern and Southern Africa's Regional Trade Units Relevant. The Brenthurst Foundation.

Gibb, R. (2009). Regional Integration and Africa's Development Trajectory: Meta-theories, Expectations and Reality. *Third World Quarterly.* 30(4). Routledge: Taylor and Francis Group. https://doi.org/10.1080/01436590902867136

Gibbons, P. (1996). Zimbabwe 1991-94. Cited in Engberg-Pederson et al., 1997. 349-351. Limits of Adjustment in Africa.

Giles, H., Coupland, N., Coupland, J. (1991). Accommodation Theory: Communication, Context, and Consequence. In Giles, H., Coupland, J., Coupland, N. (eds.), Contexts of Accommodation. 1–68. Cambridge University Press. New York. https://doi.org/10.1017/CBO9780511663673.001

Giles, H., Edwards, J.R. (2010). Attitudes to Language: Past, Present and Future. In Malmkjaer, K. (ed.), The Routledge Linguistics Encyclopedia (3rd edn). 35–40. Routledge. London.

Giles, H., Gasiorek, J. (2017). Parameters of non-accommodation: Refining and Elaborating Communication Accommodation Theory. In Forgas, J., László, J., Orsolya, V., Gillespie, A. (eds.) (2013). International Politics: A New Introduction. Routledge. London.

Gilpin, R. (1987). The Political Economy of International Relations. Yale University Press. Princeton. https://doi.org/10.1515/9781400882779

Gilpin, R. (2001). Global Political Economy: Understanding the International Economic Order. Princeton University Press. Princeton. https://doi.org/10.1515/9781400831272

Giovanni, A.C., Van der Hoeven, R., Mkandawire, T. (eds.) (1992). Africa's Recovery in the 1990s: From Stagnation and Adjustment to Human Development. Macmillan. Basingstoke.

Gomes, P.J. Ngandu, K.Y. (2014). The African Union, preventive diplomacy, mediation and the Panel of the Wise: Review and reflection on the Panel's first six years. *African Security.* 7(3). 181-206. https://doi.org/10.1080/19392206.2014.952582

Goodison, P., Stoneman, C. (2005). Trade Development and Cooperation: Is the EU Helping Africa. Nordiska Afrikainstitutet, Elanders Infologistics Vast. Goteberg.

Goodison, P. (2006a). Regional Integration and EPAs: A case study of the sugar sector in Southern Africa. European Research Office, Brussels.

Gonzalez, L. (2016). Genocide and International Law: A South African Perspective. *International Journal of African Studies.* 4(2). 65-80.

Gottsschalk, K. Schmidt, S. (2004). The African Union and the New Partnership for Africa's Development: Strong Institutions for Weak States? *Internationale Politik und Gesellschaft.* 4(1). 138-158.

Graham, V. (2008). Politics and transformation in a global and local context. *Journal for Contemporary History Volume.* 33(2). 117-135.

Grant, J., Soderbaum, F. (2003). Introduction: the new regionalism in Africa. In the New Regionalism in Africa. Grant, J., Soderbaum F. (eds.). Ashagate. Aldershot.

Grieco, J. (1995). The Maastricht Treaty, Economic and Monetary Union and the Neo-Realist Research Programme. *Review of International Studies.* 21(1). 21-40. https://doi.org/10.1017/S0260210500117504

Griffith, J.S. (2002). Governance of the World Bank. Report prepared for DFID.

Grosfoguel, R. (2000). Developmentalism, Modernity and Dependency. *Theory in Latin America', Neplanta.* 1(2). 347–74.

Grosfoguel, R. (2002). Colonial Difference, Geopolitics of Knowledge and Global Coloniality in the Modern and Colonial Capitalist World-system. *Review.* 25(3). 203-224.

Grosfoguel, R. (2009). A Decolonial Approach to Political Economy. *Kult 6* Special Issue Epistemologies of Transformation. 10(38). 25-27.

Grovogui, S.N. (2011). Looking Beyond Spring for the Season: An African Perspective on the World Order after the Arab Revolt, *Globalisations.* 8(5). 567-572. https://doi.org/10.1080/14747731.2011.622868

Gumede, V. (2021). The African Continental Free Trade Agreement and the Future of Regional Economic Communities. *Journal of Contemporary African Studies.* 39:3. 470-483. https://doi.org/10.10 80/02589001.2020.1852198

Guzzini, S. (2000). A Reconstruction of Constructivism in International Relations. *European Journal of International Relations.* 6(2). 147-182. https://doi.org/10.1177/1354066100006002001

Gyekye, K. (2010). The African Development Dilemma: An Examination of Economic Development in Sub-Saharan Africa. University of Ghana Press.

Haas, E.B. (1958). The Uniting of Europe: Political, Social and Economic Forces, 1950-7. Stevens. London.

Haas, E.B. (1960). Consensus Formation in the Council of Europe. University of California Press. Berkeley.

Haas, E.B. (1961). International Integration: The European and Universal Process. *International Organisation.* (15). 366-92. https://doi. org/10.1017/S0020818300002198

Haas, E.B. (1964). Technocracy, Pluralism and the New Europe. In Graubard, S. (ed.) A New Europe? 62-88. Houghton Mifflin. Boston, MA.

Haas, E.B. (1970). The Study of Regional Integration: Reflections on the Joy and Anguish of Pretheorizing. *International Organisation.* (24). 607-44. https://doi.org/10.1017/S0020818300017495

Haas, E.B. (1971). The study of regional integration". In: L.L. Lindberg and S.A. Scheingold, (eds). Regional Integration: Theory and Research. Cambridge: Harvard University Press.

Haas, E.B. (1976). Turbulent fields and the theory of regional integration', *International Organisation* 30: 173-212. https://doi.org/10.1017/ S0020818300018245

Haas, P. M. 1992. Introduction: Epistemic Communities and International Policy Coordination. *International Organisation.* 46(1). 1-35. https://doi.org/10.1017/S0020818300001442

Haas, E. B. 2001. Does Constructivism Subsume Neo-functionalism? A "Soft Rationalist" Solution. In Christiansen, T. Joergensen K.E., Wiener, A. (eds) The Social Construction of Europe. 22-31 SAGE. London. https://doi.org/10.4135/9781446221105.n2

Haas, E. B. (2004). Introduction: Institutionalism or constructivism? in The Uniting of Europe: Politics, Social and Economic Forces, 1950-1957 (3rd edn.). xiii-lvi. University of Notre Dame Press. Notre Dame.

Haas, M. L. (2005). Ideological Origins of Great Power Politics. Cornell University Press. Ithaca, NY.

Habib, A. (2011). Social and Political Geography of the Tunisian Revolution: the Alfa Grass Revolution. *Review of African Political Economy*. 38:129. 467-479. https://doi.org/10.1080/03056244.2011.604250

Hallward-Driemeier, M., Nayyar G. (2017). Trouble in the Making? The Future of Manufacturing-Led Development. World Bank. Washington, D.C. https://doi.org/10.1596/978-1-4648-1174-6

Hamalengwa, M., Flinterman, C., Dankwa, E.V.O. (eds) 1988. The International Law of Human Rights in Africa: Basic documents and annotated bibliography. Dordrecht: Martinus Nijhoff. https://doi.org/10.1163/9789004638167

Hammersley, M., Atkinson, P. (1983). Ethnography: Principles in Practice 2nd Edition. Routledge. New York.

Hammersley, M. (1992). What's Wrong With Ethnography? London: Routledge.

Hamouda, B, H., Rémi L., Sadni-Jallab, M. (2005). Evaluation de l'accord de partenariat économique entre l'union européenne et le Mali, African Trade Policy Centre, Work in Progress, No 24, UNECA, Addis Ababa.

Hamouda, B, H., Karingi, S., Idrissa Ouedraogo, B., Oulmane, N. Sadni-Jallab. M. (2006). Assessing the consequences of the Economic Partnership Agreement on the Ethiopian economy, African Trade Policy Centre, Work in Progress, No 43, UNECA, Addis Ababa.

Hargreavees, J.D. (1996). Decolonisation in Africa. 2nd Edition. Longman. Harlow.

Harrigan, J., Wang, W.C., Elsayid, H. (2006). The Economic and Political Determinants of IMF and World Bank Lending in the Middle East and North Africa. *World Development*. 34(2). 247-270. https://doi.org/10.1016/j.worlddev.2005.07.016

Hart, J. A. (1985). The New International Economic Order: Conflict and cooperation in North-South economic relations, 1974-1977. 2nd Edition. Houndmills, Basingstoke, Hampshire and Macmillan Press, London.

Hentz, J. (2003). Introduction: New Regionalism and the Theory of Security Studies. In New and Critical Security and Regionalism: Beyond the Nation State, (eds.) Hentz, J., Boas, M. Ashagate. Aldershot.

Herbst, J. (1990). The Structural Adjustment of Politics in Africa. *World Development*. 18(7). 949-958. https://doi.org/10.1016/0305-750X(90)90078-C

Herbst, J. (2000). States and Power in Africa: Comparative Lessons in Authority and Control. Princeton University Press.

Hereros, S. (2019). The Failure of the Free Trade Agreement of the Americas: A Cautionary Tale for the African Continental Free Trade Area. In Inclusive Trade in Africa: The African Continental Free Trade Area in Comparative Perspective (ed.) Lukeand, D. MacLeod J. Routledge. London. https://doi.org/10.4324/9780429401121-4

Hertel, T.W. and Tsigas, M.E. (1997). Structure of the GTAP. In Hertel, T.W. (ed.), Global Trade Analysis: Modeling and Applications. 13 – 73. Cambridge University Press. London. https://doi.org/10.1017/CBO9781139174688.003

Hertel, T.W., Winters, L.A. (2006). Poverty and the WTO: Impacts of the Doha Development Agenda. World Bank. Washington D.C.

Hertel, T. W., Hummels, D., Ivanic, M., Keeney, R. (2007). How Confident Can we be of CGE-based Assessments of Free Trade Agreements. *Economic Modelling*. 24(4). 661-635. https://doi.org/10.1016/j.econmod.2006.12.002

Hertel, T.W., Narayanan, B., McDougall, R.A. (2008). Behavioral Parameters. In: Narayanan, B., Walmsley, T.L. (eds) Global Trade, Assistance, and Production: The GTAP 7 Data Base. Center for Global Trade Analysis, Purdue University. West Lafayette.

Hertel, T. W. (2013). Global Applied General Equilibrium Analysis Using the Global Trade Analysis Project Framework. In Dixon P.B. and Jorgenson, D.W. (eds.), Handbook of Computable General Equilibrium Modeling, Volume 1. 815-876. North Holland. United States. https://doi.org/10.1016/B978-0-444-59568-3.00012-2

Hettne, B., Soderbaum, F. (1998). The new regionalism approach. *Politeia.* Vol. 17(3).

Hettne, B. and Soderbaum, F. (1999). "Theorising the rise of regionness. *New Political Economy.* 5(3). Pre-publication Manuscript. https://doi.org/10.1080/713687778

Hettne, B., Inotai, A., Osvaldo Sunkel, O. (1999). Globalism and the New Regionalism, Volume I. Palgrave Macmillan. London. https://doi.org/10.1007/978-1-349-27268-6

Heywood, A. (2007). Politics. 3rd edition. Basingstoke: Palgrave Macmillan.

Higginbottom, A. (2013) The Political Economy of Foreign Investment in Latin America: Dependency Revisited. *Latin American Perspectives.* 40(190). 184–206. https://doi.org/10.1177/0094582X13479304

Higginbottom, A. (2014). 'Imperialist Rent" in Practice and Theory. *Globalizations.* 11(1). 23–33. https://doi.org/10.1080/14747731.2014.860321

Hinkle, L. (2005). Beyond Cotonou: Economic Partnership Agreements in Africa. In Newfarmer, R. (ed.) Trade, Doha, and Development: A Window into the Issues. 267-80. The World Bank. Washington DC.

Hinkle, L., Newfarmer, R. (2006). Risks and Rewards of Regional Trading Arrangements. In Africa: Economic Partnership Agreements between the European Union and Sub-Saharan Africa. Newfarmer, R (Ed.). Trade and Development: World Bank. Washington.

Hirsch, A. (2021) The African Union's Free Movement of Persons Protocol: Why has it Faltered and how can its Objectives be Achieved? *South African Journal of International Affairs.* 28:4. 497-517. https://doi.org/10.1080/10220461.2021.2007788

Hix, S, (1994). The Study of the European Community: The Challenge to Comparative Politics. *West European Politics.* 17. 1-30. https://doi.org/10.1080/01402389408424999

Hodler, R., Raschky, P. (2015). Regional Favouritism. *The Quarterly Journal of Economics.* 129(2). 995–1033. https://doi.org/10.1093/qje/qju004

Hoffmann, S. (1964). The European Process at Atlantic Cross purposes. *Journal of Common Market Studies.* III(2). 85-101. https://doi.org/10.1111/j.1468-5965.1964.tb01096.x

Hoffmann, S. (1966). Obstinate or Obsolete: the Fate of the Nation State and the Core of Western Europe. *Daedalus.* 95(3). 862–915.

Hoffmann, S. (1995). Obstinate or Obsolete? France, European Integration and the Fate of the Nation-State. In Hoffmann, S. (1995). The European Sisyphus: Essays on Europe 1964-1994. Boulder, CO: Westview Press [reprinted from: Hoffmann, S. 1964. Decline or Renewal? France Since the 1930s, Viking Penguin].

Hoffmann, S. (2003). Obstinate or Obsolete? The Face of the Nation-State and the Case of Western Europe. An Article from *Daedalus*, 95(3), reprinted in The European Union. Readings on the Theory and Practice of European Integration (3rd edition) by Nelsen and Stubb (eds.). Palgrave Macmillan, Hampshire.

Holsti, K.J. (1995). International Politics: Framework for Analysis. 7th Edition. Prentice Hall. London,

Hogwood, B.W., Gunn, L A. (1984). Policy Analysis for the Real World. Oxford University Press. Oxford.

Hooghe, L., Marks, G. (2009). A Post Functionalist Theory of European Integration: from Permissive Consensus to Constraining Dissensus. *British Journal of Political Science.* 39:(1). 1–23. https://doi.org/10.1017/S0007123408000409

Hope, R. K. Sr. (2002). From Crisis to Renewal: Towards a Successful Implementation of the New Partnership for Africa's Development. African Affairs, *The Journal of the Royal African Society.* 101(404). 387-402. https://doi.org/10.1093/afraf/101.404.387

Hope, K.R., (2005). Toward Good Governance and Sustainable Development: The African Peer Review Mechanism. *Governance: An International Journal of Policy, Administration, and Institutions.* 18(2). 283-311. https://doi.org/10.1111/j.1468-0491.2005.00276.x

Hope, A., (2018). What is COMESA's Digital Free Trade Area and Should SADC Have One Too? "TRALAC Trade Brief T18TB01/2018, TRALAC (Trade Law Centre), Stellenbosch, South Africa.

Hopf, T. (1998). The Promise of Constructivism in International Relations Theory. *International Security.* 23 (1). 171-200. https://doi.org/10.1162/isec.23.1.171

Hove, V. S. (2015). An Analysis of How the Online Non-Tariff Barriers Mechanism Facilitates Reporting, Monitoring and Elimination of NTBs in the COMESA, EAC and SADC Region. Research Report, Graduate School of Business, University of Cape Town.

Hull, C., Svensson, E. (2008). African Union Mission in Somalia (AMISOM): Exemplifying African Union Peacekeeping Challenges. Swedish Defence Research Agency (FOI). Stockholm.

ICSID. (2015). ICSID 2015 Annual Report. Washington, DC.

IEG. (2011). The Development Potential of Regional Programs: An Evaluation of World Bank Support of Multicountry Operations. World Bank. Washington, DC.

IISD and UN Environment. (2016). A Sustainability Toolkit for Trade Negotiations: Trade and Investment as Vehicles for Achieving the 2030 Sustainable Development Agenda. IISD. Winnipeg, MB.

ILO. (2010). Newsletter. ILO. London.

ILO., UNCTAD. (2013). Assessment Report: Towards a Continental Free Trade Area in Africa—Modeling Assessment with a Focus on Agriculture.

ILO. (2014). Social Protection Global Policy Trends 2010–2015. From Fiscal Consolidation to Expanding Social Protection: Key to Crisis Recovery, Inclusive Development and Social Justice. Social Protection Policy Papers, Paper 12. Retrieved from: http://www.ilo.org/wcmsp5/groups/public/---dgreports/-dcomm/documents/publication/wcms_319641.pdf.

ILO. (2016). World Employment and Social Outlook 2016: Trends for Youth. Geneva. https://doi.org/10.1002/wow3.76

ILO. (2018). World Employment Social Outlook: Trends for WomenGlobalSnapshot.ILO. Geneva. Retrieved from:https://www.ilo.org/wcmsp5/groups/public/wcms_619577.pdf.

IMF (2008). Regional Economic Outlook, Sub-Saharan Africa. Washington, DC.

IMF (2010). Regional Economic Outlook, Sub-Saharan Africa. Washington, DC.

IMF., World Bank. (2014). Natural Resource Revenue Administration Handbook. International Monetary Fund and World Bank. Washington, DC.

IMF. (2017a). Benin Staff Report for the 2017 Article IV Consultation and First Review under the Extended Credit Facility Arrangement and Request for Modifications of Performance Criteria. IMF. Washington, DC.

IMF. (2018). Regional Economic Outlook for Sub-Saharan Africa: Domestic Revenue Mobilization and Private Investment. IMF. Washington, DC.

IMF. (2018). World Economic Outlook: Challenges to Steady Growth. IMF. Washington, DC.

IMF. (2018a). Fiscal Policy and Development Spending Needs for Achieving Selected SDGs. IMF Fiscal Affairs Department. Washington, DC.

Inotia, A. (1991). Regional Integration Among Developing Countries Revisited. The World Bank, Washington DC. Country Economics Department. April, 1991.

Inglehart, R., Ronald, F., Norris. P. (2016). Trump, Brexit, and the Rise of Populism: Economic Have-Nots and Cultural Backlash. Faculty Research Working Paper Series RWP16-026. Harvard Kennedy School. Cambridge, MA. https://doi.org/10.2139/ssrn.2818659

ISS. (2009b). Consultative Meeting on the Situation in the Republic of Guinea. 30 January 2009, (online). Retrieved from: http://www.iss.co.za/uploads/AUGUINEA30JAN09.PDF, (13 July 2010).

ISS. (2012). Institute for Security Studies, Peace and Security Council Report, Issue 33, April 2012, (online). Retrieved from: http://www.iss.co.za/uploads/No33April_12_WEB.pdf, (22 August 2012).

Ismail, F. (2017). The AGOA Extension and Enhancement Act of 2015, the SA-US AGOA Negotiations and the Future of AGOA. *World Trade Review*. 0:0. 1-18. https://doi.org/10.1017/S147474561600063X

Ismi, A. (2004). Impoverishing a Continent: The World Bank and the IMF in Africa: Canadian Centre for Policy Alternatives.

Issoufou, M., Songwe, V. (2018). Africa's Continental FTA, Boost to Growth, Development. Fortune.

ISS PSC Report. (2014). Tension between AU and ECOWAS. Peace and Security Council Report. Institute for Security Studies, Issue 58.

ITU. (2017). ICT Facts and Figures 2017. ITU. Geneva. Retrieved from: https://www.itu.int/en/ITU-D/Statistics/Documents/facts/ICTFactsFigures2017.pdf

ITC. (2010). Market Access, Transparency and Fairness in Global Trade: Export Impact for Good 2010. United Nations Publication. Sales No. E.11. III.T. Geneva.

ITC. (2015). The Invisible Barriers to Trade: How Businesses Experience Non-tariff Measures. Geneva.

ITC. (2017). SMEs [Small and medium-sized enterprises] Competitiveness Outlook 2017: The Region – A Door to Global Trade. SME Competitiveness Outlook Series (United Nations Publication. Sales No. E.17.III.T.2. Geneva.

Isichei, E. (1997). A History of African Societies to 1870. Cambridge University Press. Cambridge.

Jackson, R.H. Rosberg, C.G. (1982) Personal Rule in Black Africa: Prince, Autocrat, Prophet, Tyrant. University of California Press. Berkely.

Jackson, S. (2006). The United Nations Operation in Burundi (ONUB) – Political and Strategic Lessons Learned. United Nations Peacekeeping Best Practices - Independent External Study.

Jean, P., Seraphin, M. (1998). The economic impact of aid on recipients. Draft prepared for AERC/ODC Collaborative Research Project on Managing the Transition from Aid Dependency in Sub-Saharan Africa, Nairobi. May 21-22, 1998.

Jegede, A. (2009). The African Union Peace and Security Architecture: Can the Panel of the Wise Make a Difference? *African Human Rights Journal.* 9(2). 401-433.

Jibril, A. (2010). Past and Future of UNAMID: Tragic Failure or Glorious Success, HAND Briefing Paper, July. HAND. Kampala.

JICA (2009). The research on the cross-border transport infrastructure: Phase 3. Final Report. Mitsubishi UFJ Research and Consulting Co., Ltd., Tokyo.

Johnson, H. (1967). Economic policies toward less developed countries. The Brookings Institute. Washington DC.

Jordaan, A. (2011). Analysing the Trade Effects of the EU-SA and SADC Trading Agreement: A Panel Data Approach. *South African Journal of Economic and Management Sciences.* 14(2). 229-244. https://doi.org/10.4102/sajems.v14i2.56

Kagame, P. (2017). The Imperative to Strengthen our Union: Report on the Proposed Recommendations for the Institutional Reform of the African Union.

Kakonen, J. (1975). The World Bank: A Bridgehead of Imperialism. *Instant Research on Peace and Violence.* 5(3). 150-164.

Karingi, M. (2005). Economic and Welfare Impacts of the EU-Africa Economic Partnerships Agreements, UNECA, ATPC, Work in Progress. No. 10.

Karingi, S., Mevel. S. (2012). Deepening Regional Integration in Africa: A Computable General Equilibrium Assessment of the Establishment of a Continental Free Trade Area followed by a Continental Customs Union. Paper for presentation at the 15th Global Trade Analysis Project Conference, Geneva, 27–29 June.

Karingi, S., Mevel, S. (2013). Towards a Continental Free Trade Area in Africa: A CGE Modelling Assessment with a Focus on Agriculture. In Shared Harvests: Agriculture, Trade, and Employment. Cheong, D., Jansen, M., Peters, R. (eds.). ILO and United Nations. Geneva.

Karingi, S., Davis, W. (2017). Mimeo. Towards a transformative African Integration Process: Rethinking the Conventional Approaches. Submitted to the *Journal of Africa Economies*, pending decision.

Kasaija, P.A. (2011). The Principle of African Solutions to African Problems Under the Spotlight: The African Union (AU) and the Libya Crisis. Africa Governance Monitoring and Advocacy Project (AfriMAP). Retrieved from: http//www.afrimap.org/English/images/paper/AfriMAP_NAfrica_Kasaija_EN.pdf (Accessed 7 September 2021).

Kasaija, P.A. (2012). The African Union's Notion of 'African Solutions to African Problems' and the Crises in the Cote d'Ivoire (2010-2011) and Libya (2011). *African Journal on Conflict Resolution (ACCORD)*. 12(2). 135-159.

Kasaija. P.A (2013a). The African Union, the Libyan Crisis and the Notion of African solutions to African Problems. *Journal of Contemporary African Studies*. 31(1). 117-138. https://doi.org/10.1080/02589001.2 012.761463

Kasaia, P..A. (2013b). The African Capacity for Immediate Response to Crises (ACIRC) and the Establishment of the African Standby Force (ASF). *Journal of African Union Studies*. 2(1). 63-88.

Kasaija, P. A. (2018). The African Union and Regional Integration in Africa, In Levine, D.H., Dawn, N. (eds.) Political Regional-Building in Africa and Economic Challenges. 143-156. Palgrave Macmillan. Cape Town.

Kasaija, P. A. (2018). The African Union's Peace and Security Architecture (APSA): The African Standby Force (ASF). In Karbo, T. Murithi, T. (eds.), The Africa Union: Autocracy, Diplomacy and Peace-building in Africa. 149-182. I.B. Tauris. London.

Kasaija, P. A. (2018). The African Union's New Funding Mechanism: Self Financing at Last? In Onditi et al. (eds.), Contemporary Africa and the Foreseeable World Order. 77-91. Lexington Books. Lanham.

Katzenstein, P. (1996). Introduction: Alternative Perspectives on National Security. In Katzenstein, P. (ed.), The Culture of National Security: Norms and Identity in World Politics. 1-32. Columbia University Press. New York.

Kay, C. (1989). Latin American Theories of Development and Underdevelopment. Routledge. London. https://doi. org/10.20446/JEP-2414-3197-05-1-3

Kedir, A., Elhiraika, A., Chinzara. Z., Sandjong, D. (2017). Growth and Development Finance Required for Achieving Sustainable Development Goals (SDGs) in Africa. *African Development Review*. 29(1). 15–26. https://doi.org/10.1111/1467-8268.12230

Keet, D. (1999). Globalisation and Regionalisation: Contradictory Tendencies, Counteractive Tactics, or Strategic Possibilities? Braamfontein: Foundation for Global Dialogue.

Kelley, J.R. (2010). The New Diplomacy: Evolution of a Revolution. *Diplomacy and Statecraft.* 21(2). 286-305. https://doi.org/10.1080/09592296.2010.482474

Kelley, K, (2011). How 'Quiet Americans' Helped Defeat Al Shabaab, The East African, Nairobi, 22 August.

Keohane, R.O., Nye, J. (1977). Power and Interdependence: World Politics in Transition. Boston: Little, Brown.

Keohane, R.O. (1988). International institutions: Two approaches. *International Studies Quarterly.* 32. 379-396. https://doi.org/10.2307/2600589

Keohane, R., Martin, L. (1995). The Promise of Institutionalist Theory. *International Security.* 20(1). 39-51. https://doi.org/10.2307/2539214

Khaldun, I. (1967). The Muqaddimah: An Introduction to History, Volume 1. 2nd Edition. Translated by F. Rosenthal. Princeton University Press. Princeton, NJ.

Khadiagala, G. M., Lyons, T. (eds.) (2001). African Foreign Policies: Power and Process Lynne Rienner. Boulder and London. https://doi.org/10.1515/9781685850210

Khadiagala, G.M. (2010). Forging Regional Foreign Policies in SADC: A Framework for Analysis. In Proceedings of the 2009 FOPRISA Annual Conference. Harvey, C. (ed.). Lightbooks Lentswe La Lesedi. Botswana.

Khadiagala, G.M. (2012). The SADCC and its Approaches to African Regionalism. In Region Building in Southern Africa: Progress, Problems and Prospects. Saunders, D. Nagar, D. (eds.). Zed Books. London. https://doi.org/10.5040/9781350222212.ch-001

Khadiagala, G.M. (1994). Allies in Adversity: The Frontline States in Southern Africa Security 1975-1993. Ohio University Press. Athens.

Khadiagala, G. M. (2003). Burundi. In Boulden, J (ed.), Dealing with Conflict in Africa. Palgrave. New York. https://doi.org/10.1057/9781403982209_9

Khadiagala, G. M. (1996). Regionalism and Leadership in African Security. In South Within Africa: Emerging Policy Frameworks. African Center for Development and Strategic Studies. Institute for African Alternatives. Nigeria.

Khadiagala, G. M. (2010). Forging Regional Foreign Policies in SADC: A Framework for Analysis. In Proceedings of the 2009 FOPRISA Annual Conference, REPORT 8.

Khandelwal, P. (2004). COMESA and SADC: Prospects and Challenges for Regional Trade Integration, IMF Working Paper, Policy Development and Review Department. https://doi.org/10.5089/9781451875447.001

Kimaryo, L. (2013). Africa's Rocky Road to Continental Unity. Paper presented at a Workshop to commemorate 50 years of OAU/AU. Moshi University College of Co-operative and Business Studies (MUCCoBS).

Kingston, K.G. (2011). The Impacts of the World Bank and IMF Structural Adjustment Programmes on Africa: The Case Study of Cote D'Ivoire, Senegal, Uganda, Zimbabwe. *Sacha Journal of Policy and Strategic Studies.* 1(2). 110–130.

Kioko, B. (2003). The Right of Intervention Under the African Union Constitutive Act: From Non-Interference to Non-Intervention. IRRC, Vol. 85 No. 852. https://doi.org/10.1017/S0035336100179948

Kitipor, J. (2007). Mercury: Multilateralism and the EU in the Contemporary Global Order (7th EU Framework Programme).

Klingebiel, S. (2007). Peace and Security Policy of the African Union and the Regional Security Mechanism, in Gebrewold-Tochalo, B (ed), Africa and Fortress Europe. Ashgate. Aldershot:

Klingebiel, S., Blohm, T. M., Echle, R., Grunow, K., (2008). Donor Contributions to the Strengthening of the African Peace and Security Architecture. Bonn: German Development Institute (DIE).

Kobbie, J. P. 2009. 'The Role of the African Union in African Peacekeeping Operations [online]. Retreived from <http://www.dtic.mil/cgibin/GetTRDoc?AD=ADA500610&Location=U2&doc=GetTRDoc.pdf> [17 September 09]

Komey, G. K., Osman, A.A., Melakedingel, N. (2013) Operationalizing African-led Solutions in Peace and Security: Case Studies from South Sudan and Somalia. Institute for Peace and Security Studies (IPSS). African-led Solutions (AfSol) Research Project. Addis Ababa. Retrieved from: https://www.academia.edu/7782970/Operationalizing_African_Led_Solutions_in_Peace_and_Security_Case_Studies_From_South_Sudan_and_Somalia [accessed 07 September 2021].

Kongwa, I. (2002). The African Union: Problems and Promises of African Integration in Africa in the Context of North–South relations. 9th Conference of Africanists. *Journal of Institute of African Studies.* RAS, Moscow. 21-23. May

Koslowski, R. (1999). A Constructivist Approach to Understanding the European Union as a Federal Polity. *Journal of European Public Policy.* 6(4). 561-578. https://doi.org/10.1080/135017699343478

Koslowski, R and Kratochwil, F, (994). Understanding Change in International Politics: The Soviet Empire's Demise and the International System. *International Organisation.* 48 (2): 215 - 247. https://doi.org/10.1017/S0020818300028174

Kouassi, N.R. (2007). The Itinerary of the African Integration Process: An Overview of Historical Landmarks*Afri. can Integration Review.* 1(2). 1-30.

Krueger, A.O., Bhagwati. J. (1995). The Dangerous Drift to Preferential Trade Agreements. Washington, DC: American Enterprise Institute Press.

Kvangraven, I.H. (2017). A Dependency Pioneer – Samir Amin', in Kufakurinani U. (ed.) Dialogues on Development – Dependency Theory. 12–17. Institute for New Economic Thinking. New York.

Kvangraven, I.H. (2018). Unpacking and Repackaging Dependency Theory, in I.H. Kvangraven Essays on Global Development, Trade and Finance.1–55. ProQuest LLC. Ann Arbor, MI.

Kvangraven, I.H. (2019). Samir Amin: A Third World Activist and Pioneering Marxist'. *Development and Change.* 51(3). 631–49. https://doi.org/10.1111/dech.12562

Laffer, A.B. (2004). The Laffer Curve: Past, Present and Future. Backgrounder 1765 (June). The Heritage Foundation. Washington, DC.

Lakatos, I. (1978). The Methodology of Scientific Research Programmes: Philosophical Papers Volume 1. Cambridge University Press. Cambridge. https://doi.org/10.1017/CBO9780511621123

Lakner, C., Mahler, D.G., Negre, M., Prydz, E. B. (2022). How Much Does Reducing Inequality Matter for Global Poverty? *The Journal of Economic Inequality.* 20. 559–585. https://doi.org/10.1007/s10888-021-09510-w

Lamberte, M.B. (2004). Part of 1 Programme to Support Regional Economic Cooperation in Asia. High Level Certificate on Asia's Economic Cooperation and Integration. 1-2 July. ADB Headquarters. Manila, Philippines.

Lamy, S.L. (2005). Contemporary Mainstream Approaches: Neo-realism and Neoliberalism. In Baylis, J., Smith, S. (eds.) The Globalization of World Politics: An introduction to international relations (3rd edition). 205-224. Oxford University Press. Oxford.

Lamy, P. (2010).Regional Integration in Africa: Ambitions and Vicissitudes. Policy Paper 43. Jacques Delors Institute.

Landsberg, M. (1979). Export-Led Industrialisation in the Third World; Manufacturing Imperialism. *Review of Radical Political Economics.* 2(4). 50-63. https://doi.org/10.1177/048661347901100405

Landsberg, C. (2004). The Quiet Diplomacy of Liberation: International Politics and South Africa's Transition. Jacana Media. Johannesburg.

Landsberg, C. (2012a). Reflections on the African Union after Decade One: Looking Back in Order to Look Forward. In The African Union at 10 Years. Africa Institute of South Africa. Pretoria.

Landsberg, C. (2012b). Reflection on the African Union after decade one. *Africa Insight*, 42(3). 1-12.

Landsberg, C. (2016). African Solutions for African Problems: Quiet Diplomacy and South Africa's Diplomatic Strategy towards Zimbabwe. *Journal for Contemporary History.* 41(1). 126-148. https://doi.org/10.18820/24150509/jch.v41i1.7

Laprevote, F-C., Can, B., Frisch, S. (2015). Competition Policy within the Context of Free Trade Agreements. Think Piece, E15 Initiative. International Centre for Trade and Sustainable Development. Geneva.

Lawrence, R. (1996). Regionalism, Multilateralism, and Deeper Integration. Brookings Institution. Washington DC.

LeBillon, P. (2011). Extractive Sectors and Illicit Financial Flows: What Role for Revenue Governance Initiatives? U4 Issue 2011 (13). CHR. Michelsen Institute. Bergen, Norway.

Lee, S. (2002). Global Monitor: The International Monetary Fund. *New Political Economy.* 7(2). 283-98. https://doi.org/10.1080/13563460220138880

Legum, C. (1962). Pan-Africanism: A Short Political Guide. Pall Mall Press Ltd. London.

Le Pere, G., Tjønneland. E.N. (2005). Which Way SADC? Advancing Cooperation and Integration in Southern Africa. Institute for Global Dialogue Occasional Paper, no. 50.

Le Pere, G, Vickers, B. (2011). The Dark Side of Globalisation: The African Connection. In Heine, J., Thakur, R. (eds.) The Dark Side of Globalisation. Tokyo: The UN University Press.

Le Pere, G. (2012). AU-EU Security and Governance Cooperation. In Adebajo, A., Whiteman, K. (eds.) The EU and Africa: From Eurafrique to Afro-Europa. Columbia University Press. New York. https://doi.org/10.1057/9780230362154_9

Le Pere, G, Ikome, F. (2012). The Future of Africa's Development and Global Governance. In Lundsgaarde, E. (ed) Africa Toward 2030: Challenges for Development Policy. 224–55. Palgrave Macmillan. London.

Le Pere, G. (2014). The Long Road from Revolution to Democracy in the Middle East and North Africa: Challenges and Threats Facing States in Transition. In Jeenah, N. (ed.) MENA Uprisings and Transformations and their Impact on Africa. The Afro-Middle East Centre. Johannesburg.

Lesser, C., Moisé-Leeman, E. (2009). Informal Cross-border Trade and Trade Facilitation Reform in sub-Saharan Africa. Trade Policy Paper No. 86. Organisation for Economic Co-operation and Development. Paris.

Lieberman, D.E., Bramble, D.M., Raichlen, D.A., Shea, J.J. (2007). The Evolution of Endurance Running and the Tyranny of Ethnography: A reply to Pickering and Bunn. *Journal of Human Evolution.* 53:4. 34-7. https://doi.org/10.1016/j.jhevol.2007.07.002

Lieberman, E.S. 2005. 'Nested Analysis as a Mixed-Method Strategy for Comparative Research.' *American Political Science Review* 99(03): 435-452. https://doi.org/10.1017/S0003055405051762

Limão, N., Anthony, J. Venables, A.J., (2000). Infrastructure, geographical disadvantage, transport costs and trade. London: London School of Economics. (20 December). https://doi.org/10.1596/17438

Lindberg, L. (1963). The Political Dynamics of European Integration. Princeton University Press. Stanford, CA.

Lindberg, L., Scheingold, S. (1970). Europe's Would-Be Polity. Prentice Hall. Englewood Cliffs. NJ.

Linklater, S (2010). The English School Conception of International Society: Reflections on Western and non-Western perspectives, *Ritsumeikan Annual Review of International Studies*. 9. 1-13.

Lloyd, P.J. (2002). Facilitating Free Movement of People in an Australia-US FTA. Paper prepared for "The impact of an Australia US free trade agreement: foreign policy challenges and economic opportunities" conference held at the National Press Club Canberra, August 29–30.

Lor, P. (2011). Preparing for Research: Metatheoretical Considerations. International & Comparative Librarianship-Encyclopaedia of Library and Information Sciences, 4–15.

Lotze, W. (2011). A Tale of Two Councils, the African Union, the United Nations and the Protection of Civilians in Cote d'Ivoire. *Global Responsibility to Protect*. 3. 365-375. https://doi.org/10.1163/187598411X589617

Lotze, W. (2016). Mission Support for African Peace Operations. In de Coning, C., Gelot, L., Karlsrud, J. (eds.), The Future of African Peace Operations: From the Janjaweed to Boko Haram. 76–89. Zed Books. London. https://doi.org/10.5040/9781350251038.ch-006

Lotze, W., Williams, P.D. (2016). The Surge to Stabilize: Lessons for the UN from the AU's Experience in Somalia. International Peace Institute. New York.

Love, J.L. (1980). Raúl Prebisch and the Origins of the Doctrine of Unequal Exchange. *Latin American Research Review*. 15(3). 45–72. https://doi.org/10.1017/S0023879100033100

Makinda, S. M., Okumu, F.W. (2007). The African Union: Challenges of Globalization, Security, and Governance. Routledge. New York. https://doi.org/10.4324/9780203940112

Makinda, S.M. Okumu, F.W. (2008). The African Union: Challenges of Globalization, Security, and Governance. Routledge. London. https://doi.org/10.4324/9780203940112

Maloka, E. (2002). Nepad and Africa's Future. *Africa Insight.* 32(2). 65-67. https://doi.org/10.4314/ai.v32i2.22290

Marquette, C. (1997). "Current Poverty, Structural Adjustment, and Drought in Zimbabwe. *World Development.* 25:7. https://doi. org/10.1016/S0305-750X(97)00019-3

Martin, G. (1992). African Regional Cooperation and Integration: Achievements, Problems and Prospects. In Seidman, A., Anang, F. (eds) Twenty-First Century Africa: Towards a New Vision for Self Sustainable Development. Trenton: Africa World Press.

Marsh, R. (2013). Understanding Africa and the Events that Shaped its Destiny. LAPA. Johannesburg.

Marston, S., Jones III J., Woodward, K. (2005). Human Geography Without Scale, Transitions of the Institute of British Geographers. *New Series.* 30. 416-432. https://doi.org/10.1111/j.1475-5661.2005.00180.x

Marx, K. (1967_. Capital, Vol. I. International Publishers. New York.

Mashele, P. (2006). The New Partnership for Africa's Development – Four Years of a Promising Attempt or Hollow Optimism? ISS Occasional Paper 125. February 2006.

Mathoho, M. (2003). An African Peer Review Mechanism: a Panacea for Africa. Some reflections on African development strategies in the 21st Century, 17 governance challenges? Policy Brief 29. Center for Policy Studies. Johannesburg. South Africa.

Matlosa, M. (1996). The Role of the State in Development in the SADC: Does NEPAD Provide a New Paradigm? SAPES Trust, Harare.

Matlosa, K., Pule N. (1995). The Military in Lesotho. *African Security Review.* 10(2). 34-76. https://doi.org/10.1080/10246029.2001.9627937

Mattli, W. (1999). The Logic of Regional Integration: Europe and Beyond. Cambridge University Press. Cambridge. https://doi.org/10.1017/CBO9780511756238

Maur, J. C., Shepherd, B. (2015). Connecting Food Staples and Input Markets in West Africa. World Bank. Washington, DC. https://doi.org/10.1596/22276

Maystadt, J.-F., De Luca, G., Sekeris, P.G., Ulimwengu, J., Folledo, R. (2014). Mineral Resources and Conflicts in DRC: A Case of Ecological Fallacy?" *Oxford Economic Papers.* 66(3). 721–749. https://doi.org/10.1093/oep/gpt037

Mbeki, T. (2012). Is Africa There for the Taking? *New African.* (515). 70-76. https://doi.org/10.2307/j.ctv125jpdf.98

Mbengue, M.M. (2018). Facilitating Investment for Sustainable Development: It Matters for Africa. Columbia FDI Perspectives on Topical Foreign Direct Investment Issues 222. Columbia Center on Sustainable Investment, New York.

Mbengue, M.M., Schacherer. S. (2017). The Africanisation of International Investment Law: The Pan-African Investment Code and the Reform of the International Investment Regime. *Journal of World Investment and Trade* 18(3). 414-448. https://doi.org/10.1163/22119000-12340047

McAllister, R. (1997). From EC to EU, a Historical and Political Survey. Routledge. London. https://doi.org/10.1007/978-1-349-15196-7_2

McDonald, M. (2008). Constructivism. In Williams, P. (ed.), Security Studies: An Introduction. 59-72. Routledge. London and New York.

McGowan, P. (2003). African Military Coups d'etat, 1956-2001: Frequency, Trends and Distribution, *Journal of Modern African Studies.* 41(3). 339-370. https://doi.org/10.1017/S0022278X0300435X

McKinsey Global Institute. (2016). Lions on the Move II: Realizing the Potential of Africa's Economies. McKinsey and Company. Available at http://www.mckinsey.com/ global-themes/ middle-east-and-africa/lions-on-the-move-realizing-the-potentialof-africas-economies.

McLure, J. (2011). The Troubled Horn of Africa: Can the War-Torn Region be Stabilized?' In Issues in Peace and Conflict Studies: Selections From CQ Researcher. 231-258. Sage Publications. London. https://doi.org/10.4135/9781483349244.n9

McMichael, P. (2012). Development and Social Change: A Global Perspective. Sage Publications. Thousand Oaks, California.

Melendez-Ortiz, R. (2014). The Impact of Mega-regionals: Discriminatory and Multilateralizing Potential of TPP and TTIP Provisions. In WEF (ed.), Mega-regional Trade Agreements: Game-Changers or Costly Distractions for the World Trading System? WEF. Geneva.

Melitz, M.J. (2003). The Impact of Trade on Intra-industry Reallocations and Aggregate Industry Productivity. *Econometrica.* 71(6). 1695–1725. https://doi.org/10.1111/1468-0262.00467

Melitz, M.J., Ottaviano, G.I.P. (2008). Market Size, Trade, and Productivity. *The Review of Economic Studies.* 75. 295–316. https://doi. org/10.1111/j.1467-937X.2007.00463.x

Melitz, M.J. Redding, S.J. (2015). New Trade Models, New Welfare Implications. *American Economic Review.* 105. 1105–46. https:// doi.org/10.1257/aer.20130351

Mendez-Parra, M., te Velde, D.W., Winters, L.A. (2016). The Impact of the UK's Post-Brexit Trade Policy on Development. London. ODI, UK Trade Policy Observatory (UKTPO).

Mendez-Parra, M., Papadavid, P., te Velde, D.W. (2016). Brexit and Development: How will Developing Countries be Affected? Briefing Paper. Overseas Development Institute. London. www. odi.org/publications/10480-brexit-and-developmenthowwill-developing-countries-be-affected.

Mengisteab, K. (1995). Beyond Economic Liberalization in Africa: Structural Adjustment and Alternatives. Zed Books. London.

Mengisteab, K.(1996). Globalisation and Autocentricity in Africa's Development in the Twenty First Century. Africa World Press. New Jersey.

Mevel, S., Karingi S. (2012). Deepening Regional Integration in Africa: A Computable General Equilibrium Assessment of the Establishment of a Continental Free Trade Area Followed by a Continental Customs Union. Presented at the seventh African Economic Conference. 30 October to 2 November. Kigali.

Mevel S, Ofa S.V., Karingi, S. (2013). Quantifying Illicit Financial Flows from Africa Through Trade Mispricing and Assessing their Incidence on African Economies. Presented at the sixteenth Global Trade Analysis Project conference. 12–14 June.

Mikic, M., Shang, W. (2019). ASEAN at 50 and Beyond. In Luke, D. MacLeod, J. (eds.), Inclusive Trade in Africa: The African Continental Free Trade Area in Comparative Perspective. Routledge. London. https://doi.org/10.4324/9780429401121-5

Milner, C. (2006). An assessment of the Overall Implementation and Adjustment Costs for the ACP Countries of Economic Partnership Agreements with the EU. In Grynberg, R., Clarke, A. (2006). The European Development Fund and Economic Partnership Agreements, Commonwealth Secretariat Economic Affairs Division.

Miller, T. (2017). China's Asian Dream: Empire Building along the New Silk Road. Zed Books. London. https://doi.org/10.5040/9781350219120

Mistry, P. S. (2000). Africa's Record of Regional Co-operation and Integration. *African Affairs, The Journal of the Royal African Society.* 99(397). 553–573. https://doi.org/10.1093/afraf/99.397.553

Mitrany, D. (1943). A Working Peace System – An Argument for the Functional Development of International Organisations (4th edition). National Peace Council. London.

Mitrany, D. (1966). A Working Peace System. Chicago.

Mitrany, D. (1968). The Prospect of Integration: Federal or Functional? In Nye J. (ed.), International Regionalism. Little, Brown and Company. Boston, MA.

Mkandawire, T., Soludo, C. (1999). Our Continent, Our Future: African Perspectives on Structural Adjustment. Africa World Press. Trenton, NJ and Asmara, Eritrea.

Mkandawire, T. (2004). Thinking About Development States in Africa. *Cambridge Journal of Economics Vol.* 25. 289–313. https://doi.org/10.1093/cje/25.3.289

Mkandawire, T. (2011). The African State in a Global Era: A Structural Analysis of the Crisis of Development. Palgrave Macmillan.

Mkandawire, T. (2012). The African Union and the African State. African Development Bank.

Mkapa, B. (2016). EPA has Never Made Much Sense for Tanzania. Daily News. Retrieved from: http://dailynews.co.tz/index.php/home-news/52107-epa-has-never-made-much-sense-fortanzania#. V7K2IvSx76k.twitter. 28 July.

Uniting Africa

Mohammed, A. (2008). Toward an Effective African Union: Participation, Institutions, and Leadership. In Adejumobi, S., Olukoshi, A. (eds), The African Union and New Strategies for Development in Africa. Cambria Press. Amherst, NY, USA.

Mokeona, S.S. (2003). Deputy Director General, NEPAD Secretariat and Member of the NEPAD Steering Committee. Midrand, South Africa.

Mold, A. (2006). Tackling the Commodity Price Problem – New Proposals and Revisiting Old Solutions. In Meyn, M. African Development Yearbook 2006, Institute for World Economics and International Management (IWIM), University of Bremen.

Mold, A., Mukwaya, R. (2015). The Effects of the Tripartite Free Trade Area: Towards a New Economic Geography in Southern Eastern and Northern Africa. Centre for Research in Economic Development and International Trade, University of Nottingham Research Paper, 15 (04). 1-38.

Mold, A. (2017). Much ado about nothing? The Impact of Brexit on the East African Community. Forthcoming.

Mold, A., Mveyange, A. (2020).The Impact of the COVID-19 Crisis on Trade: Recent Evidence from East Africa.

Möller, B. (2009). Africa's Sub-regional Organisations: Seamless Web or Patchwork?", Crisis States Working Papers Series No. 2, August 2009. Retrieved from: http://eprints.lse.ac.uk/28486/1/ WP56.2MollerRO.pdf, (2 September,2010).

Monnet, J. (1997). Muistelmat [Mémoires]. Edita, Helsinki.

Moore, M., Prichard, W. Fjeldstad, O.H. (2018). Taxing Africa: Coercion, Reform and Development. Zed Press (London) and the International Africa Institute. https://doi. org/10.5040/9781350222861

Moravcsik, A. (1991). Negotiating the Single European Act. In Keohane and Hoffmann (eds.) The New European Community. Decision- making and Institutional Change 41-84. Westview Press, Boulder. https://doi.org/10.4324/9780429496189-2

Moravcsik, A. (1993). Preferences and Power in the European Community: A Liberal Intergovernmental Approach. *Journal of Common Market* *Studies.* 31(4). 473-524. https://doi.org/10.1111/j.1468-5965.1993. tb00477.x

442

Moravcsik, A. (1995). Liberal Intergovernmentalism and Integration: A Rejoinder. *Journal of Common Market Studies.* 33(4). 611-628. https://doi.org/10.1111/j.1468-5965.1995.tb00554.x

Moravcsik, A. (1998). The Choice for Europe. Social Purpose & State Power from Messina to Maastricht. UCL Press Limited. London.

Moravcsik, A. (1999). Is Something Rotten in the State of Denmark? Constructivism and European integration? *Journal of European Public Policy.* (6:6). 669-681. https://doi.org/10.1080/135017699343531

Morse, J.M. (2003). Principles of Mixed Methods and Multimethod Research Designs. In Akashorri A., Teddlie, C. (eds). Handbook of Mixed Methods in Social and Behavioural Research. Sage Publications. Thousand Oaks, CA.

Moyo, D. (2009). Dead Aid: Why Aid is Not Working and How There is a Better Way for Africa. Farrar, Straus, and Giroux.

Mpyisi, K. (2009). Policy Paper: How EU Support of the African Peace and Security Architecture Impacts Democracy Building and Human Security Enhancement in Africa. Stockholm: International Institute for Democracy and Electoral Assistance.

Muchena, D.T. (2006). The China Factor in Southern Africa. *Openspace.* 1(4). 22-26.

Muchie, M. (2003). A Theory of a Pan-African Unification-Nation for the Structural Transformation of Africa. Paper prepared for CODESRIA's 30th Anniversary celebrations, Dakar, Senegal, 8-1 December 2003. Retreived from: http://www.codesria.org/Links/conferences/anniversary-dakar/muchie.pdf. Accessed on 29 September 2021.

Mueller, H. (2004(. Arguing, Bargaining, and All That. Reflections on the Relationship of Communicative Action and Rationalist Theory in Analysing International Negotiation. *European Journal of International Relations.* 10(3). 395-495. https://doi.org/10.1177/1354066104045542

Mukwaya, R., Mold, A. (2014). Effect of the COMESA-SADC-EAC FTA on the East African Region: Towards a New Economic Geography. 2014 Conference Paper, 17th Annual Conference on Global Economic Analysis, Dakar, Senegal.

Mullins, P. (2010). International Tax Issues for the Resources Sector. In Daniel, P., Keen, M., McPherson, C. (eds.), The Taxation of Petroleum and Minerals: Principles, Problems and Practice. Routledge. New York.

Murray, C. (1998) Changing Livelihoods in Qwaqwa: Research Questions and Methods of Study in Multiple Livelihoods and Social Change. Working Paper No. 1. Institute for Development Policy and Management, Manchester University, Manchester.

Murithi, T. (2005). The African Union: Pan-Africanism, Peacebuilding and Development. Ashgate. Aldershot.

Murithi, T. (2007). Institutionalising Pan-Africanism. Transforming African Union Values and Principles into Policy and Practice. ISS Paper 143.

Murithi, T. (2008). The African Union and its Institutions, Auckland Park: Centre for Conflict Resolution.

Murithi, T., Gueli, R. (2008). The African Union's Evolving Role in Peace Operations: the African Union Mission in Burundi, the African Union Mission in Sudan and the African Union Mission in Somalia. *African Security Review*. 17(1). 70–82. https://doi.org/10.1080/10246029.2008.9627460

Murithi, T. (2009). The African Union's Transition from Non-Intervention to Non Indifference: An Ad Hoc Approach to the Responsibility to Protect? Independent Publishers Group 2009. 90-106.

Murithi, T., Hallelujah, L. (eds.) 2012. The African Union Peace and Security Council: a Five Year Appraisal. Institute for Security Studies (ISS), Monograph Number 187.

Murithi, T. (2014). The Role of the African Peace and Security Architecture in Implementation of Article 4(h). In Kuwali, D. Viljoen, F. (eds), Africa and the Responsibility to Protect. Article 4(h) of the African Union Constitutive Act. Routledge. Oxford.

Mutanda, D., (2017). What Makes Terrorism Tick in Africa? Evidence from Al-Shabaab and Boko Haram. *Jadavpur Journal of International Relations*. 21(1). 20-40. https://doi.org/10.1177/0973598417706590

Mutasa, C. (2018). The African Union's Socioeconomic Challenges. In Karbo. T. Murithi, T. (eds.) The African Union. Autocracy, Diplomacy and Peacebuilding in Africa. Tauris: London and New York. https://doi.org/10.5040/9781350988422.ch-008

Mwanabiningo, N. (2015). Deriving Maximum Benefit from Small-Scale Cross Border Trade between DRC and Rwanda. London: International Alert.

Mwega, F. (2005). Implications of Economic Partnership Agreement Negotiations for Regional Integration for the East African Countries: the Case of Kenya, University of Nairobi.

Nabudere, D.W. (2001). The African Renaissance in the Age of Globalisation. *African Journal of Political Science.* 6(2). 11-27. https://doi.org/10.4314/ajps.v6i2.27321

Nagar, D. (2012). Economic Integration. In Dzinesa, S., Nagar, D. (eds.), Region-Building in Southern Africa: Progress, Problems, and Prospects. Zed Books. London.

Nagar, D. "(2013). Towards a New Pax Africana. The Politics of Peacekeeping in Africa. CCR seminar paper. (August).

Nagar, D., Mutasa, C. (2018). Africa and The World: Bilateral and Multilateral International Diplomacy. Springer International Publishing. Switzerland.

Nagar, D. (2020). Politics and Pan-Africanism: Diplomacy, Regional Economies and Peace-Building in Contemporary Africa. Bloomsbury Publishing. New York. https://doi.org/10.5040/9781788318754

Nagar, D. (2022). Challenging the United Nations Peace and Security Agenda in Africa. Springer International Publishing. Switzerland. https://doi.org/10.1007/978-3-030-83523-1

Naiman, R., Watkins, N. (1999). A Survey of IMF Structural Adjustment in Africa: Growth, Social Spending and Debt Relief. Centre for Economic and Policy Research (CEPR). 4-7.

Nakamura, R., Smallwood, F. (1980). The Policy Implementation. 12–18. St. Martin's. New York.

Nanjira, D.D. (2010). African Foreign Policy and Diplomacy: From Antiquity to the 21st century. Volume 2. Praeger. Santa Barbara CA. https://doi.org/10.5040/9798400608117

Narayanan, B., Aguiar, A., McDougall, R. (eds) (2012). Global Trade, Assistance, and Production: The GTAP 8 Database. Centre for Global Trade Analysis, Purdue University. West Lafayette.

Nabudere, D. (2002). NEPAD: Historical Background and its Prospects. Paper presented at 'Africa Forum for Envisioning Africa Focus on NEPAD', Nairobi 26-29 April 2002. http://www.eldis.org. Accessed on 04 June 2021

Nayyar, D. (2013). Catch-Up: Developing Countries in the World Economy. Oxford University Press. Oxford. https://doi.org/10.1093/acprof:oso/9780199652983.001.0001

Ncube, M. (2015). China the Biggest External Risk to Africa's Growth Outlook. Terence Creamer Media. 3 September.

Ncube, C. (2016). Intellectual Property Policy, Law and Administration in Africa: Exploring Continental and Sub-regional Co-operation. Routledge. https://doi.org/10.4324/9781315743714

Ncube, C., Schonwetter, T., de Beer, J., Oguamanam, C. (2017). Intellectual Property Rights and Innovation: Assessing Regional Integration in Africa (ARIA VIII). Open AIR Working Paper 5. https://doi.org/10.2139/ssrn.3078997

Ndaguba, E A. (2016). Financing Regional Peace and Security in Africa: A Critical Analysis of the Southern African Development Community Standby Force (Master Dissertation). UFH Library. South Africa.

Ndaguba, E.A., Okonkwo, C. (2017). Feasibility of Funding Peace Operation in Africa: Understanding the challenges of Southern African Development Community Standby force (SADCSF). Africa Review, 9(2). 140−153. https://doi.org/10.1080/09744053.2017.1329807

Ndlovu-Gatsheni, S.J. (2001). Imperial Hypocrisy, Settler Colonial Double Standards and Denial of Human Rights to Africans in Colonial Zimbabwe. In Bhebe, N., Ranger, T (eds), The Historical Dimensions of Democracy and Human Rights in Zimbabwe: Volume One: Pre-Colonial and Colonial Legacies. University of Zimbabwe Publications. Harare.

Ndlovu-Gatsheni, S.J. (2012a). The African Neo-Colonised World. Dakar: CODESRIA Books. https://doi.org/10.1093/acref/9780195301731.013.49596

Ndlovu-Gatsheni, S.J. (2012b). Fiftieth Anniversary of Decolonization in Africa: A Moment of Celebration or Critical Reflection? *Third World Quarterly*. 33(1). 71-89. https://doi.org/10.1080/01436597.2012.627236

Ndlovu-Gatsheni, S. (2013a). Coloniality of Power in Postcolonial Africa: Myth of Decolonisation. CODESRIA Books. Dakar, Senegal.

Ndlovu-Gatsheni, S. (2013b). Empire, Global Coloniality and African Subjectivity. Berghahn Books. New York and Oxford. https://doi.org/10.3167/9780857459510

Ndlovu-Gatsheni, S. (2013c) The Entrapment of Africa within the Global Colonial Matrices of Power: Eurocentrism, Coloniality, and Deimperialization in the Twenty first Century. *Journal of Developing Societies*. 29(4), 331–353. https://doi.org/10.1177/0169796X13503195.

Ndlovu-Gatsheni, S. (2007). Tracking the Historical Roots of Post-Apartheid Citizenship Problems: The Native Club, Restless Natives, Panicking Settlers and the Politics of Nativism in South Africa. African Studies Centre. Leiden.

Ndlovu-Gatsheni, S. (2008). Black Republican Tradition, Nativism and Populist Politics in South Africa. *Transformation*. 68(1). 53–86. https://doi.org/10.1353/trn.0.0013

Ndlovu-Gatsheni, S. (2012). Beyond the Equator There Are No Sins: Coloniality and Violence in Africa. *Journal of Developing Societies*. 28(4). 419–440.https://doi.org/10.1177/0169796X12463143

Ndlovu-Gatsheni, S. (2013a) Coloniality of Power in Postcolonial Africa: Myths of Decolonisation. Council for the Development of Social Science Research in Africa. Dakar, Senegal. https://doi.org/10.1017/CBO9781107415324.004

Ndlovu-Gatsheni, S. (2013b). Why Decoloniality in the 21st Century?' *The Thinker*. 48. 10–13.

Ndlovu-Gatsheni, S. (2015). Decoloniality as the Future of Africa. History Compass.13(10). 485–496.https://doi.org/10.1111/hic3.12264.

Ndlovu-Gatsheni, S. (2016) The Decolonial Mandela: Peace, Justice and the Politics of Life. Berghahn Books. New York and Oxford. https://doi.org/10.2307/j.ctvgs0c16

Ndlovu-Gatsheni, S.J. (2018). Introduction: Seek Ye Epistemic Freedom First. In NdlovuGatsheni, S.J. (ed.), Epistemic Freedom in Africa: Deprovincialization and Decolonization. 1–41. Routledge. London and New York. https://doi.org/10.4324/9780429492204-1

Ndonga, D., Laryea, E., Murendere, C. (2020) Assessing the Potential Impact of the African Continental Free Trade Area on Least Developed Countries: A Case Study of Malawi. *Journal of Southern African Studies.* 46:4. 773-792. https://doi.org/10.1080/03057070.2020.1767888

Ndulu, B.J., O'Connell, S.A. (1999). Governance and Growth in Sub-Saharan Africa. *Journal of Economic Perspectives.* 13(3). 41–66. https://doi.org/10.1257/jep.13.3.41

Ndulu, B. (2007). Challenges of African growth. World Bank. https://doi.org/10.1596/978-0-8213-6882-4

Ndulu, B., O'Connell, S.A., Azam, J-P., Collier, P., Soludo, C., Bates, R.H., Fosu, A.K., Gunning, J.W., Nijinkeu, D. (eds.) (2008). The Political Economy of Growth in Africa: 1960-2000, Volume 1. Cambridge University Press. Cambridge. (for African Economic Research Consortium).

Ndulu, B, O'Connell, S.A., Azam, J-P., Bates, R.H., Fosu, A.K., Gunning, J.W., Nijinkeu, D. (eds.) (2008). The Political Economy of Growth in Africa: 1960-2000, Volume 2, Country Case Studies. Cambridge University Press. Cambridge. (for African Economic Research Consortium).

Ndulo, M.B. (2009). The United Nations Responses to the Sexual Abuse and Exploitation of Women and Girls by Peacekeepers during Peacekeeping Missions. *Berkeley Journal of International Law.* 27. 127–61.

Ndzendze, B., Monyae, D. (2019). China's Belt and Road Initiative: Linkages with the African Union's Agenda 2063 in Historical Perspective. *Transnational Corporation Review.* 11(1) 38-49. https://doi.org/10.1080/19186444.2019.1578160

Neocosmos, M. (2010). Democracy, Citizenship, and the Politics of Belonging in Africa. Palgrave Macmillan.

NEPAD. (2001). October. The Reader's Digest Oxford Wordfinder. 1993. Oxford University Press. Oxford. 1129.

NEPAD. (2001). October 2001.

NEPAD. (2001). A Historical Overview of the New Partnership for Africa's Development (NEPAD). NEPAD Background Document (November).

NEPAD. (2002). October 2002.

NEPAD. (2002). Initial Action Plan, July 2002.

NEPAD. (2002). Declaration on Democracy, Political, Economic and Corporate Governance. AHG/235(XXXVIII) Annex 1 (18 June 2002). 8-17.

NEPAD (2005). Implementing the Comprehensive African Agriculture Development Programme and Restoring Food Security in Africa: The Roadmap. Midrand, South Africa.

NEPAD (2017). Annual Results Based Report (2017): Fast Tracking the Implementation of Africa's Development Agenda. Mirand, South Africa.

Ngoma, N. (2004). Coups and Coup Attempts in Africa: Is There a Missing Link, *African Security Review*. 13(3). 85-94. https://doi.org/10.1080/10246029.2004.9627307

Nguyen, M., Ananthalakshmi, A. (2017). TPP trade deal members seek to move ahead without U.S. Reuters. 19 May.

Nhara, A. (2006). SADC and COMESA Integration: Separating Myth from Reality. Trade and Development Studies Centre, Harare, Zimbabwe.

Nicholson, M. (2002). The Global Political Economy. In Nicholson M. (ed.). International Relations: A Concise Introduction. Palgrave. Basingstoke.

Niemann, A. (1998). The PHARE Programme and the Concept of Spillover: Neo-Functionalism in the Making. *Journal of European Public Policy* (5). 428-46. https://doi.org/10.1080/135017698343901

Niemann, A. (2000). The Internal and External Dimensions of European Union Decision-Making: Developing and Testing a Revised Neo-functionalist Framework, Ph.D. Thesis, University of Cambridge.

Niemann, A. (2004). From Pre-theory to Theory? Developing a Revised Neo-functionalist Framework for Explaining EU Decision-making Outcomes. Dresdner Arbeitspapiere Internationale Beziehungen, No. 11.

Niemann, A. (2006). Explaining decisions in the European Union, Cambridge University Press. Cambridge. https://doi.org/10.1017/CBO9780511492044

Niemann, A., Schmitter, P. (2009). Neo-functionalism. In: Wiener, A., Diez, T. (eds), Theories of European Integration (2nd edition). Oxford University Press.

Niemann, A., Demosthenes. I. (2015). European economic integration in times of crisis: a case of neo-functionalism? *Journal of European Public Policy.* 22:(2). 196-218. https://doi.org/10.1080/13501763.2014.994021

Nkrumah, K. (1957). Ghana: The Autobiography of Kwame Nkrumah. Thomas Nelson. Edinburgh.

Nkrumah, K. (1961). I Speak Freedom. Panaf Books. London.

Nkrumah, K. (1963). Africa Must Unite. Panaf Books. London.

Nkrumah, K. (1965). Neo-Colonialism: The Last Stage of Imperialism. International Publisher. New York.

Nkrumah, K. (1968). Dark Days in Ghana. International Press. New York.

Nkrumah, K. (1969). Handbook of Revolutionary Warfare. International Press. New York.

Nkrumah, K. (1970). Africa Must Unite, International Press. New York.

Nkrumah, K. (1970). Class Struggle in Africa, New York: International Press. New York.

Nkrumah, K. (1973). Autobiography. Panaf Books. London.

Nkrumah, K. (1973). Revolutionary Path. Panaf Books. London.

Nkrumah, K. (1974). Consciencism: Philosophy and Ideology for Decolonization and Development with Particular Reference to the African Revolution. Panaf Books. London.

Nkrumah, K. (1980). Axioms of Kwame Nkrumah. Panaf Books. London.

Nkuhlu, W. (2004). Keynote lecture, in "Can Africa Half its Poverty by 2015? The Challenge to the NEPAD," compiled by the Southern African Regional Poverty Network (SARPN) and the Human Science Research Council (Pretoria, April 4 2004): 6-7. Retrieved from: http://www.sarpn.org.za/Eventpapers/April2002/clareshor/lecture.php

Nugent, N. (1989). The Government and Politics of the European Union. Duke University Press. Durham. https://doi.org/10.1007/978-1-349-20251-5

Nugent, P., Asimaju, A.I. (1996). African Boundaries: Barriers, Conduits and Opportunities. Pinter. London.

Nugent, N. (1999). The Government and Politics of the European Union. (Fourth edition). Duke University Press, Durham. https://doi.org/10.1007/978-1-349-27605-9

Nwonwu, F. (2006). NEPAD: A New Agenda or Another Rhetoric in Africa's Political Adventurism? *Africa Policy Journal*. 2. 1-30.

Nyaba, A. (2005). Righting the Past Wrongs Against the African People. In Prah, K.K. (ed) Reflections on Arab-led Slavery of Africans. CASAS Book Series. Cape Town.

Nye, J. (1971). Comparing Common Markets: A Revised Neo-Functionalist Model. In Lindberg and Scheingold (eds.) Regional Integration. Theory and Research. Harvard University Press, Cambridge.

Nyerere, J.K. (1966). Freedom and Socialism. Dar Es Salam, Oxford University Press.

Nyerere, J. (1967). Ujaama −The Basis of African Socialism. In Friedland. W.H., Rosberg, C.G. (eds.), African Socialism.238-247. Stanford University Press. Standard.

Nyerere, J. (1979). Crusade for Liberation, Dar es Salaam: Oxford University Press.

Nyerere, J.K. (1993). Statement by J.K. Nyerere on Security, Stability and Development in Africa.

Nyuur, R.B., Ofori, D.F. Yaw A.D. (2015). The Impact of FDI Inflow on Domestic Firms Uptake of CSR Activities: The Moderating Effects of Host Institutions. *Thunderbird International Business Review.* 58(2).147-159. https://doi.org/10.1002/tie.21744

OAU (1963). :Charter of the Organisation of African Unity," "Protocol of the Commission of Mediation, Conciliation, and Arbitration," and "Functions and Regulations of the General Secretariat." Addis Ababa.

OAU. (1981). Lagos Plan of Action for the Economic Development of Africa. 1980−2000. Addis Ababa.

OAU. (1991). Treaty Establishing the African Economic Community. Abuja.

OAU. (2000). Constitutive Act of the African Union. Addis Ababa.

OAU. (1990). Declaration of the Assembly of Heads of State and Government of the OAU on the Political and Socio-Economic Situation in Africa and the Fundamental Change Taking Place in the World. Addis Ababa.

OAU, (1991). Treaty Establishing The African Economic Community. Abuja, Nigeria.

OAU. (1992). OAU Charter and Rules of Procedure. Addis Ababa.

Obare, G. (2011). Lessons from Structural Adjustment Programmes and their Effects in Africa. *Quarterly Journal of International Agriculture.* 50(1). 55-64.

Ochieng, E.D. (1999). Factors, Preventing the Realisation of the OAU'S aims. In VIII Conference of Africanists held in Moscow: Africa at the Threshold of the New Millennium. Abstracts of Institute of African Studies, RAS, Moscow. 28 – 30 September 1999. 91-92.

OECD (2011). OECD Guide to Measuring the Information Society 2011. OECD Publishing. Paris.

OECD (2016). Social Expenditure Update 2016: Social Spending Stays at Historically Highly Levels in Many OECD Countries. OECD Publishing. Paris.

OECD. (2018). Implications of E-commerce for Competition Policy: Background Note. OECD Publishing. Paris.

OECD., Inter-American Development Bank. (2018). Mapping of Investment Promotion Agencies in OECD Countries. OECD Publishing. Paris.

Ogbeide, M.M. (2010). Comparative integration: A Brief Analysis of the European Union (EU) and the Economic Community of West African States (ECOWAS). *The Journal of International Social Research.* 3(10). Uluslararas Sosyal Arasturmalar Dergesi.

Ogbonnaya, U.M. (2016) Terrorism, Agenda 2063 and the Challenges of Development in Africa. *South African Journal of International Affairs.* 23:2. 185-199. https://doi.org/10.1080/10220461.2016.120 8114

Oguamanam, C. (2018a). Breeding Apples for Oranges: Africa's Misplaced Priority over Plant Breeders' Rights. *World Intellectual Property.* 18. 165-195. doi:10.1111/jwip.12039, 2015. https://doi.org/10.1111/jwip.12039

Oguamanam, C. (2018b). Tiered or Differentiated Approach to Traditional Knowledge and Traditional Cultural Expressions: The Evolution of a Concept. CIGI Papers No. 185, August 2018. https://doi.org/10.2139/ssrn.3265807

Oguamanam, C. (2011). Beyond "Nollywood" and Piracy: In Search of an Intellectual Property Policy for Nigeria (2011) NJIP 3. Retrieved from: https://papers.ssrn.com/ sol3/papers.cfm?abstract_id=2291267. Accessed 19 June 2021.

Okhonmina, S. (2009). The African Union: Pan-Africanist aspirations and the Challenges of African Unity. *The Journal of Pan-African Studies.* 3(4). 86-95.

Okhonmina, S. (2009). The African Union: Pan-Africanist Aspirations and the Challenges of African Unity. *The Journal of Pan-African Studies.* 3(4). 86-95.

Okou, C., Spray, J., Unsal, D.F. (2022). Staple Food Prices in Africa: An Empirical Assessment. IMF Working Paper WP/22/135, International Monetary Fund, Washington, DC. https://doi.org/10.5089/9798400216190.001

Okumu, W. (2009). The African Union; Pitfalls and Prospects for Uniting Africa. *Journal of International Affairs.* 62(2). 93-111.

Okunade, S.K., Ogunnubi,O. (2021). A "Schengen" Agreement in Africa? African Agency and the ECOWAS Protocol on Free Movement. *Journal of Borderlands Studies.* 36:1. 119-137. https://doi.org/10.1080/08865655.2018.1530128

Olanrewaju, J. (2015). Globalization of Terrorism: A Case Study of Boko Haram in Nigeria. *International Journal of Politics and Good Governance.* (6). 1-22.

Olu-Adeyemi, L., Ayodele, B. (2007). The Challenges of Regional Integration for Development in Africa: Problems and Prospects. *Journal of Social Sciences.* 15(3). 213-218. https://doi.org/10.1080/09718923.2007.11892585

Olu-Adeyemi, L., Ayodele, B. (2007). The Challenges of Regional Integration for Development in Africa: Problems and Prospects. *Journal of Social Sciences*. 15(3). 213-218. https://doi.org/10.1080/0 9718923.2007.11892585

O'Neill, W., Cassis, V. (2005). Protecting Two Million Internally Displaced: The Successes and Shortcomings of the African Union in Darfur. Washington, D.C.: The Brooking Institution, University of Bern.

Onimode, B. (2004). Mobilisation for the Implementation of Alternative Development Paradigm in the 21st Century Africa. In Onimode, B. et al. (ed.), African development and Governance Strategies in the 21st Century, Looking Back to Move Forward. Zeb Books. New York. 20-29.

Onuf, N. G. (1989). World of Our Making: Rules and Rule in Social Theory and International Relations. University of South Carolina Press. Columbia.

Oppong, R.F. (2009). Redefining the Relations between the African Union and the Regional Economic Communities in Africa. In: Bösl, A., Erasmus, G., Hartzenberg, T., McCarthy, C. (eds). Monitoring Regional Integration in Southern Africa Yearbook. Stellenbosch, South Africa. TRALAC & Windhoek, Namibia: Konrad-Adenauer-

Oppong, R.F. (2010). The African Union, African Economic Community and Africa's Regional Economic Communities: Untangling a Complex Web. *African Journal of International and Comparative Law*. 18(1). 92–103. https://doi.org/10.3366/E0954889009000528

Oppong, R.F. (2011). Legal Aspects of Economic Integration in Africa. Cambridge University Press. New York. https://doi.org/10.1017/ CBO9780511835186

Ostrom, E. (1999). Institutional Rational Choice: an Assessment of the Institutional Analysis and Development Framework. In Sabatier, P. A. Theories of the Policy Process. USA. Westview Press. UK. Oxford.

Oxfam (1995). A Case for Reform: Fifty Years of the IMF and the World Bank. Policy Paper. Oxford UK. 1995.

Oxfam (2006). Unequal Partners: How EU–ACP Economic Partnership Agreements (EPAs) Could Harm the Development Prospects of Many of the World's Poorest Countries, Oxford. Oxfam International.

Oyejide, A., Elbadawi, I., Collier P. (eds.) (1997). Regional Integration and Trade Liberalization in Sub-Saharan Africa. Volume 1. Macmillan. London. https://doi.org/10.1007/978-1-349-25636-5_1

Oyejide, T.A. (2000). Regional Economic Integration. The Challenges of Regional Integration in Africa. Page 15, Paper 145, June 2007. Economic Research Papers No 2. African Development Bank. Abidjan.

Oyejkide, A., Njinkeu, D. (2001). African Preparation for Trade Negotiations in the Context of ACP-EU Cotonou Partnership Agreements. Background Document Prepared for the Conference of African Trade Ministers held in Abuja (Nigeria), August.

Oyejide, T. A. (2005). National and Regional Trade and Investment Policies of Sub-Saharan African countries in the Context of post-Doha Multilateral Trading System. In UNCTAD, UNDP. (eds), Trade capacity development for Africa. United Nations. Geneva.

Oyejide, A., Njinkeu, D. (2007). Introduction and overview. In Oyejide, A. Njinkeu, D. (eds), Africa and the World Trading System. Africa World Press. Asmara/Trenton NJ.

Paez, L. (2017). Bilateral Investment Treaties and Regional Investment Regulation in Africa: Towards a Continental Investment Area? *Journal of World Investment and Trade.* 18(3). 379-413. https://doi.org/10.1163/22119000-12340046

Parshotam, A. (2018). Can the African Continental Free Trade Area offer a New Beginning for Trade in Africa? South African Institute of International Affairs. Occasional paper 290, 1-26.

Patel, I.G. (ed). (1992). Policies for African development from the 1980's to the 1990's. International Monetary Fund. Washington, DC.

Patnaik, P. (2008). The Accumulation Process in the Period of Globalisation. Weekly *Economic and Political Weekly.* 28. 108-113.

Patton, D.W. (1996). Policy Development and Implementation. In Magill, F.N. (ed.) International Encyclopedia of Government and Politics. One: 1-9. 927-975. Fitzroy Dearborn Publishers. Chicago-London.

Patton, M.Q. (1980). Qualitative Evaluation Methods. SAGE Publications. Berverly Hills. London.

Patton, M.Q., Cochran, M. (2002). A Guide to Using Qualitative Research Methodology. Medicines San Frontiers.

Pawson, R., Tilley, N. (2001). Realistic Evaluation. Sage. London. https://doi.org/10.1177/109821400102200305

Pearson, K., Horridge, M. (2003. Hands-on Computing with RunGTAP and WinGEM to Introduce GTAP and GEMPACK. Centre of Policies Studies. Monash.

Pearson, M. (2012). Trade Facilitation in the COMESA-EAC-SADC Tripartite Free Trade Area. In Hartzenberg, T et al. (ed.), The Tripartite Free Trade Area: Towards a New African Integration Paradigm? 142-79.Trade Law Centre for Southern Africa. Stellenbosch.

Perkins, J. (2004). Confessions of an Economic Hitman: How the US uses Globalisation to Cheat Poor Countries Out of Trillions. Ebury Press. New York.

Petras, J., Veltmeyer, H. 2001. Globalization Unmasked: Imperialism in the 21st Century. Zed Books.

Pham, P.J. (2010). State Collapse, Insurgency, and Famine in the Horn of Africa: Legitimacy and the Ongoing Somali Crisis. *Journal of the Middle East and Africa*. 2. 153-187. https://doi.org/10.1080/215208 44.2011.617238

Pham, J. (2011). AFRICOM from Bush to Obama. *South African Journal of International Affairs*. 18(1). 107–124. https://doi.org/10.1080/1022 0461.2011.564429

Pienkowski, A. (2017). Debt Limits and the Structure of Public Debt. Working Paper WP/17/117. IMF. Washington, DC. https://doi.org/10.5089/9781484300657.001

Pieterse, J.N. (2002). Global Inequality: Bringing Politics Back *Third World Quarterly*. 23 (6). 1023-1046. https://doi.org/10.1080/0143659022000036667

Pirozzi, N. (2009). EU Support to African Security Architecture: Funding and Training Components. European Union Institute for Security Studies Occasional Paper 76.

Pirozzi, N. (2010). Towards an Effective Africa-EU Partnership on Peace and Security: Rhetoric or Facts? *The International Spectator*. 45(2). 85-101. https://doi.org/10.1080/03932721003790753

Plano, J.C., Olton, R. (1988). The International Relations Dictionary (4th edition). Longman. California.

Pomeranz, K. (2000). The Great Divergence: China, Europe, and the Making of the Modern World Economy. Princeton University Press. https://doi.org/10.1515/9781400823499

Posthumus, B. (2003). A Conference Report. In Posthumus, B. (ed.), NEPAD: A New Partnership? Netherlands Institute for Southern Africa. Amsterdam.

Powell, K. (2005). The African Union's Emerging Peace and Security Regime: Opportunities and Challenges for Delivering on The Responsibility to Protect. Institute for Security Studies.

Powell, J. (2013). Subordinate Financialisation: A Study of Mexico and its Non-financial Corporations. PhD dissertation, SOAS, University of London.

PPIAF (2005). Towards Growth and Poverty Reduction: Lessons from Private Participation in Infrastructure in Sub-Saharan Africa. Cape Town.

Prah, K.K. (2006). Challenges to the Promotion of Indigenous Languages in South Africa. Review Commissioned by the Foundation for Human Rights in South Africa. The Center for Advanced Studies of African Society. Cape Town.

Prah, K.K. (2014). The African Cause is on the Course, Closing Address; 8th PAC, 16 January 16, Johannesburg: South Africa.

Prebisch, R. (1939). El Ciclo Económico y la Politica Monetaria ['The Economie Cycle and Monetary Policy']. In E. Garcia Vasquez (ed.) Obras de Raul Prebisch, Vol. 2 [The Works of Raul Prebisch, Vol. 2]. 647–57. Fundación Raul Prebisch. Buenos Aires.

Prebisch, R. (1950). The Economic Development of Latin America and its Principal Problems. United Nations Economic Commission for Latin America (United Nations publication. Sales No. 50.II.G.2.New York).

Preston, P.W. (1996).. Development theory – an Introduction. Blackwell. Oxford.

Pricewaterhouse Coopers (2008). Global sourcing: Shifting strategies – A survey of retail and consumer companies.

Pricewaterhouse Coopers, (2015). Food Security in Africa: Water on Oil. London.

Pritchett, L. (1997). Divergence, Big Time. *Journal of Economic Perspectives.* 11(3). 3–17. https://doi.org/10.1257/jep.11.3.3

Pritchett, L. (2010). The Cliff at the Border. In Equity and Growth in a Globalizing World, In (ed.) Kanbur, R., Spence. M. (ed.), Commission on Growth and Development. Washington, DC.

Pritchett L., Smith, R. (2016). Is There a Goldilocks Solution? "Just right" Promotion of Labour Mobility. Policy Paper No. 94. Centre for Global Development.

Przeworkski, A., Vreeland, J. (2000). The Effects of IMF Programs on Economic Growth. *The Journal of Development Economics.* 62. 385–421. https://doi.org/10.1016/S0304-3878(00)00090-0

Punch, K. (2005). Grounded Theory, the Analysis of Qualitative Data, Computer Software and Qualitative Analysis, Drawing and Verifying Conclusions in Qualitative Data Analysis. In: Introduction to Social Research. Quantitative and Qualitative Approaches. (2nd Edition). Sage, London.

Putnam, R. (1988). Diplomacy and Domestic Politics: the Logic of Two-level Games. *International Organisation.* 42(3). 427-460. https://doi.org/10.1017/S0020818300027697

Qobo, M. (2007). The Challenges of Regional Integration in Africa; In the Context of Globalisation and the Prospects for a United States of Africa. *Institute of Security Studies.* 145. 1-16.

Radelet, S. (1997). Regional Integration and Cooperation in Sub-Saharan Africa: Are Formal Trade Agreements the Right Strategy? Development Discussion Paper 592.

Radlicki, M. (2015). Back to Basics: What ISIS, Al-Shabaab and Boko Haram Have in Common, and How They Preach Water and Drink Wine. *Mail and Guardian.* 11 June. 2015 [Accessed 17 October 2021].

Ratha D, Mohapatra S, Scheja E. (2011). Impact of Migration on Economic and Social Development: A Review of Evidence and Emerging Issues. Policy Research Working Paper No. 5558. World Bank. https://doi.org/10.21648/arthavij/2011/v53/i3/117558

Ratha, D., Mohapatra, S., Özden, Ç., Plaza, S., Shaw, W. Shimeles, A. (2011). Leveraging Migration for Africa: Remittances, Skills and Investments. World Bank. Washington D.C.

Ravallion, M. (2016). The World Bank: Why it is Still Needed and Why it Still Disappoints. *The Journal of Economic Perspectives.* 30(1). 77–94. https://doi.org/10.1257/jep.30.1.77

Ravenhill, J. (1985). The Future of Regionalism in Africa. In Onwuka, and Sesay (eds.), The Future of Regionalism in Africa, Macmillan Education.

Ravenhill, J. (1986). Africa in Economic Crisis. Macmillan. Basingstoke. https://doi.org/10.1007/978-1-349-18371-5

Ravenhill, J. (2010). The 'New East Asian Regionalism': A Political Domino Effect. *Review of International Political Economy.* 17(2). 2010. https://doi.org/10.1080/09692290903070887

Ravenhill, J. (2014). Regional Integration in Africa: Theory and Practice. Paper Presented on Region-building and Regional Integration in Africa. Centre for Conflict Resolution, April 2014. Cape Town, South Africa.

Ravenhill, J. (2014). Global Political Economy. New York. Oxford University Press.

Rehder. B., Hastie, R. (2001). Causal Knowledge and Categories: The Effects of Causal Beliefs on Categorisation, Induction and Similarity. *Journal of Experimental Psychology General.* 130. 323–360. https://doi.org/10.1037/0096-3445.130.3.323

Reinert, S., Patalano, R. (2016). Antonio Serra and the Economics of Good Government. Palgrave Macmillan. London. https://doi.org/10.1057/9781137539960

Renwick, D. (2015). Peace Operations in Africa. At Council on Foreign Relations.

Reuters. (2017). Brandy Chases Whisky in South African Spirit Wars. 13 October.

Risse, T. (2000). "Let's Argue!" Communicative Action in World Politics. *International Organisation.* 54. 1–39. https://doi.org/10.1162/002081800551109

Roberts, A. (2009). The Incredible Human Journey: The Story of How we Colonised The Planet: Bloomsburg Publishing. London.

Robinson, W.I. (2002). Remapping Development in the Light of
Globalisation: From a Territorial to a Social Cartography.
Third World Quarterly. 23(6). 1047-1071. https://doi.
org/10.1080/0143659022000036658

Rodney, W. (1973). How Europe Underdeveloped Africa. Dar es Salaam:
Tanzania Publishing House.

Rodrik D. (2018). New Technologies, Global Value Chains and the
Developing Economies. Pathways for Prosperity Commission
Background Paper Series No. 1. University of Oxford. https://doi.
org/10.3386/w25164

Rodt, A. P. (2011). The African Mission in Burundi: The Successful
Management of Violent Ethno Political Conflict? Exceps
Ethnopolitics Papers no. 10

Romans, H. (2006). Transit Migration in Egypt. Euro-Mediterranean
Consortium for Applied Research on International Migration,
European University Institute, Florence, Italy.

Roodman, D.M. (2001). Still Waiting for the Jubilee; Pragmatic Solutions
for the Third World Debt Crisis. World Watch Paper No. 155.
Washington, DC: World watch.

Rosamond, B. (2000). Regional Identities and Inter-regional
Dialogue: The European Union and the ASEM Process.
Global Economic Review. 29(1). 79-96. https://doi.
org/10.1080/12265080008449783

Rozhnov, K. (2010). Brics Tries to Shift Power Balance. BBC News, July 16.

Ruggie, J.G. (1998). What Makes the World Hang Together? Neo-
utilitarianism and the Social Constructivist Challenge.
International Organisation. 52. 855-885. https://doi.
org/10.1162/002081898550770

Ruggiero, R. (2000). Reflections from Seattle. In Schott, J. (ed.) The WTO
After Seattle. Institute for International Economics. Washington,
DC.

Sabatier, P. A. (1997). Top-Down and Bottom-Up Approaches to
Implementation Research. In Hill, M. (ed.) The Policy Process, a
Reader. (2nd edition). Prentice Hall. London.

Sabatier, P.A. (ed.) (1999). Theories of Policy Process. Westview Press.
Boulder, CO.

Sachs, J. (2005). The End of Poverty: Economic Possibilities for Our Time. Penguin Press.

SACU. (2002). The Southern African Customs Union Agreement – Draft Final between the Governments of the Republic of Botswana, the Kingdom of Lesotho, the Republic of Namibia, the Republic of South Africa and the Kingdom of Swaziland. Retrieved from: http://www.tralac.org/documents/sacu_2002.htm, accessed 05/07/2021.

SADC. (1994). A Framework for Building the Community. The Management of Regional Cooperation Report. SADC Unpublished Document. Gaborone.

SADC. (2001). SADC Communique on Civil Society Conference in Lesotho.

SADC. (2009). The SADC Communique on Harare, Zimbabwe's Global Political Agreement (GPA). August 2.

SADC (2011). The SADC Communique on Namibia, Windhoek, Summit. August.

SADC (2012). The SADC Communique on Maputo, Mozambique – on the Dissolution of the SADC Tribunal. August.

Sandjong, T., D'Estaing, D.G. (2015). Foreign Direct Investment, Economic Growth and Structural Transformation: The Case of West African Economies and Monetary Union Countries. Munich Personal RePEc Archive. Munich, Germany. Retreived from: https://mpra.ub.uni-muenchen.de/62230/1/MPRA_paper_62230.pdf

SAPRIN. (2002). The Policy Roots of Economic Crisis and Poverty: A Multi-Country Participatory Assessment of Structural Adjustment. April 2002. Executive Summary, p.21.

SAPRIN. (2002). African Civil Society Declaration on NEPAD: 'We do not Accept NEPAD!! Africa is not for Sale!!' Retteived from: <http://www.sarpn.org.za/NEPAD/july2002/acs_declaration/African_Civil_Society.pdf> [15 July 2020].

Saqndrey, R., Jensen, H.G. (2012). Manufacturing and Regional Free Trade Areas: A Computer Analysis of the Impacts. In Hartzenberg T. et al. (ed.) The Tripartite Free Trade Area: Towards a New African Integration Paradigm? 70-141. Trade Law Centre for Southern Africa: Stellenbosch.

Saurombe, A. (2012). An Analysis of Economic Integration in Africa with Specific Reference to the African Union and the African Economic Community. *South African Journal of Public Law.* 27(1). 292-314.

Sayer, A. (2000). Realism and Social Science. Sage. London. https://doi.org/10.4135/9781446218730

Saygili M., Peters, R., Knebel, C. (2017). African Continental Free Trade Area: Challenges and Opportunities of Tariff Reductions. Policy Issues in International Trade and Commodities. United Nations. New York and Geneva.

Saygili, M., Peters, R. Knebel. C. (2018). African Continental Free Trade Area: Challenges and Opportunities of Tariff Reductions. Research Paper 15, UNCTAD (United Nations Conference on Trade and Development). Geneva.

Schimmelfennig, F. (2003). Liberal Intergovernmentalism. In Wiener, A., Diez,T. (eds.) European Integration Theory. 75-94. Oxford University Press. Oxford.

Schimmelfennig, F. (2000). International Socialization in the New Europe: Rational Action in an Institutional Environment. *European Journal of International Relations.* 6(1). 109-139. https://doi.org/10.1177/1354066100006001005

Schiavone, G. (1997). International Organisations: a Dictionary. (4th edition). Macmillan Press. London.

Schidt-Traub, G. (2015). Investment Needs to Achieve the Sustainable Development Goals: Understanding the Billions and Trillions. Working Paper Version 2. Sustainable Development Solutions Network.

Schlager, E. (1999). A Comparison of Frameworks, Theories, and Models of Policy Processes. In Sabatier, P.A. (ed.) Theories of the Policy Process. Westview Press. Boulder, Colorado.

Schmitter, P.C. (1969). Three Neo-functional Hypotheses About International Integration. *International Organisation.* 23. 161-6. https://doi.org/10.1017/S0020818300025601

Schmitter, P.C. (1970). A Revised Theory of Regional Integration. *International Organisation* 24: 836-868. https://doi.org/10.1017/S0020818300017549

Schmitter, P. C. (200). Neo-Neo-functionalism. In Wiener, A., Diez,T. (eds.). European Integration Theory. (1ˢᵗ Edition). 46-74. Oxford University Press. Oxford.

Schmitter, P.C. Lefkofridi, Z. (2016). Neo-Functionalism as a Theory of Disintegration.In: *Chinese Political Science Review.* 1(1). 1-29. https://doi.org/10.1007/s41111-016-0012-4

Schutt, R.K. (2012) Qualitative Data Analysis. In: Schutt, R.K. (ed.) Investigating the Social World: The Process and Practice of Research. Chapter 10. Retrieved from: http://www.sagepub.com/upm-data/43454_10.pdf [Accessed 14 July 2021].

Schwab, K. (2015). Global Competitiveness Report. Davos, Switzerland: World Economic Forum.

Senghor, L. (1964). On African Socialism. Frederick A Praeger. New York.

Senghor, J.G. (1989). Towards a Dynamic African Economy: Selected Speeches and Lectures by Adebayo Adedeji, 1975 – 1986. Frank Cass and Co. London.

Serafino, N.M. (2009). The Global Peace Operations Initiative: Background and Issues for Congress, 11 June. Congressional Research Service. Washington, D.C.

Sesay, A. (1991). The Limits of Peace-keeping by Regional Organisation: OAU Peacekeeping Force in Chad. *Conflict Quarterly.* 111. 7-26.

Sesay. A., Omotosho, M. (2011). The Politics of Regional Integration in West Africa. West African Civil Society (WAC) Series. Vol. 2. No. 2. West African Civil Society Institute.

Shank, M. (2007). Understanding Political Islam in Somalia. *Contemporary Islam.* 1(1). 89–103. https://doi.org/10.1080/096922997347724

Shaw, M. (1997). The State of Globalisation: Towards a Theory of State Transformation', *Review of International Political Economy.* 4(3). 497-513. https://doi.org/10.1080/096922997347724

Shaw, M.N. (2008). International Law. (6ᵗʰ edition). Cambridge University Press. Cambridge. https://doi.org/10.1017/CBO9780511841637

Shepperson, G. (1962). Pan-Africanism and Pan-Africanism: Some Historical Notes. *Phylon.* 23. 346-358. https://doi.org/10.2307/274158

Shingal, A., Mendez-Parra, M. (2020). African Greenfield Investment and the Likely Effect of the African Continental Free Trade Area. Indian Council for Research on International Economic Relations Working Paper 387.

Shivji, I. (2008). The African Union: A New Dawn or a New Dawn in Name Only? Dar es Salaam University Press.

Shivji, I.G. (2008). The African Union and the African State: Reclaiming the Agenda for Pan-Africanism and African Development. Dar es Salaam University Press.

Shivji, I.G. (2009). Accumulation in the African Periphery: A Theoretical Framework. Mkuki na Nyota Publishers. Dar es Salaam.

Sicurelli, D. (2007). 'The European Commission and EU Peacekeeping in Africa. Pushing for a Supranational Security Policy. Paper prepared for the XXI Conferenza della Societa Italiana di Scienza Politica. 20-22 September.

Sicurelli, D. (2008). Framing Security and Development in the EU Pillar Structure. How the Views of the European Commission Affect EU Africa Policy. *European Integration.* 30(2). 217-234. https://doi.org/10.1080/07036330802005433

Sicurelli, D. (2010). Competing Models of Peacekeeping: the Role of the EU and China in Africa. Paper prepared for the Fifth Pan-European Conference on EU Politics Porto, Portugal, 23-26 June.

Sikkink, K. (1997). Development Ideas in Latin America: Paradigm Shift and the Economic Commission for Latin America. In Cooper, F., Packard, R. (eds), International Development and the Social Sciences: Essays on the History and Politics of Knowledge. University of California Press. California. https://doi.org/10.1525/9780520919440-011

Simuyemba, S. (2000). Linking Africa Through Regional Infrastructures, Economic Research Papers No. 64. African Development Bank. Abidjan.

Singh, A. (1992). The Lost Decade: The Economic Crisis of the Third World in the 1980s: How the North Caused the South's Crisis. *Contention.* 2. 58-80.

Singer, H.W. (1950). U.S. Foreign Investment in Underdeveloped Areas: The Distribution of Gains between Investing and Borrowing Countries. *American Economic Review, Papers and Proceedings*. 40. 473-485.

Singer, H. (1950). The Distribution of Gains between Investing and Borrowing Countries', *American Economic Review*, 40(2). 473–85.

Singer, H. (1953). Obstacles to Economic Development. *Social Research*. 20(1). 19–31.

Singer, H. (1965). Social Development: Key Growth Sector., *International Development Review*. 7(1). 3–8.

Singer, H. (1970). Multinational Corporations and Technology Transfer: Some Problems and Suggestions. In Cairncross, A., Puri, M. (eds), The Strategy of International Development: Essays in the Economics of Backwardness. 208–33. International Arts and Sciences Press. White Plains, NY. https://doi.org/10.1007/978-1-349-04228-9_13

Singer, H. (1992) Lessons of Post-war Development Experience: 1945–1988. In Sharma, S. (ed.), Development Policy. 35–80. Palgrave Macmillan. London. https://doi.org/10.1007/978-1-349-22385-5_3

Smith, A. (1999). The Wealth of Nations. Book I-IV. Penguin. London.

Smith, P. (1993). The politics of integration: Concepts and themes. In Smith, P. (ed.), The Challenge of Integration. Europe and the America's. University of Miami North-South Centre.

Smuts, J.C. (1918). The League of Nations: A Practical Suggestion. Hodder and Stoughton. London.

Soderbaum, F. (2002). The Political Economy of Regionalism in Southern Africa. Department of Peace and Development Research. Goteborg University.

Soderbaum, F. (2004). The Political Economy of Regionalism: The Case of Southern Africa. Palgrave Macmillan. London.

Sodipo, B. (2019). Governance for an Effective AfCFTA. In Luke. D., MacLeod, J. (eds.), Inclusive Trade in Africa: The African Continental Free Trade Area in Comparative Perspective. Routledge. London. https://doi.org/10.4324/9780429401121-8

Sommer, L., MacLeod, J. (2019). How Important is Special and Differential Treatment for an Inclusive AfCFTA?" In Luke. D., MacLeod, J. (eds.), Inclusive Trade in Africa: The African Continental Free Trade Area in Comparative Perspective. Routledge. London. https://doi.org/10.4324/9780429401121-6

Sousa, F.J. (2010). Chapter 9: Metatheories in research: Positivism, Postmodernism, and Critical Realism. In Woodside, A.G. (ed.), Organisational Culture, Business-to-Business Relationships, and Interfirm Networks. 455–503. Emerald Group. Bingley, England. https://doi.org/10.1108/S1069-0964(2010)0000016012

Stevens, C. (2005). Economic Partnership Agreements and African Integration: a Help or a Hindrance. University of Sussex. Brighton.

Stevens, C., Kennan, J. (2005). What Role for South Africa in EPAs and Regional Economic Integration? Paper Prepared for a Conference on Regional Integration and Economic Partnership Agreements, South Africa

Stevenson, J. (2007). The Somali Model? *The National Interest.* 90. 41-45.

Stiglitz, J. (1989). Market, market imperfections, and development', *American Economic Review.* 79(2): 197-303.

Stiglitz, J. (1996). Some Lessons from the East Asian Miracle. *The World Bank Research Observer.* 11(2). 155-77. https://doi.org/10.1093/wbro/11.2.151

Stiglitz, J. (2002). Globalisation and its Discontents. W.W. Norton and Company. New York.

Stiglitz, J., Charlton, A. (2005). Fair Trade for All: How Trade can Promote Development. Oxford University Press. New York.

Stiglitz, J. (2006). Making Globalisation Work. New York. W.W. Norton and Company

Stiglitz, Joseph E. (2007). Regulating Multinational Corporations: Towards Principles of Cross-Border Legal Frameworks in a Globalised World Balancing Rights with Responsibilities. *American University International Law Review.* 23(3). 451-558. https://doi.org/10.1017/S0272503700025179

Stiglitz, J. (2010). Freefall: America, Free Markets, and the Sinking of the World Economy. W.W. Norton and Company. New York.

Stiglitz, J. (2017). Globalization and Its Discontents – Revisited. W.W. Norton & Company. London.

Sunkel, O. (1972) Big Business and "Dependencia. A Latin American View. *Foreign Affairs.* 50(3). 517–31. https://doi.org/10.2307/20037926

Sunkel, O. (1973). Transnational Capitalism and National Disintegration in Latin America', *Social and Economic Studies* 22(1). 132–71

Suwandi, I. (2019). Value Chains – The New Economic Imperialism. Monthly Review. New York. https://doi.org/10.14452/MR-070-10-2019-03_1

Svensson, E. (2008a). The African Mission in Burundi: Lessons Learned from the African Union's First Peace Operation. Swedish Defence Research Agency (FOI). Stockholm.

Svensson, E. (2008b.) The African Union's Operations in the Comoros: MAES and Operation Democracy. Swedish Defence Research Agency (FOI). Stockholm.

Sy, A., Sow, M. (2017). Four questions on the State of the West African Economic and Monetary Union and the Implications for other Regional Economic Communities. Brookings Institute. Retrieved from: https://www.brookings.edu/blog/africa-in-focus/2016/03/15.

Tardy, T. (2012). The Dangerous Liaisons of the Responsibility to Protect and the Protection of Civilians in Peacekeeping Pperations. *Global Responsibility to Protect.* 4(4). 424-448. https://doi.org/10.1163/1875984X-00404003

Tardy, T. (2014). Hybrid Peace Operations: Rationale and Challenges. *Global Governance.* 20(1). 95–118. https://doi.org/10.1163/19426720-02001007

Tavares, R., Tang, V. (2011). Regional Economic Integration in Africa: Impediments to Progress. *South African Journal of International Affairs.* 18(2). 217-233. https://doi.org/10.1080/10220461.2011.588826

Taylor, L., Black S.L. (1974). Practical General Equilibrium Estimation of Resource Pulls Under Trade Liberalisation. *Journal of International Economics.* 4(1). 37-58. https://doi.org/10.1016/0022-1996(74)90032-4

Taylor, L. (1981). 'South—North Trade and Southern Growth: Bleak Prospects from a Structuralist Point of View. *Journal of International Economics*. 11(4). 589—601. https://doi.org/10.1016/0022-1996(81)90036-2

Taylor, L. (19970. Editorial. The Revival of the Liberal Creed: The IMF and the World Bank in a Globalised Economy. *World Development*. 25(2). 145-52. https://doi.org/10.1016/S0305-750X(96)00117-9

Taylor, I. (2003). The Failure of the New Economic Partnership for Africa's Development. *Contemporary Review*. 282(1648). 281-285.

Taylor, I. (2013). African Unity at 50: From Non-Interference to Non-Indifference. E-International Relations. 25 June.

Taylor, I. (2015). Dependency Redux: Why Africa is Not Rising. *Review of African Political Economy*. 43(157). 8—25. https://doi.org/10.1080/0 3056244.2015.1084911

Taylor, P., Groom, A.J.R. (2006). International Institutions at Work. Pinter. London.

Teddlie, C., Yu, F. (2007). Mixed Methods Sampling: A Typology with Examples. *Journal of Mixed Methods Research*. 1(1). 77-100. https://doi.org/10.1177/1558689806292430

Tella, O. (2023). Africa-China Relations; Building a Multipolar World Order. Palgrave Macmillan.

Telo, M. (2001). Introduction: Globalisation, New Regionalism and the Role of the European Union. In Telo., M. (ed.), European Union and New Regionalism. Ashgate. Aldershot.

Teravaninthorn, S., Raballand, G. (2008). Transport Prices and Costs in Africa: a Review of the Main International Corridors. World Bank. Washington, DC.

Teravaninthorn, S., Raballand, G. (2009). Transport Prices and Costs in Africa: A Review of the Main International Corridors. The International Bank for Reconstruction and Development / The World Bank.

te Velde, D. W. (2016). Scenarios for UK Trade Policy Towards Developing Countries After the Vote to Leave the EU. In Mendez-Parra, M., te Velde, D.W., Winters, L.A. (eds.), The Impact of the UK's Post-Brexit Trade Policy on Development: An Essay Series. Overseas Development Institute. London. Retreived from: www. odi.org/publications/10480-brexit-and-developmenthowwill-developing-countries-be-affected.

The Europa Dictionary of International Organisations (1st edition) (1999). Europa. London.

Thompson, V.B. (1969). Africa and Unity: The Evolution of Pan-Africanism. Longmans, Green and Company. Ltd. London.

Thompson, D. (2000). The Pan-Africanist. Ian Randle Publishers. Jamaica.

Thonke, O., Spliid, A. (2012). What to Expect from Regional Integration in Africa. *African Security Review*. 21(1). 42-66. https://doi.org/10.108 0/10246029.2011.629452

Thucydides. (1954). History of the Peloponnesian War. Translated by Warner, R. Penguin. Baltimore.

Tieku, T.K. (2004). Explaining the Clash and Accommodation of Interests of Major Actors in the Creation of the African Union. *African Affairs*. 103. 249-267. https://doi.org/10.1093/afraf/adh041

Tondi, P.T. (2005). Pan African Thought and Practice, Alternation Special Edition

Touray, O. A. (2005). The Common African Defence and Security Policy. *African Affairs* 104(417). 635−656. https://doi.org/10.1093/afraf/adi066

TRALAC. (2017). African Production and Trade of Coffee and Tea in Perspective: What are the Implications for Continental Trade Liberalization? Retrteived from: www. tralac.org/publications/article/12329-african-production-and-trade-of-coffee-andtea-in-perspective-what-are-the-implications-for-continental-trade-liberalisation. html (accessed 21 August 2021).

TRALAC. (2018). Egypt: Intra-African Trade and Tariff Profile. Retrieved from: www. tralac.org/resources/our-resources/13144-egypt-intra-african-trade-and-tariffprofile.html (accessed 21 August 2021).

Tranholm-Mikkelsen, J. (1991). Neo-functionalism: Obstinate or Obsolete? A Reappraisal in the Light of the New Dynamism of the EC. *Millenium.* 20. 1-22. https://doi.org/10.1177/03058298910200 010201

Trudi, H. (2011). Regional Integration in Africa. WTO Staff Working Paper (ERSD-2011-14) 1-28.

Tutu, D. (1999). No Future Without Forgiveness. Doubleday. https://doi. org/10.1111/j.1540-5842.1999.tb00012.x

Tyson, L.D., Robinson, S. (1983). Modelling Structural Adjustment: Micro and Macro Elements in a General Equilibrium Framework. In Scarf, H.E., Shoven, J. (eds.), Applied General Equilibrium Analysis. Cambridge University Press. Cambridge.

UMA. (1989). Treaty of Marrakech. February 17, Rabat.

UN. (1945). Charter of the United Nations, 24 October, 1 UNTS XVI [online]. Retrieved from: <http://www.unhcr.org/refworld/ docid/3ae6b3930.html> [17 July 11].

UN. (2001). Global agenda for dialogue among civilisations. A/Res/56/6, 21 November.

UN (2008). United Nations Peacekeeping Operations: Principles and Guidelines. New York.

UN. (2010a). Charter of the United Nations. Retreived from: http://www. un.org/en/documents/charter/index.shtml, (June 23, 2010).

UN. (2011c). Review of the Ten-year Capacity-building Programme for the African Union: Report of the Secretary-General [A/65/716–S/2011/54]. 2 February.

UNCTAD. (1996). World Investment Report 1996: Investment, Trade and International Policy Arrangements. UN. New York and Geneva.

UNCTAD. (2008). Cocoa Study: Industry Structures and Competition. UN publication. Geneva. https://doi.org/10.1177/0015732515960306

UNCTAD. (2009). Economic Development in Africa Report 2009: Strengthening Regional Economic Integration for Africa's Development. Sales No. E.09.II.D.7. UN publication. New York and Geneva).

UNCTAD. (2013). Economic Development in Africa Report 2013: Intra-African Trade –Unlocking Private Sector Dynamism. Sales No. E.13.II.D.2. UN publication. New York and Geneva.

UNCTAD. (2014). Pan-African Cotton Road Map: A Continental Strategy to Strengthen Regional Cotton Value Chains for Poverty Reduction and Food Security. UN publication. New York and Geneva.

UNCTAD. (2015a). Deep Regional Integration and Non-tariff Measures: A Methodology for Data Analysis. Policy Issues in International Trade and Commodities Research Study Series No. 69.

UNCTAD. (2015b). Economic Development in Africa Report 2015: Unlocking the Potential of Africa's Services Trade for Growth and Development (United Nations publication. Sales No. E.15.II.D.2. UN publication. New York and Geneva.

UNCTAD. (2015c). Commodities and Development Report 2015: Smallholder Farmers and Sustainable Commodity Development. UN publication. New York and Geneva.

UNCTAD. (2016a). Sand in the Wheels: Non-tariff Measures and Regional Integration in SADC. Policy Issues in International Trade and Commodities Research Study Series No. 71. Made in Africa – Rules of Origin for Enhanced Intra-African Trade.

UNCTAD. (2016b). Cocoa Industry: Integrating Small Farmers into the Global Value Chain UN publication. New York and Geneva.

UNCTAD. (2016c). African Continental Free Trade Area: Policy and Negotiation Options for Trade in Goods. United Nations publication. New York and Geneva.

UNCTAD. (2017). Commodity Dependence and the Sustainable Development Goals. TD/B/C.I/MEM.2/37. Geneva. 3 August.

UNCTAD. (2018a). Trade and Development Report 2018: Power, Platforms and the Free Trade Delusion. Sales No. E.18. II. D.7. UN publication. New York and Geneva.

UNCTAD. (2018b). World Investment Report 2018: Investment and New Industrial Policies. Sales No. E.18. II. D.4. UN publication. New York and Geneva.

UNCTAD. (2018c). The Least Developed Countries Report 2018: Entrepreneurship for Structural Transformation – Beyond Business as Usual. No. E.18. II. D.6. UN publication. New York and Geneva.

UNCTAD. (2018d). Economic Development in Africa Report 2018: Migration for Structural Transformation. Sales No. E.18. II. D.2. UN publication. New York and Geneva.

UNCTAD. (2018e.) The Djibouti City–Addis Ababa Transit and Transport Corridor: Turning Diagnostics into Action. UN publication. New York and Geneva.

UNCTAD. (2018f). African Continental Free Trade Area: Challenges and opportunities of tariff reductions. Research Paper No. 15.

UNCTAD. (2018g). Handbook on Duty-Free Quota-Free Market Access and Rules of Origin for Least Developed Countries, Part I. United Nations publication. New York and Geneva.

UNCTAD. (2018h). The Treatment of Goods Originating in Special Economic Arrangements/Zones in the African Continental Free Trade Area, Technical Paper. Retreived from: https://unctad.org/meetings/en/SessionalDocuments/aldc2019_AfCFTA_of origin11_tn_SEZs.pdf (accessed 26 August 2021).

UNCTAD. (2018i). The Methodologies of Drafting the Ad-valorem Percentage Criterion. Presentation made at the seventh session of the Technical Working Group Meeting on Rules of Origin. 30 and 31 July. Geneva.

UNCTAD., FAO. (2017). Commodities and Development Report 2017: Commodity Markets, Economic Growth and Development. United Nations and FAO. Sales No. E.17. II. D.1. UN publication. New York and Geneva.

UNCTAD. (2001). Economic development in Africa: performance, prospects and policy issues. UNCTAD. Geneva.

UNCTAD. (2003). FDI policies for development: national and international perspectives. World Investment Report 2003. UN publication. Geneva.

UNCTAD. (2006). The Least Developed Countries Report: Developing Productive Capacities. UN publication. Geneva

UNCTAD. (2007). Bilateral Investment Treaties 1995-2006: Trends in Investment Rulemaking. UN publication. New York and Geneva.

UNCTAD. (2008). Cocoa Study: Industry Structures and Competition. UN publication. Geneva.

UNCTAD. (2009). Economic Development in Africa Report 2009: Strengthening Regional Economic Integration for Africa's Development. United Nations Conference on Trade and Development, Geneva, Switzerland.

UNCTAD. (2009a). The Role of International Investment Agreements in Attracting Foreign Direct Investments to Developing Countries. UN publication. New York and Geneva.

UNCTAD. (2011). World Investment Report 2011: Non-equity Modes of International Production and Development. New UN publication. New York and Geneva.

UNCTAD. (2012). Trade and Development Report: The Role of Fiscal Policy in Income Distribution. UN publication. Geneva.

UNCTAD. (2013). World Investment Report 2013: Global Value Chains— Investment and Trade for Development. UN publication. Geneva.

UNCTAD. (2014). Virtual Institute Teaching Material on Trade and Gender – Volume 1: Unfolding the Links. UN publication. New York and Geneva.

UNCTAD. (2015). The Continental Free Trade Area: Making it work for Africa 44:1-4. (accessed July 2021): http://unctad.org/en/ PublicationsLibrary.

UNCTAD. (2015a). Investment Policy Framework for Sustainable Development. UN publication. Geneva.

UNCTAD. (2016). Trade Misinvoicing in Primary Commodities in Developing Countries: The Cases of Chile, Côte d'Ivoire, Nigeria, South Africa and Zambia. UN publication. New York and Geneva.

UNCTAD. (2016b). Trading into Sustainable Development: Trade, Market Access, and the Sustainable Development Goals." Developing Countries in International Trade Studies. UN publication. Geneva.

UNCTAD. (2017). African Continental Free Trade Area: Challenges and Opportunities of Tariff Reductions. Policy Issues in International Trade and Commodities. UN publication. New York.

UNCTAD. (2017a). Global Action Menu for Investment Facilitation. UN publication. Geneva.

UNCTAD. (2017b). World Investment Report 2017: Investment and the Digital Economy. UN publication. New York Geneva.

UNCTAD. (2018). Key statistics and trends in international trade: 2016/2017. UN publication. New York and Geneva.

UNCTAD. (2018a). World Investment Report 2018: Investment and New Industrial Policies. UN publication. Geneva.

UNCTAD. (2018i). The Methodologies of Drafting the Ad-valorem Percentage Criterion. Presentation made at the Seventh Session of the Technical Working Group Meeting on Rules of Origin. 30 and 31 July. Geneva.

UNCTAD. (2019). Investment Policy Hub.Geneva: UNCTAD. Retreived from: https://investmentpolicyhub.u ctad.org/.

UNCTAD. (2022). World Investment Report 2022: International Tax Reform and Sustainable Investment. UN publication. New York.

UNDESA. (2015). World Population Projected to Reach 9.7 Billion by 2050. Retreived from: http://www.un.org/en/ development/desa/news/ population/2015-report.html. Accessed 7 July 2022.

UNDESA. (2017). Expanding Productive Capacity: Lessons Learned from Graduating Least Developed Countries. UN publication. New York.

UNDESA. (2018a). World Economic Situation and Prospects 2018. UN publication. New York.

UNDESA, (2018b). World Economic Situation and Prospects as of mid-2018. UN publication. New York.

UNDESA. (2019). World Economic Situation and Prospects 2019. UN publication. New York.

UNDP. (2009). Human Development Report 2009 Overcoming Barriers: Human Mobility and Development. UN publication. New York.

UNDP. (2011). Regional Integration and Human Development: a Pathway for Africa. UN publication. New York.

UNDP. (2016). African Human Development Report. New York.

UNECA. (2002). The African Peer Review Mechanism: Process and Procedure. *African Security Review.* 11(4). 7-13. https://doi.org/10.1 080/10246029.2002.9628140

UNECA. (2004). Assessing the Integration in UNECA. Addis Ababa.

UNECA. (2005b). Assessment of the Impact of the Economic Partnership Agreement between COMESA Countries and the European Union. September 2005.

UNECA. (2005c). Assessment of the Economic Partnership Agreement between the ECOWAS Countries and the European Union. Draft paper, 18–20. December 2005.

UNECA. (2006). Assessing Regional Integration in Africa II: Rationalizing Regional Economic Communities, United Nations Economic Commission for Africa and African Union, Addis Ababa. http://www.uneca.org/aria

UNECA 2006a.'EPA Negotiations: African Countries Continental Review', Draft Report, 18 December 2006.

UNECA 2008. UN System-wide Support to the African Union and its New Partnership for Africa's Development (NEPAD) Programme [E/ECA/COE/27/15]. Addis Ababa, 25 February

UNECA (2010). Addis Ababa: UNECA.

UNECA. (2012). Assessing Regional Integration in Africa V: Towards an African Continental Free Trade Area. United Nations Economic Commission for Africa: Addis Ababa.

UNECA. (2016). Investment Policies and Bilateral Investment Treaties in Africa Implications for Regional Integration. Addis Ababa, Ethiopia: ECA.

UNECA. (2020). The African Continental Free Trade Area: An Opportunity for Growth and Development. UN Economic Commission for Africa.

UNESCO. (2015). Education for All 2000-2015: Achievements and Challenges. Paris: UNESCO.

UNIDO. (2001, 2003, and 2005). Africa Foreign Investor Surveys. United Nations. Vienna.

UNIDO. (2011). Africa Investors Report: Towards Evidence Based Investment Promotion Strategies. United Nations. Vienna.

UNSC. (2002). Statement by the President of the Security Council [S/PRST/2002/2]. Made at the 4465th meeting, 31 January.

UNSC. (2004). First Report of the Secretary-General on the United Nations Operation in Burundi [S/2004/682]. 25 August.

UNSC. (2005a). Fourth Report to the Secretary-General on the United Nations operation in Burundi [S/2005/328]. 19 May.

UNSC. (2005b). Monthly Report of the Secretary-General. on Darfur [S/2005/467]. 18 July.

UNSC. (2006a). Eighth Report of the Secretary-General on the United Nations Operation in Burundi [S/2006/852]. 25 October.

UNSC. (2006b). Resolution 1706 (2006) [S/RES/1706]. Adopted by the Security Council at its 5519th meeting. 31 August.

UNSC. (2007a). First Report of the Secretary-General. on the United Nations Integrated Office in Burundi [S/2007/287]. 17 May.

UNSC. (2007b). Resolution 1744 [S/RES/1744]. Adopted by the Security Council at its 5633rd meeting. 20 February.

UNSC. (2007c). Resolution 1769 (2007) [S/RES/1769]. Adopted by the Security Council at its 5727th Meeting, 31 July.

UNSC. (2008). Third Report of the Secretary-General on the United Nations Integrated Office in Burundi [S/2008/330]. 15 May.

UNSC. (2009). Resolution 1863 (2009) [S/RES/1863 (2009)]. Adopted by the Security Council at its 6068th Meeting. 16 January.

UNSC. (2010). Resolution 1964 (2010). Adopted by the Security Council at its 6461st meeting. 22 December.

UNWTO. (2022). *World Tourism Barometer.* 20(5).

Usov, V. (2002). Evolution of African Integration: from OAU to AU. (In 9th Conference of Africanists held in Moscow by the Council for the Problems of Economic, Social, Political, and Cultural Development of African Studies. Abstracts of the Russian Academy of Sciences. Moscow. 29-30 May 2002. 21-23.).

USTR. (2016). Beyond AGOA: Looking to the future of US-Africa and investment. Washington. https://ustr.gov/sites/default/files/2016-AGOA-Report.pdf.

Valensisi G and Karingi S. (2017). From Global Goals to Regional Strategies: Towards an African Approach to SDGs [the Sustainable Development Goals]. *African Geographical Review.* 36(1). 45–60. https://doi.org/10.1080/19376812.2016.1185738

Valensisi G, Lisinge R., Karingi, S. (2016). The Trade Facilitation Agreement and Africa's Regional Integration. *Canadian Journal of Development Studies.* 37(2). 239–259. https://doi.org/10.1080/02255189.2016.1131672

Valenzuela, J.S., Valenzuela, A. (1978). Modernization and Dependency: Alternative Perspectives in the Study of Latin American Underdevelopment. *Comparative Politics* 10(4). 535–57. https://doi.org/10.2307/421571

Van Hoeymissen, S. (2011). Regional Organisations in China's Security Strategy for Africa: The Sense of Supporting "African Solutions to African Problems. *Journal of Current Chinese Affairs.* 40(4). 91-118. https://doi.org/10.1177/186810261104000404

Van Meter, D.S., Van Horn, C.E. (1975). The Policy Implementation Process: *A Conceptual Framework. - Administration & Society.* 6(4). 445–488. https://doi.org/10.1177/009539977500600404

Van Wyk, J.A. (2007). Political Leaders in Africa: Presidents, Patrons or Profiteers. Occasional Paper Series, Vol 2 (1). The African Centre for the Constructive Resolution of Disputes. South Africa.

Van Wyk, J-A. (2016). High–Level Panels as Diplomatic Instruments: The African Union Panel of the Wise and The Emergence of an African Peace Diplomacy Architecture, *Journal of Contemporary History.* 41(1). 57-79. https://doi.org/10.18820/0258-2422/jch.v41i1.4

Vanzetti, D., Peters, R., Knebel, C. (2018). Nontariff Measures: Lifting CFTA and ACP Trade to the Next Level. Research Paper 14 (UNCTAD/SER. RP/2017/14), UN publication. Geneva.

Vayrynen, R. (2003). Regionalism: Old and New. *International Studies Review.* (5). 25-51. https://doi.org/10.1111/1521-9488.501002

Vasconi, T.A. (1971). Dependencia superestructura' ['Dependency and Superstructure'], in T.A. Vasconi and I. Reca (eds) Modernizacion y Crisis en la Universidad Latinoamericana [Modernization and Crisis in the Latin American University]. 9–38. Santiago: Centro de Esudios Socio-Economicos (CESO), Universidad de Chile.

Vasconi, T.A. (1977). Ideologia, lucha de clases y aparatos educativos en el desarrollo de America Latina' ['Ideology, Class Struggle and Educational Equipment in the Development of Latin America'], in G. Labarca et al. (eds) La Educacion Burgesa [The Bourgeois Education]. 173–236. Mexico: Nueva Imagen

Venter, D.J., Neuland, E.W. (2005). NEPAB and the African Renaissance. Johannesburg: Richard Havenga.

Verwey, L. (2005). Nepad & Civil Society Participation in the APRM. Occasional Papers, IDASA–Budget Information Service – Africa Budget Project. Retrieved from: http://www.idasa.org.za.

Vickers, B. (2007). States, Markets and Industrial Developments in the 21st Century. What Options for Developing Countries. Institute for Global Dialogue, Occasional Paper No 56. Midrand: Institute for Global Dialogue.

Vickers, B. (2017). A Handbook on Regional Integration in Africa. Towards Agenda 2063. The Commonwealth Secretariat: United Kingdom. 155.

Vickers, B., Cawood, R. (2018). South Africa's Corporate Expansion: Towards a 'SA Inc.' Approach in Africa. In Adebayo, A., Virk, K. (eds), Foreign Policy in Post- Apartheid South Africa. Security, Diplomacy and Trade. IB Taurus: New York and London. https://doi.org/10.5040/9781350986480.ch-005

Victor, P. (2010). Questioning Economic Growth. *Nature*, 468. 370–371. https://doi.org/10.1038/468370a

Vincze (Eds.), Social Cognition and Communication. 155–172. Psychology Press. New York.

Viner, J. (1950). The Customs Union Issue. New York: Carnegie Endowment for International Peace.

Vines, A., Middleton, R. (2008). Options for the EU to Support the African Peace and Security Architecture, European Parliament Policy Department External Policy Report prepared by Chatham House [online] available from [08 August 2010].

Walters, R.S., Blake, D.H. (1992). The Politics of Global Economic Relations. (4th edition). Princetice-Hall Inc. New Jersey.

Walters, L., Bohlmann, H.R., Clance, M.W. (2016). The Impact of the COMESA–EAC–SADC Tripartite Free Trade Agreement on the South African Economy. Working Paper 635, Economic Research Southern Africa, 13 September.

Wapmuk, S. (2009). In Search of Greater Unity: African States and the Quest for an African Union Government. *Journal of Alternative Perspectives in the Social Sciences*. 1(3). 647–651.

Warthon, K. (2010). Peace and Security Advisor at the United States Mission to the African Union [interview by J. Wood] Addis Ababa, 12 May 2010.

WB. (1981). Accelerated Development in Sub-Saharan Africa: An Agenda for Action World Bank. Washington, DC.

WB. (1998). Southern Africa Sub-Regional Strategy. World Bank. Washington, DC.

WB. (2000). Can Africa Claim the 21st Century? World Bank. Washington, DC.

WB. (2001). World Development Indicators. World Bank. Washington, DC.

WB. (2002). Capital Market Integration in the East African Community. World Bank. Washington, DC.

WB. (2003). Global Economic Prospects and the Developing Countries 2003: Investing to Unlock Global Opportunities. World Bank. Washington, DC.

WB. (2011). Partnering for Africa's Regional Integration: Progress Report on the Regional Integration Assistance Strategy for Sub-Saharan Africa. World Bank. Washington, DC. Retreived from: http://documents.worldbank.org/curated/en/151701468006936079/Africa-Partnering-for-Africas-regional-integrationprogress-report-on-the-regional-integrationassistance-strategy-for-Sub-Saharan-Africa.

WB. (2012). Transformation Through Infrastructure. World Bank. Washington, DC.

WB. (2015). International Debt Statistics 2015. World Bank. Washington, DC.

WB. (2017). Policies that Promote SME Participation in Public Procurement. Business Environment Working Group (BEWG) of the Donor Committee for Enterprise Development (DCED). World Bank. Washington, DC.

WB. (2017a). Illicit Financial Flows (IFFs). 27 June 2017. World Bank. Washington, DC. Available at: http://www.worldbank.org/en/topic/financialsector/brief/illicit-financialflows-iffs.

WB. (2017b). World Development Indicators [database]. Contribution of Natural Resources to Gross Domestic Product. World Bank. Washington, DC. Available at: http://wdi.worldbank.org/table/3.14.

WB. (2018). Poverty and Shared Prosperity 2018: Piecing Together the Poverty Puzzle. World Bank. Washington, DC.

WB. (2018a). Africa's Pulse. Boosting Productivity in Sub-Saharan Africa: The Role of Human Capital. World Bank. Washington, DC.

WB. (2018b). World Development Indicators [database]. World Bank. Washington, DC.

WB. (2021). Connecting Africa: The Role of Infrastructure in Regional Trade.

WB. (2022). World Bank Commodity Price Data (The Pink Sheet), https://www.worldbank.org/en/research/ commodity-markets (accessed on 20 June 2023).

WB. (2022). World Bank Country and Lending Groups, https://datahelpdesk.worldbank.org/knowledgebase/ articles/906519 (accessed on 22 June 2023).

WB. (2022). World Development Indicators, https://data.worldbank.org/ (accessed on 9 June 2023).

WB., KNOMAD. (Global Knowledge Partnership on Migration and Development). (2022). Remittances Brave Global Headwinds. Migration and Development Brief 37. World Bank, Washington, DC.

WEF., WB., and AfDB. (2009). The Africa Competitiveness Report 2009. Geneva.

Weir, S., Beetham, D. (1999). Political Power and Democratic Control in Britain: The Democratic Audit of the United Kingdom. Routledge. London.

Weiss, L. (1997). Globalisation and the Myth of the Powerless State. *New Left Review* 225. 3-27. https://doi.org/10.7591/9781501711732

Weltz, M. (2014). A Culture of Conservatism; How and Why African Union Member States Obstruct the Deepening of Integration. *Strategic Review for Southern Africa*. 36(1). 4-24. https://doi.org/10.35293/srsa.v36i1.148

Wendt, A. (1992). Anarchy is What States Make of it: The Social Construction of Power Politics. *International Organisation*. 46. 391-425. https://doi.org/10.1017/S0020818300027764

Wendt, A. (1999). Social Theory of International Politics. Cambridge University Press. Cambridge. https://doi.org/10.1017/CBO9780511612183

Wheatley, J. (2017). Ivorian Prime Minister Warns of Brexit Fallout. UK's vote to Leave the EU Could Have Unintended Effect on Cocoa Farms in West Africa. Financial Times. London. September 2017.

Wiener, A. (2007). The Dual Quality of Norms and Governance beyond the State: Sociological and Normative Approaches to Interaction. *Critical Review of International Social and Political Philosophy*. 10 1 https://doi.org/10.1080/13698230601122412

Willenbockel, D. (2004). Specification Choice and Robustness in CGE Trade Policy Analysis with Imperfect Competition. *Economic Modelling* 21(6). 1065-1099. https://doi.org/10.1016/j.econmod.2004.03.003

Willenbockel, D. (2013). General Equilibrium Analysis of the COMESA-EACSADC Tripartite FTA. TMSA Regional Integration Research Network.

Williams, P.D. (2004). Britain and Africa after the Cold War: Beyond Damage Limitation? In Taylor, I., Williams, P. (eds.), Africa in International Politics: External Involvement on the Continent. Routledge. London.

Williams, P.D. (2006). Military Responses to Mass Killing: The African Union Mission in Sudan.' *International Peacekeeping*. 13(2), 168–183. https://doi.org/10.1080/13533310500436565

William, P.D. (2007). From Non-intervention to Non-indifference: The Origins and Development of the African Union's Security Culture. *African Affairs*. 106(423). 253-279. https://doi.org/10.1093/afraf/adm001

Williams, P.D. (2007) Thinking about Security in Africa. *International Affairs*. 83(6).1021–1038. https://doi.org/10.1111/j.1468-2346.2007.00671.x

Williams, P.D. (2006a). The African Union: Prospects for Regional Peacekeeping After Burundi & Sudan. *Review of African Political Economy*. 33(108). 352–357.

Williams, P.D. (2006b). Military Responses to Mass Killing: The African Union Mission in Sudan. *International Peacekeeping*.13(2). 168–183. https://doi.org/10.1080/13533310500436565

Williams, P. D. (2007). From Non-Intervention to Non-Indifference: The Origins and Development of the African Union's Security Culture. *African Affairs*. 106(423). 253–279. https://doi.org/10.1093/afraf/adm001

Williams, P.D. (2009). The African Union's Peace Operations: A Comparative Analysis.*African Security*. 2(2–3). 97–118. https://doi.org/10.1080/19362200903361937

Williams, P.D. (2013a). AMISOM in Transition: The Future of the African Union Mission in Somalia. Rift Valley Institute. February 13.

Williams, P. D. (2013b). Peace Operations in Africa: Lessons Learned Since 2000. Africa Security Brief No. 25, Africa Center for Strategic Studies. https://doi.org/10.21236/ADA587312

Williams, P.D., Boutellis, A. (2014). Partnership Peacekeeping: Challenges and Opportunities in the United Nations–African Union Relationship. *African Affairs*. 113 451). 254–278. https://doi.org/10.1093/afraf/adu021

Williams, P.D., Dersso, S.A. (2015). Saving Strangers and Neighbors: Advancing UN-AU Cooperation on Peace Operations, New York: International Peace Institute, February.

Williams, P.D. (2016) AMISOM Under Review. *RUSI Journal*. 161(1). 40–49. https://doi.org/10.1080/03071847.2016.1152120

Williams, P.D. (2017b). A Navy SEAL Was Killed in Somalia. Here's What You Need to Know About U.S. Operations There. *Monkey Cage*. May 8.

Williams, P.D. (2018). Paying for AMISOM: Are Politics and Bureaucracy Undermining the AU's Largest Peace Operation? Retrieved from: https://theglobalobservatory.org/2017/01/amisom-african-union-peacekeeping-financing/ [January 11, 2017a. As of August 30, 2018].

Williams, P.D. (2018a). Fighting for Peace in Somalia: A History and Analysis of the African Union Mission (AMISOM), 2007–2017. Oxford University Press. Oxford.

Bibliography

Williams, P.D. (2018b). Joining AMISOM: Why Six African States Contributed Troops to the African Union Mission in Somalia. *Journal of Eastern African Studies*. 12(1). 172–192. https://doi.org/10.1080/17531055.2018.1418159

Woldemichael, A. Kidane, D., Shimeles, A. 2022. Food Inflation and Child Health. *The World Bank Economic Review*. 36(3). 757–773. https://doi. org/10.1093/wber/lhac009.

Wolfer, L. (2007). Real Research: Conducting and Evaluating Research in the Social Sciences. Pearson Education. Boston, MA.

Woodward, D. (2007). IMF Voting Reform; Need, Opportunity and Options: (49)

World Customs Organisation. (2012). Rules of Origin Handbook. Available at http://www. wcoomd.org/en/topics/origin/overview/origin-handbook.aspx.

WTO. (1995). Agreement on Trade-related Aspects of Intellectual Property Rights (TRIPS). Geneva.

WTO. (2014). Challenges faced by LDCs in complying with preferential rules of origin under unilateral preference schemes. G/RO/W/148. Geneva. 28 October.

WTO. (2015). World Trade Report 2015: Speeding Up Trade – Benefits and Challenges of Implementing the WTO Trade Facilitation Agreement. Geneva.

WTO. (2017). Minutes of the Meeting Held in the Centre William Rappard on 7 December 2016. Geneva.

WTO. (2017a). List of all RTAs. Retrieved from: http://rtais. wto.org/UI/PublicAllRTAList.aspx./WDSP/IB/2015/04/20/000442464_20150420122912/ Rendered/PDF/ACS125280REVIS0itive0Private0Sector.pdf.

WTO. (2018). Utilization Rates Under Preferential Trade Arrangements for LDCs Under the LDC Duty Scheme. G/RO/W/179. Geneva. 10 October.

Yarbrough, B, Yarbrough, R. (1992). Cooperation and Governance in International Trade: The Strategic Organisational Approach. Princeton University Press. Princeton. https://doi. org/10.1515/9781400862900

Yaya, S., Otu, A., Labonté, R. (2020). Globalisation in the Time of COVID-19: Repositioning Africa to Meet the Immediate and Remote Challenges. *Globalization and Health.* 16(1). 1-7. https://doi.org/10.1186/s12992-020-00581-4

Yihdego, Z. (2011). The African Union: Founding Principles, Frameworks and Prospects. *European Law Journal.* 17(5). 568-594. https://doi.org/10.1111/j.1468-0386.2011.00567.x

Zandile, Z., Phiri, A. (2018). FDI as a Contributing Factor to Economic Growth in Burkina Faso: How True is this? Available at: https//mpra.ub.uni-muenchen.de/87282/1/MPRA_paper_87282.pdf.

Zehfuss, M. (1998). Sprachlosigkeit Schränkt Ein. Zur Bedeutung von Sprache in konstruktivistischen Theorien. *Zeitschrift für internationale Beziehungen.* 5. 109-137.

Zehfuss, M. (2002). Constructivism in International Relations: The Politics of Reality, Cambridge University Press. Cambridge. https://doi.org/10.1017/CBO9780511491795

Zekos, G. (2005). Foreign Direct Investment in a Digital Economy. *European Business Review.* 17(1). 52-68. https://doi.org/10.1108/09555340510576267

Zhengyu, W.. Taylor, I. (2011). From Refusal to Engagement: Chinese Contribution to Peacekeeping in Africa. *Journal of Contemporary African Studies.* 29(2).137-154. https://doi.org/10.1080/02589001.2011.555190

Zoellick, R.B. (2012). "Why we still need the World Bank: looking beyond aid: *Foreign Affairs.* 91(2). 66-78.

Zondi, S. (2013). South Africa and SADC Mediation in Zimbabwe. In Rupiya, M. (ed.) Zimbabwe's Military: Examining its Veto Power in the Transition to Democracy, 2008–2013. 49–79. African Public Policy Research Institute. Pretoria.

Zondi, S., Khaba, B. 2014. The Madagascar Crisis, SADC Mediation and the Changing Indian Oceanic Order. *Africa Insight.* 43(4). 1–17.

Zondi, S. (2016a). A Decolonial Turn In Diplomatic Theory: Unmasking Epistemic Injustice. In Masters, L., and Shilaho, W. K. (eds.) 2016. *African Diplomacy: A special edition for Journal for Contemporary History.* 41(1). June 2016. University of Free State. https://doi.org/10.18820/24150509/jch.v41i1.2

Zondi, S. (2016b). Decolonisation and the African Agenda: Towards Another Model of the World. Presented at NRF/ UJ SARCHI Chair of Foreign Policy and African Diplomacy, University of Johannesburg, 10 June 2016.

Zuern, M., Checkel, J. (2005). Getting Socialized to Build Bridges: Constructivism and Rationalism, Europe and the Nation-State. *International Organisation.* (59). 1045-1079. https://doi.org/10.1017/S0020818305050356

Zulu, J.J. (2004). Zambia's Experience with HIPC. Policy Brief: Promotion of Social Justice and Concern for the Poor. Jesuit Center for Theological Reflection, at http://www.jctr.org.zm/downloads/HIPCbrief_280604.pd.

Zulu, J.J., Assefa, K., Sinha, S. (2016). Exploring the Linkages between Informal Employment and Inequality in Africa: The Case of Tanzania." Paper presented at the Global Conference on Prosperity, Equality and Sustainability: Perspectives and Policies for the Better World, New Delhi, India, 25–27 April 2016.

Zuma, N.D. (2013). Welcome Remarks. Opening Session of the 20th Ordinary Session of the Assembly of Heads of State and Government of the AU. Addis Ababa, Ethiopia. 27 January. Retrieved from: http://cpauc.au.int/en/sites/default/files/AUC %20Chairperson%20Statement%20to%2020th%20 Assembly%20(Final).pdf. [2013, December 20]

www.ingramcontent.com/pod-product-compliance
Lightning Source LLC
Chambersburg PA
CBHW071727270326
41928CB00013B/2586